EVERYMAN, I will go with thee,

and be thy guide,

In thy most need to go by thy side

FRANCES (FANNY) BURNEY

Born at King's Lynn, Norfolk, in 1752. Her
family moved to London in 1760, and her
literary career began with the publication of
Evelina in 1778. Mistress of the Robes to
Queen Charlotte, 1786–91. In 1793 she
married M. d'Arblay, a French officer, and
died in 1840.

The Diary of Fanny Burney

EDITED WITH AN
INTRODUCTION BY
LEWIS GIBBS

DENT: LONDON
EVERYMAN'S LIBRARY
DUTTON: NEW YORK

All rights reserved
Made in Great Britain
at the
Aldine Press · Letchworth · Herts
for
J. M. DENT & SONS LTD
Aldine House · Bedford Street · London
This edition first included in Everyman's Library 1940
Last reprinted 1971

NO. *1960*

ISBN: 0 460 01960 0

INTRODUCTION

When Mr Burney's third child, a daughter who was named Frances after her godmother, was born at King's Lynn in 1752, it seemed highly unlikely that her diary, if she should take it into her head to keep one, would have any of the interest which arises from the fact that the author has enjoyed the familiar society of the great. Mr Burney played the organ and gave music lessons, occupations which rarely lead to fame or fortune, especially when practised in a country town.

And when, in 1760, he moved to London, the likelihood was not much increased, for though he had more pupils than he could easily find time for, Fanny, at the age of eight, did not know her letters. Indeed, except for a very short period at a boarding-school in Queen's Square, in 1761, when her mother was dying, she had no regular education whatever. James, her elder brother, went to sea as a midshipman, Charles was sent to Charterhouse, her sisters, Esther and Susan, went to school in Paris for two years, but Fanny stayed at home. She was a prim, shy girl. When she was no more than ten years old, visitors to the house used to call her 'the old lady.' Her father spoke of her indulgently as a prude, and on her return from Paris, Susan, then fourteen, recorded that Fanny's characteristics were 'sense, sensibility, and bashfulness, and even a degree of prudery,' going on, however, to say that she and Esther were 'both charming girls—*des filles comme il y en a peu.*'

To this it may be added that she was slight in build and short-sighted. True, Mrs Thrale could later address her, in her enthusiastic way, as 'my lovely Burney,' but she was not, in fact, more than passably good-looking. She was past forty when she married, and when she did marry, her husband was a penniless French exile. She was never rich, though she learned in the end to drive a good bargain with a publisher. For some years—and this was when she was at the height of her fame—she lived at 'Camilla Cottage' with her husband and her son, on a bare £125 a year. And later she managed in Paris to keep house on M. D'Arblay's *retraite* of £62 10s. 0d., plus his meagre salary as a clerk in the civil department of 'les Bâtimens.' When she was Assistant Keeper of the Robes to Queen Charlotte, her allowance, as Macaulay observes with disgust, was £200 a year.

And yet it is impossible to turn the pages of her diary without being struck by the profusion of great names with which they are studded. People of genius, rank, wealth, and fashion move in a long procession through these volumes. And they move there naturally, not having been dragged in by the heels after the reprehensible custom of so many writers of diaries and memoirs. It is Dr Johnson who calls her his 'dear little Burney,' kisses her, and tells her to be a good girl. It is Sheridan who undertakes to accept a comedy of hers, 'unsight, unseen,' and to make her a bow and his best thanks into the bargain. The telescope through which she walks 'quite upright and without the least inconvenience' is Herschel's. The Paymaster of the Forces who writes her such an eloquent letter of compliment upon her second novel is Burke. The lady in whose carriage she escapes from Paris, a few hours before Napoleon arrives on his return from Elba, is the Princesse d'Hénin. The stout person who 'catches her fist' and declares that he has long wanted to know her is Louis XVIII. And the good-humoured gentleman who measures her arm with his thumb and forefinger, and says she is growing fatter, is George III.

Fanny, however, was used to good company before she herself became a celebrity. Her father, a man of remarkable energy, was made a Doctor of Music by the University of Oxford in 1769. Between 1770 and 1773 he travelled on the Continent and produced, as the fruit of these tours, books on *The Present State of Music* in France, Italy, Germany, and the United Provinces. In 1776 the first volume of his *General History of Music* was published. Moreover, he had a talent for making friends, and visitors at his house ranged from 'Omy,' the South Sea islander, to His Highness Alexis Orlov, taking in by the way Pacchierotti, the Italian tenor; Miss Davies, the English *prima donna*; Bruce, the traveller; Garrick, and Johnson —to mention only a few. They were all observed by the quiet and retiring girl with a keenness which they did not suspect.

Dr Burney found Fanny useful in copying his manuscripts, but she contrived to scribble a good deal on her own account. When she was only fifteen, she made a bonfire of her writings as a dutiful sacrifice to the opinions of her stepmother, who considered that literary composition did not become a young lady. Among the works delivered to the flames was a story called 'The History of Caroline Evelyn,' which contained a hint of *Evelina*. From this time onwards she kept a diary, addressing it at first to Nobody—'since to Nobody can I be wholly unreserved.'

Actually she had no wish to be wholly unreserved. It was not in her nature to 'reveal every thought, every wish of my heart.' Her impulse was to re-create the scenes she witnessed, and to make the characters who figured in them talk in their natural style. She had a quick eye for oddities of character and conduct, and a remarkable talent for reproducing dialogue—a talent which fairly rivals that of Boswell.

The *Diary and Letters*, as edited by Charlotte Barrett, does not begin until 1778, when Fanny was twenty-five. The reason given for this is that, in the earlier part, 'the interest is of a more private and personal nature than that which attaches to the Journal after its writer became universally known as the authoress of *Evelina*, *Cecilia*, etc.' The *Early Diary* was, in fact, not published until 1889. Whatever may be thought of Mrs Barrett's judgment in this matter, it cannot be denied that there was a certain dramatic fitness in beginning with 1778, for in the January of that year *Evelina* was published, and Fanny, secure in the knowledge that her name was not on the title-page, and that the publisher had never seen her, was able to savour the delight of beholding her work in print, and of feeling Mr Lowndes's twenty guineas in her pocket. Before many months had passed the secret was out; *Evelina* was the talk of the town, and Fanny, torn between her pleasure in magnificent compliments and her distress at finding herself in the public eye, was a 'lyon.'

From this time onwards her place was in the great world, and notable events as well as notable people supplied material for her diary. Indeed, the pulse of history beats distinctly in the work. Not that she concerned herself very much with history—she had, for instance, hardly anything to say about the American War. It was rather that history concerned itself with her, from the time when it set her writing urgent letters home about the Gordon Riots, to the time when it placed her in Brussels during the Waterloo campaign. And we are reminded of the passing of an age when Mrs Piozzi, the vivacious Mrs Thrale of old, writes to her: 'How changed is the taste of verse, prose, and painting since *le bon vieux temps*, dear Madam.' So it was indeed, when a young lady's novel could take the form of 'a wild and hideous tale called *Frankenstein*.

But the *Diary* does not depend for all its interest upon great people and striking events. Certainly we are glad to know what sort of life was led by an Assistant Keeper of the Robes, and to learn that the face of the First Consul was 'pale even to sallowness.' But the lady who persisted in calling: 'M'Ami, M'Ami!' is as memorable in her own way as the great Napoleon, and more entertaining. Such figures are plentiful in the *Diary*, and nobody was better qualified than the shy authoress to do them justice. We are not likely, for instance, to forget the lovely S. S. with her tearful eyes, or the infidel Miss W——, or Colonel

Goldsworthy declining barley water offered by his sovereign, or Colonel Manners denouncing the tax on *bacheldors*, or Lady Hawke and the *Mausoleum of Julia*.

Fanny's diary, once confided to Nobody, was later written for such readers as her sisters — especially Susan — her father, Mr Crisp, and Mrs Lock. Until she was well advanced in years she does not seem to have contemplated the possibility of publication, and even then she was much more concerned with what it would be proper to make public than with what would prove interesting. No doubt there is something to be said for the criticism that the work in its complete form is too long; it is a criticism which would necessarily apply to any diary genuinely addressed to relatives or close friends and covering an equal period. Moreover, it is a criticism of less weight than might appear. How many works in seven volumes are there which have no dull patches? And how many of Fanny's admirers would willingly part with a page of the *Diary*?

When all is said, the work offers a wonderful freshness and variety of interest. *Evelina* may rank as a minor classic, *Cecilia* finds a few select readers, the pages of *Camilla* are rarely disturbed, and though between three and four thousand copies of *The Wanderer* were sold, it has been doubted whether any one ever read it. It may well be that the *Diary* gives Fanny her best claim to the regard and gratitude of posterity.

LEWIS GIBBS.

SELECT BIBLIOGRAPHY

WORKS. *Evelina*, 3 vols., 1778 (ed. F. D. Mackinnon, 1930); *Cecilia*, 5 vols., 1782; *Camilla*, 5 vols., 1796; *The Wanderer*, 5 vols., 1814; *Memoirs of Doctor Burney*, 3 vols., 1832; *The Diary and Letters of Madame d'Arblay*, 7 vols., 1842–6; *The Early Diary of Frances Burney*, ed. A. R. Ellis, 2 vols., 1889; reprinted with additional material, 1907; *Diary and Letters, 1768–1840*, ed. A. Dobson, 6 vols., 1904; *The Queeney Letters*, ed. Lord Lansdowne, 1934.

BIOGRAPHY. A. Dobson, *Fanny Burney*, 1903; R. Brimley Johnson, *Fanny Burney and the Burneys*, 1926; C. Lloyd, *Fanny Burney*, 1936; P. A. Scholes, *The Great Dr Burney*, 1948; E. Hahn, *A Degree of Prudery*, 1951; J. Hemlow, *The History of Fanny Burney*, 1958.

THE TEXT

The text of the present volume is selected from that of the first edition of *The Diary and Letters of Madame D'Arblay*, and, in the case of Volumes I and II, from the first impression. In the second impression certain passages were omitted from these volumes. The editor has refrained from inserting sub-titles or comments in the text, and the only editorial interruptions which occur are those of Charlotte Barrett. Fanny's own injunction 'that whatever might be effaced or omitted, NOTHING should in any wise be altered or added,' has been scrupulously observed.

The four parts into which the book has been divided do not correspond to any divisions in the original or any other edition. It is hoped that the notes will give the reader all the help he needs, without unduly interrupting his enjoyment of the text.

Dates are given throughout, but an entry under a particular date is not, of course, necessarily reproduced in full. All things considered, it seemed better, as a rule, not to mark omitted passages in the diary. They are, however, always indicated in the letters. A note at the beginning of each section shows from what part of the first edition the material has been taken.

CONTENTS

PART ONE

JANUARY, 1778–DECEMBER, 1784

PART ONE

January, 1778–December, 1784[1]

THIS year was ushered in by a grand and most important event! At the latter end of January, the literary world was favoured with the first publication of the ingenious, learned, and most profound Fanny Burney! I doubt not but this memorable affair will, in future times, mark the period whence chronologers will date the zenith of the polite arts in this island!

This admirable authoress has named her most elaborate performance, *Evelina; or, a Young Lady's Entrance into the World.*

Perhaps this may seem a rather bold attempt and title for a female whose knowledge of the world is very confined, and whose inclinations, as well as situation, incline her to a private and domestic life. All I can urge is, that I have only presumed to trace the accidents and adventures to which a 'young woman' is liable; I have not pretended to show the world what it actually *is*, but what it *appears* to a girl of seventeen: and so far as that, surely any girl who is past seventeen may safely do?

My little book, I am told, is now at all the circulating libraries. I have an exceeding odd sensation when I consider that it is now in the power of *any* and *every* body to read what I so carefully hoarded even from my best friends, till this last month or two; and that a work which was so lately lodged, in all privacy, in my bureau, may now be seen by every butcher and baker, cobbler and tinker, throughout the three kingdoms, for the small tribute of threepence.

My aunt and Miss Humphries being settled at this

[1] Vol. i, p. 5–vol. ii, p. 339.

time at Brompton, I was going thither with Susan to tea, when Charlotte acquainted me that they were then employed in reading *Evelina* to the invalid, my cousin Richard.

This intelligence gave me the utmost uneasiness—I foresaw a thousand dangers of a discovery—I dreaded the indiscreet warmth of all my confidants. In truth, I was quite sick with apprehension, and was too uncomfortable to go to Brompton, and Susan carried my excuses.

Upon her return, I was somewhat tranquillized, for she assured me that there was not the smallest suspicion of the author, and that they had concluded it to be the work of a *man!* [1]

Finding myself more safe than I had apprehended, I ventured to go to Brompton next day. On my way upstairs, I heard Miss Humphries in the midst of Mr Villars's letter of consolation upon Sir John Belmont's rejection of his daughter; and just as I entered the room, she cried out: 'How pretty that is!'

How much in luck would she have thought herself, had she known *who* heard her!

In a private confabulation which I had with my Aunt Anne, she told me a thousand things that had been said in its praise, and assured me they had not for a moment doubted that the work was a *man's*.

I must own I suffered great difficulty in refraining from laughing upon several occasions—and several times, when they praised what they read, I was on the point of saying: 'You are very good!' and so forth, and I could scarcely keep myself from making acknowledgments, and bowing my head involuntarily. However, I got off perfectly safe.

It seems, to my utter amazement, Miss Humphries has guessed the author to be Anstey,[2] who wrote the *Bath*

[1] Fanny's younger sister, Susan, and her aunt, Anne, were among the few to whom the secret was known. She had confessed to her father that she had written a book which she thought of publishing, but he did not take the information seriously enough to ask the title. It was June before he discovered the truth.

[2] Christopher Anstey (1724–1805), celebrated in his day as the author of *The New Bath Guide, or Memoirs of the Blunderhead Family*.

Guide! How improbable and how extraordinary a supposition! But they have both of them done it so much honour, that, but for Richard's anger at Evelina's bashfulness, I never could believe they did not suspect me.

Chesington,[1] June 18th.

Here I am, and here I have been this age; though too weak to think of journalizing; however, as I never had so many curious anecdotes to record, I will not, at least this year, the first of my appearing in public—give up my favourite old hobby-horse.

I came hither the first week in May. My recovery, from that time to this, has been slow and sure; but as I could walk hardly three yards in a day at first, I found so much time to spare, that I could not resist treating myself with a little private sport with *Evelina*, a young lady whom I think I have some right to make free with. I had promised *Hetty* [2] that *she* should read it to Mr Crisp, at her own particular request; but I wrote my excuses, and introduced it myself.

I told him it was a book which Hetty had taken to Brompton, to divert my cousin Richard during his confinement. He was so indifferent about it, that I thought he would not give himself the trouble to read it, and often embarrassed me by unlucky questions, such as, 'If it was reckoned clever?' and 'What I thought of it?' and 'Whether folks laughed at it?' I always evaded any direct or satisfactory answer; but he was so totally free from any idea of suspicion, that my perplexity escaped his notice.

At length, he desired me to begin reading to him. I

[1] Chesington (or Chessington) Hall, a country house near Epsom, where Samuel Crisp lodged in retirement. He was a close friend of Dr Burney and his family. Himself a disappointed author—his tragedy, *Virginia*, had been produced with little success by Garrick in 1754—he gave Fanny, who expressed her affection for him by calling him her 'Daddy,' much sensible advice about her writing.

[2] Dr Burney's eldest daughter.

dared not trust my voice with the little introductory ode,[1] for as *that* is no romance, but the sincere effusion of my heart, I could as soon read aloud my own letters, written in my own name and character: I therefore skipped it, and have so kept the book out of his sight, that, to this day, he knows not it is there. Indeed, I have, since, heartily repented that I read *any* of the book to him, for I found it a much more awkward thing than I had expected: my voice quite faltered when I began it, which, however, I passed off for the effect of remaining weakness of lungs; and, in short, from an invincible embarrassment, which I could not for a page together repress, the book, by my reading, lost all manner of spirit.

Nevertheless, though he has by no means treated it with the praise so lavishly bestowed upon it from other quarters, I had the satisfaction to observe that he was even greedily eager to go on with it; so that I flatter myself the *story* caught his attention: and, indeed, allowing for my *mauling* reading, he gave it quite as much credit as I had any reason to expect. But, now that I was sensible of my error in being my own mistress of the ceremonies, I determined to leave to Hetty the third volume, and therefore pretended I had not brought it. He was in a delightful ill-humour about it, and I enjoyed his impatience far more than I should have done his forbearance. Hetty, therefore, when she comes, has undertaken to bring it.

Well, I cannot but rejoice that I published the book, little as I ever imagined how it would fare; for hitherto it has occasioned me no small diversion, and *nothing* of the disagreeable sort. But I often think a change *will* happen, for I am by no means so sanguine as to suppose such success will be uninterrupted. Indeed, in the midst of the greatest satisfaction that I feel, an inward *something* which I cannot account for, prepares me to expect a reverse; for the more the book is drawn into notice, the more exposed it becomes to criticism and remark.

[1] The ode, discreetly headed *To* ——, is addressed to her father. It begins: 'O Author of my being!'

JULY 25. Mrs Cholmondeley[1] has been reading and praising *Evelina*, and my father is quite delighted at her approbation, and told Susan that I could not have had a greater compliment than making two such women my friends as Mrs Thrale[2] and Mrs Cholmondeley, for they were severe and knowing, and afraid of praising *à tort et à travers*, as their opinions are liable to be quoted.

Mrs Thrale said she had only to complain it was too short. She recommended it to my mother[3] to read!— how droll!—and she told her she would be much entertained with it, for there was a great deal of human life in it, and of the manners of the present times, and added that it was written 'by somebody who knows the top and the bottom, the highest and the lowest of mankind.' She has even lent her set to my mother, who brought it home with her!

AUGUST 3. I now come to last Saturday evening, when my beloved father came to Chesington, in full health, charming spirits, and all kindness, openness, and entertainment.

In his way hither he had stopped at Streatham, and he settled with Mrs Thrale that he would call on her again in his way to town, and carry me with him! and Mrs Thrale said: 'We all long to know her.'

I have been in a kind of twitter ever since, for there seems something very formidable in the idea of appearing as an authoress! I ever dreaded it, as it is a title which must raise more expectations than I have any chance of answering. Yet I am highly flattered by her invitation, and highly delighted in the prospect of being introduced to the Streatham society.

My dear father communicated this intelligence, and a great deal more, with a pleasure that almost surpassed that with which I heard it, and he seems quite eager for

---

[1] This lively lady was the sister of Peg Woffington, the actress.

[2] Hester Lynch Salusbury, married in 1763 to Henry Thrale, the wealthy brewer.

[3] Actually, her stepmother.

me to make another attempt. He desired to take upon himself the communication to my Daddy Crisp, and as it is now in so many hands that it is possible accident might discover it to him, I readily consented.

Sunday evening, as I was going into my father's room, I heard him say: 'The variety of characters—the variety of scenes—and the language—why she has had very little education but what she has given herself—less than any of the others!' and Mr Crisp exclaimed: 'Wonderful!— it's wonderful!'

I now found what was going forward, and therefore deemed it most fitting to decamp.

About an hour after, as I was passing through the hall, I met my daddy [Crisp]. His face was all animation and archness; he doubled his fist at me, and would have stopped me, but I ran past him into the parlour.

Before supper, however, I again met him, and he would not suffer me to escape; he caught both my hands, and looked as if he would have looked me through, and then exclaimed: 'Why, you little hussy—you young devil!— an't you ashamed to look me in the face, you *Evelina*, you! Why, what a dance have you led me about it! Young friend, indeed! Oh, you little hussy, what tricks have you served me!'

LONDON, AUGUST. I have now to write an account of the most consequential day I have spent since my birth; namely, my Streatham visit.

Our journey to Streatham was the least pleasant part of the day, for the roads were dreadfully dusty, and I was really in the fidgets from thinking what my reception might be, and from fearing they would expect a less awkward and backward kind of person that I was sure they would find.

Mr Thrale's house is white, and very pleasantly situated, in a fine paddock. Mrs Thrale was strolling about, and came to us as we got out of the chaise.

She then received me, taking both my hands, and with mixed politeness and cordiality welcoming me to Streatham. She led me into the house, and addressed herself almost wholly for a few minutes to my father, as if to give me an assurance she did not mean to regard me as a show, or to distress or frighten me by drawing me out. Afterwards she took me upstairs, and showed me the house, and said she had very much wished to see me at Streatham, and should always think herself much obliged to Dr Burney for his goodness in bringing me, which she looked upon as a very great favour.

But though we were some time together, and though she was so very civil, she did not *hint* at my book, and I love her much more than ever for her delicacy in avoiding a subject which she could not but see would have greatly embarrassed me.

When we returned to the music room, we found Miss Thrale was with my father. Miss Thrale is a very fine girl, about fourteen years of age, but cold and reserved, though full of knowledge and intelligence.

Soon after, Mrs Thrale took me to the library; she talked a little while upon common topics, and then, at last, she mentioned *Evelina*.

'Yesterday at supper,' said she, 'we talked it all over, and discussed all your characters; but Dr Johnson's favourite is Mr Smith. He declares the fine gentleman *manqué* was never better drawn, and he acted him all the evening, saying "he was all for the ladies"! He repeated whole scenes by heart. I declare I was astonished at him. Oh, you can't imagine how much he is pleased with the book; he "could not get rid of the rogue," he told me. But was it not droll,' said she, 'that I should recommend to Dr Burney? and tease him so innocently to read it?'

I now prevailed upon Mrs Thrale to let me amuse myself, and she went to dress. I then prowled about to choose some book, and I saw, upon the reading-table, *Evelina*—I had just fixed upon a new translation of Cicero's *Laelius*, when the library door was opened, and Mr Seward[1]

[1] William Seward. He had a slender connection with literature as the author of *Anecdotes of Distinguished Persons*.

entered. I instantly put away my book, because I dreaded being thought studious and affected. He offered his service to find anything for me, and then, in the same breath, ran on to speak of the book with which I had myself 'favoured the world'!

The exact words he began with I cannot recollect, for I was actually confounded by the attack; and his abrupt manner of letting me know he was *au fait* equally astonished and provoked me. How different from the delicacy of Mr and Mrs Thrale!

When we were summoned to dinner, Mrs Thrale made my father and me sit on each side of her. I said that I hoped I did not take Dr Johnson's place—for he had not yet appeared.

'No,' answered Mrs Thrale, 'he will sit by you, which I am sure will give him great pleasure.'

Soon after we were seated, this great man entered.[1] I have so true a veneration for him, that the very sight of him inspires me with delight and reverence, notwithstanding the cruel infirmities to which he is subject; for he has almost perpetual convulsive movements, either of his hands, lips, feet, or knees, and sometimes all together.

Mrs Thrale introduced me to him, and he took his place. We had a noble dinner, and a most elegant dessert. Dr Johnson, in the middle of dinner, asked Mrs Thrale what was in some little pies that were near him.

'Mutton,' answered she, 'so I don't ask you to eat any, because I know you despise it.'

'No, madam, no,' cried he; 'I despise nothing that is good of its sort; but I am too proud now to eat of it. Sitting by Miss Burney makes me very proud to-day!'

'Miss Burney,' said Mrs Thrale, laughing, 'you must take great care of your heart if Dr Johnson attacks it; for I assure you he is not often successless.'

---

[1] Dr Johnson was now sixty-eight years old. He had been introduced to the Thrales by Arthur Murphy, and from 1766 onwards spent much of his time at Streatham.

'What's that you say, madam?' cried he; 'are you making mischief between the young lady and me already?'

A little while after he drank Miss Thrale's health and mine, and then added:

''Tis a terrible thing that we cannot wish young ladies well without wishing them to become old women!'

'But some people,' said Mr Seward, 'are old and young at the same time, for they wear so well that they never look old.'

'No, sir, no,' cried the doctor, laughing; 'that never yet was; you might as well say they are at the same time tall and short. I remember an epitaph to that purpose, which is in——'

(I have quite forgot what—and also the name it was made upon, but the rest I recollect exactly:)

'————— lies buried here;
So early wise, so lasting fair,
That none, unless her years you told,
Thought her a child, or thought her old."

Mrs Thrale then repeated some lines in French, and Dr Johnson some more in Latin. An epilogue of Mr Garrick's to *Bonduca* [1] was then mentioned, and Dr Johnson said it was a miserable performance, and everybody agreed it was the worst he had ever made.

'And yet,' said Mr Seward, 'it has been very much admired; but it is in praise of English valour, and so I suppose the subject made it popular.'

'I don't know, sir,' said Dr Johnson, 'anything about the subject, for I could not read on till I came to it; I got through half a dozen lines, but I could observe no other subject than eternal dullness. I don't know what is the matter with David; I am afraid he is grown superannuated, for his prologues and epilogues used to be incomparable.'

'Nothing is so fatiguing,' said Mrs Thrale, 'as the life of a wit; he and Wilkes [2] are the two oldest men of their

[1] By John Fletcher.

[2] Johnson's meeting with Wilkes at Mr Dilly's dinner had occurred two years before this.

ages I know, for they have both worn themselves out by being eternally on the rack to give entertainment to others.'

'David, madam,' said the doctor, 'looks much older than he is; for his face has had double the business of any other man's; it is never at rest; when he speaks one minute, he has quite a different countenance to what he assumes the next; I don't believe he ever kept the same look for half an hour together in the whole course of his life; and such an eternal, restless, fatiguing play of the muscles must certainly wear out a man's face before its real time.'

'Oh, yes,' cried Mrs Thrale; 'we must certainly make some allowance for such wear and tear of a man's face.'

We left Streatham at about eight o'clock, and Mr Seward, who handed me into the chaise, added his interest to the rest, that my father would not fail to bring me again next week to stay with them for some time. In short, I was loaded with civilities from them all. And my ride home was equally happy with the rest of the day, for my kind and most beloved father was so happy in *my* happiness, and congratulated me so sweetly, that he could, like myself, think on no other subject.

Yet my honours stopped not here; for Hetty, who, with her *sposo*, was here to receive us, told me she had lately met Mrs Reynolds, sister of Sir Joshua; and that she talked very much and very highly of a new novel called *Evelina*; though without a shadow of suspicion as to the scribbler; and not contented with her own praise, she said that Sir Joshua, who began it one day when he was too much engaged to go on with it, was so much caught, that he could think of nothing else, and was quite absent all the day, not knowing a word that was said to him: and, when he took it up again, found himself so much interested in it, that he sat up all night to finish it!

Sir Joshua, it seems, vows he would give fifty pounds to know the author! I have also heard, by the means of Charles, that other persons have declared they *will* find him out!

This intelligence determined me upon going myself to Mr Lowndes, and discovering what sort of answers he made to such curious inquirers as I found were likely to address him. But as I did not dare trust myself to speak, for I felt that I should not be able to act my part well, I asked my mother to accompany me.

We introduced ourselves by buying the book, for which I had a commission from Mrs G——. Fortunately Mr Lowndes himself was in the shop; as we found by his air of consequence and authority, as well as his age; for I never saw him before.

The moment he had given my mother the book, she asked if he could tell her who wrote it.

'No,' he answered; 'I don't know myself.'

'Pho, pho,' said she; 'you mayn't choose to tell, but you must know.'

'I don't, indeed, ma'am,' answered he; 'I have no honour in keeping the secret, for I have never been trusted. All I know of the matter is, that it is a gentleman of the other end of the town.'

My mother made a thousand other enquiries, to which his answers were to the following effect: that for a great while, he did not know if it was a man or a woman; but now, he knew that much, and that he was a master of his subject, and well versed in the manners of the times.

'For some time,' continued he, 'I thought it had been Horace Walpole's; for he once published a book in this snug manner; [1] but I don't think it is now. I have often people come to inquire of me who it is; but I suppose he will come out soon, and then, when the rest of the world knows it, I shall. Servants often come for it from the other end of the town, and I have asked them divers questions myself, to see if I could get at the author; but I never got any satisfaction.'

Just before we came away, upon my mother's still further pressing him, he said, with a most important face:

'Why, to tell you the truth, madam, I have been

[1] *The Castle of Otranto*, which Lowndes had published.

informed that it is a piece of real secret history; and, in that case, it will never be known.'

This was too much for me; I grinned irresistibly, and was obliged to look out at the shop door till we came away.

STREATHAM, SUNDAY, AUG. 23. I know not how to express the fullness of my contentment at this sweet place. All my best expectations are exceeded, and you know they were not very moderate. If, when my dear father comes, Susan and Mr Crisp were to come too, I believe it would require at least a day's pondering to enable me to form another wish.

Our journey was charming. The kind Mrs Thrale would give courage to the most timid. She did not ask me questions, or catechize me upon what I knew, or use any means to draw me out, but made it her business to draw herself out—that is, to start subjects, to support them herself, and to take all the weight of the conversation, as if it behoved her to find me entertainment. But I am so much in love with her, that I shall be obliged to run away from the subject, or shall write of nothing else.

When we arrived here, Mrs Thrale showed me my room, which is an exceeding pleasant one, and then conducted me to the library, there to divert myself while she dressed.

Miss Thrale soon joined me: and I begin to like her. Mr Thrale was neither well nor in spirits all day. Indeed, he seems not to be a happy man, though he has every means of happiness in his power. But I think I have rarely seen a very rich man with a light heart and light spirits.

Dr Johnson was in the utmost good humour.

SATURDAY MORNING. Dr Johnson was again all himself; and so civil to me!—even admiring how I dressed myself! Indeed, it is well I have so much of his favour; for it seems he always speaks his mind concerning the dress of ladies, and all ladies who are here obey his injunctions implicitly, and alter whatever he disapproves. This is a part of his character that much surprises me: but notwithstanding he is sometimes so absent, and always so near-sighted, he scrutinizes into every part of almost everybody's appearance. They tell me of a Miss Brown, who often visits here, and who has a slovenly way of dressing. 'And when she comes down in a morning,' says Mrs Thrale, 'her hair will be all loose, and her cap half off; and then Dr Johnson, who sees something is wrong, and does not know where the fault is, concludes it is in the cap, and says, "My dear, what do you wear such a vile cap for?" "I'll change it, sir," cries the poor girl, "if you don't like it." "Aye, do," he says; and away runs poor Miss Brown; but when she gets on another, it's the same thing, for the cap has nothing to do with the fault. And then she wonders that Dr Johnson should not like the cap, for she thinks it very pretty. And so on with her gown, which he also makes her change; but if the poor girl were to change through all her wardrobe, unless she could put her things on better, he would still find fault.'

And now let me try to recollect an account he gave us of certain celebrated ladies of his acquaintance: an account which, had you heard from himself, would have made you die with laughing, his manner is so peculiar, and enforces his humour so originally.

It was begun by Mrs Thrale's apologizing to him for troubling him with some question she thought trifling— Oh, I remember! We had been talking of colours, and of the fantastic names given to them, and why the palest lilac should be called *soupir étouffé*; and when Dr Johnson came in she applied to him.

'Why, madam,' said he, with wonderful readiness, 'it is called a stifled sigh because it is checked in its progress, and only half a colour.'

I could not help expressing my amazement at his universal readiness upon all subjects, and Mrs Thrale said to him:

'Sir, Miss Burney wonders at your patience with such stuff; but I tell her you are used to me, for I believe I

torment you with more foolish questions than anybody
else dares do.'

'No, madam,' said he, 'you don't torment me—you
tease me, indeed, sometimes.'

'Aye, so I do, Dr Johnson, and I wonder you bear with
my nonsense.'

'No, madam, you never talk nonsense; you have as
much sense, and more wit, than any woman I know!'

'Oh,' cried Mrs Thrale, blushing, 'it is my turn . . .
this morning, Miss Burney!'

'And yet,' continued the doctor, with the most comical
look, 'I have known all the wits, from Mrs Montagu [1]
down to Bet Flint!'

'Bet Flint!' cried Mrs Thrale; 'pray who is she?'

'Oh, a fine character, madam! She was habitually a
slut and a drunkard, and occasionally a thief and a harlot.'

'And, for heaven's sake, how came you to know her?'

'Why, madam, she figured in the literary world, too!
Bet Flint wrote her own life, and called herself Cassandra,
and it was in verse; it began:

> When Nature first ordain'd my birth,
> A diminutive I was born on earth:
> And then I came from a dark abode,
> Into a gay and gaudy world.

So Bet brought me her verses to correct; but I gave her
half a crown, and she liked it as well. Bet had a fine
spirit; she advertised for a husband, but she had no
success, for she told me no man aspired to her! Then
she hired very handsome lodgings and a footboy; and
she got a harpsichord, but Bet could not play; however,
she put herself in fine attitudes, and drummed.'

Then he gave an account of another of these geniuses,
who called herself by some fine name, I have forgotten
what.

'She had not quite the same stock of virtue,' continued

[1] The celebrated blue-stocking. She was the author of an *Essay
on the Genius and Learning of Shakespeare*, which, according to Johnson
had not one sentence of true criticism in it.

he, 'nor the same stock of honesty as Bet Flint; but I suppose she envied her accomplishments, for she was so little moved by the power of harmony, that while Bet Flint thought she was drumming very divinely, the other jade had her indicted for a nuisance!'

'And pray what became of her, sir?'

'Why, madam, she stole a quilt from the man of the house, and he had her taken up: but Bet Flint had a spirit not to be subdued; so when she found herself obliged to go to jail, she ordered a sedan-chair, and bid her footboy walk before her. However, the boy proved refractory, for he was ashamed, though his mistress was not.'

'And did she ever get out of jail again, sir?'

'Yes, madam; when she came to her trial, the judge acquitted her. "So now," she said to me, "the quilt is my own and now I'll make a petticoat of it." Oh, I loved Bet Flint!'

Oh, how we all laughed! Then he gave an account of another lady, who called herself Laurinda, and who also wrote verses and stole furniture; but he had not the same affection for her, he said, though she too 'was a lady who had high notions of honour.'

Then followed the history of another, who called herself Hortensia, and who walked up and down the park repeating a book of Virgil.

'But,' said he, 'though I know her story, I never had the good fortune to see her.'

After this he gave an account of the famous Mrs Pinkethman; 'And she,' he said, 'told me she owed all her misfortunes to her wit; for she was so unhappy as to marry a man who thought himself also a wit, though I believe she gave him not implicit credit for it, but it occasioned much contradiction and ill-will.'

'Bless me, sir!' cried Mrs Thrale, 'how can all these vagabonds contrive to get at *you*, of all people?'

'Oh, the dear creatures!' cried he, laughing heartily, 'I can't but be glad to see them!'

'Why I wonder, sir, you never went to see Mrs Rudd[1] among the rest?'

'Why, madam, I believe I should,' said he, 'if it was not for the newspapers; but I am prevented many frolics that I should like very well since I am become such a theme for the papers.'

Now would you ever have imagined this? Bet Flint, it seems, once took Kitty Fisher to see him, but to his no little regret he was not at home. 'And Mrs Williams,'[2] he added, 'did not love Bet Flint, but Bet Flint made herself very easy about that.'

How Mr Crisp would have enjoyed this account! He gave it all with so droll a solemnity, and it was all so unexpected, that Mrs Thrale and I were both almost equally diverted.

Mr Crisp to Miss F. Burney

6th Nov., 1778.

My dear Fannikin,

. . . I do entirely acquit you of all wish or design of being known to the world as an author. I believe it is ever the case with writers of real merit and genius, on the appearance of their first productions: as their powers are finer and keener than other people's, so is their sensibility. On these occasions they are as nervous as Lady Louisa in *Evelina*. But surely these painful feelings ought to go off when the salts of general applause are continually held under their nose. It is then time to follow your friend Dr Johnson's advice, and learn to be a swaggerer, at least so far as to be able to face the world, and not be ashamed of the distinction you have fairly earned, especially when it is apparent you do not court it.

[1] Mrs Rudd was notorious for having given evidence against two brothers who were executed for forgery.

[2] Anna Williams, a blind woman whom Johnson allowed to live in his house. She was the daughter of a Welsh physician.

I now proceed to assume the daddy, and consequently the privilege of giving counsel. Your kind and judicious friends are certainly in the right in wishing you to make your talents turn to something more solid than empty praise. When you come to know the world half so well as I do, and what yahoos mankind are, you will then be convinced that a state of independence is the only basis on which to rest your future ease and comfort. You are now young, lively, gay. You please, and the world smiles upon you—this is your time. Years and wrinkles in their due season (perhaps attended with want of health and spirits) will succeed. You will then be no longer the same Fanny of 1778, feasted, caressed, admired, with all the soothing circumstances of your present situation. The Thrales, the Johnsons, the Sewards, Cholmondeleys, etc., etc., who are now so high in fashion, and might be such powerful protectors as almost to ensure success to anything that is tolerable, may then themselves be moved off the stage. I will no longer dwell on so disagreeable a change of the scene; let me only earnestly urge you to act vigorously (what I really believe is in your power) a distinguished part in the present one—'now while it is yet day, and before the night cometh, when no man can work.'

I must again and again repeat my former admonitions regarding your posture in reading and writing; it is of infinite consequence, especially to such lungs, and such a frame as yours.

Lastly, if you do resolve to undertake anything of the nature your friends recommend, keep it (if possible) an impenetrable secret that you are even about such a work. Let it be all your own till it is finished entirely in your own way; it will be time enough then to consult such friends as you think capable of judging and advising. If you suffer any one to interfere till then, 'tis ten to one 'tis the worse for it—it won't be all of a piece. In these cases generally the more cooks the worse broth, and I have more than once observed those pieces that have stole privately into the world, without midwives, or godfathers and godmothers—like your own, and the *Tale of a Tub*, and a few others, have far exceeded any that followed.

Your loving daddy,

S. C.

Diary resumed

Saturday evening Mr and Mrs Thrale took me quite round the paddock, and showed me their hothouses, kitchen gardens, etc. Their size and their contents are astonishing; but we have not once missed a pineapple since I came, and therefore you may imagine their abundance; besides grapes, melons, peaches, nectarines, and ices.

While Mrs Thrale and I were dressing, and, as usual, confabbing, a chaise drove into the park, and word was brought that Mr Seward was arrived.

'You don't know much of Mr Seward, Miss Burney?' said Mrs Thrale.

I could have told her I wished he had not known much of me; but her maid was in my way, and I only said: 'No.'

'But I hope you will know more of him,' said she, 'for I want you to take to him. He is a charming young man, though not without oddities. Few people do him justice, because, as Dr Johnson calls him, he is an abrupt young man; but he has excellent qualities, and an excellent understanding. He has the misfortune to be an hypochondriac, so he runs about the world to borrow spirits, and to forget himself. But after all, if his disorders are merely imaginary, the imagination is disorder sufficient, and therefore I am sorry for him.'

The day passed very agreeably, but I have no time for particulars. I fight very shy with Mr Seward, and as he has a great share of sense and penetration, and not a little one of pride and reserve, he takes the hint; and I believe he would as soon bite off his own nose as mention *Evelina* again. And, indeed, now that the propriety of his after-conduct has softened me in his favour, I begin to think of him much in the same way Mrs Thrale does, for he is very sensible, very intelligent, and very well bred.

MONDAY.   In the evening the company divided pretty much into parties and almost everybody walked upon the gravel walk before the windows.   I was going to have joined some of them, when Dr Johnson stopped me, and asked how I did.

'I was afraid, sir,' cried I, 'you did not intend to know me again, for you have not spoken to me before since your return from town.'

'My dear,' cried he, taking both my hands, 'I was not sure of you, I am so near-sighted, and I apprehended making some mistake.'

Then drawing me very unexpectedly towards him, he actually kissed me!

To be sure, I was a little surprised, having no idea of such facetiousness from him.   However, I was glad nobody was in the room but Mrs Thrale, who stood close to us, and Mr Embry, who was lounging on a sofa at the farthest end of the room.   Mrs Thrale laughed heartily, and said she hoped I was contented with his amends for not knowing me sooner.

A little after she said she would go and walk with the rest, if she did not fear for my reputation in being left with the doctor.

'However, as Mr Embry is yonder, I think he'll take some care of you,' she added.

'Aye, madam,' said the doctor, 'we shall do very well; but I assure you I shan't part with Miss Burney!'

And he held me by both hands; and when Mrs Thrale went, he drew me a chair himself facing the window, close to his own; and thus tête-à-tête we continued almost all the evening.   I say tête-à-tête because Mr Embry kept at an humble distance, and offered us no interruption.   And though Mr Seward soon after came in, he also seated himself in a distant corner, not presuming, he said, to break in upon us!   Everybody, he added, gave way to the doctor.

JAN. 1779. And now, my dear Susan, to relate the affairs of an evening, perhaps the most important of my life. To say that, is, I am sure, enough to interest you, my dearest girl, in all I can tell you of it.

On Monday last, my father sent a note to Mrs Cholmondeley, to propose our waiting on her the Wednesday following; she accepted the proposal, and accordingly on Wednesday evening, my father, mother, and self went to Hertford Street.

Well, we were received by Mrs Cholmondeley with great politeness, and in a manner that showed she intended to entirely throw aside Madame Duval,[1] and to conduct herself towards me in a new style.

Mr and the Misses Cholmondeley and Miss Forrest were with her; but who else think you?—why Mrs Sheridan![2] I was absolutely charmed at the sight of her. I think her quite as beautiful as ever, and even more captivating; for she has now a look of ease and happiness that animates her whole face.

Miss Linley was with her; she is very handsome, but nothing near her sister: the elegance of Mrs Sheridan's beauty is unequalled by any I ever saw, except Mrs Crewe.[3] I was pleased with her in all respects. She is much more lively and agreeable than I had any idea of finding her; she was very gay, and very unaffected, and totally free from airs of any kind.

Miss Linley was very much out of spirits; she did not speak three words the whole evening, and looked wholly unmoved at all that passed. Indeed she appeared to be heavy and inanimate.

Mrs Cholmondeley sat next me. She is determined, I believe, to make me like her; and she will, I believe, have full success; for she is very clever, very entertaining, and very much unlike anybody else.

[1] In *Evelina*. *Ma foi* (p. 24) refers to her.
[2] Before her marriage she was the lovely and celebrated singer, Miss Linley, daughter of the composer, Thomas Linley.
[3] Daughter of Fulke Greville, who had been Dr Burney's patron.

The first subject started was the Opera, and all joined in the praise of Pacchierotti. Mrs Sheridan declared she could not hear him without tears, and that he was the first Italian singer who ever affected her to such a degree.

Then they talked of the intended marriage of the Duke of Dorset with Miss Cumberland, and many ridiculous anecdotes were related. The conversation naturally fell upon Mr Cumberland, and he was finely cut up!

A rat-tat-tat-tat ensued, and the Earl of Harcourt was announced. When he had paid his compliments to Mrs Cholmondeley:

'I knew, ma'am,' he said, 'that I should find you at home.'

'I suppose then, my lord,' said she, 'that you have seen Sir Joshua Reynolds; for he is engaged to be here.'

'I have,' answered his lordship; 'and heard from him that I should be sure to find you.'

And then he added some very fine compliment, but I have forgot it.

'Oh, my lord,' cried she, 'you have the most discernment of anybody! His lordship (turning another way) always says these things to me, and yet he never flatters.'

Lord Harcourt, speaking of the lady from whose house he was just come, said:

'Mrs Vesey [1] is vastly agreeable, but her fear of ceremony is really troublesome: for her eagerness to break a circle is such, that she insists upon everybody's sitting with their backs one to another; that is, the chairs are drawn into little parties of three together, in a confused manner, all over the room.'

'Why, then,' said my father, 'they may have the pleasure of caballing and cutting up one another, even in the same room.'

'Oh, I like the notion of all things,' cried Mrs Cholmondeley; 'I shall certainly adopt it!'

[1] A blue-stocking. Her salon in Bolton Street rivalled that of Mrs Montagu.

And then she drew her chair into the middle of our circle. Lord Harcourt turned his round, and his back to most of us, and my father did the same. You can't imagine a more absurd sight.

Just then the door opened, and Mr Sheridan entered.

Was I not in luck? Not that I believe the meeting was accidental; but I had more wished to meet him and his wife than any people I know not.

I could not endure my ridiculous situation, but replaced myself in an orderly manner immediately. Mr Sheridan stared at them all, and Mrs Cholmondeley said she intended it as a hint for a comedy.

Mr Sheridan has a very fine figure, and a good though I don't think a handsome face. He is tall, and very upright, and his appearance and address are at once manly and fashionable, without the smallest tincture of foppery or modish graces. In short, I like him vastly, and think him every way worthy his beautiful companion.

And let me tell you what I know will give you as much pleasure as it gave me—that, by all I could observe in the course of the evening, and we stayed very late, they are extremely happy in each other: he evidently adores her, and she as evidently idolizes him. The world has by no means done him justice.

When he had paid his compliments to all his acquaintance, he went behind the sofa on which Mrs Sheridan and Miss Cholmondeley were seated, and entered into earnest conversation with them.

Upon Lord Harcourt's again paying Mrs Cholmondeley some compliment, she said:

'Well, my lord, after this I shall be quite sublime for some days! I shan't descend into common life till—till Saturday, and then I shall drop into the vulgar style—I shall be in the *ma foi* way.'

I do really believe she could not resist this, for she had seemed determined to be quiet.

When next there was a rat-tat, Mrs Cholmondeley and Lord Harcourt, and my father again, at the command of the former, moved into the middle of the room, and then Sir Joshua Reynolds and Dr Warton [1] entered.

No further company came. You may imagine there was a general roar at the breaking of the circle, and when they got into order, Mr Sheridan seated himself in the place Mrs Cholmondeley had left, between my father and myself.

And now I must tell you a little conversation which I did not hear myself till I came home; it was between Mr Sheridan and my father.

'Dr Burney,' cried the former, 'have you no older daughters? Can this possibly be the authoress of *Evelina*?'

And then he said abundance of fine things, and begged my father to introduce him to me.

'Why, it will be a very formidable thing to her,' answered he, 'to be introduced to you.'

'Well then, by and by,' returned he.

Some time after this, my eyes happening to meet his, he waived the ceremony of introduction, and in a low voice said:

'I have been telling Dr Burney that I have long expected to see in Miss Burney a lady of the gravest appearance, with the quickest parts.'

I was never much more astonished than at this unexpected address, as among all my numerous puffers the name of Sheridan has never reached me, and I did really imagine he had never deigned to look at my trash.

Of course I could make no verbal answer, and he proceeded then to speak of *Evelina* in terms of the highest praise; but I was in such a ferment from surprise (not to say pleasure), that I have no recollections of his expressions. I only remember telling him that I was much amazed he had spared time to read it, and that he repeatedly called it a most surprising book; and some time after he added: 'But I hope, Miss Burney, you don't intend to throw away your pen?'

[1] Joseph Warton (1722–1800), author of the *Essay on the Genius and Writings of Pope*.

'You should take care, sir,' said I, 'what you say: for you know not what weight it may have.'

He wished it might have any, he said; and soon after turned again to my father.

I protest, since the approbation of the Streathamites, I have met with none so flattering to me as this of Mr Sheridan, and so very unexpected.

About this time Mrs Cholmondeley was making much sport, by wishing for an acrostic on her name. She said she had several times begged for one in vain, and began to entertain thoughts of writing one herself.

'For,' said she, 'I am very famous for my rhymes, though I never made a line of poetry in my life.'

'An acrostic on your name,' said Mr Sheridan, 'would be a formidable task; it must be so long that I think it should be divided into cantos.'

'Miss Burney,' cried Sir Joshua, who was now reseated, 'are not you a writer of verses?'

F. B.: No, sir.

Mrs. Chol.: Oh, don't believe her. I have made a resolution not to believe anything she says.

Mr Sheridan: I think a lady should not write verses till she is past receiving them.

Mrs Chol.: [*Rising and stalking majestically towards him*] Mr Sheridan, pray, sir, what may you mean by this insinuation; did I not say I writ verses?

Mr Sheridan: Oh, but you——

Mrs. Chol.: Say no more, sir! You have made your meaning but too plain already. There now, I think that's a speech for a tragedy!

Some time after, Sir Joshua returning to his standing-place, entered into confab with Miss Linley and your slave, upon various matters, during which Mr Sheridan, joining us, said:

'Sir Joshua, I have been telling Miss Burney that she must not suffer her pen to lie idle—ought she?'

Sir Joshua: No, indeed, ought she not.

Mr Sheridan: Do you then, Sir Joshua, persuade her.

But perhaps you have begun something? May we ask? Will you answer a question candidly?

F. B.: I don't know, but as candidly as *Mrs Candour* [1] I think I certainly shall.

Mr Sheridan: What then are you about now?

F. B.: Why, twirling my fan, I think!

Mr Sheridan: No, no; but what are you about at home? However, it is not a fair question, so I won't press it.

Yet he looked very inquisitive; but I was glad to get off without any downright answer.

Sir Joshua: Anything in the dialogue way, I think, she must succeed in; and I am sure invention will not be wanting.

Mr Sheridan: No, indeed; I think, and say, she should write a comedy.

Sir Joshua: I am sure I think so; and hope she will.

I could only answer by incredulous exclamations.

'Consider,' continued Sir Joshua, 'you have already had all the applause and fame you can have given you in the closet; but the acclamation of a theatre will be new to you.'

And then he put down his trumpet,[2] and began a violent clapping of his hands.

I actually shook from head to foot! I felt myself already in Drury Lane, amidst the hubbub of a first night.

'Oh, no!' cried I, 'there may be a noise, but it will be just the reverse.' And I returned his salute with a hissing.

Mr Sheridan joined Sir Joshua very warmly.

'Oh, sir!' cried I, 'you should not run on so—you don't know what mischief you may do!'

Mr Sheridan: I wish I may—I shall be very glad to be accessory.

Sir Joshua: She has, certainly, something of a knack at characters—where she got it, I don't know, and how she got it, I can't imagine; but she certainly has it. And to throw it away is——

---

[1] *The School for Scandal* was first produced in May, 1777.
[2] Sir Joshua was deaf.

Mr Sheridan: Oh, she won't—she will write a comedy—she has promised me she will!

F. B.: Oh!—if you both run on in this manner, I shall——

I was going to say get under the chair, but Mr Sheridan, interrupting me with a laugh, said:

'Set about one? Very well, that's right!'

'Ay,' cried Sir Joshua, 'that's very right. And you (to Mr Sheridan) would take anything of hers, would you not?—unsight, unseen?'

What a point-blank question! Who but Sir Joshua would have ventured it!

'Yes,' answered Mr Sheridan, with quickness, 'and make her a bow and my best thanks into the bargain.'

Now, my dear Susy, tell me, did you ever hear the fellow to such a speech as this!—it was all I could do to sit it.

'Mr Sheridan,' I exclaimed, 'are you not mocking me?'

'No, upon my honour! this is what I have meditated to say to you the first time I should have the pleasure of seeing you.'

To be sure, as Mrs Thrale says, if folks are to be spoilt, there is nothing in the world so pleasant as spoiling! But I was never so much astonished, and seldom have been so much delighted, as by this attack of Mr Sheridan. Afterwards he took my father aside, and formally repeated his opinion that I should write for the stage, and his desire to see my play—with encomiums the most flattering of *Evelina*.

BRIGHTHELMSTONE,[1] MAY 26. I have not had a moment for writing, my dear Susy, since I came hither, till now, for we have been perpetually engaged either with sights or company; for notwithstanding this is not the season, here are folks enough to fill up time from morning to evening.

The road from Streatham hither is beautiful: Mr, Mrs, Miss Thrale, and Miss Susan Thrale, and I, travelled in a

---

[1] Although it had not yet been made fashionable by the Prince of Wales, Brighton was becoming popular as a health resort, chiefly owing to the 'salt water cure.'

coach, with four horses, and two of the servants in a
chaise, besides two men on horseback; so we were obliged
to stop for some time at three places on the road.

Reigate, the first town, is a very old, half-ruined borough,
in a most neglected condition. A high hill, leading to it,
afforded a very fine prospect, of the Malvern Hill nature,
though inferior.

At Cuckfield, which is in Sussex, and but fourteen miles
hence, we dined.

The view of the South Downs from Cuckfield to this
place is very curious and singular. We got home by
about nine o'clock. Mr Thrale's house is in West Street,
which is the court end of the town here as well as in
London. 'Tis a neat, small house, and I have a snug,
comfortable room to myself. The sea is not many yards
from our windows. Our journey was delightfully
pleasant, the day being heavenly, the roads in fine order,
the prospects charming, and everybody good-humoured
and cheerful.

THURSDAY. We pass our time here most delectably.
This dear and most sweet family grow daily more kind
to me; and all of them contrive to make me of so much
consequence, that I can now no more help being easy
than, till lately, I could help being embarrassed. Mrs
Thrale has, indeed, from the first moment of our acquaintance, been to me all my heart could wish; and now her
husband and daughter gain ground in my good grace
and favour every day.

Dr Delap arrived in the morning, and is to stay two
days. He is too silent for me to form much judgment
of his companionable talents, and his appearance is snug
and reserved. Mrs Thrale is reading his play, and likes
it much. It is to come out next season. It is droll
enough that there should be, at this time, a tragedy and
comedy [1] in exactly the same situation, placed so accidentally in the same house.

[1] Strongly urged by Mrs Thrale, Murphy, Sheridan, and others,
Fanny had been at work on a comedy which she called *The Witlings*.

We afterwards went on the parade, where the soldiers were mustering, and found Captain Fuller's men all half intoxicated, and laughing so violently as we passed by them, that they could hardly stand upright. The captain stormed at them most angrily; but, turning to us, said: 'These poor fellows have just been paid their arrears, and it is so unusual to them to have a sixpence in their pockets, that they know not how to keep it there.'

The wind being extremely high, our caps and gowns were blown about most abominably; and this increased the risibility of the merry light infantry. Captain Fuller's desire to keep order made me laugh as much as the men's incapacity to obey him; for finding our flying drapery provoked their mirth, he went up to the biggest grinner, and, shaking him violently by the shoulders, said: 'What do you laugh for, sirrah? Do you laugh at the ladies?' and, as soon as he had given the reprimand, it struck him to be so ridiculous, that he was obliged to turn quick round, and commit the very fault he was attacking most furiously.

I broke off where we were all assembled on Thursday—which, by the way, is exactly opposite to the inn in which Charles II hid himself after the battle of Worcester, previous to his escaping from the kingdom. So I fail not to look at it with loyal satisfaction: and his black-wigged Majesty has, from the time of the Restoration, been its sign.

FRIDAY, MAY 28. In the morning, before breakfast, came Dr Delap; and Mrs Thrale, in ambiguous terms, complimented him upon his play, and expressed her wish that she might tell me of it; upon which hint he instantly took the manuscript from his pocket, and presented it to me, begging me, at the same time, to tell him of any faults that I might meet with in it.

There, Susy! am I not grown a grand person; not merely looked upon as a writer, but addressed as a critic! Upon my word this is fine!

By the way, it is really amazing the fatigue these militia officers go through, without compulsion or interest to spur them. Major H. is a man of at least £8,000 a year, and has a noble seat in this country, and quits ease, pleasure, retirement in the country, and public diversions in London, to take charge of the Sussex militia! Captain Fuller, too, has an estate of £4,000 or £5,000 a year—is but just of age —has figure, understanding, education, vivacity, and independence—and yet voluntarily devotes almost all his time, and almost all his attention, to a company of light infantry![1]

Instances such as these, my dear Susy, ought to reconcile all the penniless sons of toil and industry to their cares and labours; since those whom affluence invites to all the luxuries of indolence, sicken of those very gifts which the others seem only to exist to procure.

SATURDAY, MAY 29. After breakfast, Mrs and Miss Thrale took me to Widget's, the milliner and library woman on the Steyne. After a little dawdling conversation, Captain Fuller came in to have a little chat. He said he had just gone through a great operation—'I have been,' he said, cutting off the hair of all my men.'

'And why?'

'Why, the Duke of Richmond ordered that it should be done, and the fellows swore that they would not submit to it—so I was forced to be the operator myself. I told them they would look as smart again when they had got on their caps; but it went much against them; they vowed, at first, they would not bear such usage; some said they would sooner be run through the body, and others, that the duke should as soon have their heads. I told them I would soon try that, and fell to work myself with them.'

'And how did they bear it?'

'Oh, poor fellows, with great good nature, when they found his honour was their barber: but I thought proper to submit to hearing all their oaths, and all their jokes;

[1] The War of American Independence was now at its height, and by this time France and Spain had entered the struggle.

for they had no other comfort but to hope I should have enough of it, and such sort of wit. Three or four of them, however, escaped, but I shall find them out. I told them I had a good mind to cut my own hair off too, and then they would have a Captain Crop. I shall soothe them to-morrow with a present of new feathers for all their caps.'

Presently we were joined by Dr Delap and Mr Murphy.[1]

Different occupations, in a short time, called away all our gentlemen but Dr Delap; and he, seating himself next me, began to question me about his tragedy. I soon said all I wanted to say upon the subject—and, soon after, a great deal more—but not soon after he was satisfied; he returned to the same thing a million of times, asked the same questions, exacted the same compliments, and worked at the same passages, till I almost fell asleep with the sound of the same words: and at last, with what little animation was left me, I contrived to make Miss Thrale propose a walk on the Steyne, and crawling out of the shop, I sought —and found—revival from the breezes.

STREATHAM, SUNDAY, JUNE 13. After church, we all strolled round the grounds, and the topic of our discourse was Miss Streatfeild.[2] Mrs Thrale asserted that she had a power of captivation that was irresistible; that her beauty, joined to her softness, her caressing manners, her tearful eyes, and alluring looks, would insinuate her into the heart of any man she thought worth attacking.

Sir Philip [3] declared himself of a totally different opinion, and quoted Dr Johnson against her, who had told him that, taking away her Greek, she was as ignorant as a butterfly.

Mr Seward declared her Greek was all against her with

---

[1] Arthur Murphy, the dramatist (1727–1805).

[2] Miss Streatfeild—'the S. S.,' as Fanny often calls her—was a favourite of Dr Johnson and Mr Thrale. The latter's fondness for her, indeed, accounts for the slightly malicious character of Mrs Thrale's remarks. In spite of the fair Sophy's attractions, which included a knowledge of Greek, she died unmarried.

[3] Sir Philip Jennings Clerke.

him, for that, instead of reading Pope, Swift, or the *Spectator*—books from which she might derive useful knowledge and improvement—it had led her to devote all her reading time to the first eight books of Homer.

'But,' said Mrs Thrale, 'her Greek, you must own, has made all her celebrity—you would have heard no more of her than of any other pretty girl, but for that.'

'What I object to,' said Sir Philip, 'is her avowed preference for this parson.   Surely it is very indelicate in any lady to let all the world know with whom she is in love!'

'The parson,' said the severe Mr Seward, 'I suppose, spoke first—or she would as soon have been in love with you, or with me!'

You will easily believe I gave him no pleasant look. He wanted me to slacken my pace, and tell him, in confidence, my private opinion of her: but I told him, very truly, that as I knew her chiefly by account, not by acquaintance, I had not absolutely formed my opinion.

'Were I to live with her four days,' said this odd man, 'I believe the fifth I should want to take her to church.'

'You'd be devilish tired of her, though,' said Sir Philip, 'in half a year.   A crying wife will never do!'

'Oh, yes,' cried he, 'the pleasure of soothing her would make amends.'

'Ah,' cried Mrs Thrale, 'I would ensure her power of crying herself into any of your hearts she pleased.   I made her cry to Miss Burney, to show how beautiful she looked in tears.'

'If I had been her,' said Mr Seward, 'I would never have visited you again.'

'Oh, but she liked it,' answered Mrs T., 'for she knows how well she does it.   Miss Burney would have run away, but she came forward on purpose to show herself.   I would have done so by nobody else; but Sophy Streatfeild is never happier than when the tears trickle from her fine eyes in company.'

WEDNESDAY, JUNE 16. We had, at breakfast, a scene, of its sort, the most curious I ever saw.

The persons were Sir Philip, Mr Seward, Dr Delap, Miss Streatfeild, Mrs and Miss Thrale, and I.

The discourse turning, I know not how, upon Miss Streatfeild, Mrs Thrale said:

'Aye, I made her cry once for Miss Burney as pretty as could be: but nobody does cry so pretty as the S. S. I'm sure, when she cried for Seward, I never saw her look half so lovely.'

'For Seward?' cried Sir Philip; 'did she cry for Seward? What a happy dog! I hope she'll never cry for me, for, if she does, I won't answer for the consequences!'

'Seward,' said Mrs Thrale, 'had affronted Johnson, and then Johnson affronted Seward, and then the S. S. cried.'

'Oh,' cried Sir Philip, 'that I had but been here!'

'Nay,' answered Mrs Thrale, 'you'd only have seen how like three fools three sensible persons behaved: for my part, I was quite sick of it, and of them, too.'

Sir Philip: But what did Seward do? Was he not melted?

Mrs Thrale: Not he; he was thinking only of his own affront, and taking fire at that.

Mr Seward: Why, yes, I did take fire, for I went and planted my back to it.

S. S.: And Mrs Thrale kept stuffing me with toast-and-water.

Sir Philip: But what did Seward do with himself? Was not he in ecstasy? What did he do, or say?

Mr Seward: Oh, I said: 'Pho, pho, don't let's have any more of this—it's making it of too much consequence: no more piping, pray.'

Sir Philip: Well, I have heard so much of these tears, that I would give the universe to have a sight of them.

Mrs Thrale: Well, she shall cry again, if you like it.

S. S.: No, pray, Mrs Thrale.

Sir Philip: Oh, pray do! Pray let me see a little of it.

Mrs Thrale: Yes, do cry a little, Sophy [*in a wheedling voice*], pray do! Consider now, you are going to-day, and it's very hard if you won't cry a little; indeed, S. S., you ought to cry.

Now for the wonder of wonders. When Mrs Thrale, in a coaxing voice, suited to a nurse soothing a baby, had run on for some time—while all the rest of us, in laughter, joined in the request—two crystal tears came into the soft eyes of the S. S., and rolled gently down her cheeks! Such a sight I never saw before, nor could I have believed. She offered not to conceal or dissipate them: on the contrary, she really contrived to have them seen by everybody. She looked, indeed, uncommonly handsome; for her pretty face was not, like Chloe's,[1] blubbered; it was smooth and elegant, and neither her features nor complexion were at all ruffled; nay, indeed, she was smiling all the time.

'Look, look!' cried Mrs Thrale; 'see if the tears are not come already.'

Loud and rude bursts of laughter broke from us all at once. How, indeed, could they be restrained? Yet we all stared, and looked and re-looked again and again, twenty times, ere we could believe our eyes. Sir Philip, I thought, would have died in convulsions; for his laughter and his politeness, struggling furiously with one another, made him almost black in the face. Mr Seward looked half vexed that her crying for him was now so much lowered in its flattery, yet grinned incessantly; Miss Thrale laughed as much as contempt would allow her; but Dr Delap seemed petrified with astonishment.

When our mirth abated, Sir Philip, colouring violently with his efforts to speak, said:

'I thank you, ma'am; I'm much obliged to you.'

But I really believe he spoke without knowing what he was saying.

'What a wonderful command,' said Dr Delap, very gravely, 'that lady must have over herself!'

She now took out a handkerchief and wiped her eyes.

'Sir Philip,' cried Mr Seward, 'how can you suffer her to dry her own eyes?—you, who sit next her?'

[1] 'Dear Cloe, how blubber'd is that pretty face!'—PRIOR.

'I dare not dry them for her,' answered he, 'because I am not the right man.'

'But if I sat next her,' returned he, 'she should not dry them herself.'

'I wish,' cried Dr Delap, 'I had a bottle to put them in; 'tis a thousand pities they should be wasted.'

'There, now,' said Mrs Thrale, 'she looks for all the world as if nothing had happened; for, you know, nothing *has* happened!'

'Would you cry, Miss Burney,' said Sir Philip, 'if we asked you?'

'Oh,' cried Mrs Thrale, 'I would not do thus by Miss Burney for ten worlds! I dare say she would never speak to me again. I should think she 'd be more likely to walk out of my house than to cry because I bid her.'

'I don't know how that is,' cried Sir Philip; 'but I 'm sure she 's gentle enough.'

'She can cry, I doubt not,' said Mr Seward, 'on any proper occasion.'

'But I must know,' said I, 'what for.'

Miss F. Burney to Dr Burney

The fatal knell, then, is knolled, and 'down among the dead men' sink the poor *Witlings*—for ever, and for ever, and for ever![1]

I give a sigh, whether I will or not, to their memory! for, however worthless, they were *mes enfans*, and one must do one's nature, as Mr Crisp will tell you of the dog.

You, my dearest sir, who enjoyed, I really think, even more than myself, the astonishing success of my first attempt, would, I believe, even more than myself, be hurt at the failure of my second; and I am sure I speak from the bottom of a very honest heart, when I most solemnly declare, that upon your account any disgrace would mortify

[1] Fanny suppressed the comedy in deference to the opinion of her father and Mr Crisp. The latter discovered in it a resemblance to Molière's *Femmes Savantes*, which, however, she had not read.

and afflict me more than upon my own; for whatever appears with your knowledge, will be naturally supposed to have met with your approbation, and, perhaps, your assistance; therefore, though all particular censure would fall where it ought—upon me—yet any general censure of the whole, and the plan, would cruelly, but certainly, involve you in its severity.

Of this I have been sensible from the moment my 'authorshipness' was discovered, and, therefore, from that moment, I determined to have no opinion of my own in regard to what I should thenceforth part with out of my own hands. I would long since have burnt the fourth act, upon your disapprobation of it, but that I waited, and was by Mrs Thrale so much encouraged to wait, for your finishing the piece.

You have finished it now in every sense of the word. Partial faults may be corrected; but what I most wished was, to know the general effect of the whole; and as that has so terribly failed, all petty criticisms would be needless. I shall wipe it all from my memory, and endeavour never to recollect that I ever wrote it.

You bid me open my heart to you—and so, my dearest sir, I will, for it is the greatest happiness of my life that I dare be sincere to you. I expected many objections to be raised—a thousand errors to be pointed out—and a million of alterations to be proposed; but the suppression of the piece were words I did not expect; indeed, after the warm approbation of Mrs Thrale, and the repeated commendations and flattery of Mr Murphy, how could I?

I do not, therefore, pretend to wish you should think a decision, for which I was so little prepared, has given me no disturbance; for I must be a far more egregious witling than any of those I tried to draw, to imagine you could ever credit that I wrote without some remote hope of success now—though I literally did when I composed *Evelina*!

But my mortification is not at throwing away the characters, or the contrivance—it is all at throwing away the time—which I with difficulty stole, and which I have buried in the mere trouble of writing.

What my Daddy Crisp says, 'that it would be the best policy, but for pecuniary advantages, for me to write no more,' is exactly what I have always thought since *Evelina* was published. But I will not now talk of putting it in practice—for the best way I can take of showing that I have a true and just sense of the spirit of your condemnation, is not to sink sulky and dejected under it, but to exert myself to the utmost of my power in endeavours to produce something less reprehensible. . . .

Adieu, my dearest, kindest, truest, best friend. I will never proceed so far again without your counsel, and then I shall not only save myself so much useless trouble, but you, who so reluctantly blame, the kind pain which I am sure must attend your disapprobation. The world will not always go well, as Mrs Sapient [1] might say, and I am sure I have long thought I have had more than my share of success already.

. . . Once more, adieu, dearest sir! and never may my philosophy be put to the test of seeing any abatement of true kindness from you—for that would never be decently endured by

> Your own,
> FRANCES BURNEY.

OCTOBER. On Tuesday, Mr, Mrs, Miss Thrale, and 'yours, ma'am, yours,' set out on their expedition. The day was very pleasant, and the journey delightful; but that which chiefly rendered it so was Mr Thrale's being apparently the better for it.

I need not tell you how sweet a county for travelling is Kent, as you know it so well. We stopped at Sevenoaks, which is a remarkably well-situated town; and here, while

---

[1] A character in *The Witlings*.

dinner was preparing, my kind and sweet friends took me
to Knowle, though they had seen it repeatedly themselves.

We dined very comfortably at Sevenoaks, and thence
made but one stage to Tunbridge. It was so dark when
we went through the town that I could see it very in-
distinctly. The Wells, however, are about seven miles
yet farther—so that we saw that night nothing; but I
assure you, I felt that I was entering into a new country
pretty roughly, for the roads were so *sidelum* and *jumblum*,
as Miss L—— called those of Teignmouth, that I expected
an overturn every minute. Safely, however, we reached
the Sussex Hotel, at Tunbridge Wells.

Having looked at our rooms, and arranged our affairs,
we proceeded to Mount Ephraim, where Miss Streatfeild
resides. We found her with only her mother, and spent
the evening there.

Mrs Streatfeild is very—very little, but perfectly well
made, thin, genteel, and delicate. She has been quite
beautiful and has still so much of beauty left, that to call
it only the remains of a fine face seems hardly doing her
justice. She is very lively, and an excellent mimic, and
is, I think, as much superior to her daughter in natural
gifts as her daughter is to her in acquired ones: and how
infinitely preferable are parts without education to education without parts!

The fair S. S. is really in higher beauty that I have ever
yet seen her; and she was so caressing, so soft, so amiable,
that I felt myself insensibly inclining to her with an
affectionate regard. 'If it were not for that little gush,'
as Dr Delap said, I should certainly have taken a very
great fancy to her: but tears so ready—oh, they blot out
my fair opinion of her! Yet whenever I am with her, I
like, nay, almost love her, for her manners are exceedingly
captivating; but when I quit her, I do not find that she
improves by being thought over—no, nor talked over;
for Mrs Thrale, who is always disposed to half adore her
in her presence, can never converse about her without
exciting her own contempt by recapitulating what has

passed. This, however, must always be certain, whatever may be doubtful, that she is a girl in no respect like any other.

But I have not yet done with the mother; I have told you of her vivacity and her mimicry, but her character is not yet half told. She has a kind of whimsical conceit, and odd affectation, that, joined to a very singular sort of humour, makes her always seem to be rehearsing some scene in a comedy. She takes off, if she mentions them, all her own children, and, though she quite adores them, renders them ridiculous with all her power. She laughs at herself for her smallness and for her vagaries, just with the same ease and ridicule as if she were speaking of some other person; and, while perpetually hinting at being old and broken, she is continually frisking, flaunting, and playing tricks, like a young coquette.

When I was introduced to her by Mrs Thrale, who said: 'Give me leave, ma'am, to present to you a friend of your daughter's—Miss Burney,' she advanced to me with a tripping pace, and, taking one of my fingers, said: 'Allow me, ma'am, will you, to create a little acquaintance with you.'

And, indeed, I readily entered into an alliance with her, for I found nothing at Tunbridge half so entertaining, except, indeed, Miss Birch, of whom hereafter.

The next morning the S. S. breakfasted with us: and then they walked about to show me the place.

The Sussex Hotel, where we lived, is situated at the side of the Pantiles, or public walk, so called because paved with pantiles; it is called so also, like the long room at Hampstead, because it would be difficult to distinguish it by any other name; for it has no beauty in itself, and borrows none from foreign aid, as it has only common houses at one side, and little millinery and Tunbridge-ware shops at the other, and at each end is choked up by buildings that intercept all prospect. How such a place could first be made a fashionable pleasure walk, everybody must wonder.

Tunbridge Wells is a place that to me appeared very singular: the country is all rock, and every part of it is either up or down hill; scarce ten yards square being level ground in the whole place: the houses, too, are scattered about in a strange, wild manner, and look as if they had been dropped where they stand by accident, for they form neither streets nor squares, but seem strewed promiscuously, except, indeed, where the shopkeepers live, who have got two or three dirty little lanes, much like dirty little lanes in other places.

Mrs Streatfeild and I increased our intimacy marvellously. She gave me the name of '*the dove*,' for what reason I cannot guess, except it be that the dove has a sort of greenish grey eye, something like mine: be that as it may, she called me nothing else while I stayed at Tunbridge.

In the evening we all went to the rooms. The rooms, as they are called, consisted, for this evening, of only one apartment, as there was not company enough to make more necessary; and a very plain, unadorned, and ordinary apartment that was.

There were very few people, but among them Mr Wedderburne, the Attorney-General.[1] You may believe I rather wished to shrink from him, if you recollect what Mrs Thrale said of him, among the rest of the Tunbridge coterie, last season, who discussed *Evelina* regularly each evening; and that he, siding with Mrs Montagu, cut up the Branghtons, and had, as well as Mrs Montagu, almost a quarrel with Mrs Greville upon the subject, because she so warmly vindicated, or rather applauded them. Lady Louisa, however, I remember he spoke of with very high praise, as Mrs Montagu did of the Dedication; and if such folks can find anything to praise, I find myself amply recompensed for their censures, especially when they censure what I cannot regret writing, since it is the part most favoured by Dr Johnson.

Mr Wedderburne joined us immediately. Mrs Thrale

[1] Alexander Wedderburn, afterwards Lord Loughborough.

presently said: 'Mr Wedderburne, I must present my daughter to you—and Miss Burney.'

I curtsied mighty gravely, and shuffled to the other end of the party.

Amongst the company, I was most struck with the Hon. Mrs W——, lately Miss T——. She ran away with a Mr W——, a man nearly old enough to be her father, and of most notorious bad character, both as a sharper and a libertine. This wretch was with her—a most hackneyed, ill-looking object as I ever saw; and the foolish girl, who seems scarce sixteen, and looks a raw schoolgirl, has an air of so much discontent, and seems in a state of such dismal melancholy, that it was not possible to look at her without compassionating a folly she has so many years to live regretting. I would not wish a more striking warning to be given to other such forward, adventurous damsels, than to place before them this miserable runaway, who has not only disgraced her family, and enraged her friends, but rendered herself a repentant mourner for life.

The next morning we had the company of two young ladies at breakfast—the S. S. and a Miss Birch, a little girl but ten years old, whom the S. S. invited, well foreseeing how much we should all be obliged to her.

This Miss Birch is a niece of the charming Mrs Pleydell, and so like her, that I should have taken her for her daughter, yet she is not, now, quite so handsome; but as she will soon know how to display her beauty to the utmost advantage, I fancy, in a few years, she will yet more resemble her lovely and most bewitching aunt. Everybody, she said, tells her how like she is to her aunt Pleydell.

As you, therefore, have seen that sweet woman, only imagine her ten years old, and you will see her sweet niece. Nor does the resemblance rest with the person; she sings like her, laughs like her, talks like her, caresses like her, and alternately softens and animates just like her.

Her conversation is not merely like that of a woman already, but like that of a most uncommonly informed, cultivated, and sagacious woman; and at the same time that her understanding is thus wonderfully premature, she can, at pleasure, throw off all this rationality, and make herself a mere playful, giddy, romping child. One moment, with mingled gravity and sarcasm, she discusses characters, and the next, with schoolgirl spirits, she jumps round the room; then, suddenly, she asks: 'Do you know such, or such a song?' and instantly, with mixed grace and buffoonery, singles out an object, and sings it; and then, before there has been time to applaud her, she runs into the middle of the room, to try some new step in a dance; and after all this, without waiting till her vagaries grow tiresome, she flings herself, with an affectionate air, upon somebody's lap, and there, composed and thoughtful, she continues quiet till she again enters into rational conversation.

Her voice is really charming — infinitely the most powerful, as well as sweet, I ever heard at her age. Were she well and constantly taught, she might, I should think, do anything—for, two or three Italian songs, which she learnt out of only five months' teaching by Parsons, she sung like a little angel, with respect to taste, feeling, and expression; but she now learns of nobody, and is so fond of French songs, for the sake, she says, of the sentiment, that I fear she will have her wonderful abilities all thrown away. Oh, how I wish my father had the charge of her!

She has spent four years out of her little life in France, which has made her distractedly fond of the French operas, *Rose et Colas*, *Annette et Lubin*, etc., and she told us the story quite through of several I never heard of, always singing the *sujet* when she came to the airs, and comically changing parts in the duets. She speaks French with the same fluency as English, and every now and then, addressing herself to the S. S.—'*Que je vous adore!*'—'*Ah, permettez que je me mette à vos pieds!*' etc., with a dying languor that was equally laughable and lovely.

When I found, by her taught songs, what a delightful singer she was capable of becoming, I really had not patience to hear her little French airs, and entreated her to give them up; but the little rogue instantly began pestering me with them, singing one after another with a comical sort of malice, and following me round the room, when I said I would not listen to her, to say: 'But is not this pretty? —and this?—and this?' singing away with all her might and main.

She sung without any accompaniment, as we had no instrument; but the S. S. says she plays too, very well. Indeed, I fancy she can do well whatever she pleases.

We hardly knew how to get away from her when the carriage was ready to take us from Tunbridge, and Mrs Thrale was so much enchanted with her that she went on the Pantiles and bought her a very beautiful inkstand.

'I don't mean, Miss Birch,' she said, when she gave it to her, 'to present you this toy as to a child, but merely to beg you will do me the favour to accept something that may make you now and then remember us.'

She was much delighted with this present, and told me, in a whisper, that she should put a drawing of it in her journal.

So you see, Susy, other children have had this whim. But something being said of novels, the S. S. said:

'Selina, do you ever read them?' And with a sigh, the little girl answered:

'But too often!—I wish I did not!'

The only thing I did not like in this seducing little creature was our leave-taking. The S. S. had, as we expected, her fine eyes suffused with tears, and nothing would serve the little Selina, who admires the S. S. passionately, but that she, also, must weep—and weep, therefore, she did, and that in a manner as pretty to look at, as soft, as melting, and as little to her discomposure, as the weeping of her fair exemplar. The child's success in this pathetic art made the tears of both appear to the whole party to be lodged, as the English merchant says, 'very near the eyes'!

Doubtful as it is whether we shall ever see this sweet siren again, nothing, as Mrs Thrale said to her, can be more certain than that we shall hear of her again, let her go whither she will.

Charmed as we all were with her, we all agreed that to have the care of her would be distraction! 'She seems the girl in the world,' Mrs Thrale wisely said, 'to attain the highest reach of human perfection as a man's mistress! —as such she would be a second Cleopatra, and have the world at her command.'

Poor thing! I hope to heaven she will escape such sovereignty and such honours!

We left Tunbridge Wells, and got, by dinner time, to our first stage, Uckfield, which afforded me nothing to record, except two lines of a curious epitaph which I picked up in the churchyard:

> A wife and eight little children had I,
> And two at a birth who never did cry.

BATH, APRIL, 1780. Don't be angry that I have been absent so long without writing, for I have been so entirely without a moment to myself, except for dressing, that I really have not had it in my power. This morning, being obliged to have my hair dressed early, I am a prisoner, that I may not spoil it by a hat, and therefore I have made use of my captivity in writing to my dear Susy; and, briefly, I will now chronicle what has occupied me hitherto.

The journey was very comfortable; Mr Thrale was charmingly well and in very good spirits, and Mrs Thrale must be charming, well or ill. We only went to Maidenhead Bridge the first night, where I found the caution of not attempting to travel near Windsor on a hunting day, was a very necessary one, as we were with difficulty accommodated even the day after the hunt, several stragglers yet remaining at all the inns, and we heard of nothing but the king and royal huntsmen and hunts-women.

The second day we slept at Speen Hill, and the third day we reached Devizes.

And here, Mrs Thrale and I were much pleased with our hostess, Mrs Lawrence, who seemed something above her station in her inn. While we were at cards before supper, we were much surprised by the sound of a piano-forte. I jumped up, and ran to listen whence it proceeded. I found it came from the next room, where the overture to the *Buona Figliuola* was performing. The playing was very decent, but as the music was not quite new to me, my curiosity was not whole ages in satisfying, and there-fore I returned to finish the rubber.

Don't I begin to talk in an old-cattish manner of cards?

Well, another deal was hardly played, ere we heard the sound of a voice, and out I ran again. The singing, however, detained me not long, and so back I whisked: but the performance, however indifferent in itself, yet surprised us at the 'Bear' at Devizes, and, therefore, Mrs Thrale determined to know from whom it came. Accord-ingly, she tapped at the door. A very handsome girl, about thirteen years old, with fine dark hair upon a finely-formed forehead, opened it. Mrs Thrale made an apology for her intrusion, but the poor girl blushed and retreated into a corner of the room: another girl, however, advanced, and obligingly and gracefully invited us in, and gave us all chairs. She was just sixteen, extremely pretty, and with a countenance better than her features, though those were also very good. Mrs Thrale made her many compliments, which she received with a mingled modesty and pleasure, both becoming and interesting. She was, indeed, a sweetly pleasing girl.

We found they were both daughters of our hostess, and born and bred at Devizes. We were extremely pleased with them, and made them a long visit, which I wished to have been longer. But though those pretty girls struck us so much, the wonder of the family was yet to be

produced. This was their brother,[1] a most lovely boy
of ten years of age, who seems to be not merely the
wonder of their family, but of the times, for his astonishing
skill in drawing. They protest he has never had any
instruction, yet showed us some of his productions that
were really beautiful. Those that were copies were
delightful—those of his own composition amazing,
though far inferior. I was equally struck with the boy
and his works.

We found that he had been taken to town, and that all
the painters had been very kind to him, and Sir Joshua
Reynolds had pronounced him, the mother said, the most
promising genius he had ever met with. Mr Hoare[2]
has been so charmed with this sweet boy's drawings that
he intends sending him to Italy with his own son.

This house was full of books, as well as paintings,
drawings, and music; and all the family seem not only
ingenious and industrious, but amiable; added to which,
they are strikingly handsome.

I hope we shall return the same road, that we may see
them again.

SUNDAY. We went to St James's Church, heard a very
indifferent preacher, and returned to read better sermons
of our own choosing.

In the evening we had again an engagement. This,
however, was far more agreeable than our last. It was
at Mrs Lambart's. Mrs Lambart is a widow of General
Lambart, and a sister of Sir Philip Jennings. She is an
easy, chatty, sensible woman of the world.

TUESDAY, JUNE 7. In the evening we went to Mrs
Lambart's; but of that visit, in which I made a very extraordinary new acquaintance, in my next packet; for this
will not hold the account.

WEDNESDAY. To go on with Mrs Lambart. The party

---

[1] Afterwards Sir Thomas Lawrence (1769–1830). He succeeded
Benjamin West as President of the Royal Academy.
[2] William Hoare, the portrait painter. His son, Prince Hoare, was
also interested in Lawrence ,who, however ,was not sent to Italy.

was Mr and Mrs Vanbrugh—the former a good sort of
man—the latter, Captain Bouchier says, reckons herself
a woman of humour, but she kept it prodigious snug;
Lord Huntingdon, a very deaf old lord; Sir Robert Pigot,
a very thin old baronet; Mr Tyson, a very civil master of
the ceremonies; Mr and Mrs White, a very insignificant
couple; Sir James C——, a bawling old man; two Misses
C——, a pair of tonish misses; Mrs and Miss Byron;[1]
Miss W——, and certain others I knew nothing of.

Augusta Byron, according to custom, had entered into
conversation with me, and we were talking about her
sisters, and her affairs, when Mr E—— (whose name I forgot to mention) came to inform me that Mrs Lambart
begged to speak to me. She was upon a sofa with Miss
W——, who, it seemed, desired much to be introduced
to me, and so I took a chair facing them.

Miss W—— is young and pleasing in her appearance,
not pretty, but agreeable in her face, and soft, gentle, and
well-bred in her manners. Our conversation, for some
time, was upon the common Bath topics; but when Mrs
Lambart left us—called to receive more company—we
went insensibly into graver matters.

As soon as I found, by the looks and expressions of this
young lady, that she was of a peculiar cast, I left all choice
of subjects to herself, determined quietly to follow as she
led; and very soon, and I am sure I know not how, we
had for topics the follies and vices of mankind, and,
indeed, she spared not for lashing them. The women
she rather excused than defended, laying to the door of
the men their faults and imperfections; but the men, she
said, were all bad—all, in one word, and without exception,
sensualists!

I stared much at a severity of speech for which her
softness of manner had so ill prepared me; and she,
perceiving my surprise, said:

'I am sure I ought to apologize for speaking my opinion

[1] Mrs and Miss Byron were the wife and daughter respectively of
Admiral Byron—'Foul-weather Jack.'

to you—you, who have so just and so uncommon a knowledge of human nature. I have long wished ardently to have the honour of conversing with you; but your party has, altogether, been regarded as so formidable, that I have not had courage to approach it.'

I made — as what could I do else? — disqualifying speeches, and she then led to discoursing of happiness and misery: the latter she held to be the invariable lot of us all; and 'one word,' she added, 'we have in our language, and in all others, for which there is never any essential necessity, and that is—*pleasure*!' And her eyes filled with tears as she spoke.

'How you amaze me!' cried I; 'I have met with misanthropes before, but never with so complete a one; and I can hardly think I hear right when I see how young you are!'

She then, in rather indirect terms, gave me to understand that she was miserable at home, and in very direct terms, that she was wretched abroad; and openly said, that to affliction she was born, and in affliction she must die, for that the world was so vilely formed as to render happiness impossible for its inhabitants.

There was something in this freedom of repining that I could by no means approve, and, as I found by all her manner that she had a disposition to even respect whatever I said, I now grew very serious, and frankly told her that I could not think it consistent with either truth or religion to cherish such notions.

'One thing,' answered she, 'there is, which I believe might make me happy, but for that I have no inclination: it is an amorous disposition; but that I do not possess. I can make myself no happiness by intrigue.'

'I hope not, indeed!' cried I, almost confounded by her extraordinary notions and speeches; 'but, surely, there are worthier subjects of happiness attainable!'

'No, I believe there are not, and the reason the men are happier than us, is because they are more sensual!'

'I would not think such thoughts,' cried I, clasping my hands with an involuntary vehemence, 'for worlds!'

The Misses C—— then interrupted us, and seated themselves next to us; but Miss W—— paid them little attention at first, and soon after none at all; but, in a low voice, continued her discourse with me, recurring to the same subject of happiness and misery, upon which, after again asserting the folly of ever hoping for the former, she made this speech:

'There may be, indeed, one moment of happiness, which must be the finding one worthy of exciting a passion which one should dare own to himself. That would, indeed, be a moment worth living for! But that can never happen—I am sure, not to me—the men are so low, so vicious, so worthless! No, there is not one such to be found!'

What a strange girl! I could do little more than listen to her, from surprise at all she said.

'If, however,' she continued, 'I had your talents, I could, bad as this world is, be happy in it. There is nothing, there is nobody I envy like you. With such resources as yours there can never be *ennui*; the mind may always be employed, and always be gay! Oh, if I could write as you write!'

'Try,' cried I, 'that is all that is wanting: try, and you will soon do much better things!'

'Oh, no! I have tried, but I cannot succeed.'

'Perhaps you are too diffident. But is it possible you can be serious in so dreadful an assertion as that you are never happy? Are you sure that some real misfortune would not show you that your present misery is imaginary?'

'I don't know,' answered she, looking down, 'perhaps it is so—but in that case, 'tis a misery so much the harder to be cured.'

'You surprise me more and more,' cried I; 'is it possible you can so rationally see the disease of a disordered imagination, and yet allow it such power over your mind?'

'Yes, for it is the only source from which I draw any

shadow of felicity. Sometimes when in the country, I give way to my imagination for whole days, and then I forget the world and its cares, and feel some enjoyment of existence.'

'Tell me what is then your notion of felicity? Whither does your castle-building carry you?'

'Oh, quite out of the world—I know not where, but I am surrounded with sylphs, and I forget everything besides.'

'Well, you are a most extraordinary character, indeed; I must confess I have seen nothing like you!'

'I hope, however, I shall find something like myself, and, like the magnet rolling in the dust, attract some metal as I go.'

'That you may attract what you please is, of all things the most likely; but if you wait to be happy for a friend resembling yourself, I shall no longer wonder at your despondency.'

'Oh!' cried she, raising her eyes in ecstasy, 'could I find such a one!—male or female—for sex would be indifferent to me. With such a one I would go to live directly.'

I half laughed, but was perplexed in my own mind whether to be sad or merry at such a speech.

'But then,' she continued, 'after making, should I lose such a friend, I would not survive.'

'Not survive?' repeated I, 'what can you mean?'

She looked down, but said nothing.

'Surely you cannot mean,' said I, very gravely indeed, 'to put a violent end to your life?'

'I should not,' she said, again looking up, 'hesitate a moment.'

I was quite thunderstruck, and for some time could not say a word; but when I did speak, it was in a style of exhortation so serious and earnest, that I am ashamed to write it to you, lest you should think it too much.

She gave me an attention that was even respectful, but

when I urged her to tell me by what right she thought
herself entitled to rush unlicensed on eternity, she said:
'By the right of believing I shall be extinct.'

I really felt horror-struck.

'Where, for heaven's sake,' I cried, 'where have you
picked up such dreadful reasoning?'

'In Hume,' said she; 'I have read his essays repeatedly.'[1]

'I am sorry to find they have power to do so much
mischief.   You should not have read them, at least till a
man equal to Hume in abilities had answered him.   Have
you read any more infidel writers?'

'Yes, Bolingbroke,[2] the divinest of all writers.'

'And do you read nothing upon the right side?'

'Yes, the Bible, till I was sick to death of it, every Sunday
evening to my mother.'

'Have you read Beattie on *The Immutability of Truth*?'[3]

'No.'

'Give me leave, then, to recommend it to you.   After
Hume's *Essays* you ought to read it.   And even for
lighter reading, if you were to look at Mason's *Elegy on
Lady Coventry*, it might be of no disservice to you.'[4]

Poor misguided girl!   I heartily indeed wish she was
in good hands.   She is in a very dangerous situation,
with ideas so loose of religion, and so enthusiastic
of love.   What, indeed, is there to restrain an infidel,
who has no belief in a future state, from sin and evil of
any sort?

---

[1] Hume's *Essays* were published in 1741–2.

[2] Miss W—— was thinking of the essays *On Authority in Matters of
Religion*, etc., published by Mallet after Bolingbroke's death, and
vigorously denounced by Johnson.

[3] James Beattie, the poet (1735–1803).   The full title of the work
in question was *Essay on the Nature and Immutability of Truth in Opposition to Sophistry and Scepticism.*

[4] William Mason (1724–1797), best known for his edition of the
life and poems of Gray.

Miss F. Burney to Dr Burney

Bath, June 9, 1780.

MY DEAREST SIR,

How are you? Where are you? And what is to come next? These are the questions I am dying with anxiety to have daily announced. The accounts from town are so frightful that I am uneasy, not only for the city at large, but for every individual I know in it. I hope to heaven that ere you receive this, all will be once more quiet; but till we hear that it is so, I cannot be a moment in peace.[1]

Does this martial law confine you quite to the house? Folks here say that it must, and that no business of any kind can be transacted. Oh, what dreadful times! Yet I rejoice extremely that the opposition members have fared little better than the ministerial. Had such a mob been confirmed friends of either or of any party, I think the nation must have been at their disposal; for if headed by popular or skilful leaders, who and what could have resisted them?—I mean, if they are as formidable as we are here told.

Dr Johnson has written to Mrs Thrale, without even mentioning the existence of this mob; perhaps at this very moment he thinks it 'a humbug upon the nation,' as George Bodens called the Parliament.

A private letter to Bull, the bookseller, brought word this morning that much slaughter has been made by the military among the mob. Never, I am sure, can any set of wretches less deserve quarter or pity; yet it is impossible not to shudder at hearing of their destruction. Nothing less, however, would do; they were too outrageous and powerful for civil power.

But what is it they want? Who is going to turn papist? Who indeed, is thinking in an alarming way of religion— this pious mob, and George Gordon excepted?

I am very anxious indeed about our dear Etty. Such

[1] The Gordon Riots had broken out on the 2nd June.

disturbance in her neighbourhood I fear must have greatly
terrified her; and I am sure she is not in a situation or
state of health to bear terror. I have written and begged
to hear from her.

All the stage coaches that come into Bath from London
are chalked over with 'No Popery,' and Dr Harrington
called here just now, and says the same was chalked this
morning upon his door, and is scrawled in several places
about the town. Wagers have been laid that the popish
chapel here will be pulled or burnt down in a few days;
but I believe not a word of the matter, nor do I find that
anybody is at all alarmed. Bath, indeed, ought to be
held sacred as a sanctuary for invalids; and I doubt not
but the news of the firing in town will prevent all tumults
out of it.

Now, if, after all the intolerable provocation given by
the mob, after all the leniency and forbearance of the
Ministry, and after the shrinking of the minority, we shall
by and by hear that this firing was a massacre—will it
not be villainous and horrible? And yet as soon as safety
is secured—though by this means alone all now agree
it can be secured—nothing would less surprise me than
to hear the seekers of popularity make this assertion.

Will you, dear sir, beg Charlotte to answer this letter
by your directions, and tell me how the world goes? We
are sure here of hearing too much or too little. Mr
Grenville says he knows not whether anything can be
done to Lord George; and that quite shocks me, as it is
certain that, in all equity and common sense, he is either mad
enough for Moorfields, or wicked enough for the Tower,
and, therefore, that to one of these places he ought to go.

FRIDAY NIGHT. The above I writ this morning, before
I recollected this was not post day, and all is altered here
since. The threats I despised were but too well grounded,
for, to our utter amazement and consternation, the new
Roman Catholic chapel in this town was set on fire at about
nine o'clock. It is now burning with a fury that is
dreadful, and the house of the priest belonging to it is in

flames also. The poor persecuted man himself has, I believe, escaped with life, though pelted, followed, and very ill-used. Mrs Thrale and I have been walking about with the footmen several times. The whole town is still and orderly. The rioters do their work with great composure, and though there are knots of people in every corner, all execrating the authors of such outrages, nobody dares oppose them. An attempt indeed was made, but it was ill-conducted, faintly followed, and soon put an end to by a secret fear of exciting vengeance.

Alas! to what have we all lived!—the poor invalids here will probably lose all chance of life, from terror. Mr Hay, our apothecary, has been attending the removal of two, who were confined to their beds, in the street where the chapel is burning. The Catholics throughout the place are all threatened with destruction, and we met several porters, between ten and eleven at night, privately removing goods, walking on tiptoe, and scarcely breathing.

I firmly believe, by the deliberate villainy with which this riot is conducted, that it will go on in the same desperate way as in town, and only be stopped by the same desperate means. Our plan for going to Bristol is at an end. We are told it would be madness, as there are seven Romish chapels in it; but we are determined upon removing somewhere to-morrow; for why should we, who can go, stay to witness such horrid scenes?

SATURDAY AFTERNOON, JUNE 10. I was most cruelly disappointed in not having one word to-day. I am half crazy with doubt and disturbance in not hearing. Everybody here is terrified to death. We have intelligence that Mr Thrale's house in town is filled with soldiers, and threatened by the mob with destruction. Perhaps he may himself be a marked man for their fury. We are going directly from Bath, and intend to stop only at villages. To-night we shall stop at Warminster, not daring to go to Devizes. This place is now well guarded, but still we dare not await the event of to-night; all the Catholics in the town have privately escaped.

I know not now when I shall hear from you. I am in agony for news. Our headquarters will be Brighthelmstone, where I do most humbly and fervently entreat you to write—do, dearest sir, write, if but one word—if but only you name YOURSELF! Nothing but your own hand can now tranquillize me. The reports about London here quite distract me. If it were possible to send me a line by the diligence to Brighton, how grateful I should be for such an indulgence! I should then find it there upon our arrival. Charlotte, I am sure, will make it into a sham parcel, and Susy will write for you all but the name. God bless—defend—preserve you! my dearest father. Life is no life to me while I fear for your safety.

God bless and save you all! I shall write to-morrow from wherever we may be—nay, every day I shall write, for you will all soon be as anxious for news from the country as I have been for it from town. Some infamous villain has put it into the paper here that Mr Thrale is a papist. This, I suppose, is an Hothamite report, to inflame his constituents.[1]

Miss F. Burney to Dr Burney

Salisbury, June 11, 1780.

Here we are, dearest sir, and here we mean to pass this night.

We did not leave Bath till eight o'clock yesterday evening, at which time it was filled with dragoons, militia, and armed constables, not armed with muskets, but bludgeons: these latter were all chairmen, who were sworn by the mayor in the morning for petty constables. A popish private chapel, and the houses of all the Catholics, were guarded between seven and eight, and the inhabitants ordered to keep house.

[1] Mr Thrale was M.P. for Southwark.

We set out in the coach and four, with two men on horseback, and got to Warminster, a small town in Wiltshire, a little before twelve.

This morning two more servants came after us from Bath, and brought us word that the precautions taken by the magistrates last night had had good success, for no attempt of any sort had been renewed towards a riot.

But the happiest tidings to me were contained in a letter which they brought, which had arrived after our departure, by the diligence, from Mr Perkins,[1] with an account that all was quiet in London, and that Lord G. Gordon was sent to the Tower.[2]

I am now again tolerably easy, but I shall not be really comfortable, or free from some fears, till I hear from St Martin's Street.[3]

The Borough House has been quite preserved. I know not how long we may be on the road, but nowhere long enough for receiving a letter till we come to Brighthelmstone.

We stopped in our way at Wilton, and spent half the day at that beautiful place.

Just before we arrived there, Lord Arundel had sent to the officers in the place, to entreat a party of guards immediately, for the safety of his house, as he had intelligence that a mob was on the road from London to attack it—he is a Catholic. His request was immediately complied with.

We intended to have gone to a private town, but find all quiet here, and, therefore, prefer it as much more commodious. There is no Romish chapel in the town; mass has always been performed for the Catholics of the place at a Mrs Arundel's in the Close—a relation of his lordship's, whose house is fifteen miles off. I have inquired about the Harrises: I find they are here, and all well.

[1] Mr Perkins was the superintendent of Thrale's brewery.
[2] He was eventually acquitted.
[3] Dr Burney's house. It belonged formerly to Sir Isaac Newton.

Peace now, I trust, will be restored to the nation—at least as soon as some of the desperate gang that may escape from London, in order to spread confusion in the country, are dispersed or overcome.

I will continue to write while matters are in this doubtful state, that you may have no anxiety added to the great stock you must suffer upon my account.

We are all quite well, and when I can once hear you are so, I shall be happy.

Adieu, most dear sir! Love, duty, and compliments to all from

Your most dutiful

And most affectionate,

F. B.

Miss Charlotte Burney to Miss F. Burney

I am very sorry, my dear Fanny, to hear how much you have suffered from your apprehension about us. Susan will tell you why none of us wrote before Friday; and she says she has told you what dreadful havoc and devastation the mob have made here in all parts of the town. However, we are pretty quiet and tranquil again now. Papa goes on with his business pretty much as usual, and so far from the military keeping people within doors (as you say, in your letter to my father, you suppose to be the case), the streets were never more crowded — everybody is wandering about in order to see the ruins of the places that the mob have destroyed.

There are two camps, one in St James's, and the other in Hyde Park, which, together with the military law, makes almost every one here think he is safe again. I expect we shall all have 'a passion for a scarlet-coat' now.

I hardly know what to tell you that won't be stale news. They say that duplicates of the handbill that I have enclosed were distributed all over the town on Wednesday and Thursday last; however, thank heaven, everybody says now that Mr Thrale's house and brewery are as safe as we can wish them. There was a brewer in Turnstile that had his house gutted and burnt, because, the mob said, 'he was a *papish*, and sold popish beer.' Did you ever hear of such diabolical ruffians?

Sister Hetty is vastly well, and has received your letter; I think she has stood the fright better, and been a greater heroine, than any of us.

To add to the pleasantness of our situation, there have been gangs of women going about to rob and plunder. Miss Kirwans went on Friday afternoon to walk in the Museum gardens, and were stopped by a set of women and robbed of all the money they had. The mob had proscribed the mews, for they said, 'the king should not have a horse to ride upon'! They besieged the new Somerset House, with intention to destroy it, but were repulsed by some soldiers placed there for that purpose.

Mr Sleepe has been here a day or two, and says the folks at Watford, where he comes from, 'approve very much of having the Catholic chapels destroyed, for they say it's a shame the pope should come here'! There is a house hereabouts that they had chalked upon last week: 'Empty, and No Popery!'

I am heartily rejoiced, my dearest Fanny, that you have got away from Bath, and hope and trust that at Bright-helmstone you will be as safe as we are here.

It sounds almost incredible, but they say, that on Wednesday night last, when the mob were more powerful, more numerous, and outrageous than ever, there was, nevertheless, a number of exceedingly genteel people at Ranelagh, though they knew not but their houses might be on fire at the time!

God bless you, my dear Fanny—for heaven's sake keep up your spirits!

Yours ever, with the greatest affection,
CHARLOTTE ANN BURNEY.

Miss F. Burney to Mr Crisp

Streatham, April 29th, 1781.

Have you not, my dearest daddy, thought me utterly lost? and, indeed, to all power of either giving or taking comfort, I certainly have been for some time past. I did not, it is true, *hope* that poor Mr Thrale could live very long, as the alteration I saw in him only during my absence while with you had shocked and astonished me. Yet, still the suddenness of the blow gave me a horror from which I am not even now recovered. The situation of sweet Mrs Thrale, added to the true concern I felt at his loss, harassed my mind till it affected my health, which is now again in a state of precariousness and comfortless restlessness that will require much trouble to remedy.

You have not, I hope been angry at my silence; for, in truth, I have had no spirits to write, nor, latterly, ability of *any* kind, from a headache that has been incessant.

I now begin to long extremely to hear more about yourself, and whether you have recovered your sleep and any comfort. The good nursing you mention is always my consolation when I have the painful tidings of your illness; for I have myself experienced the kindness, care, and unwearied attention of the ever good and friendly Kitty, who, indeed, as you well say, can by no one be excelled in that most useful and most humane of all sciences.

Mrs Thrale flew immediately upon this misfortune to Brighthelmstone, to Mr Scrase—*her* Daddy Crisp—both for consolation and counsel; and she has but just quitted him, as she deferred returning to Streatham till her presence was indispensably necessary upon account of proving the will. I offered to accompany her to Brighthelmstone; but she preferred being alone, as her mind was cruelly disordered, and she saw but too plainly I was too sincere a mourner myself to do much besides adding to her grief. The moment, however, she came back, she solicited me to meet her—and I am now here with her, and en-

deavour, by every possible exertion, to be of some use
to her. She looks wretchedly indeed, and is far from well;
but she bears up, though not with calm intrepidity, yet
with flashes of spirit that rather, I fear, spend than relieve
her. Such, however, is her character, and were this
exertion repressed, she would probably sink quite.

Miss Thrale is steady and constant, and very sincerely
grieved for her father.

The four executors, Mr Cator, Mr Crutchley, Mr
Henry Smith, and Dr Johnson, have all behaved generously
and honourably, and seem determined to give Mrs Thrale
all the comfort and assistance in their power. She is to
carry on the business jointly with them.[1] Poor soul!
It is a dreadful toil and worry to her.

Adieu, my dearest daddy. I will write again in a week's
time. I have now just been blooded; but am by no
means *restored* by that loss. But well and ill, equally and
ever,

Your truly affectionate child,
F. B.

Diary resumed

Streatham, May, 1781. Miss Owen and I arrived here
without incident, which, in a journey of six or seven miles,
was really marvellous! Mrs Thrale came from the
Borough with two of the executors, Dr Johnson and Mr
Crutchley, soon after us. She had been sadly worried,
and in the evening frightened us all by again fainting
away. Dear creature! she is all agitation of mind and
of body: but she is now wonderfully recovered, though
in continual fevers about her affairs, which are mightily
difficult and complicate indeed. Yet the behaviour of all
the executors is exactly to her wish. Mr Crutchley, in

---

[1] Mr Thrale died of apoplexy, a natural result of his habit of over-
eating. He seems to have been an indifferent man of business, and
left his affairs in great disorder. The brewery was sold almost
immediately.

particular, were he a darling son or only brother, could not possibly be more truly devoted to her. Indeed, I am very happy in the revolution in my own mind in favour of this young man, whom formerly I so little liked; for I now see so much of him, business and inclination uniting to bring him hither continually, that if he were disagreeable to me, I should spend my time in a most comfortless manner.

THURSDAY. This was the great and most important day to all this house, upon which the sale of the brewery was to be decided. Mrs Thrale went early to town, to meet all the executors, and Mr Barclay, the Quaker,[1] who was the *bidder*. She was in great agitation of mind, and told me if all went well she would wave a white pocket-handkerchief out of the coach window.

Four o'clock came and dinner was ready, and no Mrs Thrale. Five o'clock followed, and no Mrs Thrale. Queeny and I went out on to the lawn, where we sauntered in eager expectation, till near six, and then the coach appeared in sight, and a white pocket-handkerchief was waved from it.

I ran to the door of it to meet her, and she jumped out of it, and gave me a thousand embraces while I gave my congratulations. We went instantly to her dressing-room, where she told me, in brief, how the matter had been transacted, and then we went down to dinner.

SUNDAY. I had new specimens to-day of the oddities of Mr Crutchley, whom I do not yet quite understand, though I have seen so much of him. In the course of our walks to-day we chanced, at one time, to be somewhat before the rest of the company, and soon got into a very

[1] David Barclay. The brewery was sold for £135,000. Readers of Boswell will remember the account of Johnson on this occasion 'bustling about with an inkhorn and pen in his buttonhole,' and exclaiming: 'We are not here to sell a parcel of boilers and vats, but the potentiality of growing rich beyond the dreams of avarice.'

Mr Perkins, the superintendent of the brewery, was subsequently taken into partnership, and thus was founded the celebrated firm of Barclay & Perkins.

serious conversation; though we began it by his relating a most ludicrous incident which had happened to him last winter.

There is a certain poor wretch of a villainous painter, one Mr Lowe, who is in some measure under Dr Johnson's protection, and whom, therefore, he recommends to all the people he thinks can afford to sit for their pictures. Among these he made Mr Seward very readily, and then applied to Mr Crutchley.

'But now,' said Mr Crutchley, as he told me the circumstance, 'I have not a notion of sitting for my picture—for who wants it? I may as well give the man the money without, but no, they all said that would not do so well, and Dr Johnson asked me to give *him* my picture. "And I assure you, sir," says he, "I shall put it in very good company, for I have portraits of some very respectable people in my dining-room." "Aye, sir," says I, "that's sufficient reason why you should not have mine, for I am sure it has no business in such society." So then Mrs Thrale asked me to give it to *her*. "Aye sure, ma'am," says I, "you do me great honour; but pray, first, will you do me the favour to tell me what door you intend to put it behind?" However, after all I could say in opposition, I was obliged to go to the painter's. And I found him in such a condition! A room all dirt and filth, brats squalling and wrangling, up two pair of stairs, and a closet, of which the door was open, that Seward well said was quite Pandora's box—it was the repository of all the nastiness, and stench, and filth, and food, and drink, and—oh, it was too bad to be borne! And "Oh!" says I, "Mr Lowe, I beg your pardon for running away, but I have just recollected another engagement"; so I poked the three guineas in his hand, and told him I would come again another time, and then ran out of the house with all my might.'

Well, when we had done laughing about this poor unfortunate painter, the subject turned upon portraits in general, and our conference grew very grave: on *his* part it soon became even melancholy. I have not time to *dialogue* it; but he told me he could never bear to have himself the picture of any one he loved, as, in case of their death or absence, he should go distracted by looking at it: and that, as for himself, he never had, and never would sit for his own, except for one miniature by Humphreys,[1] which his sister begged of him, as he could never flatter himself there was a human being in the world to whom it could be of any possible value: 'And now,' he added, 'less than ever!'

This, and various other speeches to the same purpose, he spoke with a degree of dejection that surprised me, as the coldness of his character, and his continually boasted insensibility, made me believe him really indifferent both to love and hatred.

WEDNESDAY. We had a terrible noisy day. Mr and Mrs Cator came to dinner, and brought with them Miss Collison, a niece. Mrs Nesbitt was also here, and Mr Pepys.[2]

The long war which has been proclaimed among the wits concerning Lord Lyttelton's *Life*, by Dr Johnson,[3] and which a whole tribe of *blues*, with Mrs Montagu at their head, have vowed to execrate and revenge, now broke out with all the fury of the first actual hostilities, stimulated by long-concerted schemes and much spiteful information. Mr Pepys, Dr Johnson well knew, was one of Mrs Montagu's steadiest abettors; and, therefore, as he had some time determined to defend himself with the first of them he met, this day he fell the sacrifice to his wrath.

In a long tête-à-tête which I accidentally had with Mr Pepys before the company was assembled, he told me his

---

[1] Ozias Humphry (1742–1810), chiefly known as a painter of miniatures.

[2] W. W. Pepys, a master in Chancery. He was the brother of Dr (afterwards Sir Lucas) Pepys, who frequently appears in the *Diary*.

[3] Johnson's estimate of Lord Lyttelton gives no offence to the modern reader, who is merely surprised to find his Lordship included in a set of Lives of the Poets. Mrs Montagu had contributed to Lyttelton's *Dialogues of the Dead*.

apprehensions of an attack, and entreated me earnestly to
endeavour to prevent it; modestly avowing he was no
antagonist for Dr Johnson; and yet declaring his personal
friendship for Lord Lyttelton made him so much hurt
by the *Life*, that he feared he could not discuss the matter
without a quarrel, which, especially in the house of Mrs
Thrale, he wished to avoid.

It was, however, utterly impossible for me to serve him.
I could have stopped Mrs Thrale with ease, and Mr Seward
with a hint, had either of them begun the subject; but,
unfortunately, in the middle of dinner, it was begun by
Dr Johnson himself, to oppose whom, especially as he
spoke with great anger, would have been madness and folly.

Never before have I seen Dr Johnson speak with so
much passion.

'Mr Pepys,' he cried, in a voice the most enraged, 'I
understand you are offended by my *Life of Lord Lyttelton*.
What is it you have to say against it? Come forth, man!
Here am I, ready to answer any charge you can bring!'

'No, sir,' cried Mr Pepys, 'not at present; I must beg
leave to decline the subject. I told Miss Burney before
dinner that I hoped it would not be started.'

I was quite frightened to hear my own name mentioned
in a debate which began so seriously; but Dr Johnson made
not to this any answer: he repeated his attack and his
challenge, and a violent disputation ensued, in which this
great but *mortal* man did, to own the truth, appear unreason-
ably furious and grossly severe. I never saw him so
before, and I heartily hope I never shall again. He has
been long provoked, and justly enough, at the *sneaking*
complaints and murmurs of the Lytteltonians; and,
therefore, his long-excited wrath, which hitherto had met
no object, now burst forth with a vehemence and bitterness
almost incredible.

Mr Pepys meantime never appeared to so much advantage; he preserved his temper, uttered all that belonged
merely to himself with modesty, and all that more immediately related to Lord Lyttelton with spirit. Indeed, Dr

Johnson, in the very midst of the dispute, had the candour and liberality to make him a personal compliment, by saying:

'Sir, all that you say, while you are vindicating one who cannot thank you, makes me only think better of you than I ever did before. Yet still I think you do *me* wrong,' etc. etc.

Some time after, in the heat of the argument, he called out:

'The more my Lord Lyttelton is inquired after, the worse he will appear; Mr Seward has just heard two stories of him which corroborate all I have related.'

He then desired Mr Seward to repeat them. Poor Mr Seward looked almost as frightened as myself at the very mention of his name; but he quietly and immediately told the stories, which consisted of fresh instances, from good authorities, of Lord Lyttelton's illiberal behaviour to Shenstone; and then he flung himself back in his chair, and spoke no more during the whole debate, which I am sure he was ready to vote a bore.

One happy circumstance, however, attended the quarrel, which was the presence of Mr Cator, who would by no means be prevented talking himself, either by reverence for Dr Johnson, or ignorance of the subject in question; on the contrary, he gave his opinion, quite uncalled, upon everything that was said by either party, and that with an importance and pomposity, yet with an emptiness and verbosity, that rendered the whole dispute, when in his hands, nothing more than ridiculous, and compelled even the disputants themselves, all inflamed as they were, to laugh. To give a specimen—one speech will do for a thousand.

'As to this here question of Lord Lyttelton I can't speak to it to the purpose, as I have not read his *Life*, for I have only read the *Life of Pope*; I have got the books though, for I sent for them last week, and they came to me on Wednesday, and then I began them; but I have not yet read *Lord Lyttelton*. *Pope* I have begun, and that is what I am now reading. But what I have to say about Lord

Lyttelton is this here: Mr Seward says that Lord Lyttelton's steward dunned Mr Shenstone for his rent, by which I understand he was a tenant of Lord Lyttelton's. Well, if he was a tenant of Lord Lyttelton's, why should not he pay his rent?'

Who could contradict this?

When dinner was quite over, and we left the men to their wine, we hoped they would finish the affair; but Dr Johnson was determined to talk it through, and make a battle of it, though Mr Pepys tried to be off continually. When they were all summoned to tea, they entered still warm and violent. Mr Cator had the book in his hand, and was reading the *Life of Lyttelton*, that he might better, he said, understand the cause, though not a creature cared if he had never heard of it.

Mr Pepys came up to me and said:

'Just what I had so much wished to avoid! I have been crushed in the very onset.'

I could make him no answer, for Dr Johnson immediately called him off, and harangued and attacked him with a vehemence and continuity that quite concerned both Mrs Thrale and myself, and that made Mr Pepys, at last, resolutely silent, however called upon.

This now grew more unpleasant than ever; till Mr Cator, having some time studied his book, exclaimed:

'What I am now going to say, as I have not yet read the *Life of Lord Lyttelton* quite through, must be considered as being only said aside, because what I am going to say——'

'I wish, sir,' cried Mrs Thrale, 'it had been *all* said aside; here is too much about it, indeed, and I should be very glad to hear no more of it.'

This speech, which she made with great spirit and dignity, had an admirable effect. Everybody was silenced. Mr Cator, thus interrupted in the midst of his proposition, looked quite amazed; Mr Pepys was much gratified by the interference; and Dr Johnson, after a pause, said:

'Well, madam, you *shall* hear no more of it; yet I will defend myself in every part and in every atom!'

And from this time the subject was wholly dropped. This dear violent Doctor was conscious he had been wrong, and therefore he most candidly bore the reproof.

Mr Cator, after some evident chagrin at having his speech thus rejected, comforted himself by coming up to Mr Seward, who was seated next me, to talk to him of the changes of the climates from hot to *could* in the countries he had visited; and he prated so much, yet said so little, and pronounced his words so vulgarly, that I found it impossible to keep my countenance, and was once, when most unfortunately he addressed himself to me, surprised by him on the full grin. To soften it off as well as I could, I pretended unusual complacency, and instead of recovering my gravity, I continued a most ineffable smile for the whole time he talked, which was indeed no difficult task. Poor Mr Seward was as much off his guard as myself, having his mouth distended to its fullest extent every other minute.

When the leave-taking time arrived, Dr Johnson called to Mr Pepys to shake hands, an invitation which was most coldly and forcibly accepted. Mr Cator made a point of Mrs Thrale's dining at his house soon, and she could not be wholly excused, as she has many transactions with him; but she fixed the day for three weeks hence. They have invited me so often, that I have now promised not to fail making one.

Thursday Morning. Dr Johnson went to town for some days, but not before Mrs Thrale read him a very serious lecture upon giving way to such violence; which he bore with a patience and quietness that even more than made his peace with me; for such a man's confessing himself in the wrong is almost more amiable than another man being steadily right.

Friday, June 14th. We had my dear father and Sophy Streatfeild, who, as usual, was beautiful, caressing, amiable, sweet, and—fatiguing.

Monday, June 17th. There passed, some time ago, an agreement between Mr Crutchley and Mr Seward, that the latter is to make a visit to the former, at his country house in Berkshire; and to-day the time was settled: but a more ridiculous scene never was exhibited. The host elect and the guest elect tried which should show least expectation of pleasure from the meeting, and neither of them thought it at all worth while to disguise his terror of being weary of the other. Mr Seward seemed quite melancholy and depressed in the prospect of making, and Mr Crutchley absolutely miserable in that of receiving, the visit. Yet nothing so ludicrous as the distress of both, since nothing less necessary than that either should have such a punishment inflicted. I cannot remember half the absurd things that passed; but a few, by way of specimen, I will give.

'How long do you intend to stay with me, Seward?' cried Mr Crutchley; 'how long do you think you can bear it?'

'Oh, I don't know; I shan't fix,' answered the other; 'just as I find it.'

'Well, but—when shall you come? Friday or Saturday? I think you 'd better not come till Saturday.'

'Why yes, I believe on Friday.'

'On Friday! Oh, you 'll have too much of it! What shall I do with you?'

'Why on Sunday we 'll dine at the Lyells'. Mrs Lyell is a charming woman; one of the most elegant creatures I ever saw.'

'Wonderfully so,' cried Mr Crutchley; 'I like her extremely—an insipid idiot! She never opens her mouth but in a whisper; I never *heard* her speak a word in my life. But what must I do with you on Monday? Will you come away?'

'Oh, no; I 'll stay and see it out.'

'Why, how long shall you stay? Why I must come away myself on Tuesday.'

'Oh, I shan't settle yet,' cried Mr Seward, very dryly. 'I shall put up six shirts, and then do as I find it.'

'Six shirts!' exclaimed Mr Crutchley; and then, with

equal dryness added: 'Oh, I suppose you wear two a day.'

And so on.

MONDAY, JULY 2ND. In a tête-à-tête I chanced to have with Mr Crutchley, he again gave me reason to recollect the notion he lately put in my head, that he is still suffering in his own mind from some former bitter disappointment.

We were talking over Johnson's *Life of Pope*, and after mutually giving our opinions upon various passages, and agreeing to prefer it altogether to any other of the *Lives*, he asked me if I had remarked how beautifully he had written upon Pope's fondness for Patty Blount.[1] And then he looked out the paragraph and read it:

'Their acquaintance began early; the life of each was pictured on the other's mind; their conversation, therefore, was endearing, for when they met there was an immediate coalition of congenial notions. Perhaps he considered her unwillingness to approach the bed of sickness as female weakness or human frailty; perhaps he was conscious to himself of peevishness and impatience, or, though he was offended by her inattention, might yet consider her merit as overbalancing her fault; and, if he had suffered his heart to be alienated from her, he could have found nothing that might fill her place; he could only have shrunk within himself; it was too late to transfer his confidence or his fondness.'

The manner in which he read this paragraph was so strikingly tender and feeling, that it could not, I think, proceed merely from the words; and when he came to 'he might consider her merit as overbalancing her fault,' he exclaimed, 'How impossible that a thing one loves can ever for a moment offend one!' And when he had done it, he read it all over again, with yet more sensibility; and, not yet satisfied, he repeated it a third time.

Poor Mr Crutchley! I begin to believe his heart much

[1] Martha Blount. She and her sister, Teresa, became friends of Pope in his youth. His affection for Martha lasted until his death, and he left her the income from his property.

less stubborn than he is willing to have it thought; and I do now really but little doubt either that some former love sits heavy upon it, or that he is at this moment suffering the affliction of a present and hopeless one: if the latter is the case, Miss ——, I am next to certain, is the object. I may possibly, however, be mistaken in both conjectures, for he is too unlike other people to be judged by rules that will suit them.

We had much literary chat upon this occasion, which led us to a general discussion, not only of Pope's *Life*, but of all his works, which we tried who should out-praise. He then got a book to take to his favourite bench, and made me, as he left the room, an apology the most humble, for having interrupted or taken up any part of my time, which could not otherwise have but been spent better.

Two minutes after he came back for another book, and while he was seeking it Mr Evans came in. They then both of them sat down to chat, and Mr Seward was the subject. Mr Evans said he had met him the day before in the Park, with Mrs Nesbitt and another lady, and that he was giving Mrs Nesbitt a prescription. In his medical capacity he seems to rise daily: 'tis a most strange turn to take merely for killing *ennui*! But, added to quacking both himself and his friends, he has lately, I hear, taken also to making a rather too liberal use of his bottle, thinking, I suppose, that generous wine will destroy even the blue devils. I am really sorry, though, for this, as it may be attended with serious evil to him.

'When he was at my place,' said Mr Crutchley, 'he did himself up pretty handsomely; he ate cherries till he complained most bitterly of indigestion, and he poured down Madeira and port most plentifully, but without relief. Then he desired to have some peppermint water, and he drank three glasses; still that would not do, and he said he must have a large quantity of ginger. We had no such thing in the house. However, he had brought some, it seems, with him, and then he took that, but still to no purpose. At last, he desired some brandy, and tossed off a glass of that; and, after all, he asked for a dose of rhubarb. Then we had to send and inquire all over the house for this rhubarb, but our folks had hardly ever heard of such a thing. I advised him to take a good bumper of gin and gunpowder, for that seemed almost all he had left untried.'

Miss F. Burney to Mrs Phillips[1]

Feb., 1782.

I thank you most heartily for your two sweet letters, my ever dearest Susy, and equally for the kindness they contain and the kindness they accept. And as I have a frank and a subject, I will leave my *bothers*, and write you and my dear brother Molesworth a little account of a *rout* I have just been at, at the house of Mr Paradise.

'You will wonder, perhaps, in this time of hurry, why I went thither; but when I tell you Pacchierotti [2] was there, you will not think it surprising.

There was a crowd of company; Charlotte and I went together; my father came afterwards. Mrs Paradise received us very graciously, and led me immediately up to Miss Thrale, who was sitting by the Pac. The Miss Kirwans, you may be sure, were not far off, and so I did pretty well. There was nobody else I knew but Dr Solander,[3] Mr Coxe the traveller,[4] Sir Sampson and Lady Gideon [Streatham acquaintances], Mr Sastres, and Count Zenobia, a noble Venetian, whom I have often met lately at Mrs Thrale's.

We were very late, for we had waited cruelly for the

---

[1] Fanny's sister, Susan, who was now married to Captain Phillips, an officer in the Marines. He had been a shipmate of James, her elder brother.

[2] Pacchierotti, the Italian singer, was a great friend of the Burneys.

[3] The botanist (1736–1782).

[4] William Coxe (1747–1828), better known as a historian.

coach, and Pac. had sung a song out of *Artaxerxes*, composed for a tenor, which we lost, to my infinite regret. Afterwards he sang *Dolce speme*, set by Bertoni, less elegantly than by Sacchini, but more expressively for the words. He sang it delightfully. It was but the second time I have heard him in a room since his return to England.

After this he went into another room, to try if it would be cooler; and Mrs Paradise, leaning over the Kirwans and Charlotte, who hardly got a seat all night for the crowd, said she begged to speak to me. I squeezed my great person out, and she then said:

'Miss Burney, Lady Say and Sele desires the honour of being introduced to you.'

Her ladyship stood by her side. She seems pretty near fifty—at least turned forty; her head was full of feathers, flowers, jewels, and gew-gaws, and as high as Lady Archer's; her dress was trimmed with beads, silver, persian sashes, and all sort of fine fancies, and her face is thin and fiery, and her whole manner spoke a lady all alive.

'Miss Burney,' cried she, with great quickness, and a look all curiosity, 'I am very happy to see you; I have longed to see you a great while; I have read your performance, and I am quite delighted with it. I think it's the most elegant novel I ever read in my life. Such a style! I am quite surprised at it. I can't think where you got so much invention!'

You may believe this was a reception not to make me very loquacious. I did not know which way to turn my head.

'I must introduce you,' continued her ladyship, 'to my sister; she'll be quite delighted to see you. She has written a novel herself; so you are sister authoresses. A most elegant thing it is, I assure you; almost as pretty as yours, only not quite so elegant. She has written two novels, only one is not so pretty as the other. But I shall insist upon your seeing them. One is in letters, like yours, only yours is prettiest; it's called the *Mausoleum of Julia*!'[1]

[1] The *Mausoleum of Julia* was subsequently given the honours of print and read by Queen Charlotte.

What unfeeling things, thought I, are *my* sisters! I'm sure I never heard them go about thus praising *me*!

Mrs Paradise then again came forward, and taking my hand, led me up to her ladyship's sister, Lady Hawke, saying aloud, and with a courteous smirk: 'Miss Burney, ma'am, authoress of *Evelina*.'

'Yes,' cried my friend, Lady Say and Sele, who followed me close, 'it's the authoress of *Evelina*; so you are sister authoresses!'

Lady Hawke arose and curtsied. She is much younger than her sister, and rather pretty; extremely languishing, delicate, and pathetic; apparently accustomed to be reckoned the genius of her family, and well contented to be looked upon as a creature dropped from the clouds.

I was then seated between their ladyships, and Lady S. and S., drawing as near to me as possible, said:

'Well, and so you wrote this pretty book!—and pray did your papa know of it?'

'No, ma'am; not till some months after the publication.'

'So I've heard; it's surprising! I can't think how you invented it!—there's a vast deal of invention in it! And you've got so much humour, too! Now my sister has no humour—hers is all sentiment. You can't think how I was entertained with that old grandmother and her son!'

I suppose she meant Tom Branghton for the son.

'How much pleasure you must have had in writing it; had not you?'

'Y–e–s, ma'am.'

'So has my sister; she's never without a pen in her hand; she can't help writing for her life. When Lord Hawke is travelling about with her, she keeps writing all the way.'

'Yes,' said Lady Hawke; 'I really can't help writing. One has great pleasure in writing the things; has not one, Miss Burney?'

'Y–e–s, ma'am.'

'But your novel,' cried Lady Say and Sele, 'is in such a

style!—so elegant! I am vastly glad you made it end happily. I hate a novel that don't end happy.'

'Yes,' said Lady Hawke, with a languid smile, 'I was vastly glad when she married Lord Orville. I was sadly afraid it would not have been.'

'My sister intends,' said Lady Say and Sele, 'to print her *Mausoleum*, just for her own friends and acquaintances.'

'Yes,' said Lady Hawke; 'I have never printed yet.'

'I saw Lady Hawke's name,' quoth I to my first friend, 'ascribed to the play of *Variety*.'

'Did you indeed?' cried Lady Say, in an ecstasy. 'Sister! do you know Miss Burney saw your name in the news-papers, about the play!'

'Did she?' said Lady Hawke, smiling complacently. 'But I really did not write it; I never wrote a play in my life.'

'Well,' cried Lady Say, 'but do repeat that sweet part that I am so fond of—you know what I mean; Miss Burney *must* hear it—out of your novel, you know!'

Lady H.: No, I can't; I have forgot it.

Lady S.: Oh, no! I am sure you have not; I insist upon it.

Lady H.: But I know you can repeat it yourself; you have so fine a memory; I am sure you can repeat it.

Lady S.: Oh, but I should not do it justice! That's all —I should not do it justice!

Lady Hawke then bent forward, and repeated: '"If, when he made the declaration of his love, the sensibility that beamed in his eyes was felt in his heart, what pleasing sensations and soft alarms might not that tender avowal awaken!"'

'And from what, ma'am,' cried I, astonished, and imagin-ing I had mistaken them, 'is this taken?'

'From my sister's novel!' answered the delighted Lady Say and Sele, expecting my raptures to be equal to her own; 'it's in the *Mausoleum*—did not you know that? Well, I can't think how you can write these sweet novels! And it's all just like that part. Lord Hawke himself says it's all poetry. For my part, I'm sure I could never write so. I suppose, Miss Burney, you are producing another—a'n't you?'

'No, ma'am.' [1]

'Oh, I dare say you are. I dare say you are writing one at this very minute!'

Mrs Paradise now came up to me again, followed by a square man, middle-aged, and humdrum, who, I found, was Lord Say and Sele, afterwards from the Kirwans; for though they introduced him to me, I was so confounded by their vehemence and their manners, that I did not hear his name.

'Miss Burney,' said Mrs P., presenting me to him, 'authoress of *Evelina*.'

'Yes,' cried Lady Say and Sele, starting up, ''tis the authoress of *Evelina*!'

'Of what?' cried he.

'Of *Evelina*. You'd never think it—she looks so young, to have so much invention, and such an elegant style! Well, I could write a play, I think, but I'm sure I could never write a novel.'

'Oh, yes, you could, if you would try,' said Lady Hawke.

'Oh, no, I could not,' answered she; 'I could not get a style—that's the thing—I could not tell how to get a style! And a novel's nothing without a style, you know!'

'Why no,' said Lady Hawke; 'that's true. But then you write such charming letters, you know.'

'Letters!' repeated Lady S. and S., simpering; 'do you think so? Do you know I wrote a long letter to Mrs Ray just before I came here, this very afternoon—quite a long letter! I did, I assure you!'

Here Mrs Paradise came forward with another gentleman, younger, slimmer, and smarter, and saying to me: 'Sir Gregory Page Turner,' said to him: 'Miss Burney, authoress of *Evelina*!'

At which Lady Say and Sele, in fresh transport, again

[1] *Cecilia*, however, was published a few months later.

arose, and rapturously again repeated: 'Yes, she's authoress of *Evelina*! Have you read it?'

'No! Is it to be had?'

'Oh dear, yes! It's been printed these two years!
You'd never think it! But it's the most elegant novel I
ever read in my life. Writ in such a style!'

'Certainly,' said he, very civilly, 'I have every induce-
ment to get it. Pray where is it to be had? Everywhere,
I suppose?'

'Oh, nowhere, I hope!' cried I, wishing at that moment
it had never been in human ken.

My *square* friend, Lord Say and Sele, then putting his
head forward, said, very solemnly: 'I'll purchase it!'

Mrs Thrale to Miss F. Burney

Tuesday night.

My eyes red with reading and crying, I stop every
moment to kiss the book [1] and to wish it was my Burney.
'Tis the sweetest book, the most interesting, the most
engaging. Oh! it beats every other book, even your own
other volumes, for *Evelina* was a baby to it. . . .

Such a novel! Indeed, I am seriously and sensibly
touched by it, and am proud of her friendship who so
knows the human heart. May mine long bear the inspection of so penetrating, so discriminating an eye!

This letter is written by scraps and patches, but every
scrap is admiration, and every patch thanks you for the
pleasure I have received. I will say no more; I cannot
say half I think with regard to praise. . . .

My most ingenious, my most admirable friend, adieu!
If I had more virtue than *Cecilia*, I should half fear the censures of such an insight into the deepest recesses of the

[1] *Cecilia*, which was published by Payne and Cadell on 12th June,
1782.

mind. Since I have read this volume, I have seriously thanked heaven that all the litter of mine was in sight; none hoarded in holes, nor hastily stuffed into closets. You have long known the worst of your admiring

H. L. T.

The Right Honourable Edmund Burke to Miss F. Burney

MADAM,

I should feel exceedingly to blame if I could refuse to myself the natural satisfaction, and to you the just but poor return, of my best thanks for the very great instruction and entertainment I have received from the new present you have bestowed on the public. There are few—I believe I may say fairly there are none at all—that will not find themselves better informed concerning human nature, and their stock of observation enriched, by reading your *Cecilia*. They certainly will, let their experience in life and manners be what it may. The arrogance of age must submit to be taught by youth. You have crowded into a few small volumes an incredible variety of characters; most of them well planned, well supported, and well contrasted with each other. If there be any fault in this respect, it is one in which you are in no great danger of being imitated. Justly as your characters are drawn, perhaps they are too numerous. But I beg pardon; I fear it is quite in vain to preach economy to those who are come young to excessive and sudden opulence.

I might trespass on your delicacy if I should fill my letter to you with what I fill my conversation to others. I should be troublesome to you alone if I should tell you all I feel and think on the natural vein of humour, the tender pathetic, the comprehensive and noble moral, and the sagacious observation, that appear quite throughout that extraordinary performance.

In an age distinguished by producing extraordinary

women, I hardly dare to tell you where my opinion would place you amongst them. I respect your modesty, that will not endure the commendations which your merit forces from everybody.

I have the honour to be, with great gratitude, respect, and esteem, madam, your most obedient and most humble servant,

EDM. BURKE.[1]

Whitehall, July 29, 1782.

Diary resumed

DEC. 8TH. Now for Miss Monckton's [2] assembly.

I had begged Mrs Thrale to call for me, that I might have her countenance and assistance upon my entrance. Miss Thrale came also. Everything was in a new style. We got out of the coach into a hall full of servants, not one of which inquired our names, or took any notice of us. We proceeded, and went upstairs, and when we arrived at a door, stopped and looked behind us. No servant had followed or preceded us. We deliberated what was to be done. To announce ourselves was rather awkward, neither could we be sure we were going into the right apartment. I proposed our going up higher, till we met with somebody; Miss Thrale thought we should go down and call some of the servants; but Mrs Thrale, after a ridiculous consultation, determined to try her fortune by opening the door. This being done, we entered a room full of—tea-things, and one maid-servant!

'Well,' cried Mrs Thrale, laughing, 'what is to be done now? I suppose we are come so early that nothing is ready.'

The maid stared, but said: 'There's company in the next room.'

[1] Burke was at this time Paymaster of the Forces.
[2] Mary Monckton, afterwards Countess of Cork and Orrery. She survived until 1840, and entertained celebrities at her parties to the last.

Then we considered how to make ourselves known; and then Mrs Thrale again resolved to take courage and enter. She therefore opened another door, and went into another apartment. I held back, but looked after, and observing that she made no curtsy, concluded she was gone into some wrong place. Miss Thrale followed, and after her went little I, wondering who was to receive, or what was to become of us.

Miss Monckton lives with her mother, the old Dowager Lady Galway, in a noble house in Charles Street, Berkeley Square. The room was large and magnificent. There was not much company, for we were very early. Lady Galway sat at the side of the fire, and received nobody. She seems very old, and was dressed with a little round white cap, and not a single hair, no cushion, roll, nor anything else but the little round cap, which was flat upon her forehead. Such part of the company as already knew her made their compliments to her where she sat, and the rest were never taken up to her, but belonged wholly to Miss Monckton.

Miss Monckton's own manner of receiving her guests was scarce more laborious; for she kept her seat when they entered, and only turned round her head to nod it, and say: 'How do do?' after which they found what accommodation they could for themselves.

As soon, however, as she perceived Mrs and Miss Thrale, which was not till they had been some minutes in the room, she arose to welcome them, contrary to her general custom, and merely because it was their first visit. Our long trains making my entrance some time after theirs, gave me the advantage of being immediately seen by her, and she advanced to me with quickness, and very politely thanked me for coming, and said:

'I fear you think me very rude for taking the liberty of sending to you.'

'No, indeed, you did me much honour,' quoth I.

She then broke further into her general rules, by making way for me to a good place, and seating me herself, and then taking a chair next me, and beginning a little chat. I really felt myself much obliged to her for this seasonable attention, for I was presently separated from Mrs Thrale, and entirely surrounded by strangers, all dressed superbly, and all looking saucily; and as nobody's names were spoken, I had no chance to discover any acquaintances. Mr Metcalf, indeed, came and spoke to me the instant I came in, and I should have been very happy to have had him for my neighbour; but he was engaged in attending to Dr Johnson, who was standing near the fire, and environed with listeners.

Some new people now coming in, and placing themselves in a regular way, Miss Monckton exclaimed: 'My whole care is to prevent a circle'; and hastily rising, she pulled about the chairs, and planted the people in groups, with as dexterous a disorder as you would desire to see.

The company in general were dressed with more brilliancy than at any rout I ever was at, as most of them were going to the Duchess of Cumberland's, and attired for that purpose. Just behind me sat Mrs Hampden, still very beautiful, but insufferably affected. Another lady, in full dress, and very pretty, came in soon after, and got herself a chair just before me; and then a conversation began between her and Mrs Hampden, of which I will give you a specimen.

'How disagreeable these sacques [1] are! I am so incommoded with these nasty ruffles! I am going to Cumberland House—are you?'

'To be sure,' said Mrs Hampden; 'what else, do you think, would make me bear this weight of dress? I can't bear a sacque.'

'Why, I thought you said you should always wear them?'

'Oh, yes, but I have changed my mind since then—as many people do.'

'Well, I think it vastly disagreeable indeed,' said the

[1] Johnson defines a 'sacque' (or 'sack') as 'a woman's loose robe.' It was of silk, and hung from the shoulders of the dress, forming a train.

other; 'you can't think how I'm encumbered with these ruffles!'

'Oh, I am quite oppressed with them,' said Mrs Hampden; 'I can hardly bear myself up.'

'And I dined in this way!' cried the other; 'only think—dining in a sacque!'

'Oh,' answered Mrs Hampden, 'it really puts me quite out of spirits.'

Well, have you enough?—and has my daddy raved enough?

Mrs and Miss Thrale had other engagements, and soon went away. Miss Monckton then took a chair again next to me, which she kept till we both started at the same voice, and she cried out: 'Oh, it's Mr Burke!' and she ran to him with as much joy as, if it had been our house, I should. Cause the second for liking her better.

I grew now in a violent fidget, both to have his notice, and for what his notice would be; but I sat very still, and he was seized upon by scores, and taken to another part of the room.

Then came in Sir Joshua Reynolds, and he soon drew a chair near mine, and from that time I was never without some friend at my elbow.

'Have you seen,' said he, 'Mrs Montagu lately?'

'No, not very lately.'

'But within these few months?'

'No, not since last year.'

'Oh, you must see her, then. You ought to see and to hear her—'twill be worth your while. Have you heard of the fine long letter she has written?'

'Yes, but I have not met with it.'

'I have.'

'And who is it to?'

'The old Duchess of Portland. She desired Mrs Montagu's opinion of *Cecilia*, and she has written it at full length. I was in a party at her Grace's, and heard of nothing but you. She is so delighted, and so sensibly, so rationally, that I only wish you could have heard her.

And old Mrs Delany had been forced to begin it, though she had said she should never read any more; however, when we met, she was reading it already for the third time.'

Mr Burke very quietly came from Mrs Hampden, and sat down in the vacant place at my side. I could then wait no longer, for I found he was more near-sighted than myself; I, therefore, turned towards him and bowed; he seemed quite amazed, and really made me ashamed, however delighted, by the expressive civility and distinction with which he instantly rose to return my bow, and stood the whole time he was making his compliments upon seeing me, and calling himself the blindest of men for not finding me out sooner. And Mrs Burke, who was seated near me, said, loud enough for me to hear her:

'See, see! what a flirtation Mr Burke is beginning with Miss Burney! and before my face too!'

These ceremonies over, he sate down by me, and began a conversation which you, my dearest Susy, would be glad to hear, for my sake, word for word; but which I really could not listen to with sufficient ease, from shame at his warm eulogiums, to remember with any accuracy. The general substance, however, take as I recollect it.

After many most eloquent compliments upon the book, too delicate either to shock or sicken the nicest ear, he very emphatically congratulated me upon its most universal success; said: 'he was now too late to speak of it, since he could only echo the voice of the whole nation'; and added, with a laugh: 'I had hoped to have made some merit of my enthusiasm; but the moment I went about to hear what others say, I found myself merely one in a multitude.'

He then told me that, notwithstanding his admiration, he was the man who had dared to find some faults with so favourite and fashionable a work. I entreated him to tell me what they were, and assured him nothing would make me so happy as to correct them under his direction. He then enumerated them: and I will tell you what they are, that you may not conclude I write nothing but the fairer part of my adventures, which I really always relate very honestly, though so fair they are at this time, that it hardly seems possible they should not be dressed up.

The masquerade he thought too long, and that something might be spared from Harrel's grand assembly; he did not like Morrice's part of the pantheon; and he wished the conclusion either more happy or more miserable; 'for in a work of imagination,' said he, 'there is no medium.'

I was not easy enough to answer him, or I have much, though perhaps not good for much, to say in defence of following life and nature as much in the conclusion as in the progress of a tale; and when is life and nature completely happy or miserable?

'But,' said he, when he had finished his comments, 'what excuse must I give for this presumption? I have none in the world to offer but the real, the high esteem I feel for you; and I must at the same time acknowledge it is all your own doing that I am able to find fault; for it is your general perfection in writing that has taught me to criticize where it is not quite uniform.'

Here's an orator, dear Susy!

Sir Joshua Reynolds now joined us.

'Are you telling her,' said he, 'of our conversation with the old wits?'[1] I am glad you hear of it from Mr Burke, Miss Burney, for he can tell it so much better than I can, and remember their very words.'

'Nothing else would they talk of for three whole hours,' said he, 'and we were there at the third reading of the bill.'

'I believe I was in good hands,' said I, 'if they talked of it to you?'

'Why, yes,' answered Sir Joshua, laughing, 'we joined in from time to time. Gibbon says he read the whole five volumes in a day.'

''Tis impossible,' cried Mr Burke, 'it cost me three days; and you know I never parted with it from the time I first opened it.'

[1] In particular, the Duchess of Portland and Mrs Delany. Burke had told Fanny of their admiration.

Here are laurels, Susy! My dear daddy and Kitty, are you not doubly glad you so kindly hurried me upstairs to write when at Chesington? [1]

SATURDAY, DEC. 28TH. My father and I dined and spent the day at Sir Joshua Reynolds's, after many preceding disappointments. Our dinner party consisted merely of Mr West,[2] the painter, Mr Jackson of Exeter,[3] and Miss Reynolds. Mr West had, some time ago, desired my father to invite him to our house, to see that lion, your sister, saying to him: 'You will be safe, Dr Burney, in trusting to our meeting, for I am past forty, and married.'

The moment Miss Palmer [4] had received me with a reproachful 'At last we are met,' Sir Joshua took my hand, and insisted upon wishing me a merry Christmas according to old forms, and then presenting me to Mr West, he said:

'You must let me introduce you to one of your greatest admirers.'

Mr West is a very pleasing man, gentle, soft-mannered, cheerful, and serene. Mr Jackson you may remember our formerly seeing; he is very handsome, and seems possessed of much of that ardent genius which distinguishes Mr Young; for his expressions, at times, are extremely violent, while at other times he droops, and is so absent that he seems to forget not only all about him, but himself.

Sir Joshua had two snuff-boxes in use, a gold and a tin one; I examined them, and asked why he made use of such a vile and shabby tin one.

'Why,' said he laughing, 'because I naturally love a little of the blackguard. Aye, and so do you too, little as you look as if you did, and all the people all day long are saying, where can you have seen such company as you treat us with?'

'Why you have seen such, Sir Joshua,' said Mr West,

[1] Much of *Cecilia* was written at Chesington.
[2] Benjamin West, who succeeded Sir Joshua as President of the Royal Academy.
[3] William Jackson, the composer (1730–1803). He had also some skill as a painter.
[4] Sir Joshua's niece.

taking up the tin snuff-box, 'for this box you must certainly have picked up at Briggs's sale.'

You may believe I was eager enough now to call a new subject; and Sir Joshua, though he loves a little passing speech or two upon this matter, never insists upon keeping it up, but the minute he sees he has made me look about me or look foolish, he is most good-naturedly ready to give it up.

But how, my dearest Susy, can you wish any wishes about Sir Joshua and me? A man who has had two shakes of the palsy! What misery should I suffer if I were only his niece, from a terror of a fatal repetition of such a shock! I would not run voluntarily into such a state of perpetual apprehension for the wealth of the East. Wealth, indeed, *per se*, I never too much valued, and my acquaintance with its possessors has by no means increased my veneration for it.

I had afterwards a whispering conversation with Mrs Reynolds,[1] which made me laugh, from her excessive oddness and absurdity. It began about Chesington. She expressed her wonder how I could have passed so much time there. I assured her that with my own will I should pass much more time there, as I know no place where I had had more, if so much, happiness.

'Well, bless me!' cried she, holding up her hands, 'and all this variety comes from only one man! That 's strange indeed, for, by what I can make out, there 's nothing but that one Mr Quip there!'

'Mr *Crisp*,' said I, 'is indeed the only man, but there are also two ladies, very dear friends of mine, who live there constantly.'

'What! And they neither of them married that Mr —that same gentleman?'

'No, they never married anybody; they are single, and so is he.'

'Well, but if he is so mighty agreeable,' said she, holding her finger up to her nose most significantly, 'can you tell

[1] Sir Joshua's sister.

me how it comes to pass he should never have got a wife
in all this time?'

There was no answering this but by grinning; but I
thought how my dear Kitty [1] would again have called her
the *old sifter*.

She afterwards told me of divers most ridiculous
distresses she had been in with Mrs Montagu and Mrs Ord.

'I had the most unfortunate thing in the world happen
to me,' she said, 'about Mrs Montagu, and I always am in
some distress or misfortune with that lady. She did me
the honour to invite me to dine with her last week—and
I am sure there is nobody in the world can be more obliged
to Mrs Montagu for taking such notice of anybody—but
just when the day came I was so unlucky as to be ill, and
that, you know, made it quite improper to go and dine
with Mrs Montagu, for fear of any disagreeable consequences. So this vexed me very much, for I had nobody
to send to her that was proper to appear before Mrs
Montagu: for, to own the truth, you must know I have no
servant but a maid, and I could not think of sending such
a person to Mrs Montagu. So I thought it best to send a
chairman, and to tell him only to ring at the bell, and to
wait for no answer; because then the porter might tell
Mrs Montagu my servant brought the note, for the porter
could not tell but he might be my servant. But my maid
was so stupid, she took the shilling I gave her for the
chairman, and went to a green-shop, and bid the woman
send somebody with the note, and she left the shilling
with her: so the green-woman, I suppose, thought she
might keep the shilling, and instead of sending a chairman
she sent her own errand-girl; and she was all dirt and rags.
But this is not all; for, when the girl got to the house,
nothing would serve her but she would give the note to
Mrs Montagu, and wait for an answer; so then, you know,
Mrs Montagu saw this ragged green-shop girl. I was
never so shocked in my life, for when she brought me
back the note I knew at once how it all was. Only think

[1] Kitty Cooke, a member of the Chesington household.

what a mortification, to have Mrs Montagu see such a person as that! She must think it very odd of me indeed to send a green-shop girl to such a house as hers!'

Now for a distress equally grievous with Mrs Ord:

'I am always,' said she, 'out of luck with Mrs Ord, for . . . when she came there happened to be a great slop on the table; so, while the maid was going to the door, I took up a rag that I had been wiping my pencils with, for I had been painting, and I wiped the table: but as she got upstairs before I had put it away, I popped a handkerchief upon it. However, while we were talking, I thought my handkerchief looked like a litter upon the table, and thinks I, Mrs Ord will think it very untidy, for she is all neatness, so I whisked it into my pocket; but I quite forgot the rag with the paint on it. So, when she was gone—bless me!—there I saw it was sticking out of my pocket, in full sight. Only think what a slut Mrs Ord must think me, to put a dish-clout in my pocket!'

Miss Burney to Mr Crisp

April 12, 1782.

MY DEAREST—DEAREST DADDY,

I am more grieved at the long and most disappointing continuation of your illness than I know how to tell you; and though my last account, I thank heaven, is better, I find you still suffer so much, that my congratulations in my letter to Susan, upon what I thought your recovery, must have appeared quite crazy, if you did not know me as well as you do, and were not sure what affliction the discovery of my mistake would bring to myself.

I think I never yet so much wished to be at Chesington, as at this time, that I might see how you go on, and not be kept in such painful suspense from post to post.

Why did you tell me of the Delanys, Portlands, Cambridges, etc., as if any of them came into competition with yourself? When you are better, I shall send you a most fierce and sharp remonstrance upon this subject. At present I must be content with saying, I will undoubtedly accept your most kind invitation as soon as I possibly can. Meantime, if my letters will give you any amusement, I will write oftener than ever, and supply you with all the prog I get myself.

Susan, who is my reader, must be your writer, and let me know if such tittle-tattle as I can collect serves to divert some of those many moments of languor and weariness that creep between pain and ease, and that call more for mental food than for bodily medicine. Your love to your Fannikin, I well know, makes all trash interesting to you that seems to concern her; and I have no greater pleasure, when absent, than in letting you and my dear Susan be acquainted with my proceedings. I don't mean by this to exclude the rest of the dear Chesington set—far from it—but a sister and a daddy must come first.

God bless and restore you, my most dear daddy! You know not how kindly I take your thinking of me, and inquiring about me, in an illness that might so well make you forget us all: but Susan assures me your heart is as affectionate as ever to your ever and ever faithful and loving child,

F. B.[1]

THURSDAY, JUNE 19TH. We heard to-day that Dr Johnson had been taken ill, in a way that gave a dreadful shock to himself, and a most anxious alarm to his friends. Mr Seward brought the news here, and my father and I instantly went to his house. He had earnestly desired me, when we lived so much together at Streatham, to see him frequently if he should be ill. He saw my father, but he had medical people with him, and could not admit me upstairs, but he sent me down a most kind message, that

[1] Soon after this letter was written Mr Crisp died. Fanny was at Chesington at the time.

he thanked me for calling, and when he was better should hope to see me often. I had the satisfaction to hear from Mrs Williams that the physicians had pronounced him to be in no danger, and expected a speedy recovery.

The stroke was confined to his tongue. Mrs Williams told me a most striking and touching circumstance that attended the attack. It was at about four o'clock in the morning: he found himself with a paralytic affection; he rose, and composed in his own mind a Latin prayer to the Almighty, 'that whatever were the sufferings for which he must prepare himself, it would please Him, through the grace and mediation of our blessed Saviour, to spare his intellects, and let them all fall upon his body.' When he had composed this, internally, he endeavoured to speak it aloud, but found his voice was gone.

Miss F. Burney to Mrs Piozzi

Norbury Park, Aug. 10, 1784.

When my wondering eyes first looked over the letter I received last night, my mind instantly dictated a high-spirited vindication of the consistency, integrity, and faithfulness of the friendship thus abruptly reproached and cast away. But a sleepless night gave me leisure to recollect that you were ever as generous as precipitate, and that your own heart would do justice to mine, in the cooler judgment of future reflection. Committing myself, therefore, to that period, I determined simply to assure you, that if my last letter hurt either you or Mr Piozzi, I am no less sorry than surprised; and that if it offended you, I sincerely beg your pardon.

Not to that time, however, can I wait to acknowledge the pain an accusation so unexpected has caused me, nor the heartfelt satisfaction with which I shall receive, when you are able to write it, a softer renewal of regard.

May heaven direct and bless you! F. B.

[N.B.—This is the sketch of the answer which F. Burney most painfully wrote to the unmerited reproach of not sending *cordial congratulations* upon a marriage which she had uniformly, openly, and with deep and avowed affliction thought wrong.[1]]

Mrs Piozzi to Miss Burney

Welbeck Street, No. 33, Cavendish Square,
Friday, Aug. 13, 1784.

Give your self no serious concern, sweetest Burney. All is well, and I am too happy myself to make a friend otherwise; quiet your kind heart immediately, and love my husband if you love his and your

H. L. PIOZZI.

[N.B.—To this kind note, F. B. wrote the warmest and most affectionate and heartfelt reply; but never received another word! And here and thus stopped a correspondence of six years of almost unequalled partiality and fondness on her side; and affection, gratitude, admiration, and sincerity on that of F. B., who could only conjecture the cessation to be caused by the resentment of Piozzi, when informed of her constant opposition to the union.]

Diary resumed

NORBURY PARK, SUNDAY, NOV. 28TH. Last Thursday, Nov. 25th, my father set me down at Bolt Court, while he went on upon business. I was anxious to again see poor Dr Johnson, who has had terrible health since his return from Litchfield. He let me in, though very ill.

[1] Mrs Thrale had married Piozzi, the musician, on 23rd July. The marriage was bitterly opposed by most of her friends, including Dr Johnson. Fanny entirely disapproved of it, and her letter on the occasion had omitted all mention of Piozzi.

He was alone, which I much rejoiced at: for I had a longer and more satisfactory conversation with him than I have had for many months. He was in rather better spirits, too, than I have lately seen him; but he told me he was going to try what sleeping out of town might do for him.

'I remember,' said he, 'that my wife, when she was near her end, poor woman, was also advised to sleep out of town; and when she was carried to the lodgings that had been prepared for her, she complained that the staircase was in very bad condition—for the plaster was beaten off the walls in many places: "Oh," said the man of the house, "that's nothing but by the knocks against it of the coffins of the poor souls that have died in the lodgings!"'

He laughed, though not without apparent secret anguish, in telling me this. I felt extremely shocked, but, willing to confine my words at least to the literal story, I only exclaimed against the unfeeling absurdity of such a confession.

'Such a confession,' cried he, 'to a person then coming to try his lodging for her health, contains, indeed, more absurdity than we can well lay our account for.'

I had seen Miss T.[1] the day before.

'So,' said he, 'did I.'

I then said: 'Do you ever, sir, hear from her mother?'

'No,' cried he, 'nor write to her. I drive her quite from my mind. If I meet with one of her letters, I burn it instantly. I have burnt all I can find. I never speak of her, and I desire never to hear of her more. I drive her, as I said, wholly from my mind.'[2]

Yet, wholly to change this discourse, I gave him a history of the Bristol milk-woman,[3] and told him the tales I had heard of her writing so wonderfully, though

[1] Thrale.

[2] Dr Johnson's bitterness against Mrs Piozzi was due not only to her marriage, but also to the fact that after Mr Thrale's death he was no longer a welcome guest at Streatham, which had for so many years been a home to him. There is, however, a good deal to be said for the lady's side of the question.

[3] Ann Yearsley.

she had read nothing but Young and Milton; 'though those,' I continued, 'could never possibly, I should think, be the first authors with anybody. Would children understand them? and grown people who have not read are children in literature.'

'Doubtless,' said he; 'but there is nothing so little comprehended among mankind as what is genius. They give to it all, when it can be but a part. Genius is nothing more than knowing the use of tools; but there must be tools for it to use: a man who has spent all his life in this room will give a very poor account of what is contained in the next.'

I saw him growing worse, and offered to go, which, for the first time I ever remember, he did not oppose; but, most kindly pressing both my hands:

'Be not,' he said, in a voice of even tenderness, 'be not longer in coming again for my letting you go now.'

I assured him I would be the sooner, and was running off, but he called me back, in a solemn voice, and, in a manner the most energetic, said:

'Remember me in your prayers!'

I longed to ask him to remember me, but did not dare. I gave him my promise, and, very heavily indeed, I left him. Great, good, and excellent that he is, how short a time will he be our boast! Ah, my dear Susy, I see he is going! This winter will never conduct him to a more genial season here! Elsewhere, who shall hope a fairer? I wish I had bidden him pray for me; but it seemed to me presumptuous, though this repetition of so kind a condescension might, I think, have encouraged me. Mrs Locke,[1] however, I know does it daily; my Susan's best prayers I know are always mine; and where can I find two more innocent pleaders? So God bless you both!

DEC. 20TH. This day was the ever-honoured, ever-lamented Dr Johnson committed to the earth. Oh, how sad a day to me! My father attended, and so did Charles.

[1] Susan and her husband lived at Mickleham, near Leatherhead, where they were tenants of Mr Lock of Norbury Park.

I could not keep my eyes dry all day! Nor can I now in the recollecting it; but let me pass over what to mourn is now so vain!

I had the good fortune at night of a sweet letter from my dearest Susy; that, and another from my Fredy,[1] were alone able to draw me from this mournful day's business.

[1] Mrs Lock.

PART TWO

(NOVEMBER, 1785–JUNE, 1788)

PART TWO

(November, 1785–June, 1788)[1]

WINDSOR, SATURDAY, NOV. 25TH. I got to Hounslow almost at the same moment with Mrs Astley, my dear Mrs Delany's maid, who was sent to meet me. As soon as she had satisfied my inquiries concerning her lady, she was eager to inform me that the Queen had drunk tea with Mrs D—— the day before, and had asked when I should come, and heard the time; and that Mrs Delany believed she would be with her again that evening, and desire to see me.[2]

This was rather fidgeting intelligence. I rather, in my own mind, thought the Queen would prefer giving me the first evening alone with my dear old friend.

I found that sweet lady not so well as I had hoped, and strongly affected by afflicting recollections at sight of me. With all her gentleness and resignations, bursts of sorrow break from her still, whenever we are alone together; and with all her gratitude and all her real fondness for the Queen, her suffering heart moans internally its irreparable loss; for the Duchess of Portland was a bosom friend—a very Susan to her.

The Queen herself is most sensible of this, and while she tries, by all the means in her power, to supply the place of the lamented Duchess of Portland, she is the first to observe and to forgive the impossibility of a full success;

[1] Vol. ii, p. 357—vol. iv, p. 153.
[2] Mrs Delany was 85 years old at this time. Dr Patrick Delany, Swift's friend and the author of *Observations upon Lord Orrery's Remarks upon the Life and Writings of Dr Jonathan Swift*, was her second husband. On the death of her friend, the Duchess of Portland, the King gave her a house at Windsor, and here Fanny stayed with her.

indeed, the circumstances I am continually hearing of her sweetness and benevolence make me more than ever rejoice she has taken my dear Mrs Delany under her immediate protection.

Mrs Delany acquainted me that the Queen, in their first interview, upon her coming to this house, said to her: 'Why did you not bring your friend Miss Burney with you?'

My dear Mrs Delany was very much gratified by such an attention to whatever could be thought interesting to her, but, with her usual propriety, answered that, in coming to a house of her Majesty's, she could not presume to ask anybody without immediate and express permission. 'The King, however,' she added, 'made the very same inquiry when I saw him next.'

Now, though you, my dear father, have had an audience, and you, my dear Susan, are likely enough to avoid one, yet I think the etiquettes on these occasions will be equally new to you both; for one never inquired into them, and the other has never thought of them. Here, at Windsor, where more than half the people we see are belonging to the Court, and where all the rest are trying to be in the same predicament, the intelligence I have obtained must be looked upon as accurate; and I shall therefore give it in full confidence you will both regard it as a valuable addition to your present stock of Court knowledge, and read it with that decent awe the dignity of the topic requires!

Directions for a Private Encounter with the Royal Family

But no, they will take me so long that I had better put them on a separate sheet, and go on with my journal while all is fresh in my memory. I am sorry to have wasted so solemn a preamble, but hope you will have the generosity to remember it when I produce my directions, as I cannot possibly undertake writing another.

To come, then, now, to those particular instructions I received myself, and which must not be regarded as having anything to do with general rules.

'I do beg of you,' said dear Mrs Delany, 'when the Queen or the King speaks to you, not to answer with mere monosyllables. The Queen often complains to me of the difficulty with which she can get any conversation, as she not only always has to start the subjects, but, commonly, entirely to support them: and she says there is nothing she so much loves as conversation, and nothing she finds so hard to get. She is always best pleased to have the answers that are made her lead on to further discourse. Now, as I know she wishes to be acquainted with you, and converse with you, I do really entreat you not to draw back from her, nor to stop conversation with only answering yes, or no.'

This was a most tremendous injunction; however, I could not but promise her I would do the best I could.

To this, nevertheless, she readily agreed, that if upon entering the room, they should take no notice of me, I might quietly retire. And that, believe me, will not be very slowly! They cannot find me in this house without knowing who I am, and therefore they can be at no loss whether to speak to me or not, from incertitude.

In the midst of all this the Queen came!

I heard the thunder at the door, and, panic-struck, away flew all my resolutions and agreements, and away after them flew I!

Don't be angry, my dear father—I would have stayed if I could, and I meant to stay; but, when the moment came, neither my preparations nor intentions availed, and I arrived at my own room, ere I well knew I had left the drawing-room, and quite breathless between the race I ran with Miss Port and the joy of escaping.

FRIDAY, DEC. 16TH. Yesterday morning we had a much better account of the Princess Elizabeth;[1] and Mrs Delany said to me:

---

[1] The Princess was suffering from 'a complaint on the chest.'

'Now you will escape no longer, for if their uneasiness ceases, I am sure they will send for you, when they come next.'

After dinner, while Mrs Delany was left alone, as usual, to take a little rest—for sleep it but seldom proves—Mr B. Dewes, his little daughter, Miss Port, and myself, went into the drawing-room. And here, while, to pass the time, I was amusing the little girl with teaching her some Christmas games, in which her father and cousin joined, Mrs Delany came in. We were all in the middle of the room, and in some confusion—but she had but just come up to us to inquire what was going forwards, and I was disentangling myself from Miss Dewes, to be ready to fly off if any one knocked at the street door, when the door of the drawing-room was again opened, and a large man, in deep mourning, appeared at it, entering and shutting it himself without speaking.

A ghost could not more have scared me, when I discovered by its glitter on the black, a star! The general disorder had prevented his being seen, except by myself, who was always on the watch, till Miss P——,[1] turning round, exclaimed: 'The King!—Aunt, the King!'

O mercy! thought I, that I were but out of the room! Which way shall I escape? And how to pass him unnoticed? There is but the single door at which he entered, in the room! Every one scampered out of the way: Miss P——, to stand next the door; Mr Bernard Dewes to a corner opposite it; his little girl clung to me; and Mrs Delany advanced to meet his Majesty, who, after quietly looking on till she saw him, approached, and inquired how she did.

He then spoke to Mr Bernard, whom he had already met two or three times here.

I had now retreated to the wall, and purposed gliding softly, though speedily, out of the room; but before I had taken a single step, the King, in a loud whisper to Mrs

---

[1] Miss Port, previously named in full. She was Mrs Delany's niece.

Delany, said: 'Is that Miss Burney?' and on her answering: 'Yes, sir,' he bowed, and with a countenance of the most perfect good humour, came close up to me.

A most profound reverence on my part arrested the progress of my intended retreat.

'How long have you been come back, Miss Burney?'

'Two days, sir.'

Unluckily he did not hear me, and repeated his question; and whether the second time he heard me or not, I don't know, but he made a little civil inclination of his head, and went back to Mrs Delany.

He insisted she should sit down, though he stood himself, and began to give her an account of the Princess Elizabeth, who once again was recovering, and trying, at present, James's Powders. She had been blooded, he said, twelve times in this last fortnight, and had lost seventy-five ounces of blood, besides undergoing blistering and other discipline. He spoke of her illness with the strongest emotion, and seemed quite filled with concern for her danger and sufferings.

Mrs Delany next inquired for the younger children. They had all, he said, the whooping-cough, and were soon to be removed to Kew.

'Not,' added he, 'for any other reason than change of air for themselves; though I am pretty certain I have never had the distemper myself, and the Queen thinks she has not had it either—we shall take our chance. When the two eldest had it, I sent them away, and would not see them till it was over; but now there are so many of them that there would be no end to separations, so I let it take its course.'

Mrs Delany expressed a good deal of concern at his running this risk, but he laughed at it, and said he was much more afraid of catching the rheumatism, which has been threatening one of his shoulders lately. However, he added, he should hunt the next morning, in defiance of it.

A good deal of talk then followed about his own health,

and the extreme temperance by which he preserved it. The fault of his constitution, he said, was a tendency to excessive fat, which he kept, however, in order by the most vigorous exercise, and the strictest attention to a simple diet.

When Mrs Delany was beginning to praise his forbearance, he stopped her.

'No, no,' he cried, ''tis no virtue; I only prefer eating plain and little, to growing diseased and infirm.'

When the discourse upon health and strength was over, the King went up to the table, and looked at a book of prints, from Claude Lorraine, which had been brought down for Miss Dewes; but Mrs Delany, by mistake, told him they were for me. He turned over a leaf or two, and then said:

'Pray, does Miss Burney draw, too?'

The *too* was pronounced very civilly.

'I believe not, sir,' answered Mrs Delany; 'at least, she does not tell.'

'Oh!' cried he, laughing, 'that's nothing! She is not apt to tell; she never does tell, you know! Her father told me that himself. He told me the whole history of her *Evelina*. And I shall never forget his face when he spoke of his feelings at first taking up the book!—he looked quite frightened, just as if he was doing it that moment! I never can forget his face while I live!'

Then coming up close to me, he said:

'But what?—what?—how was it?'

'Sir,' cried I, not well understanding him.

'How came you — how happened it ? — what ? — what?'

'I—I only wrote, sir, for my own amusement—only in some odd, idle hours.'

'But your publishing—your printing—how was that?'

'That was only, sir—only because——'

I hesitated most abominably, not knowing how to tell him a long story, and growing terribly confused at these questions—besides, to say the truth, his own 'what?

what?' so reminded me of those vile *Probationary Odes*,[1] that, in the midst of all my flutter, I was really hardly able to keep my countenance.

The *What?* was then repeated with so earnest a look, that, forced to say something, I stammeringly answered:

'I thought—sir—it would look very well in print!'

I do really flatter myself this is the silliest speech I ever made! I am quite provoked with myself for it; but a fear of laughing made me eager to utter anything, and by no means conscious, till I had spoken, of what I was saying.

He laughed very heartily himself—well he might—and walked away to enjoy it, crying out:

'Very fair indeed! That's being very fair and honest!'

Then, returning to me again, he said:

'But your father—how came you not to show him what you wrote?'

'I was too much ashamed of it, sir, seriously.'

Literal truth that, I am sure.

'And how did he find it out?'

'I don't know myself, sir. He never would tell me.'

Literal truth again, my dear father, as you can testify.

'But how did you get it printed?'

'I sent it, sir, to a bookseller my father never employed, and that I never had seen myself, Mr Lowndes, in full hope by that means he never would hear of it.'

'But how could you manage that?'

'By means of a brother, sir.'

'Oh!—you confided in a brother, then?'

---

[1] *Probationary Odes for the Laureateship.* The death of William Whitehead, the poet laureate, in 1785 gave the Whig wits an opportunity of satirizing leading characters of the time in 'Odes,' supposed to have been written by them in competition for the vacant post. The allusion here is to the lines:

> 'Methinks I hear,
> In accents clear,
> Great Brunswick's voice still vibrate on my ear:
> "What?—What?—What?"'

'Yes, sir—that is, for publication.' [1]

'What entertainment you must have had from hearing people's conjectures before you were known! Do you remember any of them?'

'Yes, sir, many.'

'And what?'

'I heard that Mr Baretti [2] laid a wager it was written by a man; for no woman, he said, could have kept her own counsel.'

This diverted him extremely.

'But how was it,' he continued, 'you thought most likely for your father to discover you?'

'Sometimes, sir, I have supposed I must have dropped some of the manuscript: sometimes, that one of my sisters betrayed me.'

'Oh! your sister?—what, not your brother?'

'No, sir; he could not, for——'

I was going on, but he laughed so much I could not be heard, exclaiming:

'Vastly well! I see you are of Mr Baretti's mind, and think your brother could keep your secret, and not your sister.'

'Well, but,' cried he presently, 'how was it first known to you you were betrayed?'

'By a letter, sir, from another sister. I was very ill, and in the country; and she wrote me word that my father had taken up a review, in which the book was mentioned, and had put his finger upon its name, and said: "Contrive to get that book for me."'

'And when he got it,' cried the King, 'he told me he was afraid of looking at it! And never can I forget his face when he mentioned his first opening it. But you have not kept your pen unemployed all this time?'

---

[1] Her younger brother, Charles, had carried out the transaction with Lowndes for her.

[2] Giuseppe Baretti (1719–89). He was the author of a *Dictionary of the English and Italian Languages*, and had been tutor in Italian to Miss Thrale.

'Indeed I have, sir.'

'But why?'

'I—I believe I have exhausted myself, sir.'

He laughed aloud at this, and went and told it to Mrs Delany, civilly treating a plain fact as a mere *bon mot*.

While this was talking over, a violent thunder was made at the door. I was almost certain it was the Queen. Once more I would have given anything to escape; but in vain. I had been informed that nobody ever quitted the royal presence, after having been conversed with, till motioned to withdraw.

Miss P——, according to established etiquette on these occasions, opened the door which she stood next, by putting her hand behind her, and slid out backwards into the hall, to light the Queen in. The door soon opened again, and her Majesty [1] entered.

Immediately seeing the King, she made him a low curtsy, and cried:

'Oh, your Majesty is here!'

'Yes,' he cried, 'I ran here without speaking to anybody.'

The Queen had been at the lower Lodge, to see the Princess Elizabeth, as the King had before told us.

She then hastened up to Mrs Delany, with both her hands held out, saying:

'My dear Mrs Delany, how are you?'

Instantly after, I felt her eye on my face. I believe, too, she curtsied to me; but though I saw the bend, I was too near-sighted to be sure it was intended for me. I was hardly ever in a situation more embarrassing; I dared not return what I was not certain I had received, yet considered myself as appearing quite a monster, to stand stiff-necked, if really meant.

Almost at the same moment, she spoke to Mr Bernard Dewes, and then nodded to my little clinging girl.

I was now really ready to sink, with horrid uncertainty of what I was doing, or what I should do—when his

[1] Charlotte of Mecklenburg-Strelitz.

Majesty, who I fancy saw my distress, most good-humouredly said to the Queen something, but I was too much flurried to remember what, except these words: 'I have been telling Miss Burney——'

Relieved from so painful a dilemma, I immediately dropped a curtsy. She had made one to me in the same moment, and, with a very smiling countenance, came up to me, but she could not speak, for the King went on talking, eagerly, and very gaily repeating to her every word I had said during our conversation upon *Evelina*, its publication, etc., etc.

Then he told her of Baretti's wager, saying: 'But she heard of a great many conjectures about the author, before it was known, and of Baretti, an admirable thing! he laid a bet it must be a man, as no woman, he said, could have kept her own counsel!'

The Queen, laughing a little, exclaimed:

'Oh, that is quite too bad an affront to us! Don't you think so?' addressing herself to me, with great gentleness of voice and manner.

The King then went on, and when he had finished his narration the Queen took her seat.

She made Mrs Delany sit next her, and Miss P—— brought her some tea.

The King, meanwhile, came to me again, and said: 'Are you musical?'

'Not a performer, sir.'

Then, going from me to the Queen, he cried: 'She does not play.'

I did not hear what the Queen answered; she spoke in a low voice, and seemed much out of spirits.

They now talked together a little while, about the Princess Elizabeth, and the King mentioned having had a very promising account from her physician, Sir George Baker: and the Queen soon brightened up.

The King then returned to me, and said:

'Are you sure you never play? Never touch the keys at all?'

'Never to acknowledge it, sir.'

'Oh! that's it!' cried he; and flying to the Queen, cried: 'She does play—but not to acknowledge it!'

I was now in a most horrible panic once more; pushed so very home, I could answer no other than I did, for these categorical questions almost constrain categorical answers; and here, at Windsor, it seems an absolute point that whatever they ask must be told, and whatever they desire must be done. Think but, then, of my consternation, in expecting their commands to perform! My dear father, pity me!

The eager air with which he returned to me fully explained what was to follow. I hastily, therefore, spoke first, in order to stop him, crying: 'I never, sir, played to anybody but myself! Never!'

'No?' cried he, looking incredulous; 'what, not to——'

'Not even to me, sir!' cried my kind Mrs Delany, who saw what was threatening me.

'No? Are you sure?' cried he, disappointed; 'but—but you'll——'

'I have never, sir,' cried I, very earnestly, 'played in my life, but when I could hear nobody else—quite alone, and from a mere love of any musical sounds.'

He still, however, kept me in talk, and still upon music.

'To me,' said he, 'it appears quite as strange to meet with people who have no ear for music, and cannot distinguish one air from another, as to meet with people who are dumb. Lady Bell Finch once told me that she had heard there was some difference between a psalm, a minuet, and a country dance, but she declared they all sounded alike to her! There are people who have no eye for difference of colour. The Duke of Marlborough actually cannot tell scarlet from green!'

He then told me an anecdote of his mistaking one of those colours for another, which was very laughable, but I do not remember it clearly enough to write it. How unfortunate for true virtuosi that such an eye should possess objects worthy the most discerning—the treasures of Blenheim!

The King then, looking at his watch, said: 'It is eight o'clock, and if we don't go now, the children will be sent to the other house.'

'Yes, your Majesty,' cried the Queen, instantly rising.

Mrs Delany put on her Majesty's cloak, and she took a very kind leave of her. She then curtsied separately to us all, and the King handed her to the carriage.

It is the custom for everybody they speak to to attend them out, but they would not suffer Mrs Delany to move. Miss P——, Mr Dewes, and his little daughter, and myself, all accompanied them, and saw them in their coach, and received their last gracious nods.

When they were gone, Mrs Delany confessed she had heard the King's knock at the door before she came into the drawing-room, but would not avow it, that I might not run away. Well! being over was so good a thing, that I could not but be content.

Dec. 19TH. In the evening, while Mrs Delany, Miss P——, and I were sitting and working together in the drawing-room, the door was opened, and the King entered.

We all started up; Miss P—— flew to her modest post by the door, and I to my more comfortable one opposite the fire, which caused me but a slight and gentle retreat, and Mrs Delany he immediately commanded to take her own place again.

Our party being so small, he made all that passed general; for though he principally addressed himself to Mrs Delany, he always looked round to see that we heard him, and frequently referred to us.

I should mention, though, the etiquette always observed upon his entrance, which, first of all, is to fly off to distant quarters; and next, Miss P—— goes out, walking backwards, for more candles, which she brings in, two at a time, and places upon the tables and pianoforte. Next she goes out for tea, which she then carries to his Majesty, upon a large salver, containing sugar, cream, and bread and butter, and cake, while she hangs a napkin over her arm for his fingers.

When he has taken his tea, she returns to her station, where she waits till he has done, and then takes away his cup, and fetches more.

This, it seems, is a ceremony performed, in other places, always by the mistress of the house; but here neither of their Majesties will permit Mrs Delany to attempt it.

Well; but to return. The King said he had just been looking over a new pamphlet of Mr Cumberland's,[1] upon the character of Lord Sackville.

'I have been asking Sir George Baker,' said he, 'if he had read it, and he told me yes; but that he could not find out why Cumberland had written it. However, that, I think, I found out in the second page. For there he takes an opportunity to give a high character of himself.'

He then spoke of Voltaire, and talked a little of his works, concluding with this strong condemnation of their tendency:

'I,' cried he, 'think him a monster—I own it fairly.'

Nobody answered. Mrs Delany did not quite hear him, and I knew too little of his works to have courage to say anything about them.

He next named Rousseau, whom he seemed to think of with more favour, though by no means with approbation. Here, too, I had read too little to talk at all, though his Majesty frequently applied to me. Mrs Delany told several anecdotes which had come to her immediate knowledge of him while he was in England, at which time he had spent some days with her brother, Mr Granville, at Calwich. The King, too, told others, which had come to his own ears, all charging him with savage pride and insolent ingratitude.

Here, however, I ventured to interfere; for, as I knew he had had a pension from the King, I could not but wish his Majesty should be informed he was grateful to him. And as you, my dear father, were my authority, I thought it was

---

[1] Richard Cumberland, the dramatist (1732–1811).

but common justice to the memory of poor Rousseau to acquaint the King of his personal respect for him.

'Some gratitude, sir,' said I, 'he was not without. When my father was in Paris, which was after Rousseau had been in England, he visited him in his garret, and the first thing he showed him was your Majesty's portrait over his chimney.'

The King paused a little while upon this; but nothing more was said of Rousseau.

The sermon of the day before was then talked over. Mrs Delany had not heard it, and the King said it was no great loss. He asked me what I had thought of it, and we agreed perfectly, to the no great exaltation of poor Dr L——.

Some time afterwards, the King said he found by the newspapers that Mrs Clive [1] was dead.

Do you read the newspapers? thought I. Oh, King! you must then have the most unvexing temper in the world not to run wild.

This led on to more players. He was sorry, he said, for Henderson, [2] and the more as Mrs Siddons had wished to have him play at the same house with herself. Then Mrs Siddons took her turn, and with the warmest praise.

'I am an enthusiast for her,' cried the King, 'quite an enthusiast. I think there was never any player in my time so excellent—not Garrick himself; I own it!'

Then, coming close to me, who was silent, he said:

'What? what?'—meaning, what say you? But I still said nothing; I could not concur where I thought so differently, and to enter into an argument was quite impossible; for every little thing I said the King listened to with an eagerness that made me always ashamed of its insignificancy. And, indeed, but for that I should have talked to him with much greater fluency, as well as ease.

From players he went to plays, and complained of the great want of good modern comedies, and of the extreme immorality of most of the old ones.

---

[1] Catherine (Kitty) Clive, the actress (1711–85).
[2] John Henderson (1747–85), the 'Bath Roscius.' In popular esteem this actor stood second only to Garrick.

'And they pretend,' cried he, 'to mend them; but it is not possible.   Do you think it is?—what?'

'No, sir, not often, I believe.   The fault, commonly, lies in the very foundation.'

'Yes, or they might mend the mere speeches; but the characters are all bad from the beginning to the end.'

Then he specified several; but I had read none of them, and, consequently, could say nothing about the matter—till, at last he came to Shakespeare.

'Was there ever,' cried he, 'such stuff as great part of Shakespeare? only one must not say so!   But what think you?—What?—Is there not sad stuff?—What—what?'

'Yes, indeed, I think so, sir, though mixed with such excellences, that——'

'Oh!' cried he, laughing good-humouredly, 'I know it is not to be said! but it's true.   Only it's Shakespeare, and nobody dare abuse him.'

This led on to a good deal more dramatic criticism; but what was said was too little followed up to be remembered for writing.   His Majesty stayed near two hours, and then wished Mrs Delany good night, and having given me a bow, shut the door himself, to prevent Mrs Delany, or even me, from attending him out, and, with only Miss P—— to wait upon him, put on his own great coat in the passage, and walked away to the lower lodge, to see the Princess Elizabeth, without carriage or attendant.   He is a pattern of modest, but manly superiority to rank.

Miss F. Burney to Mrs Burney [1]

Windsor, Dec. 17th, 1785.

MY DEAREST HETTY,

I am sorry I could not more immediately write; but I really have not had a moment since your last.

Now I know what you next want is, to hear accounts

[1] Fanny's sister, Esther, Dr Burney's eldest daughter.

of kings, queens, and such royal personages. Oho! Do
you so? Well.

Shall I tell you a few matters of fact? Or, had you
rather a few matters of etiquette? Oh, matters of etiquette,
you cry! for matters of fact are short and stupid, and anybody can tell, and everybody is tired with them.

Very well, take your own choice.

To begin, then, with the beginning.

You know I told you, in my last, my various difficulties,
what sort of preferment to turn my thoughts to, and
concluded with just starting a young budding notion of
decision, by suggesting that a handsome pension for nothing at all would be as well as working night and day for a
salary.

This blossom of an idea, the more I dwelt upon, the
more I liked. Thinking served it for a hot-house and it
came out into full blow as I ruminated upon my pillow.
Delighted that thus all my contradictory and wayward
fancies were overcome, and my mind was peacably settled
what to wish and to demand, I gave over all further
meditation upon choice of elevation, and had nothing
more to do but to make my election known.

My next business, therefore, was to be presented.
This could be no difficulty; my coming hither had been
their own desire, and they had earnestly pressed its execution. I had only to prepare myself for the rencounter.

You would never believe—you, who, distant from
courts and courtiers, know nothing of their ways—the
many things to be studied, for appearing with a proper
propriety before crowned heads. Heads without crowns
are quite other sort of rotundas.

Now, then, to the etiquette. I inquired into every
particular, that no error might be committed. And as
there is no saying what may happen in this mortal life,
I shall give you those instructions I have received myself,
that, should you find yourself in the royal presence, you
may know how to comport yourself.

Directions for coughing, sneezing, or moving, before the King and Queen.

In the first place, you must not cough. If you find a cough tickling in your throat, you must arrest it from making any sound; if you find yourself choking with the forbearance, you must choke—but not cough.

In the second place, you must not sneeze. If you have a vehement cold, you must take no notice of it; if your nose membranes feel a great irritation, you must hold your breath; if a sneeze still insists upon making its way, you must oppose it, by keeping your teeth grinding together; if the violence of the repulse breaks some blood-vessel, you must break the blood-vessel—but not sneeze.

In the third place, you must not, upon any account, stir either hand or foot. If, by any chance, a black pin runs into your head, you must not take it out. If the pain is very great, you must be sure to bear it without wincing; if it brings the tears into your eyes, you must not wipe them off; if they give you a tingling by running down your cheeks, you must look as if nothing was the matter. If the blood should gush from your head by means of the black pin, you must let it gush; if you are uneasy to think of making such a blurred appearance, you must be uneasy, but you must say nothing about it. If, however, the agony is very great, you may, privately, bite the inside of your cheek, or of your lips, for a little relief; taking care, meanwhile, to do it so cautiously as to make no apparent dent outwardly. And, with that precaution, if you even gnaw a piece out, it will not be minded, only be sure either to swallow it, or commit it to a corner of the inside of your mouth till they are gone—for you must not spit.

I have many other directions, but no more paper; I will endeavour, however, to have them ready for you in time. Perhaps, meanwhile, you will be glad to know if I have myself had opportunity to put in practice these receipts?

How can I answer in this little space? My love to Mr

B. and the little ones, and remember me kindly to cousin
Edward, and believe me, my dearest Esther.

Most affectionately yours,

F. B.

Miss Burney to Mrs Francis,[1] *Aylsham, Norfolk*

St Martin's Street, June 27th, 1786.

My sweet Charlotte's kind indulgence to my long silence
has been very, very dearly accepted.   It is like your ever
affectionate mind to believe and feel for my hurries.   New
ones that you dream not of have occupied, and now occupy
me.   I must tell you them briefly, for I have scarce a
moment; but it would be very vexatious to me that any
pen but my own should communicate any event material
to me, my dear Charlotte.

Her Majesty has sent me a message, express, near a
fortnight ago, with an offer of a place at Court, to succeed
Mrs Haggerdorn, one of the Germans who accompanied
her to England, and who is now retiring into her own
country.   'Tis a place of being constantly about her own
person, and assisting in her toilette—a place of much
confidence, and many comforts; apartments in the palace;
a footman kept for me; a coach in common with Mrs
Schwellenberg;[2] 200*l.* a year, etc. etc.

I have been in a state of extreme disturbance ever since,
from the reluctance I feel to the separation it will cause
me from all my friends.   Those, indeed, whom I most
love, I shall be able to invite to me in the palace; but I see
little or no possibility of being able to make, what I most
value, excursions into the country.

When you come, however, my dearest Charlotte, I shall

---

[1] Charlotte, Dr Burney's fourth daughter.
[2] Mrs Schwellenberg had come over with the Queen, twenty-five
years before.   She was Keeper of the Robes.   Fanny's title was to
be Assistant Keeper.

certainly take measures for seeing you, either in town, or at Windsor, or both.

So new a scene, so great a change, so uncertain a success, frightens and depresses me; though the extreme sweetness of the Queen, in so unsolicited an honour, so unthought-of a distinction, binds me to her with a devotion that will make an attendance upon her light and pleasant. I repine only at losing my loved visits to the country, Mickleham, Norbury, Chesington, Twickenham, and Aylsham, as I had hoped; all these I must now forgo.

Everybody so violently congratulates me, that it seems as if *all* was gain. However, I am glad they are all so pleased. My dear father is in raptures; that is my first comfort. Write to wish him joy, my dear Charlotte, without a hint to him, or any one but Susan, of my confessions of my internal reluctance and fears.

You may believe how much I am busied. I have been presented at the Queen's Lodge in Windsor, and seen Mrs Haggerdorn in office, and find I have a place of really nothing to do, but to *attend*; and on Thursday I am appointed by her Majesty to go to St James's, to see all that belongs to me there. And I am now *fitting out* just as you were, and all the maids and workers suppose I am going to be married, and snigger every time they bring in any of my new attire. I do not care to publish the affair, till it is made known by authority; so I leave them to their conjectures, and I fancy their greatest wonder is *who* and *where* is the *sposo*; for they must think it odd he should never appear!

F. B.

Diary resumed

QUEEN'S LODGE, WINDSOR, MONDAY, JULY 17TH, 1786. With what hurry of mind and body did I rise this morning! Everything had already been arranged for Mrs Ord's carrying us to Windsor, and my father's carriage was merely to go as baggage wagon for my clothes. But I wept not then. I left no one behind me to regret; my dear father accompanied me, and all my dear sisters had already taken their flight, never more to return. Even poor little Sarah,[1] whom I love very dearly, was at Chesington.

Between nine and ten o'clock we set off. We changed carriage in Queen Anne Street, and Mrs Ord conveyed us thence to Windsor. With a struggling heart, I kept myself tolerably tranquil during the little journey. My dear father was quite happy, and Mrs Ord felt the joy of a mother in relinquishing me to the protection of a Queen so universally reverenced. Had I been in better spirits, their ecstasy would have been unbounded; but alas!— what I was approaching was not in my mind; what I was leaving had taken possession of it solely.

It was now debated whether I was immediately to go to the Lodge, or wait for orders. The accustomed method for those who have their Majesties' commands to come to them is, to present themselves to the people in waiting, and by them to be announced. My heart, however, was already sinking, and my spirits every moment were growing more agitated, and my sweet Mrs Delany determined to spare me the additional task of passing through such awe-striking formalities. She therefore employed my dear father—delighted with the employment—to write a note, in her name.

'Mrs Delany presents her most humble duty to the Queen; she found Dr Burney and his daughter at her house; Miss Burney waits the honour of her Majesty's commands.'

This, though unceremonious and unusual, she was sure the Queen would pardon. A verbal answer came that I was to go to the Lodge immediately.

Oh, my dear Susan! in what agony of mind did I obey the summons! I was still in my travelling dress, but could not stay to change it. My father accompanied me. Mrs

[1] Dr Burney's daughter by his second wife.

Delany, anxiously and full of mixed sensations, gave me her blessing. We walked; the Queen's Lodge is not fifty yards from Mrs Delany's door. My dear father's own courage all failed him in this little step; for as I was now on the point of entering—probably for ever—into an entire new way of life, and of forgoing by it all my most favourite schemes, and every dear expectation my fancy had ever indulged of happiness adapted to its taste—as now all was to be given up—I could disguise my trepidation no longer —indeed I never had disguised, I had only forborne proclaiming it. But my dear father now, sweet soul! felt it all, as I held by his arm, without power to say one word, but that if he did not hurry along I should drop by the way. I heard in his kind voice that he was now really alarmed; he would have slackened his pace, or have made me stop to breathe; but I could not; my breath seemed gone, and I could only hasten with all my might, lest my strength should go too.

A page was in waiting at the gate, who showed us into Mrs Haggerdorn's room, which was empty. My dear father endeavoured here to compose my spirits; I could have no other command over them than to forbear letting him know the afflicted state of all within, and to suffer him to keep to his own conclusions, that my emotion was all from fear of the approaching audience. Indeed was it not!— I could hardly even think of it. All that I was resigning— there, and there only went every fear, and all reluctance.

The page came in a minute or two to summon me to the Queen. The Queen was in her dressing-room. Mrs Schwellenberg was standing behind her; nobody else present.

She received me with a most gracious bow of the head, and a smile that was all sweetness. She saw me much agitated, and attributed it, no doubt, to the awe of her presence. Oh, she little knew my mind had no room in it for feelings of that sort! She talked to me of my journey, my father, my sisters, and my brothers; the weather, the roads, and Mrs Delany—any, everything she could suggest, that could best tend to compose and to make me easy; and when I had been with her about a quarter of an hour, she desired Mrs Schwellenberg to show me my apartment, and, with another graceful bow, motioned my retiring.

Mrs Schwellenberg left me at the room door, where my dear father was still waiting for me, too anxious to depart till he again saw me.

We spent a short time together, in which I assured him I would from that moment take all the happiness in my power, and banish all the regret. I told him how gratifying had been my reception, and I omitted nothing I could think of to remove the uneasiness that this day seemed first to awaken in him. Thank God! I had the fullest success; his hopes and gay expectations were all within call, and they ran back at the first beckoning.

Left to myself, I did not dare to stop to think, nor look round upon my new abode, nor consider for how long I was taking possession; I rang for my new maid, and immediately dressed for dinner.

I now took the most vigorous resolutions to observe the promise I had made my dear father. Now all was finally settled, to borrow my own words, I needed no monitor to tell me it would be foolish, useless, even wicked, not to reconcile myself to my destiny.

At night I was summoned to the Queen's apartment. Mrs Schwellenberg was there, waiting. We sat together some time. The Queen then arrived, handed into her dressing-room by the King, and followed by the Princess Royal and Princess Augusta. None other of the Princesses slept in the Queen's Lodge. The Lower Lodge, which is at the farther end of the Garden, is the dwelling-place of the four younger Princesses.

The King, with a marked appearance of feeling for the —no doubt evident—embarrassment of my situation on their entrance, with a mild good breeding inquired of me how I had found Mrs Delany; and then, kissing both his daughters, left the room.

The two Princesses each took the Queen's hand, which they respectfully kissed, and wishing her good night, curtsied condescendingly to her new attendant, and retired.

The Queen spoke to me a little of my father, my journey, and Mrs Delany, and then entered into easy conversation, in German, with Mrs Schwellenberg, who never speaks English but by necessity. I had no sort of employment given me. The Queen was only waited upon by Mrs Schwellenberg and Mrs Thielky, her wardrobe woman; and when she had put on her night *déshabillé*, she wished me good night.

MONDAY, JULY 18TH. I rose at six, and was called to the Queen soon after seven. Only Mrs Schwellenberg was with her, and again she made me a mere looker-on; and the obligation I felt to her sent me somewhat lighter-hearted from her presence.

When she was dressed, in a simple morning gown, she had her hat and cloak put on, to go to prayers at eight o'clock, at the King's Chapel in the Castle; and I returned to my room.

At noon came my dear father, and spent an hour or two with me—so happy! so contented! so big with every pleasant expectation!—I rejoice to recollect that I did nothing, said nothing this morning to check his satisfaction; it was now, suddenly and at once, all my care to increase his delight. And so henceforward it must invariably continue.

My Windsor apartment is extremely comfortable. I have a large drawing-room, as they call it, which is on the ground floor, as are all the Queen's rooms, and which faces the Castle and the venerable Round Tower, and opens at the farther side, from the windows, to the Little Park. It is airy, pleasant, clean, and healthy. My bedroom is small, but neat and comfortable; its entrance is only from the drawing room, and it looks to the garden. These two rooms are delightfully independent of all the rest of the house, and contain everything I can desire for my convenience and comfort.

MONDAY, JULY 24TH. Let me endeavour to give you, more connectedly, a concise abstract of the general method of passing the day, that then I may only write what varies, and occurs occasionally.

I rise at six o'clock, dress in a morning gown and cap, and wait my first summons, which is at all times from seven to near eight, but commonly in the exact half hour between them.

The Queen never sends for me till her hair is dressed. This, in a morning, is always done by her wardrobe woman, Mrs Thielky, a German, but who speaks English perfectly well.

Mrs Schwellenberg, since the first week, has never come down in a morning at all. The Queen's dress is finished by Mrs Thielky and myself. No maid ever enters the room while the Queen is in it. Mrs Thielky hands the things to me, and I put them on. 'Tis fortunate for me I have not the handing them! I should never know which to take first, embarrassed as I am, and should run a prodigious risk of giving the gown before the hoop, and the fan before the neckerchief.

By eight o'clock, or a little after, for she is extremely expeditious, she is dressed. She then goes out to join the King, and be joined by the Princesses, and they all proceed to the King's chapel in the Castle, to prayers, attended by the governesses of the Princesses, and the King's equerry. Various others at times attend; but only these indispensably.

I then return to my own room to breakfast. I make this meal the most pleasant part of the day; I have a book for my companion, and I allow myself an hour for it. My present book is Gilpin's description of the Lakes of Cumberland and Westmorland.[1] Mrs Delany has lent it me. It is the most picturesque reading I ever met with: it shows me landscapes of every sort, with tints so bright

---

[1] William Gilpin (1724–1804) wrote a series of books on the scenery of the Lake District, the Highlands, the Wye Valley, and the Isle of Wight.

and lively, I forget I am but reading, and fancy I see them before me, coloured by the hand of nature.

At nine o'clock I send off my breakfast things, and relinquish my book, to make a serious and steady examination of everything I have upon my hands in the way of business—in which preparations for dress are always included, not for the present day alone, but for the court days, which require a particular dress; for the next arriving birthday of any of the Royal Family, every one of which requires new apparel; for Kew, where the dress is plainest; and for going on here, where the dress is very pleasant to me, requiring no show nor finery, but merely to be neat, not inelegant, and moderately fashionable.

That over, I have my time at my own disposal till a quarter before twelve, except on Wednesdays and Saturdays, when I have it only to a quarter before eleven.

My rummages and business sometimes occupy me uninterruptedly to those hours. When they do not, I give till ten to necessary letters of duty, ceremony, or long arrears—and now, from ten to the times I have mentioned, I devote to walking.

These times mentioned call me to the irksome and quick-returning labours of the toilette. The hour advanced on the Wednesdays and Saturdays is for curling and craping the hair, which it now requires twice a week.

A quarter before one is the usual time for the Queen to begin dressing for the day. Mrs Schwellenberg then constantly attends; so do I; Mrs Thielky, of course, at all times. We help her off with her gown, and on with her powdering things, and then the hairdresser is admitted. She generally reads the newspapers during that operation.

When she observes that I have run to her but half dressed, she constantly gives me leave to return and finish as soon as she is seated. If she is grave, and reads steadily on, she dismisses me, whether I am dressed or not; but at all times she never forgets to send me away while she is powdering, with a consideration not to spoil my clothes, that one would not expect belonged to her high station.

Neither does she ever detain me without making a point of reading here and there some little paragraph aloud.

When I return, I finish, if anything is undone, my dress, and then take Baretti's *Dialogues*,[1] my dearest Fredy's *Tablet of Memory*, or some such disjointed matter, for the few minutes that elapse ere I am again summoned.

I find her then always removed to her state dressing-room, if any room in this private mansion can have the epithet of state. There, in a very short time, her dress is finished. She then says she won't detain me, and I hear and see no more of her till bedtime.

It is commonly three o'clock when I am thus set at large. And I have then two hours quite at my own disposal: but, in the natural course of things, not a moment after! These dear and quiet two hours, my only quite sure and undisturbed time in the whole day, after breakfast is over, I shall henceforward devote to thus talking with my beloved Susan, my Fredy, my other sisters, my dear father, or Miss Cambridge; with my brothers, cousins, Mrs Ord, and other friends, in such terms as these two hours will occasionally allow me. Henceforward, I say; for hitherto dejection of spirits, with uncertainty how long my time might last, have made me waste moment after moment as sadly as unprofitably.

At five, we have dinner. Mrs Schwellenberg and I meet in the eating-room. We are commonly tête-à-tête: when there is anybody added, it is from her invitation only. Whatever right my place might afford me of also inviting my friends to the table I have now totally lost, by want of courage and spirits to claim it originally.

When we have dined, we go upstairs to her apartment, which is directly over mine. Here we have coffee till the *terracing* is over; this is at about eight o'clock. Our tête-à-tête then finishes, and we come down again to the eating-room. There the equerry, whoever he is, comes to tea constantly, and with him any gentleman that the King or Queen may have invited for the evening; and when

[1] A volume of Italian-English dialogues published in 1771.

tea is over, he conducts them, and goes himself, to the concert room.

This is commonly about nine o'clock.

From that time, if Mrs Schwellenberg is alone, I never quit her for a minute, till I come to my little supper at near eleven.

Between eleven and twelve my last summons usually takes place, earlier and later occasionally. Twenty minutes is the customary time then spent with the Queen: half an hour, I believe, is seldom exceeded.

I then come back, and after doing whatever I can to forward my dress for the next morning, I go to bed—and to sleep, too, believe me: the early rising, and a long day's attention to new affairs and occupations, cause a fatigue so bodily, that nothing mental stands against it, and to sleep I fall the moment I have put out my candle and laid down my head.

Such is the day to your F. B. in her new situation at Windsor; such, I mean, is its usual destination, and its intended course. I make it take now and then another channel, but never stray far enough not to return to the original stream after a little meandering about and about it.

I think now you will be able to see and to follow me pretty closely.

With regard to those summonses I speak of, I will now explain myself. My summons, upon all regular occasions —that is, morning, noon, and night toilets—is neither more nor less than a bell. Upon extra occasions a page is commonly sent.

At first, I felt inexpressibly discomfited by this mode of call. A bell!—it seemed so mortifying a mark of servitude, I always felt myself blush, though alone, with conscious shame at my own strange degradation. But I have philosophized myself now into some reconcilement with this manner of summons, by reflecting that to have some person always sent would be often very inconvenient, and that this method is certainly less an interruption to any occupation I may be employed in, than the entrance of messengers so many times in the day. It is, besides, less liable to mistakes. So I have made up my mind to it as well as I can; and now I only feel that proud blush when somebody is by to revive my original dislike of it.

TUESDAY, JULY 25TH. I now begin my second week, with a scene a little, not much, different. We were now to go to Kew, there to remain till Friday.

I had this morning, early, for the first time, a little visit from one of the Princesses. I was preparing for my journey, when a little rap at my room door made me call out: 'Come in!' and who should enter but the Princess Royal!

I apologized for my familiar admittance, by my little expectation of such an honour. She told me she had brought the Queen's snuff-box, to be filled with some snuff which I had been directed to prepare. It is a very fine-scented and mild snuff, but requires being moistened from time to time to revive its smell.

The Princess, with a very sweet smile, insisted upon holding the box while I filled it; and told me she had seen Mrs Delany at the chapel, and that she was very well; and then she talked on about her, with a visible pleasure in having a subject so interesting to me to open upon.

When the little commission was executed, she took her leave with as elegant civility of manner as if parting with another King's daughter. I am quite charmed with the Princess Royal; unaffected condescension and native dignity are so happily blended in her whole deportment.

She had left me but a short time before she again returned. 'Miss Burney,' cried she, smiling with a look of congratulation, 'Mamma says the snuff is extremely well mixed; and she has sent another box to be filled.'

I had no more ready. She begged me not to mind, and not to hurry myself, for she would wait till it was done.

Mrs Schwellenberg, Miss Planta,[1] and myself travelled to Kew together. I have two rooms there; both small,

[1] Miss Planta had charge of the Princesses. According to Fanny, her actual post in the court calendar was that of English teacher.

and up two pairs of stairs; but tidy and comfortable enough.
Indeed all the apartments but the King's and Queen's, and
one of Mrs Schwellenberg's, are small, dark, and old-
fashioned. There are staircases in every passage, and
passages to every closet. I lost myself continually, only
passing from my own room to the Queen's.

AUGUST 8TH. An exceeding pretty scene was exhibited
to-day to their Majesties. We came, as usual on every
alternate Tuesday, to Kew. The Queen's Lodge is at
the end of a long meadow, surrounded with houses,
which is called Kew Green; and this was quite filled with
all the inhabitants of the place—the lame, old, blind, sick,
and infants, who all assembled, dressed in their Sunday
garb, to line the sides of the roads through which their
Majesties passed, attended by a band of musicians, arranged
in the front, who began *God Save the King!* the moment
they came upon the Green, and finished it with loud
huzzas. This was a compliment at the expense of the
better inhabitants, who paid the musicians themselves, and
mixed in with the group, which indeed left not a soul, I
am told, in any house in the place.

This testimony of loyal satisfaction in the King's safe
return, after the attempted assassination,[1] affected the
Queen to tears: nor were they shed alone; for almost
everybody's flowed that witnessed the scene. The Queen,
in speaking of it afterwards, said: 'I shall always love little
Kew for this!'

At the second toilette to-day, Mrs Schwellenberg, who
left the dressing-room before me, called out at the door:
'Miss Bernar, when you have done from the Queen, come
to my room.'

There was something rather more peremptory in the
order than was quite pleasant to me, and I rather dryly
answered: 'Very well, Mrs Schwellenberg.'

The Queen was even uncommonly sweet and gracious
in her manner after this lady's departure, and kept me with

[1] A woman named Margaret Nicholson had attempted to stab the
King.

her some time after she was dressed. I never go from her presence till I am dismissed; no one does, not even when they come in only with a hurried message—except the pages, who enter merely as messengers, and Mrs Schwellenberg, whose place and illness together have given her that privilege.

The general form of the dismission, which you may perhaps be curious to hear, is in these words: 'Now I will let you go'; which the Queen manages to speak with a grace that takes from them all air of authority.

At first, I must confess, there was something inexpressibly awkward to me, in waiting to be told to go, instead of watching an opportunity, as elsewhere, for taking leave before I thought myself *de trop*: but I have since found that this is, to me, a mark of honour; as it is the established custom to people of the first rank, the Princesses themselves included, and only not used to the pages and the wardrobe women, who are supposed only to enter for actual business, and therefore to retire when it is finished, without expectation of being detained to converse, or beyond absolute necessity.

I give you all these little details of interior royalty, because they are curious, from opening a new scene of life, and can only be really known by interior residence.

When I went to Mrs Schwellenberg, she said: 'You might know I had something to say to you, by my calling you before the Queen.' She then proceeded to a long prelude, which I could but ill comprehend, save that it conveyed much of obligation on my part, and favour on hers; and then ended with: 'I might tell you now, the Queen is going to Oxford, and you might go with her; it is a secret—you might not tell it nobody. But I tell you once, I shall do for you what I can; you are to have a gown.'

I stared, and drew back, with a look so undisguised of wonder and displeasure at this extraordinary speech, that I saw it was understood, and she then thought it time, therefore, to name her authority, which, with great emphasis, she did thus: 'The Queen will give you a gown! The Queen says you are not rich,' etc.

There was something in the manner of this quite intolerable to me; and I hastily interrupted her with saying: 'I have two new gowns by me, and therefore do not require another.'

Perhaps a proposed present from her Majesty was never so received before; but the grossness of the manner of the messenger swallowed up the graciousness of the design in the principal; and I had not even a wish to conceal how little it was to my taste.

The highest surprise sat upon her brow: she had imagined that a gown—that any present—would have been caught at with obsequious avidity; but indeed she was mistaken.

Seeing the wonder and displeasure now hers, I calmly added: 'The Queen is very good, and I am very sensible of her Majesty's graciousness; but there is not, in this instance, the least occasion for it.'

'Miss Bernar,' cried she, quite angrily, 'I tell you once, when the Queen will give you a gown, you must be humble, thankful, when you are Duchess of Ancaster!'

She then enumerated various ladies to whom her Majesty had made the same present, many of them of the first distinction, and all, she said, great secrets. Still I only repeated again the same speech.

I can bear to be checked and curbed in discourse, and would rather be subdued into silence—and even, if that proves a gratification that secures peace and gives pleasure, into apparent insensibility; but to receive a favour through the vehicle of insolent ostentation—no! no! To submit to ill humour rather than argue and dispute I think an exercise of patience, and I encourage myself all I can to practise it: but to accept even a shadow of an obligation upon such terms I should think mean and unworthy; and therefore I mean always, in a Court as I would elsewhere, to be open and fearless in declining such subjection.

When she had finished her list of secret ladies, I told her

I must beg to speak to the Queen, and make my own acknowledgments for her gracious intention.

This she positively forbid; and said it must only pass through her hands. 'When I give you the gown,' she added, 'I will tell you when you may make your curtsy.'

I was not vexed at this prohibition, not knowing what etiquette I might offend by breaking it; and the conversation concluded with nothing being settled.

I might have apprehended some misrepresentation of this conference; but I could not give up all my own notions of what I think everybody owes to themselves, so far as to retract, or apologize, or say anything further. I determined to run the risk of what might be related, and wait the event quietly. In situations entirely new, where our own ideas of right and wrong are not strictly and courageously adhered to from the very beginning, we are liable to fall into shackles which no after time, no future care and attention, can enable us to shake off.

How little did the sweet Queen imagine that this her first mark of favour should so be offered me as to raise in me my first spirit of resistance! How differently would she have executed her own commission herself! To avoid exciting jealousy was, I doubt not, her motive for employing another.

At night, however, this poor woman was so ill, so lost for want of her party at cards, and so frightened with apprehensions of the return of some dreadful spasmodic complaints, from which she has many years suffered the severest pain, that I was induced to do a thing you will wonder at, and against which I had resolved to struggle unrelentingly. This was to play at cards with her. She had frequently given me broad hints of desiring me to learn; but I had openly declared I disliked cards, and never wished nor meant to learn a single game. However, to-night's sufferings conquered me, and I proposed it myself. The offer was plumply accepted, and Miss Planta was sent for to help to teach me. Irksome enough is this compliance; but while I stand firm in points of honour, I must content myself to relinquish those of inclination.

AUGUST 12TH, SATURDAY. The Prince of Wales's birthday. How I grieve at whatever may be the cause which absents him from his family!—a family of so much love, harmony, and excellence, that to mix with them, even rarely, must have been the first of lessons to his heart; and here, I am assured, his heart is good, though, elsewhere, his conduct renders it so suspicious.

I come now to the Oxford expedition.

The plan was to spend one day at Lord Harcourt's, at Nuneham, one at Oxford, and one at Blenheim; dining and sleeping always at Nuneham.

I now a little regretted that I had declined meeting Lady Harcourt, when invited to see her at Mrs Vesey's, about three years ago. I was not, just then, very happy— and I was surfeited of new acquaintances; when the invitation, therefore, came, I sent an excuse. But now when I was going to her house, I wished I had had any previous knowledge of her, to lessen the difficulties of my first appearance in my new character, upon attending the Queen on a visit.

I said something of this sort to Mrs Schwellenberg, in our conversation the day before the journey; and she answered that it did not signify; for, as I went with the Queen, I might be sure I should be civilly treated.

Yes, I said, I generally had been; and congratulated myself that at least I knew a little of Lord Harcourt, to whom I had been introduced, some years ago, at Sir Joshua Reynolds's, and whom I had since met two or three times. 'Oh,' she cried, 'it is the same—that is nothing—when you go with the Queen, it is enough; they might be civil to you for that sake. You might go quite without no, what you call, fuss; you might take no gown but what you go in—that is enough; you might have no servant—for what? You might keep on your riding-dress. There is no need you might be seen. I shall do everything that I can to assist you to appear for nobody.

I leave you to imagine my thanks. But the news about the servant was not very pleasant, as I thought it most likely I could never more want one than in a strange house added to a strange situation. However, I determined upon assuming no competition in command, and therefore I left the matter to her own direction.

We arrived at Nuneham at about six o'clock.

The house is one of those straggling, half-new, half-old, half-comfortable, and half-forlorn mansions, that are begun in one generation and finished in another. It is very pleasantly situated, and commands, from some points of view, all the towers of Oxford.

In going across the park to the entrance, we saw not a creature. All were busy, either in attendance upon the royal guests, or in finding hiding-places from whence to peep at them.

We stopped at the portico—but not even a porter was there; we were obliged to get out of the carriage by the help of one of the postilions, and to enter the house by the help of wet grass, which would not suffer me to stay out of it, otherwise, I felt so strange in going in uninvited and unconducted, that I should have begged leave to stroll about till somebody appeared.

Miss Planta, more used to these expeditions, though with quite as little taste for them, led the way, and said we had best go and see for our own rooms.

I was quite of the same opinion, but much at a loss how we might find them. We went through various passages, unknowing whither they might lead us, till at length we encountered a prodigious fine servant. Miss Planta asked him for Lady Harcourt's maid; he bowed slightly, and passed on without making any answer.

Very pleasant this! I then begged we might turn back, not caring for another adventure of the same sort. Miss Planta complied; and we met two more of the yellow-laced saunterers, with whom she had precisely the same success.

I think I never remember to have felt so much shame

from my situation as at that time. To arrive at a house where no mistress or master of it cared about receiving me; to wander about, a guest uninvited, a visitor unthought of; without even a room to go to, a person to inquire for, or even a servant to speak to! It was now I felt the real want of either a man or maid, to send forward, and find out what we were to do with ourselves; and indeed I resolved, then, I would not another time be so passive to unauthorized directions.

We strayed thus, backwards and forwards, for a full quarter of an hour, in these nearly deserted straggling passages; and then, at length, met a French woman, whom Miss Planta immediately seized upon: it was Lady Harcourt's woman, and Miss Planta had seen her at Windsor.

'Pray show us,' cried Miss Planta, 'where we are to go.'

She was civil, and led us to a parlour looking very pleasantly upon the park, and asked if we would have some tea. Miss Planta assented. She told us the King and Queen were in the park, and left us.

As there was a garden door to this room, I thought it very possible the royal party and their suite might return to the house that way. This gave great addition to my discomposure, for I thought that to see them all in this forlorn plight would be still the worst part of the business; I therefore pressed Miss Planta to let us make another attempt to discover our own rooms.

Miss Planta laughed exceedingly at my disturbance, but complied very obligingly with my request.

The wardrobe women had already been shown to the rooms they were to prepare for the Queen and the Princesses.

The King and Queen's suite, then in the house, were the Duchess of Ancaster, Lady Charlotte Bertie, Colonel Fairly,[1] and Major Price; with pages whose names I know not, and footmen, and two hairdressers.

The family party in the house were, the Lord and Lady; two Miss Vernons, sisters of Lady Harcourt; General

[1] See p. 206, *note*.

Harcourt, brother to Lord Harcourt, and aide-de-camp to the King; and Mrs Harcourt, his wife.

In this our second wandering forth we had no better success than in the first; we either met nobody, or only were crossed by such superfine men in laced liveries, that we attempted not to question them. My constant dread was of meeting any of the royal party, while I knew not whither to run. Miss Planta, more inured to such situations, was not at all surprised by our difficulties and disgraces, and only diverted by my distress from them.

We met at last with Mhaughendorf,[1] and Miss Planta eagerly desired to be conducted to the Princesses' rooms, that she might see if everything was prepared for them.

When they had looked at the apartments destined for the Princesses, Miss Planta proposed our sitting down to our tea in the Princess Elizabeth's room. This was extremely disagreeable to me, as I was sensible it must seem a great freedom from me, should her Royal Highness surprise us there; but it was no freedom for Miss Planta, as she has belonged to all the Princesses these nine years, and is eternally in their sight. I could not, therefore, persuade her of the difference; and she desired Mhaughendorf to go and order our tea upstairs.

Miss Planta, followed by poor me, then whisked backwards and forwards, from one of the apartments to another, superintending all the preparations; and, as we were crossing a landing-place, a lady appeared upon the stairs, and Miss Planta called out: 'It's Lady Harcourt,' and ran down to meet her.

They talked together a few minutes. 'I must get you, Miss Planta,' said she, looking up towards me, 'to introduce me to Miss Burney.'

She then came up the stairs, said she was glad to see me, and desired I would order anything I wanted, either for the Queen or for myself.

Cold enough was my silent curtsy.

[1] Miss Mhaughendorf was a dresser to the Princesses Royal and Augusta.

She talked again to Miss Planta, who, already knowing her, from seeing her frequently when in waiting, as she is one of the ladies of the bedchamber, was much more sociable than myself.

She afterwards turned to me, and said: 'If there is anything you want, Miss Burney, pray speak for it.' And she added: 'My sisters will attend you presently; you will excuse me—I have not a moment from their Majesties.' And then she curtsied, and left us.

We returned to the Princess Elizabeth's room, and there the tea followed, but not the promised sisters.

I never saw Miss Planta laugh so heartily before nor since; but my dismay was possibly comical to behold.

The tea was but just poured out, when the door opened, and in entered all the Princesses. I was very much ashamed, and started up, but had no asylum whither to run. They all asked us how we did after our journey; and I made an apology, as well as I could, to the Princess Elizabeth, for my intrusion into her apartment; confessing I did not know where to find my own.

The Princess Royal, eagerly coming up to me, said: 'I thought you would be distressed at first arriving, and I wanted to help you; and I inquired where your room was, and said I would look at it myself; and I went round to it, but I found the King was that way, and so, you know, I could not get past him; but indeed I wished to have seen it for you.'

There was hardly any thanking her for such sweetness; they then desired us to go on with our tea, and went into the Princess Royal's room.

I was now a little revived; and soon after the Princess Elizabeth came back, and asked us if we had done, desiring us at the same time not to hurry.

When the Princesses left us, we were again at a loss what to do with ourselves; we saw several passing servants, maids as well as men, and Miss Planta applied to them all to show me my room, which I was anxious to inhabit in peace and solitude: however, they all promised to send someone else, but no one came. Miss Planta, in the midst of the diversion she received from my unavailing earnestness to get into some retreat, had the good nature to say: 'I knew how this would turn out, and wished the visit over before it began; but it must really be very new to you, unused as you are to it, and accustomed to so much attention in other places.'

At length she seized upon a woman-servant, who undertook to conduct me to this wished-for room. Miss Planta accompanied me, and off we set.

When we got to the hall leading to this parlour, we were suddenly stopped by the appearance of the King, who just then came out of that very room. Lord Harcourt attended, with a candle in his hand, and a group of gentlemen followed.

We were advanced too far to retreat, and therefore only stood still. The King stopped, and spoke to the Duchess of Ancaster; and then spoke very graciously to Miss Planta and me, inquiring when we set out, and what sort of journey we had had. He then ascended the stairs, the Princess Royal accompanying him, and all the rest following; the Duchess first pointing to the door of the eating-parlour, and bidding us go there, and expect Miss Vernons.

Lord Harcourt, during this meeting, had contrived to slip behind the King, to make me a very civil bow; and when his Majesty moved on, he slid nearer me, and whispered a welcome to his house, in very civil terms. This was all he could do, so situated.

We now entered the eating-room. We sat down—but no Miss Vernons! Presently the door opened—I hoped they were coming—but a clergyman, a stranger to us both, appeared. This gentleman, I afterwards found, was Mr Hagget, chaplain to Lord Harcourt, and rector of a living in his lordship's gift and neighbourhood; a young man, sensible, easy, and remarkably handsome, in very high favour with all the family.

With nobody to introduce us to each other, we could but rise and bow, and curtsy, and sit down again.

In a few minutes, again the door gave hopes to me of Miss Vernons; but there only appeared a party of gentlemen.

Major Price came foremost, and immediately introduced me to General Harcourt. The General is a very shy man, with an air of much haughtiness; he bowed and retreated, and sat down, and was wholly silent.

Colonel Fairly followed him, and taking a chair next mine, began some of the civilest speeches imaginable, concerning this opportunity of making acquaintance with me.

Just then came in a housemaid, and said she would show me my room. I rose hastily. Miss Planta, who knew everybody present except the clergyman, was now willing to have sat still and chatted; but nothing short of compulsion could have kept me in such a situation, and therefore I instantly accompanied the maid; and poor Miss Planta could not stay behind.

. . . I was surprised when my summons was brought me by Lady Harcourt, who tapped gently at my door, and made me a little visit, previously to telling me her errand. She informed me, also, that the Queen had given her commands for Miss Planta and me to belong to the suite the next day, in the visit to Oxford; and that a carriage was accordingly ordered for us.

The Queen said not a word to me of the day's adventures; and I was glad to have them passed over, especially as Lady Harcourt's visit, and the civility which accompanied it, appeared a little conscious of remissness. But when, in speaking of Oxford, her Majesty condescended to ask what gown I had brought with me, how did I rejoice to answer, a new Chambéry gauze, instead of only that which I have on, according to my Cerbera's [1] advice.

My next difficulty was for a hairdresser. Nuneham

[1] Mrs Schwellenberg.

is three or four miles from Oxford; and I had neither maid to dress, nor man to seek a dresser. I could only apply to Mrs Thielky, and she made it her business to prevail with one of the royal footmen to get me a messenger, to order a hairdresser from Oxford at six o'clock in the morning. The Queen, with the most gracious consideration, told me, overnight, that she should not want me till eight o'clock.

Thus ended the first night of this excursion.

AUGUST 13TH. At six o'clock my hairdresser, to my great satisfaction, arrived. Full two hours was he at work, yet was I not finished, when Swarthy, the Queen's hairdresser, came rapping at my door, to tell me her Majesty's hair was done, and she was waiting for me. I hurried as fast as I could, and ran down without any cap. She smiled at sight of my hasty attire, and said I should not be distressed about a hairdresser the next day, but employ Swarthy's assistant, as soon as he had done with the Princesses: 'You should have had him,' she added, 'to-day, if I had known you wanted him.'

When her Majesty was dressed, all but the hat, she sent for the three Princesses; and the King came also. I felt very foolish with my uncovered head; but it was somewhat the less awkward, from its being very much a custom, in the Royal Family, to go without caps; though none that appear before them use such a freedom.

As soon as the hat was on: 'Now, Miss Burney,' said the Queen, 'I won't keep you; you had better go and dress too.'

And now for the Oxford expedition.

How many carriages there were, and how they were arranged, I observed not sufficiently to recollect; but the party consisted of their Majesties, the Princesses Royal, Augusta, and Elizabeth, the Duchess of Ancaster, Lord and Lady Harcourt, Lady Charlotte Bertie, and the two Miss Vernons.

These last ladies are daughters of the late Lord Vernon, and sisters of Lady Harcourt.

General Harcourt, Colonel Fairly, and Major Price, and Mr Hagget, with Miss Planta and myself, completed the group. Miss Planta and I, of course, as the only undignified persons, brought up the rear. We were in a chaise of Lord Harcourt.

The city of Oxford afforded us a very noble view on the road, and its spires, towers, and domes soon made me forget all the little objects of minor spleen that had been crossing me as I journeyed towards them; and indeed, by the time I arrived in the midst of them, their grandeur, nobility, antiquity, and elevation impressed my mind so forcibly, that I felt for the first time since my new situation had taken place a rushing in of ideas that had no connection with it whatever.

The roads were lined with decently dressed people, and the high street was so crowded we were obliged to drive gently and carefully, to avoid trampling the people to death. Yet their behaviour was perfectly respectful and proper. Nothing could possibly be better conducted than the whole of this expedition.

At the outward gate of the theatre, the Vice-Chancellor, Dr Chapman, received their Majesties. All the Professors, Doctors, etc., then in Oxford, arrayed in their professional robes, attended him. How I wished my dear father amongst them!

The Vice-Chancellor then conducted their Majesties along the inner court to the door of the theatre, all the rest following; and there, waiting their arrival, stood the Duke and Duchess of Marlborough, the Marquis of Blandford, in a nobleman's Oxford robe, and Lady Caroline and Lady Elizabeth Spencer.

After they had all paid their duties, a regular procession followed, which I should have thought very pretty, and much have liked to have seen, had I been a mere looker-on; but I was frequently at a loss what to do with myself, and uncertain whether I ought to proceed in the suite, or stand by as a spectator; and Miss Planta was still, if possible, more fearful.

We were no sooner arranged, and the door of the theatre shut, than the King, his head covered, sat down; the Queen did the same, and then the three Princesses.

All the rest, throughout the theatre, stood.

The Vice-Chancellor then made a low obeisance to the King and producing a written paper, began the Address of the University, to thank his Majesty for this second visit, and to congratulate him and the nation on his late escape from assassination. He read it in an audible and distinct voice; and in its conclusion, an address was suddenly made to the Queen, expressive of much concern for her late distress, and the highest and most profound veneration for her amiable and exalted character.

When the address was ended, the King took a paper from Lord Harcourt, and read his answer. The King reads admirably; with ease, feeling, and force, and without any hesitation. His voice is particularly full and fine. I was very much surprised by its effect.

When he had done, he took off his hat, and bowed to the Chancellor and Professors, and delivered the answer to Lord Harcourt, who, walking backwards, descended the stairs, and presented it to the Vice-Chancellor.

Next followed music; a good organ, very well played, anthem-ed and voluntary-ed us for some time.

After this, the Vice-Chancellor and Professors begged for the honour of kissing the King's hand. Lord Harcourt was again the backward messenger; and here followed a great mark of goodness in the King: he saw that nothing less than a thoroughbred old courtier, such as Lord Harcourt, could walk backwards down these steps, before himself, and in sight of so full a hall of spectators; and he therefore dispensed with being approached to his seat, and walked down himself into the area, where the Vice-Chancellor kissed his hand, and was imitated by every Professor and Doctor in the room.

Notwithstanding this considerate good nature in his Majesty, the sight, at times, was very ridiculous. Some of the worthy collegiates, unused to such ceremonies, and unaccustomed to such a presence, the moment they had kissed the King's hand, turned their backs to him, and walked away as in any common room; others, attempting to do better, did still worse, by tottering and stumbling, and falling foul of those behind them; some, ashamed to kneel, took the King's hand straight up to their mouths; others, equally off their guard, plumped down on both knees, and could hardly get up again; and many, in their confusion, fairly arose by pulling his Majesty's hand to raise them.

As the King spoke to every one, upon Lord Harcourt's presenting them, this ceremonial took up a good deal of time; but it was too new and diverting to appear long.

At Christ Church College, where we arrived at about three o'clock, in a large hall there was a cold collation prepared for their Majesties and the Princesses. It was at the upper end of the hall. I could not see of what it consisted, though it would have been very agreeable, after so much standing and sauntering, to have given my opinion of it in an experimental way.

Their Majesties and the Princesses sat down to this table; as well satisfied, I believe, as any of their subjects so to do. The Duchess of Ancaster and Lady Harcourt stood behind the chairs of the Queen and the Princess Royal. There were no other ladies of sufficient rank to officiate for Princess Augusta and Elizabeth. Lord Harcourt stood behind the King's chair; and the Vice-Chancellor, and the head master of Christ Church, with salvers in their hands, stood near the table, and ready to hand to the three noble waiters whatever was wanted: while the other Reverend Doctors and Learned Professors stood aloof, equally ready to present to the Chancellor and the Master whatever they were to forward.

We, meanwhile, untitled attendants, stood at the other end of the room, forming a semicircle, and all strictly facing the royal collationers. We consisted of the Miss Vernons, thrown out here as much as their humble guests—Colonel Fairly, Major Price, General Harcourt,

and—though I know not why—Lady Charlotte Bertie—
with all the inferior Professors, in their gowns, and some,
too much frightened to advance, of the upper degrees.
These, with Miss Planta, Mr Hagget, and myself, formed
this attendant semicircle.

The time of this collation was spent very pleasantly—
to me, at least, to whom the novelty of the scene rendered
it entertaining. It was agreed that we must all be absolutely famished unless we could partake of some refreshment, as we had breakfasted early, and had no chance of
dining before six or seven o'clock. A whisper was soon
buzzed through the semicircle, of the deplorable state of
our appetite apprehensions; and presently it reached the
ears of some of the worthy Doctors. Immediately a new
whisper was circulated, which made its progress with great
vivacity, to offer us whatever we would wish, and to beg
us to name what we chose.

Tea, coffee, and chocolate, were whispered back.

The method of producing, and the means of swallowing
them, were much more difficult to settle than the choice
of what was acceptable. Major Price and Colonel Fairly,
however, seeing a very large table close to the wainscot
behind us, desired our refreshments might be privately
conveyed there, behind the semicircle, and that, while all
the group backed very near it, one at a time might feed,
screened by all the rest from observation.

I suppose I need not inform you, my dear Susan, that to
eat in presence of any of the Royal Family, is as much
hors d'usage as to be seated.

This plan had speedy success, and the very good
Doctors soon, by sly degrees and with watchful caution,
covered the whole table with tea, coffee, chocolate, cakes,
and bread and butter.

The further plan, however, of one at a time feasting
and the rest fasting and standing sentinels, was not equally
approved; there was too much eagerness to seize the
present moment, and too much fear of a sudden retreat,
to give patience for so slow a proceeding. We could do

no more, therefore, than stand in a double row, with one to screen one throughout the troop; and, in this manner, we were all very plentifully and very pleasantly served.

The Duchess of Ancaster and Lady Harcourt, as soon as the first serving attendance was over, were dismissed from the royal chairs, and most happy to join our group, and partake of our repast. The Duchess, extremely fatigued with standing, drew a small body of troops before her, that she might take a few minutes' rest on a form by one of the doors; and Lady Charlotte Bertie did the same, to relieve an ankle which she had unfortunately sprained.

In another college (we saw so many, and in such quick succession, that I recollect not any by name, though all by situation) I saw a performance of courtly etiquette, by Lady Charlotte Bertie, that seemed to me as difficult as any feat I ever beheld, even at Astley's or Hughes's. It was in an extremely large, long, spacious apartment. The King always led the way out, as well as in, upon all entrances and exits: but here, for some reason that I know not, the Queen was handed out first; and the Princesses, and the Aide-de-camp, and Equerry followed. The King was very earnest in conversation with some Professor; the attendants hesitated whether to wait or follow the Queen; but presently the Duchess of Ancaster, being near the door, slipped out, and Lady Harcourt after her. The Miss Vernons, who were but a few steps from them, went next. But Lady Charlotte, by chance, happened to be very high up the room, and near to the King. Had I been in her position, I had surely waited till his Majesty went first; but that would not, I saw, upon this occasion, have been etiquette. She therefore faced the King, and began a march backwards—her ankle already sprained, and to walk forward, and even leaning upon an arm, was painful to her: nevertheless, back she went, perfectly upright, without one stumble, without ever looking once behind to see what she might encounter; and with as graceful a motion, and as easy an air, as I ever saw anybody enter a long room, she retreated, I am sure, full twenty yards backwards out of one.

For me, I was also, unluckily, at the upper end of the room, looking at some portraits of founders, and one of Henry VIII in particular, from Holbein. However, as soon as I perceived what was going forward—backward, rather—I glided near the wainscot (Lady Charlotte, I should mention, made her retreat along the very middle of the room), and having paced a few steps backwards, stopped short to recover, and, while I seemed examining some other portrait, disentangled my train from the heels of my shoes, and then proceeded a few steps only more; and then observing the King turn another way, I slipped a yard or two at a time forwards; and hastily looked back, and then was able to go again according to rule, and in this manner, by slow and varying means, I at length made my escape.

Miss Planta stood upon less ceremony, and fairly ran off.

Since that time, however, I have come on prodigiously, by constant practice, in the power and skill of walking backwards, without tripping up my own heels, feeling my head giddy, or treading my train out of the plaits—accidents very frequent among novices in that business; and I have no doubt but that, in the course of a few months, I shall arrive at all possible perfection in the true court retrograde motion.

The last college we visited was Cardinal Wolsey's[1]—an immense fabric. While roving about a very spacious apartment, Mr F—— came behind me, and whispered that I might easily slip out into a small parlour, to rest a little while; almost everybody having taken some opportunity to contrive themselves a little sitting but myself. I assured him, very truly, I was too little tired to make it worth while; but poor Miss Planta was so woefully fatigued that I could not, upon her account, refuse to be of the party. He conducted us into a very neat little parlour, belonging to the master of the college, and Miss Planta flung herself on a chair, half dead with weariness.

[1] Christ Church, however, was visited first (p. 139).

Mr F—— was glad of the opportunity to sit for a moment also; for my part, I was quite alert. Alas! my dear Susan, 'tis my mind that is so weak, and so open to disorder; my body, I really find, when it is an independent person, very strong, and capable of much exertion without suffering from it.

Mr F—— now produced, from a paper repository concealed in his coat pocket, some apricots and bread, and insisted upon my eating; but I was not inclined to the repast, and saw he was half famished himself; so was poor Miss Planta; however, he was so persuaded I must both be as hungry and as tired as himself, that I was forced to eat an apricot to appease him.

Presently, while we were in the midst of this regale, the door suddenly opened, and the Queen came in!—followed by as many attendants as the room would contain.

Up we all started, myself alone not discountenanced; for I really think it quite respect sufficient never to sit down in the royal presence, without aiming at having it supposed I have stood bolt upright ever since I have been admitted to it.

Quick into our pockets was crammed our bread, and close into our hands was squeezed our fruit; by which I discovered that our appetites were to be supposed annihilated, at the same time that our strength was to be invincible.

Very soon after this we were joined by the King, and in a few minutes we all paraded forth to the carriages, and drove back to Nuneham.

Miss Burney to Mrs Phillips

August 20.

Has my dear Susan thought me quite dead?—not to write so long! and after such sweet converse as she has sent me. Oh, my beloved Susan, 'tis a refractory heart I have to deal with!—it struggles so hard to be sad—and silent—and fly from you entirely, since it cannot fly entirely to you. I do all I can to conquer it, to content it, to give it a taste and enjoyment for what is still attainable; but at times I cannot manage it, and it seems absolutely indispensable to my peace to occupy myself in anything rather than in writing to the person most dear to me upon earth! 'Tis strange—but such is the fact—and I now do best when I get those who never heard of you, and who care not about me. . . .

If to you alone I show myself in these dark colours, can you blame the plan that I have intentionally been forming —namely, to wean myself from myself—to lessen all my affections — to curb all my wishes — to deaden all my sensations? This design, my Susan, I formed so long ago as the first day my dear father accepted my offered appointment: I thought that what demanded a complete new system of life required, if attainable, a new set of feelings for all enjoyment of new prospects, and for lessening regrets at what were quitted, or lost. Such being my primitive idea, merely from my grief of separation, imagine but how it was strengthened and confirmed when the interior of my position became known to me!—when I saw myself expected by Mrs Schwellenberg, not to be her colleague, but her dependent deputy! not to be her visitor at my own option, but her companion, her humble companion, at her own command! This has given so new a character to the place I had accepted under such different auspices, that nothing but my horror of disappointing, perhaps displeasing, my dearest father, has deterred me, from the moment that I made this mortifying discovery, from soliciting his leave to resign. But oh! my Susan—kind, good, indulgent as he is to me, I have not the heart so cruelly to thwart his hopes—his views —his happiness in the honours he conceived awaiting my so unsolicited appointment. The Queen, too, is all sweetness, encouragement, and gracious goodness to me, and I cannot endure to complain to her of her old servant. You see, then, my situation; here I must remain! The die is cast, and that struggle is no more. To keep off every other, to support the loss of the dearest friends, and best society, and bear, in exchange, the tyranny, the *exigeance*, the *ennui*, and attempted indignities of their greatest contrast—this must be my constant endeavour. . . .

Diary resumed

THURSDAY, OCTOBER 5TH, was my first waiting at St James's without Mrs Schwellenberg; and Mr and Mrs Locke came to me in my rooms, and at night they carried me to *Tancred and Sigismunda*.[1] I saw also my father and my dear brother James.[2]

FRIDAY, OCTOBER 6TH. We returned to Windsor without Mrs Schwellenberg, who stayed in town for her physician's advice. The Queen went immediately to Mrs Delany; the Princess Royal came into my room.

'I beg pardon,' she cried, 'for what I am going to say; I hope you will excuse my taking such a liberty with you—but, has nobody told you that the Queen is always used to have the jewel-box carried into her bedroom?'

'No, ma'am, nobody mentioned it to me. I brought it here because I have other things in it.'

'I thought, when I did not see it in mamma's room,' cried she, 'that nobody had told you of that custom, and so I thought I would come to you myself; I hope you will excuse it?'

You may believe how I thanked her, while I promised to take out my own goods and chattels, and have it conveyed to its proper place immediately. I saw that she imagined the Queen might be displeased; and though I could never myself imagine that, for an omission of

[1] By James Thomson (1700–48).
[2] James Burney was in the navy, and had been with Captain Cook on his last voyage. He eventually attained the rank of rear-admiral. The reader will remember him as the friend of Charles Lamb.

ignorance, I felt the benevolence of her intention, and received it with great gratitude.

'My dear ma'am,' cried she, 'I am sure I should be most happy to do anything for you that should be in my power, always; and really Mrs Schwellenberg ought to have told you this.'

Afterwards I happened to be alone with this charming Princess and her sister Elizabeth, in the Queen's dressing-room. She then came up to me, and said:

'Now will you excuse me, Miss Burney, if I ask you the truth of something I have heard about you?'

'Certainly, ma'am.'

'It's such an odd thing, I don't know how to mention it; but I have wished to ask you about it this great while. Pray is it really true that, in your illness last year, you coughed so violently that you broke the whalebone of your stays in two?'

'As nearly true as possible, ma'am; it actually split with the force of the almost convulsive motion of a cough that seemed loud and powerful enough for a giant. I could hardly myself believe it was little I that made so formidable a noise.'

'Well, I could not have given credit to it if I had not heard it from yourself! I wanted so much to know the truth, that I determined, at last, to take courage to ask you.'

No sooner did I find that my coadjutrix ceased to speak of returning to Windsor, and that I became, by that means, the presidentess of the dinner- and tea-table, than I formed a grand design—no other than to obtain to my own use the disposal of my evenings.

From the time of my entrance into this court, to that of which I am writing, I had never been informed that it was incumbent upon me to receive the King's equerries at the tea-table; yet I observed that they always came to Mrs Schwellenberg, and that she expected them so entirely as never to make tea till their arrival. Nevertheless, nothing of that sort had ever been intimated to me, and I saw no necessity of falling into all her ways, without commands to that purpose: nor could I conclude that the King's gentlemen would expect from me either the same confinement, or readiness of reception, as had belonged to two invalid old ladies, glad of company, and without a single connection to draw them from home.

The first week, however, of my presidency, my dear Mrs Delany, with Miss P——, came to dine and spend the rest of the day with me regularly; and though Mrs Delany was generally called away to the royal apartments, her niece always remained with me. This not only obviated all objections to the company of the equerries, but kept me at home naturally, and for my own society and visitors.

I could not, however, but be struck with a circumstance that showed me, in a rather singular manner, my tea-making seemed at once to be regarded as indispensable: this was no other than a constant summons, which John regularly brought me every evening, from these gentlemen, to acquaint me they were come upstairs to the tea-room, and waiting for me.

I concluded this would wear away by use, and therefore resolved to give it that chance. One evening, however, when, being quite alone, I was going to my loved resource, John, ere I could get out, hurried to me: 'Ma'am, the gentlemen are come up, and they send their compliments, and they wait tea for you.'

'Very well,' was my answer to this rather cavalier summons, which I did not wholly admire; and I put on my hat and cloak, when I was called to the Queen. She asked me whether I thought Mrs Delany could come to her, as she wished to see her? I offered to go instantly and inquire.

'But don't tell her I sent you,' cried the most considerate Queen, 'lest that should make her come when it may hurt her: find out how she is, before you mention me.'

I promised implicit obedience; and she most graciously called after me:

'Will it hurt you, Miss Burney, to go—is it a fine evening?'

I assured her it was.

'Well, put on your clogs, then, and take care,' was her kind injunction.

As I now knew I must return myself, at any rate, I slipped into the tea-room before I set off. I found there Colonel Goldsworthy, looking quite glum, General Budé, Mr Fisher, Mr —— Fisher, his brother, and Mr Blomberg, chaplain to the Prince of Wales.

The moment I opened the door, General Budé presented Mr Blomberg to me, and Mr Fisher his brother; I told them, hastily, that I was running away to Mrs Delany, but meant to return in a quarter of an hour, when I should be happy to have their company, if they could wait so long; but if they were hurried, my man should bring their tea.

They all turned to Colonel Goldsworthy, who, as equerry in waiting, was considered as head of the party; but he seemed so choked with surprise and displeasure, that he could only mutter something too indistinct to be heard, and bowed low and distantly.

'If Colonel Goldsworthy can command his time, ma'am,' cried Mr Fisher, 'we shall be most happy to wait yours.'

General Budé said the same; the Colonel again silently and solemnly bowed, and I curtsied in the same manner and hurried away.

Mrs Delany was not well; and I would not vex her with the Queen's kind wish for her. I returned, and sent in, by the page in waiting, my account: for the Queen was in the concert room, and I could not go to her.

Neither would I seduce away Miss P—— from her duty; I came back, therefore, alone, and was fain to make my part as good as I was able among my beaux.

I found them all waiting. Colonel Goldsworthy received me with the same stately bow, and a look so glum and disconcerted, that I instantly turned from him to meet the soft countenance of the good Mr Fisher, who took a chair next mine, and entered into conversation with his usual intelligence and mildness.   General Budé was chatty and well-bred, and the two strangers wholly silent.

I could not, however, but see that Colonel Goldsworthy grew less and less pleased.   Yet what had I done?   I had never been commanded to devote my evenings to him, and, if excused officially, surely there could be no private claim from either his situation or mine.   His displeasure therefore appeared to me so unjust, that I resolved to take not the smallest notice of it.   He never once opened his mouth, neither to me nor to any one else.   In this strange manner we drank our tea.   When it was over, he still sat dumb; and still I conversed with Mr Fisher and General Budé.   At length a prodigious hemming showed a preparation in the Colonel for a speech: it came forth with great difficulty, and most considerable hesitation.

'I am afraid, ma'am—I am afraid you—you—that is—that we are intruders upon you.'

'N-o,' answered I faintly; 'why so?'

'I am sure, ma'am, if we are—if you think—if we take too much liberty—I am sure I would not for the world!—I only—your commands—nothing else——'

'Sir!' cried I, not understanding a word.

'I see, ma'am, we only intrude upon you; however, you must excuse my just saying we would not for the world have taken such a liberty, though very sensible of the happiness of being allowed to come in for half an hour—which is the best half-hour of the whole day—but yet, if it was not for your own commands——'

'What commands, sir?'

He grew still more perplexed, and made at least a dozen speeches to the same no purpose, before I could draw from him anything explicit; all of them listening silently the whole time, and myself invariably staring.   At last, a few words escaped him more intelligible.

'Your messages, ma'am, were what encouraged us to come.'

'And pray, sir, do tell me what messages? I am very happy to see you, but I never sent any messages at all!'

'Indeed, ma'am!' cried he, staring in his turn; 'why your servant, little John there, came rapping at our door, at the equerry room, before we had well swallowed our dinner, and said: "My lady is waiting tea, sir."'

I was quite confounded. I assured him it was an entire fabrication of my servant's, as I had never sent, nor even thought of sending him, for I was going out.

'Why to own the truth, ma'am,' cried he, brightening up, 'I did really think it a little odd to send for us in that hurry—for we got up directly from table, and said, if the lady is waiting, to be sure we must not keep her; and then —when we came—to just peep in, and say you were going out!'

How intolerable an impertinence in John!—it was really no wonder the poor Colonel was so glum.

Again I repeated my ignorance of this step; and he then said: 'Why, ma'am, he comes to us regularly every afternoon, and says his lady is waiting; and we are very glad to come, poor souls that we are, with no rest all the livelong day but what we get in this good room!—but then— to come, and see ourselves only intruders—and to find you are going out, after sending for us!'

I could scarce find words to express my amazement at this communication. I cleared myself instantly from having any the smallest knowledge of John's proceedings, and Colonel Goldsworthy soon recovered all his spirits and good humour, when he was satisfied he had not designedly been treated with such strange and unmeaning inconsistency. He rejoiced exceedingly that he had spoken out, and I thanked him for his frankness, and the evening concluded very amicably.

The evening after, I invited Miss P——, determined to spend it entirely with my beaux, in order to wholly explain away this impertinence. Colonel Goldsworthy now made me a thousand apologies for having named the matter to me at all. I assured him I was extremely glad

he had afforded me an opportunity of clearing it. In the
course of the discussion, I mentioned the constant summons
brought me by John every afternoon. He lifted up his
hands and eyes, and protested most solemnly he had never
sent a single one.

'I vow, ma'am,' cried the Colonel, 'I would not have
taken such a liberty on any account; though all the comfort of my life, in this house, is one half-hour in a day
spent in this room. After all one's labours, riding, and
walking, and standing, and bowing—what a life it is!
Well, it's honour! that's one comfort! it's all honour!
royal honour!—one has the honour to stand till one has
not a foot left; and to ride till one's stiff, and to walk till
one's ready to drop—and then one makes one's lowest
bow, d'ye see, and blesses one's self with joy for the
honour!'

This is his style of rattle, when perfectly at his ease,
pleased with every individual in his company, and completely in good humour. But the moment he sees any
one that he fears or dislikes, he assumes a look of glum
distance and sullenness, and will not utter a word, scarcely
even in answer. He is warmly and faithfully attached to
the King and all the Royal Family, yet his favourite theme,
in his very best moods, is complaint of his attendance,
and murmuring at all its ceremonials. This, however, is
merely for sport and oddity, for he is a man of fortune,
and would certainly relinquish his post if it were not to
his taste.

His account of his own hardships and sufferings here,
in the discharge of his duty, is truly comic. 'How do you
like it, ma'am?' he says to me, 'though it's hardly fair
to ask you yet, because you know almost nothing of the
joys of this sort of life. But wait till November and December, and then you'll get a pretty taste of them! Running
along in these cold passages; then bursting into rooms fit
to bake you; then back again into all these agreeable puffs!
Bless us! I believe in my heart there's wind enough in
these passages to carry a man of war! And there you'll

have your share, ma'am, I promise you that! You 'll get knocked up in three days, take my word for that.'

I begged him not to prognosticate so much evil for me.

'Oh, ma'am, there 's no help for it!' cried he; 'you won't have the hunting, to be sure, nor amusing yourself with wading a foot and a half through the dirt, by way of a little pleasant walk, as we poor equerries do! It 's a wonder to me we outlive the first month. But the agreeable puffs of the passages you will have just as completely as any of us. Let 's see, how many blasts must you have every time you go to the Queen? First, one upon your opening your door; then another, as you get down the three steps from it, which are exposed to the wind from the garden door downstairs; then a third, as you turn the corner to enter the passage: then you come plump upon another from the hall door; then comes another, fit to knock you down, as you turn to the upper passage; then, just as you turn towards the Queen's room, comes another; and last, a whiff from the King's stairs, enough to blow you half a mile off!'

'Mere healthy breezes,' I cried, and assured him I did not fear them.

'Stay till Christmas,' cried he, with a threatening air, 'only stay till then, and let 's see what you 'll say to them; you 'll be laid up as sure as fate! You may take my word for that. One thing, however, pray let me caution you about—don't go to early prayers in November; if you do, that will completely kill you! Oh, ma'am, you know nothing yet of all these matters!—only pray, joking apart, let me have the honour just to advise you this one thing, or else it 's all over with you, I do assure you!'

It was in vain I begged him to be more merciful in his prophecies; he failed not, every night, to administer to me the same pleasant anticipations.

'When the Princesses,' cried he, 'used to it as they are, get regularly knocked up before this business is over, off they drop, one by one: first the Queen deserts us; then Princess Elizabeth is done for; then Princess Royal begins coughing; then Princess Augusta gets the snuffles; and all the poor attendants, my poor sister at their head, drop off, one after another, like so many snuffs of candles: till at last, dwindle, dwindle, dwindle—not a soul goes to the chapel but the King, the parson, and myself; and there we three freeze it out together!'

One evening, when he had been out very late hunting with the King, he assumed so doleful an air of weariness, that had not Miss P—— exerted her utmost powers to revive him, he would not have uttered a word the whole night; but when once brought forward, he gave us more entertainment than ever, by relating his hardships.

'After all the labours,' cried he, 'of the chase, all the riding, the trotting, the galloping, the leaping, the—with your favour, ladies, I beg pardon, I was going to say a strange word, but the—the perspiration—and—and all that—after being wet through over head, and soused through under feet, and popped into ditches, and jerked over gates, what lives we do lead! Well, it's all honour! that's my only comfort! Well, after all this, fagging away like mad from eight in the morning to five or six in the afternoon, home we come, looking like so many drowned rats, with not a dry thread about us, nor a morsel within us—sore to the very bone, and forced to smile all the time! and then, after all this, what do you think follows? "Here, Goldsworthy," cries his Majesty: so up I comes to him, bowing profoundly, and my hair dripping down to my shoes; "Goldsworthy," cries his Majesty. "Sir," says I, smiling agreeably, with the rheumatism just creeping all over me! but still, expecting something a little comfortable, I wait patiently to know his gracious pleasure, and then, "Here, Goldsworthy, I say!" he cries, "will you have a little barley water?" Barley water in such a plight as that! Fine compensation for a wet jacket, truly!—barley water! I never heard of such a thing in my life! Barley water after a whole day's hard hunting!'

'And pray did you drink it?'

'I drink it? Drink barley water? No, no; not come

to that neither! But there it was, sure enough!—in a jug fit for a sick room; just such a thing as you put upon a hob in a chimney, for some poor miserable soul that keeps his bed! just such a thing as that! And, "Here, Goldsworthy," says his Majesty, "here's the barley water!"'

'And did the King drink it himself?'

'Yes, God bless his Majesty! but I was too humble a subject to do the same as the King! Barley water, quoth I! Ha! ha!—a fine treat truly! Heaven defend me! I'm not come to that, neither! bad enough, too, but not so bad as that.'

NOVEMBER 1ST. We began this month by steadily settling ourselves at Kew, Miss Planta, Miss Gomme, Mdlle Montmoulin, and Mr de Luc,[1] and Mrs Cheveley. Miss Goldsworthy resided at the Princess Elizabeth's house on Kew Green.

NOVEMBER 5TH. Mr Fisher read the service to us this morning, which was Sunday; and I must now tell you the manner of its being performed, which is rather singular, and, I suppose, only Royal.

There is no private chapel at Kew Lodge: the King and Queen, consequently, except by accident, as now, never pass the Sabbath there. The form, therefore, stands thus: Their Majesties and the five Princesses go into an inner room by themselves, furnished with hassocks, etc., like their closet at church: by the door of this room, though not within it, stands the clergyman at his desk: and here were assembled Mrs Delany, Mr and Mrs Smelt, Miss Goldsworthy, Miss Gomme, Miss Planta, Mdlle Montmoulin, M. de Luc, and I; the pages were all arranged at the end of the room; and, in an outer apartment, were summoned all the servants, in rows, according to their stations.

---

[1] A Swiss gentleman in the service of the Queen, in which capacity he had the honour of reading *Cecilia* to her, though, as Fanny declared with some exaggeration, he could 'hardly speak four words of English.'

November 6th. This morning happened my first disgrace of being too late for the Queen—this noon, rather; for in a morning 'tis a disaster that has never arrived to this moment.

The affair thus came to pass. I walked for some time early in Kew gardens, and then called upon Mrs Smelt. I there heard that the King and Queen were gone, privately, to Windsor, to the Lodge: probably for some papers they could not entrust with a messenger. Mr Smelt, therefore, proposed taking this opportunity for showing me Richmond gardens, offering to be my security that I should have full time. I accepted the proposal with pleasure, and we set out upon our expedition.

He saw me safe to the Lodge, and there took his leave: and I was going leisurely upstairs, when I met the Princess Amelia and Mrs Cheveley; and while I was playing with the little Princess, Mrs Cheveley announced to me that the Queen had been returned some time, and that I had been sent for immediately.

Thunderstruck at this intelligence, I hastened to her dressing-room; when I opened the door, I saw she was having her hair dressed. To add to my confusion, the Princess Augusta, Lady Effingham, and Lady Frances Howard were all in the room.

I stood still at the door, not knowing whether to advance, or wait a new summons. In what a new situation did I feel myself!—and how did I long to give way to my first impulse, and run back to my own room!

In a minute or two, the Queen, not a little dryly, said: 'Where have you been, Miss Burney?'

I told her my tale—that hearing she was gone to Windsor, I had been walking in Richmond gardens with Mr Smelt.

She said no more, and I stood behind her chair. The Princess and the two ladies were seated.

What republican feelings were rising in my breast, till she softened them down again, when presently, in a voice changed from that dryness which had wholly disconcerted me, to its natural tone, she condescended to ask me to look at Lady Frances Howard's gown, and see if it was not very pretty.

This made a dutiful subject of me again in a moment. Yet I felt a discomposure all day, that determined me upon using the severest caution to avoid such a surprise for the future. The Windsor journey having been merely upon business, had been more brief than was believed possible.

When I left the Queen, I was told that Mrs Delany was waiting for me in the parlour. What a pleasure and relief to me to run to that dear lady, and relate to her my mischance, and its circumstances! Mr Smelt soon joined us there; he was shocked at the accident; and I saw strongly by his manner how much more seriously such a matter was regarded, than any one, unused to the inside of a Court, could possibly imagine.

This discovery added not much to my satisfaction—on the contrary, I think from that time I did not, till long, long after, see noonday approach, without the extremest nervousness, if not entirely prepared for my summons.

WINDSOR, DEC. 25TH. The Queen presented me this morning with two pieces of black stuff, very prettily embroidered, for shoes. These little tokens of favour, she has a manner all her own, in its grace and elegance, of bestowing.

The next day the equerries and Miss P—— came to tea. Colonel Goldsworthy was in one of his most facetious humours, and invited us to supper at his house in town, giving a really comic account of his way of life, the great power of his domestics, their luxurious manner of living, and the ascendancy they had gained over their master.

Mrs Smelt was to be the head lady, he said, of the party, to which she readily agreed. Miss P—— made inquiries into every particular of the entertainment he was to give us; and he uttered a very solemn charge to her, not to offend one of his maids, an elderly person, so extremely tenacious of her authority, that she frequently took up a

poker, and ran furiously about with it, after any of her
fellow-servants who thwarted her will. To me also
he gave a similar charge: 'I have a poor old soul of a
man, ma'am,' says he, 'that does his business very well
for such a forlorn poor fellow as me; but now, when you
want a glass of wine or so, don't be in too great a hurry
with him—that's all I beg; don't frighten him, poor fellow,
with calling to him hastily, or angrily, or that—for if you
once do that he won't know a single thing he says or does
all the rest of the time!—he'll quite lose his wits at a stroke!'

Someone now by chance named Mrs Ariana Egerton,
the bedchamber woman; and Miss P—— said she now sent
in her name in that manner, as she must no longer be
called Miss, from her present office.

'Mrs what?' cried Colonel Goldsworthy, 'Mrs Ariana?
what name is that?'

'Why, it's her name,' said Miss P——; 'she writes it
upon her cards.'

'Ariana?' repeated he, 'I never heard the like in my life!
Why I no more believe—what will these folks tell us next!
It's nobody's name under the sun, I'll be bound for it.
All the world put together shan't make me believe it.
Ariana, forsooth! why it must be a nickname! depend
upon it it's nothing else. There, at my poor miserable
bachelor's cell in the Mews, I've got a boy that says his
name is Methusalem; he comes from Windsor, too!
Heaven help the poor people! if they are but near a court,
it turns their heads directly. I had the boy only out of the
stable, just by the bottom of the garden, yet he told me
his name was Methusalem! A likely matter, truly! ha!
ha! I'll be sworn his name is no other than Jack!'

'Pray,' cried I, 'what do you call him for short?'

'Why, ma'am, that was a great difficulty to me at first:
I'd have called him Me, for shortest, but I thought the
people would all laugh, and say: "Ah, poor gentleman, it's
all over with him now! he's calling *himself* when he wants
his man," and then I thought of Thusy. Thusy sounds
soft and pretty enough; but I thought it is like a woman's

name—Susy; to be sure, thinks I, they 'll all suppose I
mean one of the maids; and then again, "Ah," say they,
"the poor gentleman's certainly cracked! nothing else
would make him behave so comical!" And then I thought
of Lem. But it 's quite too much for me to settle such a
set of hard long names!'

In this manner he ran on, till General Budé reminded
him it was time they should appear in the concert room.

'Aye,' cried he, reluctantly, 'now for the fiddlers!
There I go, plant myself against the side of the chimney,
stand first on one foot, then on the other, hear over and
over again all that fine squeaking, and then fall fast asleep,
and escape by mere miracle from flouncing down plump
in all their faces!'

'What would the Queen say if you did that?'

'Oh, ma'am, the Queen would know nothing of the
matter; she 'd only suppose it some old double bass that
tumbled.'

'Why, could not she see what it was?'

'Oh, no, ma'am, we are never in the room with the
Queen! that 's the drawing-room, beyond, where the
Queen sits; we go no farther than the fiddling room. As
to the Queen, we don't see her week after week sometimes. The King, indeed, comes there to us, between
whiles, though that 's all as it happens, now Price is gone.
He used to play at backgammon with Price.'

'Then what do you do there?'

'Just what I tell you—nothing at all, but stand as furniture! But the worst is, sometimes, when my poor eye-
peepers are not quite closed, I look to the music books
to see what 's coming; and there I read *Chorus of Virgins*:
so then, when they begin, I look about me. A chorus of
virgins, indeed! Why, there 's nothing but ten or a
dozen fiddlers! Not a soul beside! It 's as true as I 'm
alive! So then, when we 've stood supporting the
chimney-piece about two hours, why then, if I 'm not
called upon, I shuffle back out of the room, make a profound bow to the harpsichord, and I 'm off.'

FRIDAY, DECEMBER 29TH. This day, by long arrangement, I expected to receive a visit from my father. He had engaged himself to me for three days, and was to reside at Mrs Delany's.

I acquainted the Queen with my hopes, which she heard with the most pleased expression of approbation. She told them to the King, who inquired, with an air of real satisfaction in my happiness, when he would come?

At three o'clock our dearest Padre arrived—well, gay, and sweet—and we spent near two hours wholly alone, and truly happy.

At dinner the party was enlarged by the presence of Mrs Delany and Mr Smelt; to these were added the lovely and lively Miss P——, the gentle Mlle Montmoulin, and the friendly Miss Planta.

My dear father was the principal object to all, and he seemed to enjoy himself, and to be enjoyed throughout.

We returned to my own apartment to our coffee, and the two governess ladies retired; and then came the King for Mrs Delany; and not for that solely, though ostensibly, for his behaviour to my father proved his desire to see and converse with him.

He began immediately upon musical matters, and entered into a discourse upon them with the most animated wish of both hearing and communicating his sentiments; and my dear father was perfectly ready to meet his advances. No one, at all used to the Court etiquettes, could have seen him without smiling; he was so totally unacquainted with the forms usually observed in the Royal presence, and so regardless or thoughtless of acquiring them, that he moved, spoke, acted, and debated, precisely with the same ease and freedom that he would have used to any other gentleman whom he had accidentally met.

A certain flutter of spirits, which always accompanies these interviews, even with those who are least awed by them, put my dear father off the guard which is the customary assistant upon these occasions, of watching what is done by those already initiated in these royal ceremonies:

highly gratified by the openness and good humour of the King, he was all energy and spirit, and pursued every topic that was started, till he had satisfied himself upon it, and started every topic that occurred to him, whether the King was ready for another or not.

While the rest, retreating towards the wainscot, formed a distant and respectful circle, in which the King alone moves, this dear father came forward into it himself, and, wholly bent upon pursuing whatever theme was begun, followed the King when he moved away, and came forward to meet his steps when he moved back; and while the rest waited his immediate address ere they ventured to speak a word, he began and finished, sustained or dropped, renewed or declined, every theme that he pleased, without consulting anything but his feelings and understanding.

This vivacity and this nature evidently pleased the King, whose good sense instantly distinguishes what is unconscious from what is disrespectful; and his stay in the room, which I believe was an hour, and the perfect good humour with which he received as well as returned the sprightly and informal sallies of my father, were proofs the most convincing of his approbation.

DECEMBER 30TH. This morning my dear father carried me to Dr Herschel.[1] This great and very extraordinary man received us with almost open arms. He is very fond of my father, who is one of the Council of the Royal Society this year, as well as himself, and he has much invited me when we have met at the Lodge or at Mr de Luc's.

At this time of day there was nothing to see but his instruments: those, however, are curiosities sufficient. His immense new telescope, the largest ever constructed, will still, I fear, require a year or two more for finishing, but I hope it will then reward his labour and ingenuity by the new views of the heavenly bodies, and their motions, which he flatters himself will be procured by it. Already,

[1] Sir Frederick William Herschel (1738–1822). He discovered the 'Georgium Sidus' (Uranus) in 1781. He was now living at Slough.

with that he has now in use, he has discovered fifteen hundred universes! How many more he may find who can conjecture? The moon, too, which seems his favourite object, has already afforded him two volcanoes; and his own planet, the Georgium Sidus, has now shown two satellites. From such a man what may not astronomy expect, when an instrument superior in magnitude to any ever yet made, and constructed wholly by himself or under his own eye, is the vehicle of his observation?

By the invitation of Mr Herschel, I now took a walk which will sound to you rather strange; it was through his telescope! and it held me quite upright, and without the least inconvenience; so would it have done had I been dressed in feathers and a bell hoop—such is its circumference.

TUESDAY, JANUARY 16TH, 1787, was the day appointed for removing to town for the winter; from which time we were only to come to Windsor for an occasional day or two every week.

I saw my dear father the next morning, who gave me a poem on the Queen's birthday, to present. It was very pretty; but I felt very awkward in offering it to her, as it was from so near a relation, and without any particular reason or motive.

A chance question this night from the Queen, whom I now again attended as usual, fortunately relieved me from my embarrassment about the poem. She inquired of me if my father was still writing. 'A little,' I answered, and the next morning,

THURSDAY, JANUARY 18TH, when the birthday was kept, I found her all sweetness and serenity; mumbled out my own little compliment, which she received as graciously as if she had understood and heard it; and then, when she was dressed, I followed her through the great rooms, to get rid of the wardrobe woman, and there, taking the poem from my pocket, I said: 'I told your Majesty yesterday that my father had written *a little*!—and here— the little is!'

She took it from me with a smile and a curtsy, and I ran off. She never has named it since; but she has spoken of my father with much sweetness and complacency. The modest dignity of the Queen, upon all subjects of panegyric, is truly royal and noble.

I had now, the second time, the ceremony of being entirely new dressed. I then went to St James's, where the Queen gave very gracious approbation of my gewgaws, and called upon the King to bestow the same; which his constant good humour makes a matter of great ease to him.

The Queen's dress, being for her own birthday, was extremely simple, the style of dress considered. The King was quite superb, and the Princesses Augusta and Elizabeth were ornamented with much brilliancy.

Not only the Princess Royal was missed at this exhibition, but also the Prince of Wales. He wrote, however, his congratulations to the Queen, though the coldness then subsisting between him and his Majesty occasioned his absence from Court. I fear it was severely felt by his Royal mother, though she appeared composed and content.

The two Princesses spoke very kind words, also, about my frippery on this festival; and Princess Augusta laid her positive commands upon me that I should change my gown before I went to the Lord Chamberlain's box, where only my head could be seen. The counsel proved as useful as the consideration was amiable.

When the Queen was attired, the Duchess of Ancaster was admitted to the dressing-room, where she stayed, in conversation with their Majesties and the Princesses, till it was time to summon the bedchamber women. During this, I had the office of holding the Queen's train. I knew, for me, it was a great honour, yet it made me feel, once more, so like a mute [1] upon the stage, that I could scarce believe myself only performing my own real character.

Mrs Stainforth and I had some time to stand upon the stairs before the opening of the doors. We joined Mrs

[1] i.e. a 'super.'

Fielding and her daughters, and all entered together, but
the crowd parted us; they all ran on, and got in as they
could, and I remained alone by the door. They soon
found me out, and made signs to me, which I saw not,
and then they sent me messages that they had kept room
for me just by them. I had received orders from the
Queen to go out at the end of the second country dance;
I thought, therefore, that as I now was seated by the door,
I had better be content, and stay where I could make my
exit in a moment, and without trouble or disturbance.

The sight which called me to that spot perfectly answered
all my expectations: the air, manner, and countenance of
the Queen, as she goes round the circle, are truly graceful
and engaging: I thought I could understand, by the motion
of her lips, and the expression of her face, even at the
height and distance of the Chamberlain's box, the gracious
and pleasant speeches she made to all whom she approached. With my glass, you know, I can see just as
other people see with the naked eye.

The Princesses looked extremely lovely, and the whole
court was in the utmost splendour.

At the appointed moment I slipped through the door
. . . and I passed, alone and quietly, to Mr Rhamus's
apartment, which was appropriated for the company to
wait in. Here I desired a servant I met with to call my
man: he was not to be found. I went down the stairs,
and made them call him loud, by my name; all to no
purpose. Then the chairmen were called, but called also
in vain!

What to do I knew not; though I was still in a part of
the palace, it was separated by many courts, avenues,
passages, and alleys, from the Queen's or my own apartments; and though I had so lately passed them, I could not
remember the way, nor at that late hour could I have
walked, dressed as I then was, and the ground wet with
recent rain, even if I had had a servant; I had therefore
ordered the chair allotted me for these days; but chair
and chairmen and footmen were alike out of the way.

My fright lest the Queen should wait for me was very serious. I believe there are state apartments through which she passes, and therefore I had no chance to know when she retired from the ball-room. Yet could I not stir, and was forced to return to the room whence I came, in order to wait for John, that I might be out of the way of the cold winds which infested the hall.

I now found a young clergyman standing by the fire. I suppose my anxiety was visible, for he instantly inquired if he could assist me. I declined his offer, but walked up and down, making frequent questions about my chair and John.

He then very civilly said: 'You seem distressed, ma'am; would you permit me the honour to see for your chair, or, if it is not come, as you seem hurried, would you trust me to see you home?'

I thanked him, but could not accept his services. He was sorry, he said, that I refused him, but could not wonder, as he was a stranger. I made some apologizing answer, and remained in that unpleasant situation till, at length, a hackney-chair was procured me. My new acquaintance would take no denial to handing me to the chair. When I got in, I told the men to carry me to the palace.

'We are there now!' cried they; 'what part of the palace?'

I was now in a distress the most extraordinary: I really knew not my own direction! I had always gone to my apartment in a chair, and had been carried by chairmen officially appointed; and, except that it was in St James's Palace, I knew nothing of my own situation.

'Near the park,' I told them, and saw my new esquire look utterly amazed at me.

'Ma'am,' said he, 'half the palace is in the park!'

'I don't know how to direct,' cried I, in the greatest embarrassment; 'but it is somewhere between Pall Mall and the Park.'

'I know where the lady lives well enough,' cried one of the chairmen; ''tis in St James's Street.'

'No, no,' cried I, ''tis in St James's Palace.'

'Up with the chair!' cried the other man; 'I know best
—'tis in South Audley Street; I know the lady well
enough.'

Think what a situation at the moment! I found they
had both been drinking the Queen's health till they knew
not what they said, and could with difficulty stand. Yet
they lifted me up, and though I called in the most terrible
fright to be let out, they carried me down the steps.

I now actually screamed for help, believing they would
carry me off to South Audley Street; and now my good
genius, who had waited patiently in the crowd, forcibly
stopped the chairmen, who abused him violently, and
opened the door himself, and I ran back to the hall.

He begged me to go again upstairs, but my apprehension
about the Queen prevented me. I knew she was to have
nobody but me, and that her jewels, though few, were to
be entrusted back to the Queen's house to no other hands.
I must, I said, go, be it in what manner it might. All I
could devise was to summon Mr Rhamus, the page. I
had never seen him, but my attendance upon the Queen
would be an apology for the application, and I determined
to put myself under his immediate protection.

Mr Rhamus was nowhere to be found; he was already
supposed to be gone to the Queen's house, to wait the
arrival of his Majesty. This news redoubled my fear; and
now my new acquaintance desired me to employ him in
making inquiries for me as to the direction I wanted.

It was almost ridiculous, in the midst of my distress, to
be thus at a loss for an address to myself! I felt averse to
speaking my name amongst so many listeners, and only
told him he would much oblige me by finding out a
direction to Mrs Haggerdorn's rooms.

He went upstairs; and returning, said he could now
direct the chairmen, if I did not fear trusting them.

I did fear—I even shook with fear—yet my horror of
disappointing the Queen upon such a night prevailed
over all my reluctance, and I ventured once more into the

chair, thanking this excellent Samaritan, and begging him to give the direction very particularly.

We next came to a court where we were stopped by the sentinels. They said they had orders not to admit any hackney chairs. The chairmen vowed they would make way; called out aloud to be set down; the sentinels said they would run their bayonets through the first man that attempted to dispute their orders. I then screamed out again to be set down, and my new and good friend peremptorily forced them to stop, and opening the door with violence, offered me his arm, saying: 'You had better trust yourself with me, ma'am!'

Most thankfully I now accepted what so fruitlessly I had declined, and I held by his arm, and we walked on together —but neither of us knew whither, nor the right way from the wrong! It was really a terrible situation.

The chairmen followed us, clamorous for money, and full of abuse. They demanded half a crown; my companion refused to listen to such an imposition: my shaking hand could find no purse, and I begged him to pay them what they asked, that they might leave us. He did; and when they were gone, I shook less, and was able to pay that one part of the debt I was now contracting.

We wandered about, heaven knows where, in a way the most alarming and horrible to myself imaginable; for I never knew where I was. It was midnight—I concluded the Queen waiting for me. It was wet. My head was full dressed. I was under the care of a total stranger; and I knew not which side to take, wherever we came. Inquiries were in vain. The sentinels alone were in sight, and they are so continually changed that they knew no more of Mrs Haggerdorn than if she had never resided here.

At length I spied a door open, and I begged to enter it at a venture, for information. Fortunately a person stood in the passage who instantly spoke to me by my name; I never heard that sound with more glee. To me he was a stranger, but I suppose he had seen me in some of the apartments.

I begged him to direct me straight to the Queen's rooms. He did; and I then took leave of my most humane new friend, with a thousand acknowledgments for his benevolence and services.

Was it not a strange business? I can never say what an agony of fright it cost me at the time, nor ever be sufficiently grateful for the kind assistance so providentially afforded me.

I found myself just in time; and I desired immediately to speak with Mr Nicolay, the page, of whom I requested a direction to my own rooms.

SATURDAY, JAN. 20TH. To-day began our short weekly visits for the winter to Windsor. I travelled with Mr Turbulent,[1] and with him only. He says that he and his lady were acquainted with our step-sister, Mrs Rishton, at Geneva; and I have some idea that you and I once saw him. He speaks English perfectly well. Do you remember our hearing a younger sister of his wife sing a fine French air, with all true French cadenzas?

The journey was rather awkward. To be three hours and a half tête-à-tête with a person so little known to me, and of whom I had been unable to form any precise opinion, while still in a feeble state of health, and still feebler of spirits, was by no means desirable; and yet the less as there was something in the uncertainty of my notions that led me to fear him, though I knew not exactly why.

The conversation that ensued did not remove these difficulties: wholly brought on and supported by himself, the subjects were just such as I least wish to discuss with *him*—religion and morality.

With respect to morality, his opinions seemed upon rather too large a scale for that perfect measurement which suited my more circumscribed ideas. Nothing faulty fell from him, but much was thrown out that, though not

---

[1] In this, as in certain other instances, the name is fictitious. Mr 'Turbulent' was French reader to the Queen. He was a clergyman, and his real name was Charles de Guiffardière.

positively censurable, had far better never be uttered.
He again revived the subject of Madame de Genlis:[1] again
I defended her, and again, while he palliated all the wrong
with which he charged her, he chose to disbelieve the
seriousness of my assertions in her favour. True, however, it is, I do believe her innocent of all crime but
indiscretion, and of that I know not how to clear her,
since to nothing softer can I attribute the grounds upon
which so much calumny has been raised. I imagine her,
and so I told him, to have fallen at an early and inex-
perienced period into designing and depraved hands, and
not to have been able, from cruel and distressed circumstances, to give up the unworthy protection of a profligate
patron, though her continuing under it has stained her
fair fame for evermore! Perhaps her husband, himself
worthless, would not permit her—perhaps she feared
the future ruin of her two children—perhaps, in a country
such as France, she did not, in that first youth, dare even to
think of relinquishing the protection of a Prince of the
blood. She was only fifteen when she was married—she
told me that herself. How hard do I think her lot, to fall
into hands she must ever have despised, and so to be
entangled in them as not to dare show to the world, in
the only way the world would believe her, the abhorrence
of her mind to the character of her patron, by quitting a
roof under which she could not live without censure!

The subject, however, was so nice, it was difficult to
discuss, and I wished much to avoid it, since there was so
much that I could not explain without apparent concessions
against my own case, which he instantly seized, and treated
as actual concurrences. He praised her as much as I
praised her myself, and I found he admired her with as
sincere a warmth; but, though we agreed thus far, and yet
farther, in thinking all that might be wrong in her was
venial, we differed most essentially in our opinions of

---

[1] Madame de Genlis (1746–1830), novelist and writer of memoirs,
had already been mentioned in a discussion on female virtue. Fanny
later saw reason to alter her opinion of the lady's character.

what that wrong might be. He thought her positively
fallen, yet with circumstances claiming every indulgence.
I thought her positively saved, yet with circumstances
authorizing suspicion.

I tried what was possible to fly from this disquisition,
but I found I had one to deal with not easy to control.
He kept it up, forcibly and steadily, till I was compelled
to be silent to his assertions, from want of proof beyond
opinion for answering them.

He then proceeded to a general vindication of the victims
to such sort of situations, in which I could by no means
concur; but when I resisted he startled me by naming as
individuals amongst them some characters of whom I had
conceived far superior notions. I heard him quite with
grief, and I will not write their names. I cannot look
upon him as a detractor, and I saw him by no means severe
in his exactions from female virtue. I gave, therefore, and
give implicit credit to his information, though I gave not,
and give not, any to his inferences and general comments.

'Depend upon it,' said he, 'with whatever prejudice,
and even just prejudice, you may look upon these fallen
characters at large, and considered in a class, you will
generally find them, individually, amongst the most amiable
of your sex—I had almost said amongst the most virtuous
—but amongst those who possess the greatest virtues,
though not every virtue, undoubtedly. Their own
sweetness and sensibility will generally have been the
sole source of their misconduct.'

I could neither agree nor dispute upon such a subject
with such an antagonist, and I took my usual resource,
of letting the argument die away for want of food with
which to nourish it.

I did not fare the better, however, by the next theme,
to which the death of this led us—religion.

There is no topic in the world upon which I am so
careful how I speak seriously as this. By 'seriously' I
do not mean gravely, but with earnestness; mischief here
is so easily done, so difficultly reformed. I have made it,

therefore, a rule through my life never to talk in detail upon religious opinions, but with those of whose principles I have the fullest conviction and highest respect. It is therefore very, very rarely I have ever entered upon the subject but with female friends or acquaintances, whose hearts I have well known, and who would be as unlikely to give as to receive any perplexity from the discourse. But with regard to men, I have known none with whom I have willingly conferred upon them, except Dr Johnson, Mr Locke, and Mr Smelt, and one more.

My companion was urgent to enter into a controversy which I was equally urgent to avoid; and I knew not whether most to admire or to dread the skill and capacity with which he pursued his purpose, in defiance of my constant retreat. When, in order to escape, I made only light and slight answers to his queries and remarks, he gravely said I led him into 'strange suspicions' concerning my religious tenets; and when I made to this some rallying reply, he solemnly declared he feared I was a 'mere philosopher' on these subjects, and totally incredulous with regard to all revealed religion.

This was an attack which even in pleasantry I liked not, as the very words gave me a secret shock. I therefore then spoke to the point, and frankly told him that subjects which I held to be so sacred, I made it an invariable rule never to discuss in casual conversations.

'And how, ma'am,' said he, suddenly assuming the authoritative seriousness of his professional character and dignity, 'and how, ma'am, can you better discuss matters of this solemn nature than now, with a man to whom their consideration peculiarly belongs?—with a clergyman?'

True, thought I; but I must better be apprised of your principles, ere I trust you with debating mine!—Yet, ashamed to decline so serious a call, I could only make a general answer, that as I was very well satisfied at present, I did not wish to make myself unnecessary difficulties by any discussions whatsoever.

When, afterwards, I attended the Queen, she inquired

of me particularly how the journey had passed, and if it was not very pleasant? I made some short and general answer; and she cried: 'Did you read? Did Mr Turbulent read to you?'

'No, ma'am, we had no provision of that sort; I heartily wish I had thought of it; I should have liked it exceedingly.'

'But surely you do not like reading better than conversation!'

'No, ma'am—not better than some conversation.'

'Surely not better than Mr Turbulent's? Nobody converses better than Mr Turbulent; nobody has more general knowledge, nor a more pleasing and easy way of communicating it.'

Fearing to do mischief, I assented—but faintly however, for indeed he had perplexed far more than he had pleased me. The Queen again made his panegyric, and in very warm terms, and seemed quite disappointed at the coldness of my concurrence.

Good there must be, I was sure, in a man so honoured, who for many years has been tried in his present trying situation, of teacher to the elder Princesses, and occasionally to her Majesty herself. I resolved, therefore, to suspend the judgment which was inclining on the evil side, and to wait undecided till further opportunity gave me fairer reasons for fixing my opinions.

FEB. 16TH. While I was dressing for dinner, I heard a step advancing in my parlour. I hastily shut my bedroom door, and then heard the sweet voice of the Princess Augusta, saying: 'It's only me, Miss Burney; I won't come in to disturb you.' Out I rushed all bepowdered, entreating her pardon: she said she only came for little Badine, but stayed chatting on some time, merely to recover me from the confusion of having seemed to shut her out.

The instant I was left alone with Mr Turbulent he demanded to know '*my project for his happiness*';[1] and he

[1] Bewildered and more than half offended by Mr Turbulent's unusual opinions and behaviour, Fanny had arranged not to travel with him in future.

made his claim in a tone so determined, that I saw it would be fruitless to attempt evasion or delay.

'Your captivity, then, sir,' cried I—'for such I must call your regarding your attendance to be indispensable—is at an end: the equerry coach is now wholly in your power. I have spoken myself upon the subject to the Queen, as you bid—at least, braved you me to do; and I have now her consent to discharging you from all necessity of travelling in our coach.'

He looked extremely provoked, and asked if I really meant to inform him I did not choose his company?

I laughed the question off, and used a world of civil argument to persuade him I had only done him a good office: but I was fain to make the whole debate as sportive as possible, as I saw him disposed to be seriously affronted.

A long debate ensued. I had been, he protested, excessively ill-natured to him. 'What an impression,' cried he, 'must this make upon the Queen! After travelling, with apparent content, six years with that oyster Mrs Haggerdorn—now—now that travelling is becoming really agreeable—in that coach—I am to be turned out of it! How must it disgrace me in her opinion!'

She was too partial, I said, to '*that oyster*,' to look upon that matter in such a degrading light; nor would she think of it at all, but as an accidental matter.

I then added, that the reason he had hitherto been destined to the female coach was, that Mrs Schwellenberg and Mrs Haggerdorn were always afraid of travelling by themselves; but that, as I had more courage, there was no need of such slavery.

'Slavery!' repeated he, with an emphasis that almost startled me, 'Slavery is pleasure—is happiness—when directed by our wishes!'

And then, with a sudden motion that made me quite jump, he cast himself at my feet, on both his knees:

'Your slave,' he cried, 'I am content to be! your slave I am ready to live and die!'

I begged him to rise, and be a little less rhapsodic. 'I

have emancipated you,' I cried; 'do not, therefore, throw away the freedom you have been six years sighing to obtain. You are now your own agent—a volunteer——'

'If I am,' cried he, impetuously, 'I dedicate myself to you. A volunteer, ma'am, remember that! I dedicate myself to you, therefore, of my own accord, for every journey! You shall not get rid of me these twenty years.'

I tried to get away myself—but he would not let me move; and he began, with still increasing violence of manner, a most fervent protestation that he would not be set aside, and that he devoted himself to me entirely. And, to say the simple truth, ridiculous as all this was, I really began to grow a little frightened by his vehemence and his posture; till, at last, in the midst of an almost furious vow, in which he dedicated himself to me for ever, he relieved me, by suddenly calling upon Jupiter, Juno, Mars, and Hercules, and every god, and every goddess, to witness his oath. And then, content with his sublimity, he arose.

MARCH 1ST. With all the various humours in which I had already seen Mr Turbulent, he gave me this evening a surprise, by his behaviour to one of the Princesses, nearly the same that I had experienced from him myself. The Princess Augusta came, during coffee, for a knotting shuttle of the Queen's. While she was speaking to me, he stood behind and exclaimed, *à demi-voix*, as if to himself: '*Comme elle est jolie ce soir, son Altesse Royale!*' And then, seeing her blush extremely, he clasped his hands, in high pretended confusion, and, hiding his head, called out: '*Que ferai-je?* The Princess has heard me!'

'Pray, Mr Turbulent,' cried she, hastily, 'what play are you to read to-night?'

'You shall choose, ma'am; either *La Coquette corrigée*, or——' [he named another I have forgotten].

'Oh, no!' cried she, 'that last is shocking! don't let me hear that!'

'I understand you, ma'am. You fix, then, upon *La Coquette? La Coquette* is your Royal Highness's taste?'

'No, indeed, I am sure I did not say that.'

'Yes, ma'am, by implication. And certainly, therefore, I will read it, to please your Royal Highness!'

'No, pray don't; for I like none of them!'

'None of them, ma'am?'

'No, none—no *French plays* at all!'

And away she was running, with a droll air, that acknowledged she had said something to provoke him.

'This is a declaration, ma'am, I must beg you to explain!' cried he, gliding adroitly between the Princess and the door, and shutting it with his back.

'No, no, I can't explain it; so pray, Mr Turbulent, do open the door.'

'Not for the world, ma'am, with such a stain uncleared upon your Royal Highness's taste and feeling!'

She told him she positively could not stay, and begged him to let her pass instantly.

But he would hear her no more than he has heard me, protesting he was too much shocked for her, to suffer her to depart without clearing her own credit!

He conquered at last, and thus forced to speak, she turned round to us and said: 'Well—if I must, then—I will appeal to these ladies, who understand such things far better than I do, and ask them if it is not true about these French plays, that they are all so alike to one another, that to hear them in this manner every night is enough to tire one?'

'Pray, then, madam,' cried he, 'if French plays have the misfortune to displease you, what *national* plays have the honour of your preference?'

I saw he meant something that she understood better than me, for she blushed again, and called out: 'Pray open the door at once! I can stay no longer; do let me go, Mr Turbulent.'

'Not till you have answered that question, ma'am! what *country* has plays to your Royal Highness's taste?'

'Miss Burney,' cried she impatiently, yet laughing, 'pray do you take him away!— Pull him!'

He bowed to me very invitingly for the office; but I frankly answered her: 'Indeed, ma'am, I dare not undertake him! I cannot manage him at all.'

'The *country*! the *country*! Princess Augusta! name the happy *country*!' was all she could gain.

'*Order* him away, Miss Burney,' cried she; ''tis your room: order him away from the door.'

'Name it, ma'am, name it'; exclaimed he; 'name but the *chosen nation*!'

And then, fixing her with the most provoking eyes, '*Est-ce le Danemarc?*' he cried.

She coloured violently, and, quite angry with him, called out: 'Mr Turbulent, how can you be such a fool!'

And now I found . . . the Prince Royal of Denmark was in his meaning, and in her understanding!

He bowed to the ground, in gratitude for the term *fool*, but added, with pretended submission to her will: 'Very well, ma'am, *s'il ne faut lire que les comédies Danoises.*'

'Do let me go!' cried she seriously; and then he made way, with a profound bow as she passed, saying: 'Very well, ma'am, *La Coquette*, then? Your Royal Highness chooses *La Coquette corrigée?*'

'*Corrigée?* That never was done!' cried she, with all her sweet good humour, the moment she got out; and off she ran, like lightning, to the Queen's apartments.

What say you to Mr Turbulent now?

For my part, I was greatly surprised. I had not imagined any man, but the King or Prince of Wales, had ever ventured at a *badinage* of this sort with any of the Princesses; nor do I suppose any other man ever did. Mr Turbulent is so great a favourite with the Royal Family, that he safely ventures upon whatever he pleases, and doubtless they find, in his courage and his rodomontading, a novelty extremely amusing to them, or they would not fail to bring about a change.

For myself, I own, when I perceived in him this mode of conduct with the Princesses, I saw his flights, and his rattling, and his heroics, in a light of mere innocent play, from exuberence of high spirits; and I looked upon them, and upon him, in a fairer light.

St James's Palace, June 4th. I have had a dread of the bustle of this day for some weeks, and every kind friend has dreaded it for me; yet am I at this moment more quiet than I have been any single moment since I left my dearest Susan at that last gate of sweet Norbury Park. Till we meet again, I shall feel as if always seeing that beloved sister on that very spot.

Take a little of the humours of this day, with respect to myself, as they have arisen. I quitted my downy pillow at half-past six o'clock; for bad habits in sickness have lost me half an hour of every morning; and then, according to an etiquette I discovered but on Friday night, I was quite new dressed: for I find that, on the King's birthday, and on the Queen's, both real and nominal, two new attires, one half, the other full dressed, are expected from all attendants that come into the royal presence.

This first labour was happily achieved in such good time, that I was just seated to my breakfast—a delicate bit of roll, half-eaten, and a promising dish of tea, well stirred—when I received my summons to attend the Queen.

She was only with her wardrobe woman, and accepted most graciously a little murmuring congratulation upon the day, which I ventured to whisper while she looked another way. Fortunately for me, she is always quick in conceiving what is meant, and never wastes time in demanding what is said. She told me she had bespoke Miss Planta to attend at the grand toilette at St James's, as she saw my strength still diminished by my late illness. Indeed it still is, though in all other respects I am perfectly well.

The Queen wore a very beautiful dress, of a new manufacture, of worked muslin, thin, fine, and clear, as the Chambéry gauze. I attended her from the Blue Closet, in which she dresses, through the rooms that lead to the breakfast apartment. In one of these, while she stopped for her hairdresser to finish her head-dress, the King joined her. She spoke to him in German, and he kissed her hand.

The three elder Princesses came in soon after; they all went up, with congratulatory smiles and curtsies, to their royal father, who kissed them very affectionately; they then, as usual every morning, kissed the Queen's hand. The door was thrown open to the breakfast room, which is a noble apartment, fitted up with some of Vandyke's best works; and the instant the King, who led the way, entered, I was surprised by a sudden sound of music, and found that a band of musicians were stationed there to welcome him. The Princesses followed, but Princess Elizabeth turned round to me to say she could hardly bear the sound: it was the first morning of her coming down to breakfast for many months, as she has had that repast in her own room ever since her dangerous illness. It overcame her, she said, more than the dressing, more than the early rising, more than the whole of the hurry and fatigue of all the rest of a public birthday. She loves the King most tenderly; and there is a something in receiving any person who is loved, by sudden music, that I can easily conceive to be very trying to the nerves.

As I had been extremely distressed upon the Queen's birthday, in January, where to go or how to act, and could obtain no information from my coadjutrix, I now resolved to ask for directions from the Queen herself; and she readily gave them, in a manner to make this gala day far more comfortable to me than the last. She bade me dress as fast as I could, and go to St James's by eleven o'clock; but first come into the room to her.

Then followed my grand toilette. The hairdresser was waiting for me, and he went to work first, and I second, with all our might and main.

When my adorning tasks were accomplished, I went to the Blue Closet. No one was there. I then hesitated whether to go back or seek the Queen. I have a dislike insuperable to entering a Royal presence, except by an

immediate summons: however, the directions I had had
prevailed, and I went into the adjoining apartment.
There stood Madame la Fîte,[1] talking in a low voice with
M. de Luc. They told me the Queen was in the next
room, and on I went.

She was seated at a glass, and the hairdresser was
putting in her jewels, while a clergyman in his canonicals
was standing near, and talking to her.

I imagined him some bishop unknown to me, and
stopped; the Queen looked round, and called out: 'Oh,
it's Miss Burney—come in, Miss Burney.' In I came,
curtsying respectfully to a bow from the canonicals;
but I found not out, till he answered something said by
the Queen, that it was no other than Mr Turbulent.

I then went to St James's. The Queen was most
brilliant in attire; and when she was arrayed, Mr West[2]
was allowed to enter the dressing-room, in order to give
his opinion of the disposition of her jewels, which indeed
were arranged with great taste and effect.

Aug. 15th. In the afternoon, while I was drinking
coffee with Mrs Schwellenberg—or, rather, looking at it,
since I rarely swallow any—her Majesty came into the
room, and soon, after a little German discourse with
Mrs Schwellenberg, told me Mrs Siddons had been ordered
to the Lodge, to read a play, and desired I would receive
her in my room.

I felt a little queer in the office; I had only seen her twice
or thrice, in large assemblies, at Miss Monckton's, and at
Sir Joshua Reynolds's, and never had been introduced to
her, nor spoken with her. However, in this dead and
tame life I now lead, such an interview was by no means
undesirable.

I had just got to the bottom of the stairs, when she
entered the passage gallery. I took her into the tea-room,
and endeavoured to make amends for former distance

[1] This lady, whom Fanny had known at Norbury, sometimes
officiated as reader to the Queen.
[2] Benjamin West.

and taciturnity, by an open and cheerful reception. I had heard from sundry people (in the old days) that she wished to make the acquaintance; but I thought it, then, one of too conspicuous a sort for the quietness I had so much difficulty to preserve in my ever increasing connections. Here all was changed; I received her by the Queen's commands, and was perfectly well inclined to reap some pleasure from the meeting.

But, now that we came so near, I was much disappointed in my expectations. I know not if my dear Fredy has met with her in private, but I fancy approximation is not highly in her favour. I found her the heroine of a tragedy—sublime, elevated, and solemn. In face and person, truly noble and commanding; in manners, quiet and stiff; in voice, deep and dragging; and in conversation, formal, sententious, calm, and dry. I expected her to have been all that is interesting; the delicacy and sweetness with which she seizes every opportunity to strike and to captivate upon the stage had persuaded me that her mind was formed with that peculiar susceptibility which, in different modes, must give equal powers to attract and to delight in common life. But I was very much mistaken. As a stranger, I must have admired her noble appearance and beautiful countenance, and have regretted that nothing in her conversation kept pace with their promise; and, as a celebrated actress, I had still only to do the same.

Whether fame or success have spoiled her, or whether she only possesses the skill of representing and embellishing materials with which she is furnished by others, I know not; but still I remain disappointed.

She was scarcely seated, and a little general discourse begun, before she told me—all at once—that 'there was no part she had ever so much wished to act as that of Cecilia.'

I made some little acknowledgment, and hurried to ask when she had seen Sir Joshua Reynolds, Miss Palmer, and others with whom I knew her acquainted.

The play she was to read was *The Provoked Husband*.[1]

[1] Vanbrugh's comedy, completed by Cibber in 1728.

She appeared neither alarmed nor elated by her summons, but calmly to look upon it as a thing of course, from her celebrity.

SEPTEMBER. I saw a great deal of Mr Bunbury[1] in the course of this month, as he was in waiting upon the Duke of York, who spent great part of it at Windsor, to the inexpressible delight of his almost idolizing father. Mr Bunbury did not open upon me with that mildness and urbanity that might lead me to forget the strokes of his pencil and power of his caricature; he early avowed a general disposition to laugh at, censure, or despise all around him. He began talking of everybody and everything about us, with the decisive freedom of a confirmed old intimacy.

'I am in disgrace here, already!' he cried, almost exultantly.

'In disgrace?' I repeated.

'Yes—for not riding out this morning!—I was asked—what could I have better to do?—Ha! ha!'

The next time that I saw him after your departure from Windsor, he talked a great deal of painting and painters, and then said: 'The draughtsman of whom I think the most highly of any in the world was in this room the other day, and I did not know it, and was not introduced to him!'

I immediately assured him I never did the honours of the room when its right mistress was in it, but that I would certainly have named them to each other had I known he desired it.

Another evening he gave us the history of his life at Brighthelmstone. He spoke highly of the Duke, but with much satire of all else, and that incautiously, and evidently with an innate defiance of consequences, from a consciousness of secret powers to overawe their hurting him.

Notwithstanding the general reverence I pay to extra-ordinary talents, which lead me to think it even a species

[1] Harry Bunbury, a celebrated caricaturist.

of impertinence to dwell upon small failings in their rare possessors, Mr Bunbury did not win my goodwill. His serious manner is supercilious and haughty, and his easy conversation wants rectitude in its principles. For the rest, he is entertaining and gay, full of talk, sociable, willing to enjoy what is going forward, and ready to speak his opinion with perfect unreserve.

Plays and players seem his darling theme; he can rave about them from morning to night, and yet be ready to rave again when morning returns. He acts as he talks, spouts as he recollects, and seems to give his whole soul to dramatic feeling and expression. This is not, however, his only subject. Love and romance are equally dear to his discourse, though they cannot be introduced with equal frequency. Upon these topics he loses himself wholly—he runs into rhapsodies that discredit him at once as a father, a husband, and a moral man. He asserts that love is the first principle of life, and should take place of every other; holds all bonds and obligations as nugatory that would claim a preference; and advances such doctrines of exalted sensations in the tender passion as made me tremble while I heard them.

He adores *Werter*,[1] and would scarce believe I had not read it—still less that I had begun it and left it off, from distaste at its evident tendency. I saw myself sink instantly in his estimation, though till this little avowal I had appeared to stand in it very honourably.

Nov. 27TH. I had a terrible journey indeed to town, Mrs Schwellenberg finding it expedient to have the glass down on my side, whence there blew in a sharp wind, which so painfully attacked my eyes that they were inflamed even before we arrived in town.

Mr de Luc and Miss Planta both looked uneasy, but no one durst speak; and for me, it was among the evils that I can always best bear: yet before the evening I grew so ill that I could not propose going to Chelsea,

---

[1] Goethe published this book, which attracted widespread attention, in 1774.

lest I should be utterly unfitted for Thursday's drawing-room.

The next day, however, I received a consolation that has been some ease to my mind ever since. My dear father spent the evening with me, and was so incensed at the state of my eyes, which were now as piteous to behold as to feel, and at the relation of their usage, that he charged me, another time, to draw up my glass in defiance of all opposition, and to abide by all consequences, since my place was wholly immaterial when put in competition with my health.

On the Thursday I was obliged to dress, just as if nothing was the matter.

The next day, when we assembled to return to Windsor, Mr de Luc was in real consternation at sight of my eyes; and I saw an indignant glance at my coadjutrix, that could scarce content itself without being understood.

Some business of Mrs Schwellenberg's occasioned a delay of the journey, and we all retreated back; and when I returned to my room, Miller, the old head housemaid, came to me, with a little neat tin saucepan in her hand, saying: 'Pray, ma'am, use this for your eyes: 'tis milk and butter, *such as I used to make for Madame Haggerdorn* when she travelled in the winter with Mrs Schwellenberg.'

Good heaven! I really shuddered when she added, that all that poor woman's misfortunes with her eyes, which, from inflammation after inflammation, grew nearly blind, were attributed by herself to these journeys, in which she was forced to have the glass down at her side in all weathers, and frequently the glasses behind her also!

Miss Planta presently ran into my room, to say she had hopes we should travel without this amiable being; and she had left me but a moment when Mrs Stainforth succeeded her, exclaiming: 'Oh, for heaven's sake, don't leave her behind; for heaven's sake, Miss Burney, take her with you!'

'Twas impossible not to laugh at these opposite interests, both from agony of fear, breaking through all restraint.

Soon after, however, we all assembled again, and got into the coach. Mr de Luc, who was my *vis-à-vis*, instantly pulled up the glass.

'Put down that glass!' was the immediate order.

He affected not to hear her, and began conversing.

She enraged quite tremendously, calling aloud to be obeyed without delay. He looked compassionately at me, and shrugged his shoulders, and said: 'But, ma'am——'

'Do it, Mr de Luc, when I tell you! I will have it! When you been too cold, you might bear it!'

'It is not for me, ma'am, but poor Miss Burney.'

'Oh, poor Miss Burney might bear it the same! put it down, Mr de Luc! without, I will get out! put it down, when I tell you! It is my coach! I will have it selfs! I might go alone in it, or with one, or with what you call nobody, when I please!'

Frightened for good Mr de Luc, and the more for being much obliged to him, I now interfered, and begged him to let down the glass. Very reluctantly he complied, and I leant back in the coach, and held up my muff to my eyes.

What a journey ensued! To see that face when lighted up with fury is a sight for horror! I was glad to exclude it by my muff.

Miss Planta alone attempted to speak. I did not think it incumbent on me to 'make the agreeable,' thus used; I was therefore wholly dumb: for not a word, not an apology, not one expression of being sorry for what I suffered, was uttered. The most horrible ill-humour, violence, and rudeness, were all that were shown. Mr de Luc was too much provoked to take his usual method of passing all off by constant talk: and as I had never seen him venture to appear provoked before, I felt a great obligation to his kindness.

When we were about half-way, we stopped to water the horses. He then again pulled up the glass, as if from absence. A voice of fury exclaimed: 'Let it down! Without I won't go!'

'I am sure,' cried he, 'all Mrs de Luc's plants will be killed by this frost!'

For the frost was very severe indeed.

Then he proposed my changing places with Miss Planta, who sat opposite Mrs Schwellenberg, and consequently on the sheltered side.

'Yes!' cried Mrs Schwellenberg, 'Miss Burney might sit there, and so she ought!'

I told her briefly I was always sick in riding backwards.

'Oh, ver well! when you don't like it, don't do it. You might bear it when you like it! What did the poor Haggerdorn bear it! when the blood was all running down from her eyes!'

This was too much! 'I must take, then,' I cried, 'the more warning!'

After that I spoke not a word. I ruminated all the rest of the way upon my dear father's recent charge and permission. I was upon the point continually of availing myself of both, but alas! I felt the deep disappointment I should give him, and I felt the most cruel repugnance to owe a resignation to a quarrel.

These reflections powerfully forbade the rebellion to which this unequalled arrogance and cruelty excited me; and after revolving them again and again, I—*accepted a bit of cake* which she suddenly offered me as we reached Windsor, and determined, since I submitted to my monastic destiny from motives my serious thoughts deemed right, I would not be prompted to oppose it from mere feelings of resentment to one who, strictly, merited only contempt.

I gulped as well as I could at dinner: but all civil fits are again over. Not a word was said to me; yet I was really very ill all the afternoon. The cold had seized my elbows, from holding them up so long, and I was stiff and chilled all over.

Mr de Luc called upon me next morning, and openly avowed his indignation, protesting it was an oppression he could not bear to see used, and reproving me for checking him when he would have run all risks. I thanked him most cordially, but assured him the worst of all inflammations to me was that of a quarrel, and I entreated him, therefore, not to interfere. But we have been cordial friends from that time forward.

Miss Planta also called, kindly bringing me some eye-water, and telling me she had never so longed to beat anybody in her life; 'And yet, I assure you,' she added, 'everybody remarks that she behaves, altogether, better to you than to anybody!'

DEC. 1ST. I had received for to-day an invitation to meet Lady Bute and Lady Louisa Stuart at my dearest Mrs Delany's, and I should have wished it at all times, so much I like them both. I had no opportunity to speak first to my royal mistress, but I went to her at noon, rather more dressed than usual, and when I saw her look a little surprised, I explained my reason. She seemed very well satisfied with it, but my coadjutrix appeared in astonishment unequalled; and at dinner, when we necessarily met again, new testimonies of conduct quite without example were exhibited; for when Mrs Thackeray and Miss Planta were helped, she helped herself, and appeared publicly to send me to Coventry—though the sole provocation was intending to forgo her society this evening!

I sat quiet and unhelped a few minutes, considering what to do: for so little was my appetite, I was almost tempted to go without dinner entirely. However, upon further reflection, I concluded it would but harden her heart still more to have this fresh affront so borne, and so related, as it must have been, through Windsor, and therefore I calmly begged some greens from Miss Planta.

Neither she nor Mrs Thackeray had had courage to offer me anything, my 'disgrace' being so obvious. The weakness of my eyes, which still would not bear the light, prevented me from tasting animal food all this time.

A little ashamed, she then anticipated Miss Planta's assistance, by offering me some French beans. To curb my own displeasure, I obliged myself to accept them instead of the greens, and they tasted very well by that means, though they came through such hands.

Unfortunately, however, this little softening was presently worn out, by some speeches which it encouraged from Mrs Thackeray, who seemed to seize the moment of permission to acknowledge that I was in the room, by telling me she had lately met some of my friends in town.

This again sent me to Coventry for the rest of the dinner. When it was over, and we were all going upstairs to coffee, I spoke to Columb, in passing, to have a chair for me at seven o'clock.

'For what, then,' cried a stern voice behind me, 'for what go you upstairs at all, when you don't drink coffee?'

Did she imagine I should answer: 'For your society, ma'am?' No I turned back, quick as lightning, and only saying 'Very well, ma'am,' moved towards my own room.

Again a little ashamed of herself, she added, rather more civilly: 'For what should you have that trouble?'

I simply repeated my 'Very well, ma'am,' in a voice of, I believe, rather pique than calm acquiescence, and entered my own apartment, unable to enjoy this little release, however speedy to obtain it, from the various, the grievous emotions of my mind, that this was the person, use me how she might, with whom I must chiefly pass my time!

To finish, however, with respect to the *Présidente*, I must now acquaint you that, as my eyes entirely grew well, her incivility entirely wore off, and I became a far greater favourite than I had ever presumed to think myself till that time!

My favour now was beyond the favour of all others; I was 'My good Miss Berner' at every other word, and no one else was listened to if I would speak, and no one else was accepted for a partner if I would play! I found no cause to which I could attribute this change. I believe the whole mere matter of caprice.

WEDNESDAY, JANUARY 9TH, 1788. To-day Mrs Schwellenberg did me a real favour, and with real good nature; for she sent me the letters of my poor lost friends, Dr Johnson and Mrs Thrale, which she knew me to be almost pining to procure.[1] The book belongs to the Bishop of Carlisle, who lent it to Mr Turbulent, from whom it was again lent to the Queen, and so passed on to Mrs Schwellenberg. It is still unpublished.

With what a sadness have I been reading! what scenes has it revived!—what regrets renewed! These letters have not been more improperly published in the whole, than they are injudiciously displayed in their several parts. She has given all—every word—and thinks that, perhaps, a justice to Dr Johnson, which, in fact, is the greatest injury to his memory.

The few she has selected of her own do her, indeed, much credit; she has discarded all that were trivial and merely local, and given only such as contain something instructive, amusing, or ingenious.

About four of the letters, however, of my ever-revered Dr Johnson are truly worthy his exalted powers: one is upon death, in considering its approach as we are surrounded, or not, by mourners; another, upon the sudden and premature loss of poor Mrs Thrale's darling and only son.

Our name once occurs: how I started at its sight!— 'Tis to mention the party that planned the first visit to our house: Miss Owen, Mr Seward, Mrs and Miss Thrale, and Dr Johnson. How well shall we ever, my Susan, remember that morning!

I have had so many attacks upon her subject, that at last I fairly begged quarter, and frankly owned to Mrs Schwellenberg that I could not endure to speak any more upon the matter, endeavouring, at the same time, to explain to her my long and intimate connection with the family. Yet nothing I could say put a stop to 'How can you defend her in this? How can you justify her in that?' etc. etc. Alas! that I cannot defend her is precisely the reason I can so ill bear to speak of her.

[1] *Letters to and from the Late Samuel Johnson.*

FRIDAY, FEBRUARY 1ST. To-day I had a summons in the morning to Mrs Schwellenberg, who was very ill; so ill as to fill me with compassion. She was extremely low-spirited, and spoke to me with quite unwonted kindness of manner, and desired me to accept a sedan chair, which had been Mrs Haggerdorn's, and now devolved to her, saying I might as well have it while she lived as when she was dead, which would soon happen.

I thanked her, and wished her, I am sure very sincerely, better. Nor do I doubt her again recovering, as I have frequently seen her much worse. True, she must die at last, but who must not? My Fredy, my Susan, Mr Locke, Mrs Delany, all the world's fairest ornaments, must go the same way. Ah! the survivor of all such—not the departed —will be worthy of pity.

At night, by the Queen's gracious orders, I went to the play with Miss Goldsworthy, Mlle Montmoulin, and, by the same gracious permission, at the request of Miss Goldsworthy, Mrs Gwynn.[1] I was very glad to see her in a place where I could so much better converse with her than where I had last met her. She looked as beautiful as the first day I saw her, and was all gentleness and softness. Colonels Gwynn and Goldsworthy were our beaux.

The play was *The Merchant of Venice*. Mrs Siddons played Portia; and charmingly, though not, I think, with so perfect an entrance into the character as I have observed in her performance of some other parts.

FEB. 13TH. The Trial, so long impending, of Mr Hastings, opened to-day. The Queen yesterday asked me if I wished to be present at the beginning, or had rather take another day. I was greatly obliged by her condescension, and preferred the opening. I thought it would give me a general view of the Court, and the manner of proceeding, and that I might read hereafter the speeches and evidence.

---

[1] Mrs Gwynn and her sister, Mrs Bunbury, were the beautiful Misses Horneck, whose portraits were painted by Sir Joshua Reynolds.

She then told me she had six tickets from Sir Peter
Burrell, the Grand Chamberlain, for every day; that
three were for his box, and three for his gallery. She
asked me who I would go with, and promised me a box
ticket not only for myself, but my companion. Nor was
this consideration all she showed me; for she added, that
as I might naturally wish for my father, she would have
me send him my other ticket.

I thanked her very gratefully, and after dinner went to
St Martin's Street; but all there was embarrassing: my
father could not go; he was averse to be present at the
trial, and he was a little lame from a fall. In the end I
sent an express to Hammersmith, to desire Charles to
come to me the next morning by eight o'clock.

I was very sorry not to have my father, as he had been
named by the Queen; but I was glad to have Charles.

I told her Majesty at night the step I had ventured to
take, and she was perfectly content with it. 'But I must
trouble you,' she said, 'with Miss Gomme, who has no
other way to go.'

This morning the Queen dispensed with all attendance
from me after her first dressing, that I might haste away.
Mrs Schwellenberg was fortunately well enough to take
the whole duty, and the sweet Queen not only hurried me
off, but sent me some cakes from her own breakfast table,
that I might carry them in my pocket, lest I should have
no time for eating before I went.

Charles was not in time, but we all did well in the end.
We got to Westminster Hall between nine and ten o'clock;
and, as I know, my dear Susan, like myself, was never at
any trial, I will give some account of the place and arrangements; and whether the description be new to her or old,
my partial Fredy will not blame it.

The Grand Chamberlain's box is in the centre of the
upper end of the Hall: there we sat, Miss Gomme and
myself, immediately behind the chair placed for Sir Peter
Burrell. To the left, on the same level, were the green
benches for the House of Commons, which occupied a

third of the upper end of the Hall, and the whole of the
left side: to the right of us, on the same level, was the
Grand Chamberlain's gallery.

The left side of the Hall, opposite to the green benches
for the Commons, was appropriated to the Peeresses and
Peers' daughters.

The bottom of the Hall contained the Royal Family's
Box and the Lord High Steward's, above which was a
large gallery appointed for receiving company with Peers'
tickets.

A gallery also was run along the left side of the Hall,
above the green benches, which is called the Duke of
Newcastle's Box, the centre of which was railed off into a
separate apartment for the reception of the Queen and
four eldest Princesses, who were then *incog.*, not choosing
to appear in state, and in their own Box.

Along the right side of the Hall ran another gallery,
over the seats of the Princesses, and this was divided into
boxes for various people—the Lord Chamberlain (not
the *Great* Chamberlain), the Surveyor, Architect, etc.

So much for all the raised buildings; now for the
disposition of the Hall itself, or ground.

In the middle was placed a large table, and at the head
of it the seat for the Chancellor, and round it seats for the
Judges, the Masters in Chancery, the Clerks, and all who
belonged to the Law; the upper end, and the right side of
the room, was allotted to the Peers in their robes; the left
side to the Bishops and Archbishops.

Immediately below the Great Chamberlain's Box was
the place allotted for the Prisoner. On his right side was
a Box for his own Counsel, on his left the Box for the
Managers, or Committee, for the Prosecution; and these
three most important of all the divisions in the Hall were
all directly adjoining to where I was seated.

Almost the moment I entered I was spoken to by a
lady I did not recollect, but found afterwards to be Lady
Claremont: and this proved very agreeable, for she took
Sir Peter's place, and said she would occupy it till he

claimed it; and then, when just before me, she named to me all the order of the buildings, and all the company, pointing out every distinguished person, and most obligingly desiring me to ask her any questions I wanted to have solved, as she knew, she said, 'all those creatures that filled the green benches, looking so little like gentlemen, and so much like hairdressers.'   These were the Commons. In truth, she did the honours of the Hall to me with as much good nature and good breeding as if I had been a foreigner of distinction, to whom she had dedicated her time and attention.   My acquaintance with her had been made formerly at Mrs Vesey's.

The business did not begin till near twelve o'clock. The opening to the whole then took place, by the entrance of the *Managers of the Prosecution*; all the company were already long in their boxes or galleries.

I shuddered, and drew involuntarily back, when, as the doors were flung open, I saw Mr Burke, as Head of the Committee, make his solemn entry.   He held a scroll in his hand, and walked alone, his brow knit with corroding care and deep labouring thought—a brow how different to that which had proved so alluring to my warmest admiration when first I met him! so highly as he had been my favourite, so captivating as I had found his manners and conversation in our first acquaintance, and so much as I owed to his zeal and kindness to me and my affairs in its progress!   How did I grieve to behold him now the cruel Prosecutor (such to me he appeared) of an injured and innocent man!

Mr Fox followed next, Mr Sheridan, Mr Wyndham, Messrs Anstruther, Grey, Adam, Michael Angelo Taylor, Pelham, Colonel North, Mr Frederick Montagu, Sir Gilbert Elliot, General Burgoyne, Dudley Long, etc.   They were all named over to me by Lady Claremont, or I should not have recollected even those of my acquaintance, from the shortness of my sight.

When the Committee Box was filled, the House of Commons at large took their seats on their green benches,

which stretched, as I have said, along the whole left side
of the Hall, and, taking in a third of the upper end, joined
to the Great Chamberlain's Box, from which nothing
separated them but a partition of about two feet in height.

Then began the procession, the Clerks entering first,
then the lawyers according to their rank, and the Peers,
Bishops, and Officers, all in their coronation robes;
concluding with the Princes of the Blood—Prince William,
son to the Duke of Gloucester, coming first, then the Dukes
of Cumberland, Gloucester, and York, then the Prince of
Wales; and the whole ending by the Chancellor, with his
train borne.

They then all took their seats.

A Serjeant-at-Arms arose, and commanded silence in
the Court, on pain of imprisonment.

Then some other officer, in a loud voice, called out, as
well as I can recollect, words to this purpose: 'Warren
Hastings, Esquire, come forth! Answer to the charges
brought against you; save your bail, or forfeit your
recognizance!'

Indeed I trembled at these words, and hardly could
keep my place when I found Mr Hastings was being
brought to the bar. He came forth from some place
immediately under the Great Chamberlain's Box, and was
preceded by Sir Francis Molyneux, Gentleman-Usher of
the Black Rod; and at each side of him walked his bails,
Messrs Sullivan and Sumner.

The moment he came in sight, which was not for full
ten minutes after his awful summons, he made a low bow
to the Chancellor and Court facing him. I saw not his
face, as he was directly under me. He moved on slowly,
and, I think, supported between his two Bails, to the opening of his own Box; there, lower still, he bowed again;
and then, advancing to the bar, he leant his hands upon it,
and dropped on his knees; but a voice in the same moment
proclaiming he had leave to rise, he stood up almost
instantaneously, and a third time profoundly bowed to
the Court.

What an awful moment this for such a man!—a man fallen from such height of power to a situation so humiliating—from the almost unlimited command of so large a part of the Eastern World to be cast at the feet of his enemies, of the great tribunal of his country, and of the nation at large, assembled thus in a body to try and to judge him! Could even his prosecutors at that moment look on—and not shudder at least, if they did not blush?

The crier, I think it was, made, in a loud and hollow voice, a public proclamation: 'That Warren Hastings, Esquire, late Governor-General of Bengal, was now on his trial for high crimes and misdemeanours, with which he was charged by the Commons of Great Britain; and that all persons whatsoever who had aught to allege against him were now to stand forth.'

A general silence followed, and the Chancellor, Lord Thurlow, now made his speech. I will give it to you, to the best of my power, from memory; the newspapers have printed it far less accurately than I have retained it, though I am by no means exact or secure.

'Warren Hastings, you are now brought into this Court to answer the charges brought against you by the Knights, Esquires, Burgesses, and Commons of Great Britain— charges now standing only as allegations, by them to be legally proved, or by you to be disproved. Bring forth your answers and your defence, with that seriousness, respect, and truth due to accusers so respectable. Time has been allowed you for preparation, proportioned to the intricacies in which the transactions are involved, and to the remote distances whence your documents may have been searched and required. You will still be allowed Bail, for the better forwarding your defence, and whatever you can require will still be yours, of time, witnesses, and all things else you may hold necessary. This is not granted you as any indulgence: it is entirely your due: it is the privilege which every British subject has a right to claim, and which is due to every one who is brought before this high Tribunal.'

This speech, uttered in a calm, equal, solemn manner, and in a voice mellow and penetrating, with eyes keen and black, yet softened into some degree of tenderness while fastened full upon the prisoner—this speech, its occasion, its portent, and its object, had an effect upon every hearer of producing the most respectful attention, and, out of the Committee Box at least, the strongest emotions in the cause of Mr Hastings.

Again Mr Hastings made the lowest reverence to the Court, and, leaning over the bar, answered, with much agitation, through evident efforts to suppress it: 'My Lords — impressed — deeply impressed — I come before your Lordships, equally confident in my own integrity, and in the justice of the Court before which I am to clear it.'

'Impressed' and 'deeply impressed' too, was my mind, by this short yet comprehensive speech, and all my best wishes for his clearance and redress rose warmer than ever in my heart.

A general silence again ensued, and then one of the lawyers opened the cause. He began by reading from an immense roll of parchment the general charges against Mr Hastings, but he read in so monotonous a chant that nothing could I hear or understand than now and then the name of Warren Hastings.

During this reading, to which I vainly lent all my attention, Mr Hastings, finding it, I presume, equally impossible to hear a word, began to cast his eyes around the House, and having taken a survey of all in front and at the sides, he turned about and looked up; pale looked his face—pale, ill, and altered. I was much affected by the sight of that dreadful harass which was written on his countenance. Had I looked at him without restraint, it could not have been without tears. I felt shocked, too, shocked and ashamed, to be seen by him in that place. I had wished to be present from an earnest interest in the business, joined to firm confidence in his powers of defence; but *his* eyes were not those I wished to meet

in Westminster Hall. I called upon Miss Gomme and
Charles to assist me in looking another way, and in conversing with me as I turned aside; and I kept as much
aloof as possible till he had taken his survey, and placed
himself again in front.

From this time, however, he frequently looked round,
and I was soon without a doubt that he must see me. Not
very desirable to me, therefore, was a civility I next received
from one of the managers—one, too, placed in the front
of the Committee, and in a line with the prisoner: it was
Mr Frederick Montagu, who recognized and bowed to
me. He is a most intimate friend of Mrs Delany, and a
man of excellence in all parts of his character, save politics,
and there he is always against the Administration! Why
will any man of principle join any party? Why not be
open to all, yet belong to none?

I hope Mr Hastings did not see us; but in a few minutes
more, while this reading was still continued, I perceived
Sir Joshua Reynolds in the midst of the Committee. He,
at the same moment, saw me also, and not only bowed,
but smiled and nodded with his usual good humour and
intimacy, making at the same time a sign to his ear, by
which I understood he had no trumpet; whether he had
forgotten or lost it I know not.

I would rather have answered all this dumb show anywhere else, as my last ambition was that of being noticed
from such a Box. I again entreated aid in turning away;
but Miss Gomme, who is a friend of Sir Gilbert Elliot,
one of the Managers, and an ill-wisher, for his sake, to the
opposite cause, would only laugh, and ask why I should
not be owned by them.

I did not, however, like it, but had no choice from my
near situation; and in a few seconds I had again a bow,
and a profound one, and again very ridiculously I was
obliged to inquire of Lady Claremont who my own
acquaintance might be. Mr Richard Burke, senior, she
answered. He is a brother of the great—great in defiance
of all drawbacks—Edmund Burke.

Another lawyer now arose, and read so exactly in the same manner, that it was utterly impossible to discover even whether it was a charge or an answer.

Such reading as this, you may well suppose, set everybody pretty much at their ease; and but for the interest I took in looking from time to time at Mr Hastings, and watching his countenance, I might as well have been away. He seemed composed after the first half-hour, and calm; but he looked with a species of indignant contempt towards his accusers, that could not, I think, have been worn had his defence been doubtful. Many there are who fear for him; for me, I own myself wholly confident in his acquittal.

Soon after, a voice just by my side, from the green benches, said: 'Will Miss Burney allow me to renew my acquaintance with her?' I turned about and saw Mr Crutchley.

All Streatham rose to my mind at sight of him. I have never beheld him since the Streatham society was abolished. We entered instantly upon the subject of that family, a subject ever to me the most interesting. He also had never seen poor Mrs Thrale since her return to England; but he joined with me very earnestly in agreeing that, since so unhappy a step was now past recall, it became the duty, however painful a one, of the daughters, to support, not cast off and contemn, one who was now as much their mother as when she still bore their own name.

'But how,' cried he, 'do you stand the fiery trial of this Streatham book that is coming upon us?'

I acknowledged myself very uneasy about it, and he assured me all who had ever been at Streatham were in fright and consternation.

We talked all these matters over at more length, till I was called away by an 'How d' ye do, Miss Burney?' from the Committee Box! And then I saw young Mr Burke, who had jumped up on the nearest form to speak to me.

Pleasant enough! I checked my vexation as well as

I was able, since the least shyness on my part to those
with whom formerly I had been social must instantly have
been attributed to Court influence; and therefore, since
I could not avoid the notice, I did what I could to talk
with him as heretofore. He is, besides, so amiable a
young man, that I could not be sorry to see him again,
though I regretted it should be just in that place, and at
this time.

While we talked together, Mr Crutchley went back to
his more distant seat, and the moment I was able to withdraw from young Mr Burke, Charles, who sat behind me,
leant down and told me a gentleman had just desired to
be presented to me.

'Who?' quoth I.

'Mr Wyndham,' he answered.[1]

I really thought he was laughing, and answered accordingly; but he assured me he was in earnest, and that Mr
Wyndham had begged him to make the proposition.

What could I do? There was no refusing: yet a planned
meeting with another of the Committee, and one deep in
the prosecution, and from whom one of the hardest
charges has come—could anything be less pleasant as I
was then situated?

The Great Chamberlain's Box is the only part of the hall
that has any communication with either the Committee
Box or the House of Commons, and it is also the very
nearest to the prisoner. Mr Wyndham I had seen twice
before—both times at Miss Monckton's; and anywhere
else I could have been much gratified by his desire of a
third meeting, as he is one of the most agreeable, spirited,
well-bred, and brilliant conversers I have ever spoken
with. He is a neighbour, too, now, of Charlotte's. He
is member for Norwich, and a man of family and fortune,
with a very pleasing, though not handsome face, a very
elegant figure, and an air of fashion and vivacity.

The conversations I had had with him at Miss

---

[1] William Windham (1750-1810). He remained a Whig until the
outbreak of the French Revolution, when he joined Pitt.

Monckton's had been, wholly by his own means, extremely spirited and entertaining. I was sorry to see him make one of a set that appeared so inveterate against a man I believe so injuriously treated; and my concern was founded upon the good thoughts I had conceived of him, not merely for his social talents, which are yet very uncommon, but from a reason dearer to my remembrance. He loved Dr Johnson—and Dr Johnson returned his affection. Their political principles and connections were opposite, but Mr Wyndham respected his venerable friend too highly to discuss any points that could offend him; and showed for him so true a regard, that, during all his late illnesses, for the latter part of his life, his carriage and himself were alike at his service, to air, visit, or go out, whenever he was disposed to accept them.

Charles soon told me he was at my elbow. He had taken the place Mr Crutchley had just left. The *abord* was, on my part, very awkward, from the distress I felt lest Mr Hastings should look up, and from a conviction that I must not name that gentleman, of whom alone I could then think, to a person in a Committee against him.

He, however, was easy, having no embarrassing thoughts, since the conference was of his own seeking. 'Twas so long since I had seen him, that I almost wonder he remembered me.

After the first compliments he looked around him, and exclaimed: 'What an assembly is this! How striking a *spectacle*! I had not seen half its splendour down there. You have it here to great advantage; you lose some of the Lords, but you gain all the Ladies. You have a very good place here.'

'Yes; and I may safely say I make a very impartial use of it: for since here I have sat, I have never discovered to which side I have been listening.'

He laughed, but told me they were then running through the charges.

'And is it essential,' cried I, 'that they should so run

them through that nobody can understand them? Is that a form of law?'

He agreed to the absurdity; and then, looking still at the *spectacle*, which indeed is the most splendid I ever saw, arrested his eyes upon the Chancellor. 'He looks very well from hence,' cried he; 'and how well he acquits himself on these solemn occasions! With what dignity, what loftiness, what high propriety, he comports himself!'

This praise to the Chancellor, who is a known friend of Mr Hastings, though I believe he would be the last to favour him unjustly now he is on trial, was a pleasant sound to my ear, and confirmed my original idea of the liberal disposition of my new associate.

Then, still looking at the scene before him, he suddenly laughed, and said: 'I must not, to Miss Burney, make this remark, but—it is observable that in the *King's* Box sit the Hawkesbury family, while, next to the *Speaker*, who is here as a sort of Representative of the King, sits Major Scot!' [1]

I knew his inference, of Court influence in favour of Mr Hastings, but I thought it best to let it pass quietly. I knew else, I should only be supposed under the same influence myself.

Looking, still on, he next noticed the two Archbishops. 'And see,' cried he, 'the Archbishops of York, Markham —see how he affects to read the articles of impeachment, as if he was still open to either side! My good Lord Archbishop! your Grace might, with perfect safety, spare your eyes, for your mind has been made up upon this subject before ever it was investigated. He holds Hastings to be the greatest man in the world—for Hastings promoted the interest of his son in the East Indies!'

Somewhat sarcastic, this; but I had as little time as power for answering, since now, and suddenly, his eye dropped down upon poor Mr Hastings: the expression of his face instantly lost the gaiety and ease with which it had addressed me; he stopped short in his remarks; he fixed his

[1] John Scott, Hastings's political agent.

eyes steadfastly on this new, and but too interesting object, and after viewing him some time in a sort of earnest silence, he suddenly exclaimed, as if speaking to himself, and from an impulse irresistible: 'What a sight is that! to see that man, that small portion of human clay, that poor feeble machine of earth, enclosed now in that little space, brought to that Bar, a prisoner in a spot six foot square—and to reflect on his late power! Nations at his command! Princes prostrate at his feet! What a change! How must he feel it!'

I can hardly tell you, my dearest Susan, how shocked I felt. . . . I cannot believe Mr Hastings guilty; I feel in myself a strong internal evidence of his innocence, drawn from all I have seen of him; I can only regard the prosecution as a party affair; but yet, since his adversaries now openly stake their names, fame, and character against him, I did not think it decent to intrude such an opinion. I could only be sorry and silent.

Next, Mr Wyndham pointed out Mr Francis[1] to me. 'Tis a singular circumstance, that the friend who most loves and the enemy who most hates Mr Hastings should bear the same name! Mr Wyndham, with all the bias of party, gave me then the highest character of this Mr Francis, whom he called one of the most ill-used of men. Want of documents how to answer forced me to be silent, oppositely as I thought. But it was a very unpleasant situation to me, as I saw that Mr Wyndham still conceived me to have no other interest than a common, and probably to his mind, a weak compassion for the prisoner—that prisoner who, frequently looking around, saw me, I am certain, and saw with whom I was engaged!

The subject of Mr Francis again drew him back to Mr Hastings, but with more severity of mind. 'A prouder heart,' cried he, 'an ambition more profound, were never,

[1] Philip Francis, correctly described as 'the enemy who most hates Mr Hastings.' He is supposed to have been the author of the *Letters of Junius*. The other Mr Francis was the husband of Fanny's sister, Charlotte—Clement Francis, of Aylsham, Norfolk.

I suppose, lodged in any mortal mould than in that man!
With what a port he entered! did you observe him? his
air! I saw not his face, but his air! his port!'

'Surely there,' cried I, 'he could not be to blame! He
comes upon his defence; ought he to look as if he gave
himself up?'

'Why, no; 'tis true he must look what vindication to
himself he can; we must not blame him there.'

Encouraged by this little concession, I resolved to
venture farther, and once more said: 'May I again, Mr
Wyndham, forget that you are a *Committee-man*, and say
something not fit for a *Committee-man* to hear?'

'Oh, yes!' cried he, laughing very much, and looking
extremely curious.

'I must fairly, then, own myself utterly ignorant upon
this subject, and—and—may I go on?'

'I beg you will!'

'Well, then—and originally prepossessed in favour
of the object!'

'Do you,' cried he, earnestly; 'personally know him?'

'Yes; and from that knowledge arose this prepossession
I have confessed.'

'Indeed! what you have seen of him have you then so
much approved?'

'Yes, very much! I must own the truth!'

'But you have not seen much of him?'

'No, not lately. My first knowledge of him was almost
immediately upon his coming from India: I had heard
nothing of all these accusations; I had never been in the
way of hearing them, and knew not even that there were
any to be heard. I saw him, therefore, quite without
prejudice, for or against him; and indeed, I must own, he
soon gave me a strong interest in his favour.'

'Well,' said he, very civilly, 'I begin the less to wonder,
now, that you have adhered to his side; but——'

'To see him, then,' cried I, stopping his *but*—'to see
him brought to that Bar! and *kneeling* at it!—indeed, Mr
Wyndham, I must own to you, I could hardly keep my

seat—hardly forbear rising and running out of the Hall.'

'Why, there,' cried he, 'I agree with you! 'Tis certainly a humiliation not to be wished or defended: it is, indeed, a mere ceremony, a mere formality; but it is a mortifying one, and so obsolete, so unlike the practices of the times, so repugnant from a gentleman to a gentleman, that I myself looked another way: it hurt me, and I wished it dispensed with.'

'Oh, Mr Wyndham,' cried I, surprised and pleased, 'and can you be so liberal?'

'Yes,' cried he, laughing; 'but 'tis only to take you in!'

And then he very civilly bowed, and went down to his box, leaving me much persuaded that I had never yet been engaged in a conversation so curious, from its circumstances, in my life. The warm well-wisher myself of the prisoner, though formerly the warmest admirer of his accuser, engaged, even at his trial, and in his presence, in so open a discussion with one of his principal prosecutors; and the Queen herself in full view, unavoidably beholding me in close and eager conference with an avowed member of opposition!

In the midst of the opening of a trial such as this, so important to the country as well as to the individual who is tried, what will you say to a man—a member of the House of Commons—who kept exclaiming almost perpetually, just at my side: 'What a bore!—when will it be over?—Must one come any more?—I had a great mind not to have come at all. Who's that?—Lady Hawkesbury and the Copes?—Yes. A pretty girl, Kitty. Well, when will they have done? I wish they'd call the question—I should vote it a bore at once!'[1]

In about two or three hours—this reading still lasting—Mr Crutchley came to me again. He, too, was so wearied, that he was departing; but he stayed some time to talk over our constant topic—my poor Mrs Thrale. How

[1] The trial was not concluded until 1795.

little does she suspect the interest I unceasingly take in her—the avidity with which I seize every opportunity to gather the smallest intelligence concerning her!

One little trait of Mr Crutchley, so characteristic of that queerness which distinguishes him, I must mention. He said he questioned whether he should come any more: I told him I had imagined the attendance of every member to be indispensable. 'No,' cried he, 'ten to one if another day they are able to make a house!'

'The Lords, however, I suppose, must come?'

'Not unless they like it.'

'But I hear if they do not attend they have no tickets.'

'Why, then, Miss Primrose and Miss Cowslip must stay away too!'

A far more interesting conference, however, was now awaiting me. Towards the close of the day, Mr Wyndham very unexpectedly came again from the Committee Box, and seated himself by my side. I was glad to see by this second visit that my frankness had not offended him. He began, too, in so open and social a manner, that I was satisfied he forgave it.

'I have been,' cried he, 'very busy since I left you—writing—reading—making documents.'

I saw he was much agitated; the gaiety which seems natural to him was flown, and had left in its place the most evident and unquiet emotion. I looked a little surprised, and rallying himself, in a few moments he inquired if I wished for any refreshment, and proposed fetching me some. But, well as I liked him *for a conspirator*, I could not *break bread* with him!

I thought now all was over of communication between us, but I was mistaken. He spoke for a minute or two upon the crowd—early hour of coming—hasty breakfasting, and such general nothings; and then, as if involuntarily, he returned to the sole subject on his mind. 'Our plan,' cried he, 'is all changing: we have all been busy—we are coming into a new method. I have been making preparations—I did not intend speaking for a considerable time—not till after the circuit—but now, I may be called upon, I know not how soon.'

Then he stopped—ruminating—and I let him ruminate without interruption for some minutes, when he broke forth into these reflections: 'How strange, how infatuated a frailty has man with respect to the future! Be our views, our designs, our anticipations what they may, we are never prepared for it!—it always takes us by surprise—always comes before we look for it!'

Still I said nothing, for I did not fully comprehend him, till he added: 'I will not be so affected as to say to you that I have made no preparation—that I have not thought a little upon what I have to do; yet now that the moment is actually come——'

Again he broke off; but a generous sentiment was bursting from him, and would not be withheld.

'It has brought me,' he resumed, 'a feeling of which I am not yet quite the master! What I have said hitherto, when I have spoken in the house, has been urged and stimulated by the idea of pleading for the injured and the absent, and that gave me spirit. Nor do I tell you (with a half-conscious smile) that the ardour of the prosecution went for nothing—a prosecution in favour of oppressed millions! But now, when I am to speak here, the thought of that man, close to my side—culprit as he is—that man on whom all the odium is to fall—gives me, I own, a sensation that almost disqualifies me beforehand!'

Ah, Mr Wyndham! thought I, with feelings so generous even where enmity is so strong, how came you ever engaged in so cruel, so unjust a cause? . . .

I had afterwards to relate great part of this to the Queen herself. She saw me engaged in such close discourse, and with such apparent interest on both sides, with Mr Wyndham, that I knew she must else form conjectures innumerable. So candid, so liberal is the mind of the Queen, that she not only heard me with the most favourable attention towards Mr Wyndham, but was herself touched even to tears by the relation.

You, my beloved friends, absent from the scene of
action, and only generally interested in it, can form no
idea of the warmth you would feel upon the subject, were
you here, and in the midst of it.

We stayed but a short time after this last conference;
for nothing more was attempted than reading on the
charges and answers, in the same useless manner.

APRIL. I have scarce a memorandum of this fatal
month, in which I was bereft of the most revered of
friends, and, perhaps, the most perfect of women.[1] The
two excellent persons to whom I write this will be the
first to subscribe to her worth: nearest to it themselves,
they are least conscious of the resemblance—but how
consolatory to me is it to see and to feel it!

I believe I heard the last words she uttered; I cannot
learn that she spoke after my reluctant departure. She
finished with that cheerful resignation, that lively hope,
which always broke forth when this last—awful—but, to
her, most happy change seemed approaching.

Poor Miss P—— and myself were kneeling by her
bedside. She had just given me her soft hand; without
power to see either of us, she felt and knew us. Oh,
never can I cease to cherish the remembrance of the
sweet, benign, *holy* voice with which she pronounced a
blessing upon us both! We kissed her; and, with a smile
all beaming—I thought it so—of heaven, she seemed then
to have taken leave of all earthly solicitudes. Yet then,
even then, short as was her time on earth, the same soft
human sensibility filled her for poor human objects. She
would not bid us farewell—would not tell us she should
speak with us no more—she only said, as she turned
gently away from us: 'And now *I'll go to sleep*!' But, oh,
in what a voice she said it! I felt what the sleep would
be; so did poor Miss P——.

She bid me—how often did she bid me—not to grieve
to lose her! Yet she said, in my absence, she knew I
must, and sweetly regretted how much I must miss her.

[1] Mrs Delany.

I teach myself to think of her felicity; and I never dwell upon that without faithfully feeling I would not desire her return. But, in every other channel in which my thoughts and feelings turn, I miss her with so sad a void! She was all that I dearly loved that remained within my reach; she was become the bosom repository of all the livelong day's transactions, reflections, feelings, and wishes. Her own exalted mind was all expanded when we met. I do not think she concealed from me the most secret thought of her heart; and while every word that fell from her spoke wisdom, piety, and instruction, her manner had an endearment, her spirits a native gaiety, and her smile, to those she loved, a tenderness so animated——Oh, why do I go on entering into these details? Believe me, my dear friends, now—now that the bitterness of the first blow is over, and that the dreary chasm becomes more familiar to me, I *think* and *trust* I would not call her back.

What a message she left me! Did you hear it? She told Mrs Astley to say to me, when she was gone, how much comfort I must always feel in reflecting how much her latter days had been soothed by me.[1]

But how sad was every re-entrance into Windsor!—bereft, irremediably, of all that could soften to me the total separation it causes between me and all my original and dearest friends.

It was, however, a very fortunate circumstance that for the two or three first comings Mr Fairly [2] happened to be of the King's party. Inured himself to sorrow, his soul was easily turned to pity; and far from censuring the affliction, or contemning the misfortunes, which were inferior to his own, his kind and feeling nature led him to no sensation but of compassion, which softened every feature of his face, and took place of all the hard traces of personal suffering which most severely had marked it.

---

[1] Mrs Astley (Mrs Delany's maid) later thought fit to deny this.
[2] 'Mr Fairly' was Colonel Digby. He was 'inured to sorrow' by the death of his wife.

The tone of his voice was all in sympathy with this gentleness; and there was not an attention in his power to show me that he did not exert with the most benevolent and even flattering alacrity; interesting himself about my diet, my health, my exercise; proposing walks to me, and exhorting me to take them, and even intimating he should see that I did, were not his time all occupied by royal attendance.

MAY. I must mention a laughable enough circumstance. Her Majesty inquired of me if I had ever met with Lady Hawke? Oh, yes, I cried, and Lady Say and Sele too. 'She had just desired permission to send me a novel of her own writing,' answered her Majesty.

'I hope,' cried I, ''tis not the *Mausoleum of Julia*!' [1]

But yes, it proved no less! and this she has now published and sends about. You must remember Lady Say and Sele's quotation from it. Her Majesty was so gracious as to lend it me, for I had some curiosity to read it. It is all of a piece—all love, love, love, unmixed and unadulterated with any more worldly materials.

On one of the Egham race days the Queen sent Miss Planta and me on the course, in one of the royal coaches, with Lord Templeton and Mr Charles Fairly for our beaux. Lady Templeton was then at the Lodge, and I had the honour of two or three conferences with her during her stay.

On the course we were espied by Mr Crutchley, who instantly devoted himself to my service for the morning—taking care of our places, naming jockeys, horses, bets, plates, etc. etc., and talking between times of Streatham and all the Streathamites, of Mrs Piozzi, all the Miss Thrales, Mr Seward, Mr Selwyn, Harry Cotton, Sophy Streatfeild, Miss Owen, Sir Philip Clerke, Mr Murphy, etc. etc.

We were both, I believe, very glad of this discourse. He pointed to me where his house stood, in a fine park, within sight of the race-ground, and proposed introducing me to his sister, who was his housekeeper, and asking me

[1] See p. 73.

if, through her invitation, I would come to Sunning Hill Park. I assured him I lived so completely in a monastery that I could make no new acquaintance. He then said he expected soon Susan and Sophy Thrale on a visit to his sister, and he presumed I would not refuse coming to see them. I truly answered I should rejoice to do it if in my power, but that most probably I must content myself with meeting them on the Terrace. He promised to bring them there with his sister, though he had given up that walk these five years.

It will give me indeed great pleasure to see them again.

JUNE. Another Streatham acquaintance, Mr Murphy, made much effort at this time for a meeting, through Charles, with whom he is lately become very intimate. So much passed about the matter, that I was almost compelled to agree that he should know when I was able to go to St Martin's Street. He is an extremely agreeable and entertaining man, but of so light a character in morals that I do not wish his separate acquaintance; though, when I met with him at Streatham, as associates of the same friends, I could not but receive much advantage from his notice—amusement rather I should perhaps say, though there was enough for the higher word, *improvement*, in all but a serious way. However, where, in that serious way, I have no good opinion, I wish not to cultivate, but rather to avoid, even characters in other respects the most captivating. It is not from fearing contagion—they would none of them attack me: it is simply from an internal drawback to all pleasure in their society, while I am considering their talents *at best* as useless.

Mrs Schwellenberg came to Windsor with us after the Birthday, for the rest of the summer.

Mr Turbulent took a formal leave of me at the same time, as his wife now came to settle at Windsor, and he ceased to belong to our party. He only comes to the Princesses at stated hours, and then returns to his own

home. He gave me many serious thanks for the time
passed with me, spoke in flourishing terms of its contrast
to former times, and vowed no compensation could
ever be made him for the hours he had thrown away
by compulsion on 'The Oyster.' His behaviour altogether was very well—here and there a little eccentric,
but, in the main, merely good-humoured and high-
spirited.

I am persuaded there is no manner of truth in the
report relative to Mr Fairly and Miss Fuzilier,[1] for he led
me into a long conversation with him one evening when
the party was large, and all were otherwise engaged, upon
subjects of this nature, in the course of which he asked
me if I thought any second attachment could either be as
strong or as happy as a first.

I was extremely surprised by the question, and quite
unprepared how to answer it, as I knew not with what
feelings or intentions I might war by any unwary opinions.
I did little, therefore, but evade and listen, though he kept
up the discourse in a very animated manner, till the party all
broke up.

Had I spoken without any consideration but what was
general and genuine, I should have told him that my idea
was simply this, that where a first blessing was withdrawn
by Providence, not lost by misconduct, it seemed to me
most consonant to reason, nature, and mortal life, to
accept what would come second, in this as in all other
deprivations. Is it not a species of submission to the
Divine will to make ourselves as happy as we can in what
is left us to obtain, where bereft of what we had sought?
My own conflict for content in a life totally adverse to
my own inclinations, is all built on this principle, and
when it succeeds, to this owes its success.

I presumed not, however, to talk in this way to Mr

[1] 'Miss Fuzilier' was Miss Gunning. According to Fanny, she
was 'pretty, learned, and accomplished,' but had not 'heart enough
to satisfy Mr Fairly.' The reader will learn with regret that Mr F.
married her.

Fairly, for I am wholly ignorant in what manner or to what degree his first attachment may have riveted his affections; but by the whole of what passed it seemed to me very evident that he was not merely entirely without any engagement, but entirely at this time without any plan or scheme of forming any; and probably he never may.

PART THREE

OCTOBER, 1788–JULY, 1791

PART THREE

October, 1788–July, 1791 [1]

FRIDAY, OCTOBER 17TH. Our return to Windsor is postponed till to-morrow. The King is not well: he has not been quite well some time, yet nothing I hope alarming, though there is an uncertainty as to his complaint not very satisfactory; so precious, too, is his health. [2]

SATURDAY, OCTOBER 18TH. The King was this morning better. My Royal mistress told me Sir George Baker [3] was to settle whether we returned to Windsor to-day or to-morrow.

SUNDAY, OCTOBER 19TH. The Windsor journey is again postponed, and the King is but very indifferent. Heaven preserve him! there is something unspeakably alarming in his smallest indisposition.

I am very much with the Queen, who, I see, is very uneasy, but she talks not of it. She reads Hunter's 'Discourses,' [4] and talks chiefly upon them.

We are to stay here some time longer, and so unprepared were we for more than a day or two, that our distresses are prodigious, even for clothes to wear; and as to books, there are not three amongst us; and for company, only Mr de Luc and Miss Planta; and so, in mere desperation for employment, I have just begun a tragedy. We are now in so spiritless a situation that my mind would bend to nothing less sad, even in fiction. But I am very glad something of this kind has occurred to me; it may while

[1] Vol. iv, p. 270–vol. v, p. 226.
[2] As long ago as 1765 the King had had an illness which showed traces of insanity, but this fact was carefully concealed.
[3] Physician in ordinary to the King.
[4] Dr Henry Hunter (1741–1802), a Scotch divine. The work in question is a course of lectures entitled *Sacred Biography*.

away the tediousness of this unsettled, unoccupied, unpleasant period.

MONDAY, OCTOBER 20TH. The King was taken very ill in the night, and we have all been cruelly frightened; but it went off, and, thank heaven! he is now better.

I had all my morning devoted to receiving inquiring visits. Lady Effingham, Sir George Howard, Lady Frances Howard, all came from Stoke to obtain news of the King; his least illness spreads in a moment. Lady Frances Douglas came also. She is wife of the Archibald Douglas who caused the famous Hamilton trial in the House of Peers, for his claim to the Douglas name. She is fat, and clunch, and heavy, and ugly; otherwise, they say, agreeable enough.

TUESDAY, OCT. 21ST. The good and excellent King is again better, and we expect to remove to Windsor in a day or two.

THURSDAY, OCT. 23RD. The King continues to mend, thank God! Saturday we hope to return to Windsor. Had not this composition fit seized me, societyless, and bookless, and viewless as I am, I know not how I could have whiled away my being; but my tragedy goes on, and fills up all vacancies.

SATURDAY, OCT. 25TH. Yesterday was so much the same, I have not marked it; not so to-day. The King was so much better that our Windsor journey at length took place, with permission of Sir George Baker, the only physician his Majesty will admit.

I had a sort of conference with his Majesty, or rather I was the object to whom he spoke, with a manner so uncommon, that a high fever alone could account for it; a rapidity, a hoarseness of voice, a volubility, an earnestness—a vehemence, rather—it startled me inexpressibly; yet with a graciousness exceeding even all I ever met with before—it was almost kindness!

Heaven—heaven preserve him! The Queen grows more and more uneasy. She alarms me sometimes for herself, at other times she has a sedateness that wonders me still more.

I commune now with my dearest friends every morning, upon the affairs of the preceding day. Alas! how little can I commune with them in any other way!

SUNDAY, OCT. 26TH. The King was prevailed upon not to go to chapel this morning. I met him in the passage from the Queen's room; he stopped me, and conversed upon his health near half an hour, still with that extreme quickness of speech and manner that belongs to fever; and he hardly sleeps, he tells me, one minute all night; indeed, if he recovers not his rest, a most delirious fever seems to threaten him. He is all agitation, all emotion, yet all benevolence and goodness, even to a degree that makes it touching to hear him speak. He assures everybody of his health; he seems only fearful to give uneasiness to others, yet certainly he is better than last night. Nobody speaks of his illness, nor what they think of it.

The Bishop of Peterborough is made Dean of Durham, and I am glad, for old acquaintance' sake.

OCT. 29TH. The dear and good King again gains ground, and the Queen becomes easier.

To-day Miss Planta told me she heard Mr Fairly was confined at Sir R—— F——'s, and therefore she would now lay any wager he was to marry Miss F——.

SATURDAY, NOV. 1ST. Our King does not advance in amendment; he grows so weak that he walks like a gouty man, yet has such spirits that he has talked away his voice, and is so hoarse it is painful to hear him. The Queen is evidently in great uneasiness. God send him better!

She read to me to-day a lecture of Hunter's I have named that work, I believe: it is a biographical commentary of the Old Testament, extremely well done with respect to orthodox principles and moral inferences, and in pleasing and alluring language; a book worth much commendation, but of no genius; there is nothing original in the statement of facts, or in the reflections they produce. I would not recommend it to Mr Locke, but I read it without murmuring at loss of time myself, and I would heartily recommend it to my Fredy, for her own little congregation, as it is all good, and *there* would not be all obvious.

During the reading this morning, twice, at pathetic passages, my poor Queen shed tears. 'How nervous I am!' she cried; 'I am quite a fool! Don't you think so?'

'No, ma'am!' was all I dared answer.

She revived, however, finished the lecture, and went upstairs and played upon the Princess Augusta's harpsichord.

The King was hunting. Her anxiety for his return was greater than ever. The moment he arrived he sent a page to desire to have coffee and take his bark[1] in the Queen's dressing-room. She said she would pour it out herself, and sent to inquire how he drank it.

The King is very sensible of the great change there is in himself, and of her disturbance at it. It seems, but heaven avert it! a threat of a total breaking up of the constitution. This, too, seems his own idea. I was present at his first seeing Lady Effingham on his return to Windsor this last time. 'My dear Effy,' he cried, 'you see me, all at once, an old man.'

I was so much affected by this exclamation, that I wished to run out of the room. Yet I could not but recover when Lady Effingham, in her well-meaning but literal way, composedly answered: 'We must all grow old, sir; I am sure I do.'

He then produced a walking-stick which he had just ordered. 'He could not,' he said, 'get on without it; his strength seemed diminishing hourly.'

He took the bark, he said; 'But the *Queen*,' he cried, 'is my physician, and no man need have a better; she is my *Friend*, and no man *can* have a better.'

How the Queen commanded herself I cannot conceive; but there was something so touching in this speech, from his hoarse voice and altered countenance, that it overset me very much.

Nor can I ever forget him in what passed this night.

[1] Peruvian bark, or cinchona.

When I came to the Queen's dressing-room he was still with her. He constantly conducts her to it before he retires to his own. He was begging her not to speak to him when he got to his room, that he might fall asleep, as he felt great want of that refreshment. He repeated this desire, I believe, at least a hundred times, though, far enough from needing it, the poor Queen never uttered one syllable! He then applied to me, saying he was really very well, except in that one particular, that he could not sleep.

The kindness and benevolence of his manner all this time was most penetrating: he seemed to have no anxiety but to set the Queen at rest and no wish but to quiet and give pleasure to all around him. To me he never yet spoke with such excess of benignity: he appeared even solicitous to satisfy me that he should do well, and to spare all alarm; but there was a hurry in his manner and voice that indicated sleep to be indeed wanted. Nor could I, all night, forbear foreseeing 'He sleeps now, or to-morrow he will be surely delirious!'

SUNDAY, NOVEMBER 2ND. The King was better, and prevailed upon to give up going to the early prayers. The Queen and the Princesses went. After they were gone, and I was following towards my room, the King called after me, and he kept me in discourse a full half-hour; nearly all the time they were away.

It was all to the same purport; that he was well, but wanted more rest; yet he said he had slept the last night like a child. But his manner, still, was so touchingly kind, so softly gracious, that it doubled my concern to see him so far from well.

MONDAY, NOVEMBER 3RD. The birthday of the Princess Sophia. I had received the beautiful birthday offering yesterday from my Fredy, and this morning I carried it to the Lower Lodge, where it was very prettily welcomed.

However, we are all here in a most uneasy state. The King is better and worse so frequently, and changes so, daily, backwards and forwards, that everything is to be apprehended, if his nerves are not some way quieted. I dreadfully fear he is on the eve of some severe fever. The Queen is almost overpowered with some secret terror. I am affected beyond all expression in her presence, to see what struggles she makes to support serenity. To-day she gave up the conflict when I was alone with her, and burst into a violent fit of tears. It was very, very terrible to see! How did I wish her a Susan or a Fredy! To unburthen her loaded mind would be to relieve it from all but inevitable affliction. Oh, may heaven in its mercy never, never drive me to that solitary anguish more! —I have tried what it would do; I speak from bitter recollection of past melancholy experience.

Sometimes she walks up and down the room without uttering a word, but shaking her head frequently, and in evident distress and irresolution. She is often closeted with Miss Goldsworthy, of whom, I believe, she makes inquiry how her brother has found the King, from time to time.

The Princes both came to Kew, in several visits to the King. The Duke of York has also been here, and his fond father could hardly bear the pleasure of thinking him anxious for his health. 'So good,' he says, 'is Frederick!'

To-night, indeed, at tea-time, I felt a great shock, in hearing from General Budé, that Dr Heberden had been called in. It is true more assistance seemed much wanting, yet the King's rooted aversion to physicians makes any new-comer tremendous. They said, too, it was merely for counsel, not that his Majesty was worse.

Tuesday, November 4th. Passed much the same as the days preceding it; the Queen, in deep distress, the King in a state almost incomprehensible, and all the house uneasy and alarmed. The drawing-room was again put off, and a steady residence seemed fixed at Windsor.

Wednesday, November 5th. Oh, dreadful day! My very heart has so sickened in looking over my memorandums, that I was forced to go to other employments. I will not, however, omit its narration. 'Tis too interesting ever to escape my own memory, and my dear friends have never yet had the beginning of the thread which led to all the terrible scenes of which they have variously heard.

I found my poor Royal mistress, in the morning, sad and sadder still; something horrible seemed impending, and I saw her whole resource was in religion. We had talked lately much upon solemn subjects, and she appeared already preparing herself to be resigned for whatever might happen.

I was still wholly unsuspicious of the greatness of the cause she had for dread. Illness, a breaking up of the constitution, the payment of sudden infirmity and premature old age for the waste of unguarded health and strength —these seemed to me the threats awaiting her; and great and grievous enough, yet how short of the fact!

I had given up my walks some days; I was too uneasy to quit the house while the Queen remained at home, and she now never left it. Even Lady Effingham, the last two days, could not obtain admission; she could only hear from a page how the Royal Family went on.

At noon the King went out in his chaise, with the Princess Royal, for an airing. I looked from my window to see him; he was all smiling benignity, but gave so many orders to the postilions, and got in and out of the carriage twice, with such agitation, that again my fear of a great fever hanging over him grew more and more powerful. Alas! how little did I imagine I should see him no more for so long—so black a period!

When I went to my poor Queen, still worse and worse I found her spirits. She had been greatly offended by some anecdote in a newspaper—the *Morning Herald*— relative to the King's indisposition. She declared the printer should be called to account. She bid me burn the paper, and ruminated upon who could be employed to represent to the editor that he must answer at his peril any further such treasonable paragraphs. I named to her Mr Fairly, her own servant, and one so peculiarly fitted for any office requiring honour and discretion. 'Is he here then?' she cried. No, I answered, but he was expected in a few days.

I saw her concurrence with this proposal. The Princess Royal soon returned. She came in cheerfully, and gave, in German, a history of the airing, and one that seemed comforting.

Soon after, suddenly arrived the Prince of Wales. He came into the room. He had just quitted Brighthelmstone. Something passing within seemed to render this meeting awfully distant on both sides. She asked if he should not return to Brighthelmstone? He answered yes, the next day. He desired to speak with her; they retired together.

I had but just reached my own room, deeply musing on the state of things, when a chaise stopped at the rails; and I saw Mr Fairly and his son Charles alight, and enter the house. He walked lamely, and seemed not yet recovered from his late attack.

Only Miss Planta dined with me. We were both nearly silent; I was shocked at I scarcely knew what, and she seemed to know too much for speech. She stayed with me till six o'clock, but nothing passed, beyond general solicitude that the King might get better.

Meanwhile, a stillness the most uncommon reigned over the whole house. Nobody stirred; not a voice was heard; not a motion. I could do nothing but watch, without knowing for what: there seemed a strangeness in the house most extraordinary.

At seven o'clock Columb came to tell me that the music was all forbid, and the musicians ordered away!

This was the last step to be expected, so fond as his Majesty is of his Concert, and I thought it might have rather soothed him: I could not understand the prohibition; all seemed stranger and stranger.

Later came Colonel Goldsworthy: his countenance all gloom, and his voice scarce articulating no or yes. General Grenville was gone to town.

Very late came General Budé. He asked me if I had
seen Mr Fairly; and last of all, at length he also entered.

How grave he looked! how shut up in himself! A
silent bow was his only salutation; how changed I thought
it—and how fearful a meeting, so long expected as a solace!

Colonel Goldsworthy was called away; I heard his
voice whispering some time in the passage, but he did not
return.

Various small speeches now dropped, by which I found
the house was all in disturbance, and the King in some
strange way worse, and the Queen taken ill!

At length, General Budé said he would go and see if
any one was in the music room. Mr Fairly said he
thought he had better not accompany him, for as he had
not yet been seen, his appearance might excite fresh
emotion. The General agreed and went.

We were now alone. But I could not speak: neither
did Mr Fairly; I worked—I had begun a hassock for my
Fredy. A long and serious pause made me almost turn
sick with anxious wonder and fear, and an inward trembling totally disabled me from asking the actual situation
of things; if I had not had my work, to employ my eyes
and hands, I must have left the room to quiet myself.

I fancy he penetrated into all this, though, at first, he
had concluded me informed of everything; but he now,
finding me silent, began an inquiry whether I was yet
acquainted how bad all was become, and how ill the
King?

I really had no utterance for very alarm, but my look
was probably sufficient; he kindly saved me any questions,
and related to me the whole of the mysterious horror!

Oh, my dear friends, what a history! The King, at
dinner, had broken forth into positive delirium, which
long had been menacing all who saw him most closely;
and the Queen was so overpowered as to fall into violent
hysterics. All the Princesses were in misery, and the
Prince of Wales had burst into tears. No one knew what
was to follow—no one could conjecture the event.

He stayed with me all the evening, during which we heard no voice, no sound! all was deadly still! At ten o'clock I said: 'I must go to my own room, to be in waiting.' He determined upon remaining downstairs, in the Equerries' department, there to wait some intelligence. We parted in mutual expectation of dreadful tidings. In separating, he took my hand, and earnestly recommended me to keep myself stout and firm.

If this beginning of the night was affecting, what did it not grow afterwards! Two long hours I waited—alone, in silence, in ignorance, in dread! I thought they would never be over; at twelve o'clock I seemed to have spent two whole days in waiting. I then opened my door, to listen, in the passage, if anything seemed stirring. Not a sound could I hear. My apartment seemed wholly separated from life and motion. Whoever was in the house kept at the other end, and not even a servant crossed the stairs or passage by my rooms.

I would fain have crept on myself, anywhere in the world, for some inquiry, or to see but a face, and hear a voice, but I did not dare risk losing a sudden summons.

I re-entered my room, and there passed another endless hour, in conjectures too horrible to relate.

A little after one, I heard a step—my door opened—and a page said I must come to the Queen.

I could hardly get along—hardly force myself into the room; dizzy I felt, almost to falling. But the first shock passed, I became more collected. Useful, indeed, proved the previous lesson of the evening: it had stilled, if not mortified my mind, which had else, in a scene such as this, been all tumult and emotion.

My poor Royal mistress! never can I forget her countenance—pale, ghastly pale she looked; she was seated to be undressed, and attended by Lady Elizabeth Waldegrave and Miss Goldsworthy; her whole frame was disordered, yet she was still and quiet.

These two ladies assisted me to undress her, or rather I assisted them, for they were firmer, from being longer present; my shaking hands and blinded eyes could scarce be of any use.

I gave her some camphor julep, which had been ordered her by Sir George Baker. 'How cold I am!' she cried, and put her hand on mine; marble it felt! and went to my heart's core!

The King, at the instance of Sir George Baker, had consented to sleep in the next apartment, as the Queen was ill. For himself, he would listen to nothing. Accordingly, a bed was put up for him, by his own order, in the Queen's second dressing-room, immediately adjoining to the bedroom. He would not be further removed. Miss Goldsworthy was to sit up with her, by the King's direction.

I would fain have remained in the little dressing-room, on the other side the bedroom, but she would not permit it. She ordered Sandys, her wardrobe woman, in the place of Mrs Thielky, to sit up there. Lady Elizabeth also pressed to stay; but we were desired to go to our own rooms.

How reluctantly did I come away! how hardly to myself leave her! Yet I went to bed, determined to preserve my strength to the utmost of my ability, for the service of my unhappy mistress. I could not, however, sleep. I do not suppose an eye was closed in the house all night.

THURSDAY, NOVEMBER 6TH. I rose at six, dressed in haste by candle light, and unable to wait for my summons in a suspense so awful, I stole along the passage in the dark, a thick fog intercepting all faint light, to see if I could meet with Sandys, or any one, to tell me how the night had passed.

When I came to the little dressing-room, I stopped, irresolute what to do. I heard men's voices; I was seized with the most cruel alarm at such a sound in her Majesty's dressing-room. I waited some time, and then the door opened, and I saw Colonel Goldsworthy and Mr Batterscomb. I was relieved from my first apprehension, yet shocked enough to see them there at this early hour. They had both sat up there all night, as well as Sandys. Every page, both of the King and Queen, had also sat up, dispersed in the passages and ante-rooms; and oh, what horror in every face I met!

I waited here, amongst them, till Sandys was ordered by the Queen to carry her a pair of gloves. I could not resist the opportunity to venture myself before her. I glided into the room, but stopped at the door: she was in bed, sitting up; Miss Goldsworthy was on a stool by her side!

I feared approaching without permission, yet could not prevail with myself to retreat. She was looking down, and did not see me. Miss Goldsworthy, turning round, said: ''Tis Miss Burney, ma'am.'

She leaned her head forward, and in a most soft manner said: 'Miss Burney, how are you?'

Deeply affected, I hastened up to her, but, in trying to speak burst into an irresistible torrent of tears.

My dearest friends, I do it at this moment again, and can hardly write for them; yet I wish you to know all this piercing history right.

She looked like death—colourless and wan; but nature is infectious; the tears gushed from her own eyes, and a perfect agony of weeping ensued, which once begun, she could not stop; she did not, indeed, try; for when it subsided, and she wiped her eyes, she said: 'I thank you, Miss Burney—you have made me cry; it is a great relief to me—I had not been able to cry before, all this night long.'

Oh, what a scene followed! what a scene was related! The King, in the middle of the night, had insisted upon seeing if his Queen was not removed from the house; and he had come into her room, with a candle in his hand, opened the bed-curtains, and satisfied himself she was there, and Miss Goldsworthy by her side. This observance of his directions had much soothed him; but he stayed a full half hour, and the depth of terror during that time no words can paint. The fear of such another entrance was now so strongly upon the nerves of the poor Queen that she could hardly support herself.

The King—the Royal sufferer—was still in the next room, attended by Sir George Baker and Dr Heberden, and his pages, with Colonel Goldsworthy occasionally, and as he called for him. He kept talking unceasingly; his voice was so lost in hoarseness and weakness, it was rendered almost inarticulate; but its tone was still all benevolence—all kindness—all touching graciousness.

It was thought advisable the Queen should not rise, lest the King should be offended that she did not go to him; at present he was content, because he conceived her to be nursing for her illness.

But what a situation for her! She would not let me leave her now; she made me remain in the room, and ordered me to sit down. I was too trembling to refuse. Lady Elizabeth soon joined us. We all three stayed with her; she frequently bid me listen, to hear what the King was saying or doing. I did, and carried the best accounts I could manage, without deviating from truth, except by some omissions. Nothing could be so afflicting as this task; even now, it brings fresh to my ear his poor exhausted voice. 'I am nervous,' he cried; 'I am not ill, but I am nervous: if you would know what is the matter with me, I am nervous. But I love you both very well; if you would tell me the truth: I love Dr Heberden best, for he has not told me a lie: Sir George has told me a lie— a white lie, he says, but I hate a white lie! If you will tell me a lie, let it be a black lie!'

This was what he kept saying almost constantly, mixed in with other matter, but always returning, and in a voice that truly will never cease vibrating in my recollection.

Dr Warren was sent for express, in the middle of the night, at the desire of Sir George Baker, because he had been taken ill himself, and felt unequal to the whole toil.

The Princesses sent to ask leave to come to their mother. She burst into tears, and declared she could neither see them, nor pray, while in this dreadful situation, expecting every moment to be broken in upon, and quite uncertain in what manner, yet determined not to desert her apartment, except by express direction from the physicians. Who could tell to what height the delirium might rise? There was no constraint, no power; all feared the worst, yet none dared take any measures for security. . . .

Miss Goldsworthy had now a bed put up in the Queen's new bedroom. She had by no means health to go on sitting up, and it had been the poor King's own direction that she should remain with the Queen. It was settled that Mrs Sandys and Miss Macenton should alternately sit up in the dressing-room.

The Queen would not permit me to take that office, though most gladly I would have taken any that would have kept me about her. But she does not think my strength sufficient. She allowed me, however, to stay with her till she was in bed, which I had never done till now; I never, indeed, had even seen her in her bedroom till the day before. She has always had the kindness and delicacy to dismiss me from her dressing-room as soon as I have assisted her with her night clothes; the wardrobe woman then was summoned, and I regularly made my curtsy. It was a satisfaction to me, however, now to leave her the last, and to come to her the first.

Her present dressing-room is also her dining-room, her drawing-room, her sitting room; she has nothing else but her bedroom!

I left her with my fervent prayers for better times, and saw her nearer to composure than I had believed possible in such a calamity. She called to her aid her religion, and without it what, indeed, must have become of her? It was near two in the morning when I quitted her.

In passing through the dressing-room to come away, I found Miss Goldsworthy in some distress how to execute a commission of the Queen's: it was to her brother, who was to sit up in a room adjoining to the King's; and she was undressed, and knew not how to go to him, as the Princes were to and fro everywhere. I offered to call him to her; she thankfully accepted the proposal. I cared not, just then, whom I encountered, so I could make myself of any use.

When I gently opened the door of the apartment to which I was directed, I found it was quite filled with gentlemen and attendants, arranged round it on chairs and sofas, in dead silence.

It was a dreadful start with which I retreated; for anything more alarming and shocking could not be conceived: the poor King within another door, unconscious any one was near him, and thus watched, by dread necessity, at such an hour of the night! I pronounced the words: 'Colonel Goldsworthy,' however, before I drew back, though I could not distinguish one gentleman from another, except the two Princes, by their stars.

FRIDAY, NOVEMBER 7TH. I was now arrived at a sort of settled regularity of life more melancholy than can possibly be described. I rose at six, dressed, and hastened to the Queen's apartments, uncalled, and there waited in silence and in the dark till I heard her move or speak with Miss Goldsworthy, and then presented myself to the bedside of the unhappy Queen. She sent Miss Goldsworthy early every morning, to make inquiry what sort of night his Majesty had passed; and in the middle of the night she commonly also sent for news by the wardrobe woman, or Miss Macenton, whichever sat up.

She dismissed Miss Goldsworthy, on my arrival, to dress herself. Lady Elizabeth Waldegrave accommodated her with her own room for that purpose.

I had then a long conference with this most patient sufferer; and equal forbearance and quietness during a period of suspensive unhappiness never have I seen, never could I have imagined.

At noon now I never saw her, which I greatly regretted; but she kept on her dressing-gown all day, and the Princes were continually about the passages, so that no one unsummoned dared approach the Queen's apartments.

While I was yet with my poor Royal sufferer this

morning the Prince of Wales came hastily into the room. He apologized for his intrusion, and then gave a very energetic history of the preceding night. It had been indeed most affectingly dreadful! The King had risen in the middle of the night, and would take no denial to walking into the next room. There he saw the large congress I have mentioned: amazed and in consternation, he demanded what they did there? Much followed that I have heard since, particularly the warmest eloge on his dear son Frederick,[1] his favourite, his friend. 'Yes,' he cried, 'Frederick is my friend!'—and this son was then present amongst the rest, but not seen!

Sir George Baker was there, and was privately exhorted by the gentlemen to lead the King back to his room; but he had not courage: he attempted only to speak, and the King penned him in a corner, told him he was a mere old woman—that he wondered he had ever followed his advice, for he knew nothing of his complaint, which was only nervous!

The Prince of Wales, by signs and whispers, would have urged others to have drawn him away, but no one dared approach him, and he remained there a considerable time, 'Nor do I know when he would have been got back,' continued the Prince, 'if at last Mr Fairly had not undertaken him. I am extremely obliged to Mr Fairly indeed. He came boldly up to him, and took him by the arm, and begged him to go to bed, and then drew him along, and said he must go. Then he said he would not, and cried: "Who are you?" "I am Mr Fairly, sir," he answered, "and your Majesty has been very good to me often, and now I am going to be very good to you, for you must come to bed, sir: it is necessary to your life." And then he was so surprised that he let himself be drawn along just like a child; and so they got him to bed. I believe else he would have stayed all night!'

From this time, as the poor King grew worse, general hope seemed universally to abate; and the Prince of Wales

[1] The Duke of York.

now took the government of the house into his own hands. Nothing was done but by his orders, and he was applied to in every difficulty. The Queen interfered not in anything; she lived entirely in her two new rooms, and spent the whole day in patient sorrow and retirement with her daughters.

WEDNESDAY, NOVEMBER 12TH. To-day a little brightened upon us; some change appeared in the loved Royal sufferer, and though it was not actually for the better in itself, yet any change was pronounced to be salutary, as, for some days past, there had been a monotonous continuation of the same bad symptoms, that had doubly depressed us all.

My spirits rose immediately; indeed, I thank God, I never desponded, though many times I stood nearly alone in my hopes.

In the passage, in the morning, I encountered Colonel Gwynn. I had but just time to inform him I yet thought all would do well, ere the Princes appeared. All the Equerries are now here except Major Garth, who is ill; and they have all ample employment in watching and waiting. From time to time they have all interviews; but it is only because the poor King will not be denied seeing them: it is not thought right. But I must enter into nothing of this sort—it is all too closely connected with private domestic concerns for paper.

WEDNESDAY, NOVEMBER 19TH. The account of the dear King this morning was rather better.

Sir Lucas Pepys [1] was now called in, and added to Dr Warren, Dr Heberden, and Sir George Baker. I earnestly wished to see him, and I found my poor Royal mistress was secretly anxious to know his opinion.

The moment we were alone, Sir Lucas opened upon the subject in the most comfortable manner. He assured me there was nothing desponding in the case, and that his Royal patient would certainly recover, though not immediately.

[1] See p. 64, *note*.

THURSDAY, 27TH. This morning and whole day were dreadful! My early account was given me by Mr Charles Hawkins,[1] and with such determined decision of incurability, that I left him quite in horror.

All that I dared, I softened to my poor Queen, who was now harassed to death with state affairs, and impending storms of state dissensions. I would have given the world to have spent the whole day by her side, and poured in what balm of hope I could, since it appeared but too visibly she scarce received a ray from any other.

Universal despondence now pervaded the whole house. Sir Lucas, indeed, sustained his original good opinion, but he was nearly overpowered by standing alone, and was forced to let the stream take its course with but little opposition.

Even poor Mr de Luc was silenced; Miss Planta easily yields to fear; and Mrs Schwellenberg—who thinks it treason to say the King is ever at all indisposed—not being able to say all was quite well, forbade a single word being uttered upon the subject!

The dinners, therefore, became a time of extremest pain—all was ignorance, mystery, and trembling expectation of evil.

FRIDAY, 28TH. How woeful—how bitter a day, in every part, was this!

My early account was from the King's page, Mr Stillingfleet, and the night had been extremely bad.

I dared not sink the truth to my poor Queen, though I mixed in it whatever I could devise of cheer and hope; and she bore it with the most wonderful calmness, and kept me with her a full half-hour after breakfast was called, talking over 'Hunter's Lectures,' and other religious books, with some other more confidential matters.

Dr Addington was now called in: a very old physician, but peculiarly experienced in disorders such as afflicted our poor King, though not professedly a practitioner in them.

---

[1] Surgeon to the Household.

Sir Lucas made me a visit, and informed me of all the medical proceedings; and told me, in confidence, we were to go to Kew to-morrow, though the Queen herself had not yet concurred in the measure; but the physicians joined to desire it, and they were supported by the Princes. The difficulty how to get the King away from his favourite abode was all that rested. If they even attempted force, they had not a doubt but his smallest resistance would call up the whole country to his fancied rescue! Yet how, at such a time, prevail by persuasion?

He moved me even to tears, by telling me that none of their own lives would be safe if the King did not recover, so prodigiously high ran the tide of affection and loyalty. All the physicians received threatening letters daily, to answer for the safety of their monarch with their lives! Sir George Baker had already been stopped in his carriage by the mob, to give an account of the King; and when he said it was a bad one, they had furiously exclaimed: 'The more shame for you!'

After he left me, a Privy Council was held at the Castle, with the Prince of Wales; the Chancellor, Mr Pitt, and all the officers of state were summoned, to sign a permission for the King's removal. The poor Queen gave an audience to the Chancellor—it was necessary to sanctify their proceedings. The Princess Royal and Lady Courtown attended her. It was a tragedy the most dismal!

The Queen's knowledge of the King's aversion to Kew made her consent to this measure with the extremest reluctance; yet it was not to be opposed: it was stated as much the best for him, on account of the garden: as here there is none but what is public to spectators from the terrace, or tops of houses. I believe they were perfectly right, though the removal was so tremendous.

The physicians were summoned to the Privy Council, to give their opinions, upon oath, that this step was necessary.

Inexpressible was the alarm of every one, lest the King, if he recovered, should bear a lasting resentment against the authors and promoters of this journey. To give it, therefore, every possible sanction, it was decreed that he should be seen both by the Chancellor and Mr Pitt.

The Chancellor went into his presence with a tremor such as, before, he had been only accustomed to inspire; and when he came out, he was so extremely affected by the state in which he saw his Royal master and patron that the tears ran down his cheeks, and his feet had difficulty to support him.

Mr Pitt was more composed, but expressed his grief with so much respect and attachment, that it added new weight to the universal admiration with which he is here beheld.[1]

SATURDAY, NOVEMBER 29TH. Shall I ever forget the varied emotions of this dreadful day!

I rose with the heaviest of hearts, and found my poor Royal mistress in the deepest dejection: she told me now of our intended expedition to Kew. Lady Elizabeth hastened away to dress, and I was alone with her for some time.

Her mind, she said, quite misgave her about Kew: the King's dislike was terrible to think of, and she could not foresee in what it might end. She would have resisted the measure herself, but that she had determined not to have upon her own mind any opposition to the opinion of the physicians.

The account of the night was still more and more discouraging: it was related to me by one of the pages, Mr Brawan; and though a little I softened or omitted particulars, I yet most sorrowfully conveyed it to the Queen.

Terrible was the morning!—uninterruptedly terrible! all spent in hasty packing up, preparing for we knew not

[1] Pitt's views on the subject of the King's illness and the Regency which it seemed likely to necessitate, found more favour at Court than those of Fox and Burke, who maintained that the Prince of Wales had the same rights as he would have had in the event of the King's death.

what, nor for how long, nor with what circumstances, nor scarcely with what view! We seemed preparing for captivity, without having committed any offence; and for banishment, without the least conjecture when we might be recalled from it.

The poor Queen was to get off in private: the plan settled between the Princes and the physicians was that her Majesty and the Princesses should go away quietly, and then that the King should be told that they were gone, which was the sole method they could devise to prevail with him to follow. He was then to be allured by a promise of seeing them at Kew; and, as they knew he would doubt their assertion, he was to go through the rooms and examine the house himself.

I believe it was about ten o'clock when her Majesty departed: drowned in tears, she glided along the passage, and got softly into her carriage, with two weeping Princesses, and Lady Courtown, who was to be her Lady-in-waiting during this dreadful residence.

Then followed the third Princess, with Lady Charlotte Finch. They went off without any state or parade, and a more melancholy scene cannot be imagined. There was not a dry eye in the house. The footmen, the housemaids, the porter, the sentinels—all cried even bitterly as they looked on.

The three younger Princesses were to wait till the event was known. Lady Elizabeth Waldegrave and Miss Goldsworthy had their Royal Highnesses in charge.

It was settled the King was to be attended by three of his gentlemen, in the carriage, and to be followed by the physicians, and preceded by his pages. But all were to depart on his arrival at Kew, except his own Equerry-in-waiting.

It was not very pleasant to these gentlemen to attend his Majesty at such a time, and upon such a plan, so adverse to his inclination, without any power of assistance: however, they would rather have died than refused, and it was certain the King would no other way travel but by compulsion, which no human being dared even mention.

Miss Planta and I were to go as soon as the packages could be ready, with some of the Queen's things. Mrs Schwellenberg was to remain behind, for one day, in order to make arrangements about the jewels.

In what confusion was the house! Princes, Equerries, Physicians, Pages—all conferring, whispering, plotting, and caballing, how to induce the King to set off!

At length we found an opportunity to glide through the passage to the coach; Miss Planta and myself, with her maid and Goter.[1] But the heaviness of heart with which we began this journey, and the dreadful prognostics of the duration of misery to which it led us—who can tell?

We were almost wholly silent all the way.

When we arrived at Kew, we found the suspense with which the King was awaited truly terrible. Her Majesty had determined to return to Windsor at night, if he came not. We were all to forbear unpacking in the meanwhile.

The house was all now regulated by express order of the Prince of Wales, who rode over first, and arranged all the apartments, and writ, with chalk, the names of the destined inhabitants on each door.

My own room he had given to Lady Courtown; and for me, he had fixed on one immediately adjoining to Mrs Schwellenberg's; a very pleasant room, and looking into the garden, but by everybody avoided, because the partition is so thin of the next apartment, that not a word can be spoken in either that is not heard in both.

While I was surveying this new habitation, the Princess Royal came into it, and, with a cheered countenance, told me that the Queen had just received intelligence that the King was rather better, and would come directly, and therefore I was commissioned to issue orders to Columb to keep out of sight, and to see that none of the servants were in the way when the King passed.

[1] Fanny's maid.

Eagerly, and enlivened, downstairs I hastened, to speak
to Columb. I flew to the parlour, to ring the bell for
him, as in my new room I had no bell for either man or
maid; but judge my surprise, when, upon opening the door,
and almost rushing in, I perceived a Windsor uniform!
I was retreating with equal haste, when the figure before
me started, in so theatric an attitude of astonishment, that
it forced me to look again. The arms were then wide
opened, while the figure fell back, in tragic paces.

Much at a loss, and unable to distinguish the face, I was
again retiring, when the figure advanced, but in such
measured steps as might have suited a march upon a stage.

I now suspected it was Mr Fairly; yet so unlikely I
thought it, I could not believe it without speech. 'Surely,'
I cried, 'it is not—it is not——' I stopped, afraid to make
a mistake.

With arms yet more sublimed, he only advanced, in
silence and dumb heroics. I now ventured to look more
steadily at the face, and then to exclaim: 'Is it Mr Fairly?'

The laugh now betrayed him: he could hardly believe
I had really not known him. I explained that my very little
expectation of seeing him at Kew had assisted my near-
sightedness to perplex me.

But I was glad to see him so sportive, which I found was
owing to the good spirits of bringing good news; he had
mounted his horse as soon as he had heard the King had
consented to the journey, and he had galloped to Kew,
to acquaint her Majesty with the welcome tidings.

The poor King had been prevailed upon to quit Windsor
with the utmost difficulty: he was accompanied by General
Harcourt, his aide-de-camp, and Colonels Goldsworthy
and Wellbred—no one else! He had passed all the rest
with apparent composure, to come to his carriage, for they
lined the passage, eager to see him once more! and almost
all Windsor was collected round the rails, etc., to witness
the mournful spectacle of his departure, which left them
in the deepest despondence, with scarce a ray of hope
ever to see him again.

The bribery, however, which brought, was denied
him! He was by no means to see the Queen!

When I went to her that night she was all graciousness,
and kept me till very late. I had not seen her alone so
long, except for a few minutes in the morning, that I had
a thousand things I wished to say to her. You may be
sure they were all, as far as they went, consolatory.

Princess Augusta had a small tent bed put up in the
Queen's bed-chamber: I called her Royal Highness when
the Queen dismissed me. She undressed in an adjoining
apartment.

I must now tell you how the house is disposed. The
whole of the ground floor that looks towards the garden
is appropriated to the King, though he is not indulged
within its range. In the side wing is a room for the
physicians, destined to their consultations; adjoining to
that is the Equerry's dining-room. Mrs Schwellenberg's
parlours, which are in the front of the house, one for
dining, the other for coffee and tea, are still allowed us.
The other front rooms below are for the pages to dine, and
the rest of the more detached buildings are for the servants
of various sorts.

All the rooms immediately over those which are actually
occupied by the King are locked up; her Majesty relin-
quishes them, that he may never be tantalized by footsteps overhead. She has retained only the bedroom, the
drawing-room, which joins to it, and the gallery, in which
she eats. Beyond this gallery are the apartments of the
three elder Princesses, in one of which rooms Miss Planta
sleeps. There is nothing more on the first floor.

On the second a very large room for Mrs Schwellenberg,
and a very pleasant one for myself, are over the Queen's
rooms. Farther on are three bedrooms, one for the
surgeon or apothecary in waiting, the next for the Equerry,
and the third, lately mine, for the Queen's lady—all
written thus with chalk by the Prince.

The inhabitants at present are Mr Charles Hawkins,
Colonel Goldsworthy, and Lady Courtown.

Then follows a very long dark passage, with little bedrooms on each side for the maids, viz. the two Misses Macenton, wardrobe women to the Princesses, their own maid, Lady Courtown's, Miss Planta's, Mrs Schwellenberg's two maids, Mrs Lovel and Arline, and Mr Chamberlayne, one of the pages. These look like so many little cells of a convent.

At the end of this passage there is a larger room, formerly appropriated to Mr de Luc, but now chalked 'The Physicians.'

One Physician, one Equerry, and one Surgeon or Apothecary, are regularly to sleep in the house.

This is the general arrangement.

The Prince very properly has also ordered that one of his Majesty's Grooms of the Bedchamber should be in constant waiting; he is to reside in the Prince's house, over the way, which is also fitting up for some others. This gentleman is to receive all inquiries about the King's health. The same regulation had taken place at Windsor, in the Castle, where the gentlemen waited in turn. Though, as the Physicians send their account to St James's, this is now become an almost useless ceremony, for everybody goes thither to read the bulletin.

The three young Princesses are to be in a house belonging to the King on Kew Green, commonly called Princess Elizabeth's, as her Royal Highness has long inhabited it in her illness. There will lodge Miss Goldsworthy, Mlle Montmoulin, and Miss Gomme. Lady Charlotte Finch is to be at the Prince of Wales's.

I could not sleep all night—I thought I heard the poor King. He was under the same range of apartments, though far distant, but his indignant disappointment haunted me. The Queen, too, was very angry at having promises made in her name which could not be kept. What a day altogether was this!

SUNDAY, NOVEMBER 30TH. Here, in all its dread colours, dark as its darkest prognostics, began the Kew campaign. I went to my poor Queen at seven o'clock: the Princess

Augusta arose and went away to dress, and I received her Majesy's commands to go down for inquiries. She had herself passed a wretched night, and already lamented leaving Windsor.

I waited very long in the cold dark passages below, before I could find any one of whom to ask intelligence. The parlours were without fires, and washing. I gave directions afterwards to have a fire in one of them by seven o'clock every morning.

At length I procured the speech of one of the pages, and heard that the night had been the most violently bad of any yet passed!—and no wonder!

I hardly knew how to creep upstairs, frozen both within and without, to tell such news; but it was not received as if unexpected, and I omitted whatever was not essential to be known.

Afterwards arrived Mrs Schwellenberg, so oppressed between her spasms and the house's horrors, that the oppression she inflicted ought perhaps to be pardoned. It was, however, difficult enough to bear! Harshness, tyranny, dissension, and even insult, seemed personified. I cut short details upon this subject—they would but make you sick.

KEW, MONDAY, DECEMBER 1ST. Mournful was the opening of the month! My account of the night from Gezewell, the page, was very alarming, and my poor Royal mistress began to sink more than I had ever yet seen. No wonder; the length of the malady so uncertain, the steps which seemed now requisite so shocking: for new advice, and such as suited only disorders that physicians in general relinquish, was now proposed, and compliance or refusal were almost equally tremendous.

TUESDAY, DECEMBER 2ND. This morning I was blessed with a better account of my poor King, which I received from Mr Dundas, than I have had for six days past. With what eager joy did I fly with it to my Queen! and I obtained her leave for carrying it on to the Princesses, who other-

wise might not have known it till the general breakfast, at
nine o'clock.

WEDNESDAY, DECEMBER 3RD. Worse again to-day was
the poor King: the little fair gleam, how soon did it pass
away!

I was beginning to grow ill myself, from the added
fatigue of disturbance in the night, unavoidably occasioned
by my neighbourhood to an invalid who summoned her
maids at all hours; and my Royal mistress, who knew
this to have been the case with my predecessor, Mrs
Haggerdorn, spoke to me about it herself; and, fearing
I might suffer essentially, she graciously issued orders
for a removal to take place.

In consequence of this there were obliged to be two
or three other changes. The physician in waiting was
removed, and his room made over to me; while that
which I had first occupied was deemed impracticable for
a sleeping-room to any one.

My new apartment is at the end of the long dark passage
I have mentioned, with bedroom cells on each side of it.
It is a very comfortable room, carpeted all over, with one
window looking to the front of the house and two into a
courtyard. It is the most distant from the Queen, but in
all other respects is very desirable. I have made it as neat
as I could, and its furniture is far better than that of my
own natural apartment, which my Fredy thought so
succinct!

I must now relate briefly a new piece of cruelty. I
happened to mention to *la première présidente* my waiting
for a page to bring the morning accounts.

'And where do you wait?'

'In the parlour, ma'am.'

'In my parlour? Oh, ver well! I will see to that!'

'There is no other place, ma'am, but the cold passages,
which, at that time in the morning, are commonly wet as
well as dark.'

'Oh, ver well! When everybody goes to my room I
might keep an inn—what you call hotel.'

All good humour now again vanished; and this morning, when I made my seven o'clock inquiry, I found the parlour doors both locked!

I returned so shivering to my Queen, that she demanded the cause, which I simply related; foreseeing inevitable destruction from continuing to run such a hazard. She instantly protested there should be a new arrangement.

THURSDAY, DECEMBER 4TH. No opportunity offered yesterday for my better security, and therefore I was again exposed this morning to the cold dark damp of the miserable passage. The account was tolerable, but a threat of sore throat accelerated the reform.

It was now settled that the dining-parlour should be made over to the officers of state who came upon business to the house, and who hitherto had waited in the hall; and the room which was next to Mrs Schwellenberg's, and which had first been mine, was now made our *salle à manger*.

By this means, the parlour being taken away for other people, and by command relinquished, I obtained once again the freedom of entering it, to gather my account for her Majesty. But the excess of ill-will awakened by my obtaining this little privilege, which was actually necessary to my very life, was so great, that more of personal offence and harshness could not have been shown to the most guilty of culprits.

One of the pages acquainted me his Majesty was not worse, and the night had been as usual. As usual, too, was my day; sad and solitary all the morning—not solitary, but worse during dinner and coffee.

Mr Fairly told me this evening that Dr Willis, a physician of Lincoln, of peculiar skill and practice in intellectual maladies, had been sent for by express.[1] The poor Queen had most painfully concurred in a measure which seemed

---

[1] Dr Francis Willis. He had taken Holy Orders, but subsequently devoted himself to the treatment of lunatics. His methods differed from those of the other doctors in the important articles of common sense and kindness.

to fix the nature of the King's attack in the face of the world; but the necessity and strong advice had prevailed over her repugnance.

MONDAY, DECEMBER 15TH. This whole day was passed in great internal agitation throughout the house, as the great and important business of the Regency was to be discussed to-morrow in Parliament. All is now too painful and intricate for writing a word. I begin to confine my memorandums almost wholly to my own personal proceedings.

TUESDAY, DECEMBER 16TH. Whatsoever might pass in the House on this momentous subject, it sat so late that no news could arrive. Sweeter and better news, however, was immediately at hand than any the whole senate could transmit; the account from the pages was truly cheering. With what joy did I hasten with it to the Queen, who immediately ordered me to be its welcome messenger to the three Princesses.

After breakfast I had a long conference in the parlour with Sir Lucas Pepys, who justly gloried in the advancement of his original prediction; but there had been much dissension amongst the physicians concerning the bulletin to go to St James's, no two agreeing in the degree of *better* to be announced to the world.

Dr Willis came in while we were conversing, but instantly retreated, to leave us undisturbed. He looks a very fine old man. I wished to be introduced to him.

WEDNESDAY, DECEMBER 17TH. My account this morning was most afflictive once more; it was given by Mr Hawkins, and was cruelly subversive of all our rising hopes. I carried it to the Queen in trembling; but she bore it most mildly. What resignation is hers!

Miss Planta tells me the Queen has given her commands that no one shall bring her any account of the night but me. She has been teased, I fancy, with erroneous relations, or unnecessarily wounded with cruel particulars. Be this as it may, I can hardly, when my narration is bad, get out the words to tell it; and I come upon the worst parts, if of a nature to be indispensably told, with as much difficulty as if I had been author of them. But her patience in hearing and bearing them is truly edifying.

Mr Hawkins to-day, after a recital of some particulars extremely shocking, said: 'But you need not tell that to the Queen.'

'I could not, sir,' was my true, though dry answer. Yet I never omit anything essential to be known. Detail is rarely of that character.

MONDAY, DECEMBER 22ND. With what joy did I carry, this morning, an exceeding good account of the King to my Royal mistress! It was trebly welcome, as much might depend upon it in the resolutions of the House concerning the Regency, which was of to-day's discussion.

Mr Fairly took leave, for a week, he said, wishing me my health, while I expressed my own wishes for his good journey.

But, in looking forward to a friendship the most permanent, I saw the eligibility of rendering it the most open. I therefore went back to Mrs Schwellenberg; and the moment I received a reproach for staying so long, I calmly answered: 'Mr Fairly had made me a visit, to take leave before he went into the country.'

Amazement was perhaps never more indignant. Mr Fairly to take leave of me! while not once he even called upon her! This offence swallowed up all other comments upon the communication.

The King went on, now better, now worse, in a most fearful manner; but Sir Lucas Pepys never lost sight of hope, and the management of Dr Willis and his two sons was most wonderfully acute and successful. Yet so much were they perplexed and tormented by the interruptions given to their plans and methods, that they were frequently almost tempted to resign the undertaking from anger and confusion.

KEW PALACE, THURSDAY, JANUARY 1ST, 1789. The year

opened with an account the most promising of our beloved
King. I saw Dr Willis, and he told me the night had been
very tranquil; and he sent for his son, Dr John Willis, to
give me a history of the morning. Dr John's narration
was in many parts very affecting: the dear and excellent
King had been praying for his own restoration! Both
the doctors told me that such strong symptoms of true
piety had scarce ever been discernible through so dreadful
a malady.

SATURDAY, 3RD. I have the great pleasure, now, of a
change in my morning's historiographers: I have made
acquaintance with Dr Willis and his son, and they have
desired me to summon one of them constantly for my
information.

I am extremely struck with both these physicians. Dr
Willis is a man of ten thousand; open, honest, dauntless,
light - hearted, innocent, and high - minded: I see him
impressed with the most animated reverence and affection
for his royal patient; but it is wholly for his character—
not a whit for his rank.

Dr John, his eldest son, is extremely handsome, and
inherits, in a milder degree, all the qualities of his father;
but, living more in the general world, and having his
fame and fortune still to settle, he has not yet acquired the
same courage, nor is he, by nature, quite so sanguine in
his opinions. The manners of both are extremely pleasing,
and they both proceed completely their own way, not
merely unacquainted with court etiquette, but wholly,
and most artlessly, unambitious to form any such acquaintance.

SUNDAY, 25TH. The two last days were wholly eventless;
but this morning I had so fair an account of our beloved
monarch, that I drew up a bulletin myself; not, indeed,
for St James's, but where it was certain of a flourishing
reception. Mr Smelt was going to town, and could not
call. He sent me a note of inquiry, which arrived while
I was still listening to Dr John Willis, in our late little
parlour, and hearing every interesting particular of the

night and early morning. I answered Mr Smelt's note, thus:

'Kew Palace, Sunday morning, January 25, 1789.

'His Majesty has passed a very good night, and is perfectly composed and collected this morning.

'(Signed)   JOHN WILLIS.
'(Witnessed) FRANCES BURNEY.'

The young doctor gave me his name very willingly; and with this bulletin Mr Smelt went and gladdened the hearts of every good subject of his acquaintance in town.

These Willises are most incomparable people. They take a pleasure, that brightens every particle of their countenances, in communicating what is good, and they soften all that is bad with the most sedulous kindness.

In running this morning, at seven o'clock, along my dark passage, I nearly fell over a pail, carelessly left in the way by a housemaid, and broke my shin very painfully. Unable, therefore, to walk, yet so strongly enjoined to take the air, I could not escape accompanying Mrs Schwellenberg in a little tour round Brentford, which, that we might see a little of the world, was the postilion's drive. But the ill humour of my companion during this rural ride was of so affronting a cast, that I wished myself a thousand times hopping with my broken shin over the worst ploughed land in England, rather than so to be seated in a royal vehicle.

I have not mentioned a singular present which has been sent me from Germany this month; it is an almanac, in German, containing for its recreative part an abridgment of *Cecilia*, in that language; and every month opens with a cut from some part of her history. It is sent me by M. Henouvre, a gentleman in some office in the King's establishment at Hanover. I wish I could read it—but I have only written it!

MONDAY, FEBRUARY 2ND. What an adventure had I

this morning! one that has occasioned me the severest personal terror I ever experienced in my life.

Sir Lucas Pepys persisting that exercise and air were absolutely necessary to save me from illness, I have continued my walks, varying my gardens from Richmond to Kew, according to the accounts I received of the movements of the King. For this I had her Majesty's permission, on the representation of Sir Lucas.

This morning, when I received my intelligence of the King from Dr John Willis, I begged to know where I might walk in safety? 'In Kew Gardens,' he said, 'as the King would be in Richmond.'

'Should any unfortunate circumstance,' I cried, 'at any time, occasion my being seen by his Majesty, do not mention my name, but let me run off without call or notice.'

This he promised. Everybody, indeed, is ordered to keep out of sight.

Taking, therefore, the time I had most at command, I strolled into the gardens. I had proceeded, in my quick way, nearly half the round, when I suddenly perceived, through some trees, two or three figures. Relying on the instructions of Dr John, I concluded them to be workmen and gardeners; yet tried to look sharp, and in so doing, as they were less shaded, I thought I saw the person of his Majesty!

Alarmed past all possible expression, I waited not to know more, but turning back, ran off with all my might. But what was my terror to hear myself pursued!—to hear the voice of the King himself loudly and hoarsely calling after me: 'Miss Burney! Miss Burney!'

I protest I was ready to die. I knew not in what state he might be at the time; I only knew the orders to keep out of his way were universal; that the Queen would highly disapprove of any unauthorized meeting, and that the very action of my running away might deeply, in his present irritable state, offend him. Nevertheless, on I ran, too terrified to stop, and in search of some short passage, for

the garden is full of little labyrinths, by which I might
escape.

The steps still pursued me, and still the poor hoarse and
altered voice rang in my ears—more and more footsteps
resounded frightfully behind me—the attendants all
running, to catch their eager master, and the voices of the
two Doctor Willises loudly exhorting him not to heat
himself so unmercifully.

Heavens, how I ran! I do not think I should have felt
the hot lava from Vesuvius—at least not the hot cinders—
had I so run during its eruption. My feet were not sensible that they even touched the ground.

Soon after, I heard other voices, shriller, though less
nervous, call out: 'Stop! stop! stop!'

I could by no means consent; I knew not what was
purposed, but I recollected fully my agreement with Dr
John that very morning, that I should decamp if surprised,
and not be named.

My own fears and repugnance, also, after a flight and
disobedience like this, were doubled in the thought of
not escaping: I knew not to what I might be exposed,
should the malady be then high, and take the turn of resentment. Still, therefore, on I flew; and such was my speed,
so almost incredible to relate or recollect, that I fairly
believe no one of the whole party could have overtaken
me, if these words, from one of the attendants, had not
reached me: 'Doctor Willis begs you to stop!'

'I cannot! I cannot!' I answered, still flying on, when
he called out: 'You must, ma'am; it hurts the King to
run.'

Then, indeed, I stopped—in a state of fear really amounting to agony. I turned round, I saw the two Doctors
had got the King between them, and three attendants of
Dr Willis's were hovering about. They all slackened
their pace, as they saw me stand still; but such was the
excess of my alarm, that I was wholly insensible to the
effects of a race which, at any other time, would have
required an hour's recruit.

As they approached, some little presence of mind happily came to my command: it occurred to me that, to appease the wrath of my flight, I must now show some confidence: I therefore faced them as undauntedly as I was able, only charging the nearest of the attendants to stand by my side.

When they were within a few yards of me, the King called out: 'Why did you run away?'

Shocked at a question impossible to answer, yet a little assured by the mild tone of his voice, I instantly forced myself forward, to meet him, though the internal sensation, which satisfied me this was a step the most proper to appease his suspicions and displeasure, was so violently combated by the tremor of my nerves, that I fairly think I may reckon it the greatest effort of personal courage I have ever made.

The effort answered: I looked up, and met all his wonted benignity of countenance, though something still of wildness in his eyes. Think, however, of my surprise, to feel him put both his hands round my two shoulders, and then kiss my cheek!

I wonder I did not really sink, so exquisite was my affright when I saw him spread out his arms! Involuntarily, I concluded he meant to crush me: but the Willises, who have never seen him till this fatal illness, not knowing how very extraordinary an action this was from him, simply smiled and looked pleased, supposing, perhaps, it was his customary salutation!

He now spoke in such terms of his pleasure in seeing me, that I soon lost the whole of my terror; astonishment to find him so nearly well, and gratification to see him so pleased, removed every uneasy feeling, and the joy that succeeded, in my conviction of his recovery, made me ready to throw myself at his feet to express it.

What a conversation followed! When he saw me fearless, he grew more and more alive, and made me walk close by his side, away from the attendants, and even the Willises themselves, who, to indulge him, retreated. I own myself not completely composed, but alarm I could entertain no more.

Everything that came uppermost in his mind he mentioned; he seemed to have just such remains of his flightiness as heated his imagination without deranging his reason, and robbed him of all control over his speech, though nearly in his perfect state of mind as to his opinions.

What did he not say! He opened his whole heart to me—expounded all his sentiments, and acquainted me with all his intentions.

He assured me he was quite well—as well as he had ever been in his life; and then inquired how I did, and how I went on? and whether I was more comfortable?

If these questions, in their implication, surprised me, imagine how that surprise must increase when he proceeded to explain them! He asked after the coadjutrix, laughing, and saying: 'Never mind her—don't be oppressed—I am your friend! don't let her cast you down! I know you have a hard time of it—but don't mind her!'

Almost thunderstruck with astonishment, I merely curtsied to his kind 'I am your friend,' and said nothing.

Then presently he added: 'Stick to your father—stick to your own family—let them be your objects.'

How readily I assented!

Again he repeated all I have just written, nearly in the same words, but ended it more seriously: he suddenly stopped, and held me to stop too, and putting his hand on his breast, in the most solemn manner, he gravely and slowly said: 'I will protect you!—I promise you that—and therefore depend upon me!'

I thanked him; and the Willises, thinking him rather too elevated, came to propose my walking on. 'No, no, no!' he cried, a hundred times in a breath; and their good humour prevailed, and they let him again walk on with his new companion.

He then gave me a history of his pages, animating almost into a rage, as he related his subjects of displeasure with them, particularly with Mr Ernst, who, he told me, had been brought up by himself. I hope his ideas upon these men are the result of the mistakes of his malady.

Then he asked me some questions that very greatly distressed me, relating to information given him in his illness, from various motives, but which he suspected to be false, and which I knew he had reason to suspect: yet was it most dangerous to set anything right, as I was not aware what might be the views of their having been stated wrong. I was as discreet as I knew how to be, and I hope I did no mischief; but this was the worst part of the dialogue.

He next talked to me a great deal of my dear father, and made a thousand inquiries concerning his *History of Music*. This brought him to his favourite theme, Handel; and he told me innumerable anecdotes of him, and particularly that celebrated tale of Handel's saying of himself, when a boy: 'While that boy lives, my music will never want a protector.' And this, he said, I might relate to my father.

Then he ran over most of his oratorios, attempting to sing the subjects of several airs and choruses, but so dreadfully hoarse that the sound was terrible.

Dr Willis, quite alarmed at this exertion, feared he would do himself harm, and again proposed a separation. 'No! no! no!' he exclaimed, 'not yet; I have something I must just mention first.'

Dr Willis, delighted to comply, even when uneasy at compliance, again gave way.

The good King then greatly affected me. He began upon my revered old friend, Mrs Delany; and he spoke of her with such warmth—such kindness! 'She was my friend!' he cried, 'and I loved her as a friend! I have made a memorandum when I lost her—I will show it you.'

He pulled out a pocket-book, and rummaged some time, but to no purpose.

The tears stood in his eyes—he wiped them, and Dr Willis again became very anxious. 'Come, sir,' he cried, 'now do you come in and let the lady go on her walk—

come, now, you have talked a long while—so we'll go in—if your Majesty pleases.'

'No, no!' he cried, 'I want to ask her a few questions; I have lived so long out of the world, I know nothing!'

He then told me he was very much dissatisfied with several of his state officers, and meant to form an entire new establishment. He took a paper out of his pocket-book, and showed me his new list.

This was the wildest thing that passed; and Dr John Willis now seriously urged our separating; but he would not consent; he had only three more words to say, he declared, and again he conquered.

He now spoke of my father, with still more kindness, and told me he ought to have had the post of Master of the Band,[1] and not that little poor musician Parsons, who was not fit for it: 'But Lord Salisbury,' he cried, 'used your father very ill in that business, and so he did me! However, I have dashed out his name, and I shall put your father's in—as soon as I get loose again!'

This again—how affecting was this!

'And what,' cried he, 'has your father got, at last? Nothing but that poor thing at Chelsea? Oh, fie! fie! fie! But never mind! I will take care of him! I will do it myself!'

Then presently he added: 'As to Lord Salisbury, he is out already, as this memorandum will show you, and so are many more. I shall be much better served; and when once I get away, I shall rule with a rod of iron!'

This was very unlike himself, and startled the two good doctors, who could not bear to cross him, and were exulting at my seeing his great amendment, but yet grew quite uneasy at his earnestness and volubility.

Finding we now must part, he stopped to take leave, and renewed again his charges about the coadjutrix. 'Never mind her!' he cried, 'depend upon me! I will be your friend as long as I live!—I here pledge myself to be your

---

[1] The post became vacant in 1786, and Dr Burney made an unsuccessful attempt to obtain it. He had to content himself with the place of organist at Chelsea Hospital.

friend!' And then he saluted me again just as at the meeting, and suffered me to go on.

What a scene! How variously was I affected by it! But upon the whole, how inexpressibly thankful to see him so nearly himself—so little removed from recovery!

I went very soon after to the Queen, to whom I was most eager to avow the meeting, and how little I could help it. Her astonishment, and her earnestness to hear every particular, were very great. I told her almost all. Some few things relating to the distressing questions I could not repeat; nor many things said of Mrs Schwellenberg, which would much, and very needlessly, have hurt her.

FEBRUARY 17TH. The times are now most interesting and critical. Dr Willis confided to me this morning that to-day the King is to see the Chancellor. How important will be the result of his appearance! The whole national fate depends upon it!

WEDNESDAY, 18TH. I had this morning the highest gratification, the purest feeling of delight, I have been regaled with for many months: I saw, from the road, the King and Queen, accompanied by Dr Willis, walking in Richmond Gardens, near the farm, arm in arm! It was a pleasure that quite melted me, after a separation so bitter, scenes so distressful—to witness such harmony and security! Heaven bless and preserve them! was all I could incessantly say while I kept in their sight.

I was in the carriage with Mrs Schwellenberg at the time. They saw us also, as I heard afterwards from the Queen.

The King I have seen again—in the Queen's dressing-room. On opening the door, there he stood! He smiled at my start, and saying he had waited on purpose to see me, added: 'I am quite well now—I was nearly so when I saw you before—but I could overtake you better now!' and then he left the room.

I was quite melted with joy and thankfulness at this so entire restoration.

End of February, 1789. *Dieu merci!*

JUNE. The journey to Weymouth was one scene of festivity and rejoicing. The people were everywhere collected, and everywhere delighted. We passed through Salisbury, where a magnificent arch was erected, of festoons of flowers, for the King's carriage to pass under, and mottoed with 'The King restored,' and 'Long live the King,' in three divisions. The green bowmen [1] accompanied the train thus far; and the clothiers and manufacturers here met it, dressed out in white loose frocks, flowers, and ribbons, with sticks or caps emblematically decorated from their several manufactories. And the acclamations with which the King was received amongst them—it was a rapture past description.

At Blandford there was nearly the same ceremony.

At every gentleman's seat which we passed, the owners and their families stood at the gate, and their guests or neighbours were in carriages all round.

At Dorchester the crowd seemed still increased. The city has so antique an air, I longed to investigate its old buildings. The houses have the most ancient appearance of any that are inhabited that I have happened to see: and inhabited they were indeed! every window sash was removed, for face above face to peep out, and every old balcony and all the leads of the houses seemed turned into booths for fairs. It seems, also, the most populous town I have seen; I judge not by the concourse of the young and middle-aged—those we saw everywhere alike, as they may gather together from all quarters—but from the amazing quantity of indigenous residers; old women and young children. There seemed families of ten or twelve of the latter in every house; and the old women were so numerous, that they gave the whole scene the air of a rural masquerade.

Girls, with chaplets, beautiful young creatures, strewed the entrance of various villages with flowers.

Gloucester House, which we now inhabit, at Weymouth,

[1] Dressed as foresters, they had attended the King at Lyndhurst.

is situated in front of the sea, and the sands of the bay before it are perfectly smooth and soft.

The whole town, and Melcomb Regis, and half the county of Dorset, seemed assembled to welcome their Majesties.

I have here a very good parlour, but dull, from its aspect. Nothing but the sea at Weymouth affords any life or spirit. My bedroom is in the attics. Nothing like living at a court for exaltation. Yet even with this gratification, which extends to Miss Planta, the house will only hold the females of the party. The two adjoining houses are added, for the gentlemen, and the pages, and some other of the suite, cooks, etc.—but the footmen are obliged to lodge still farther off.

The bay is very beautiful, after its kind; a peninsula shuts out Portland Island and the broad ocean.

The King, and Queen, and Princesses, and their suite, walked out in the evening; an immense crowd attended them—sailors, bargemen, mechanics, countrymen; and all united in so vociferous a volley of 'God save the King,' that the noise was stunning.

The preparations of festive loyalty were universal. Not a child could we meet that had not a bandeau round its head, cap, or hat, of 'God save the King'; all the bargemen wore it in cockades; and even the bathing-women had it in large coarse girdles round their waists. It is printed in golden letters upon most of the bathing-machines, and in various scrolls and devices it adorns every shop and almost every house in the two towns.

Gloucester House, Weymouth.

WEDNESDAY, JULY 8TH. We are settled here comfortably enough. Miss Planta and I breakfast as well as dine together alone; the gentlemen have a breakfast parlour in the adjoining house, and we meet only at tea, and seldom then. They have all acquaintance here, in this Gloucester

Row, and stroll from the terrace or the sands, to visit them during the tea vacation time.

I like this very much: I see them just enough to keep up sociability, without any necessary constraint; for I attend the tea-table only at my own hour, and they come or not, according to chance or their convenience.

The King bathes, and with great success; a machine follows the Royal one into the sea, filled with fiddlers, who play *God save the King*, as his Majesty takes his plunge!

I am delighted with the soft air and soft footing upon the sands, and stroll up and down them morning, noon, and night. As they are close before the house, I can get to and from them in a moment.

Her Majesty has graciously hired a little maid between Miss Planta and me, who comes for the day. We have no accommodation for her sleeping here; but it is an unspeakable relief to our personal fatigues.

Miss Burney to Dr Burney

Gloucester House, Weymouth, July 13, 1789.

My dearest Padre's kind letter was most truly welcome to me. When I am so distant, the term of absence or of silence seems always doubly long to me.

The bay here is most beautiful; the sea never rough, generally calm and gentle, and the sands perfectly smooth and pleasant. I have not yet bathed, for I have a cold in my head, which I caught at Lyndhurst, and which makes me fear beginning; but I have hopes to be well enough to-morrow, and thenceforward to ail nothing more. It is my intention to cast away all superfluous complaints into the main ocean, which I think quite sufficiently capacious to hold them; and really my little frame will find enough to carry and manage without them. . . .

His Majesty is in delightful health, and much improved

spirits. All agree he never looked better. The loyalty of all this place is excessive; they have dressed out every street with labels of 'God save the King'; all the shops have it over the doors; all the children wear it in their caps—all the labourers in their hats, and all the sailors *in their voices*; for they never approach the house without shouting it aloud—nor see the King, or his shadow, without beginning to huzza, and going on to three cheers.

The bathing machines make it their motto over all their windows; and those bathers that belong to the royal dippers wear it in bandeaux on their bonnets, to go into the sea; and have it again, in large letters, round their waists, to encounter the waves. Flannel dresses, tucked up, and no shoes nor stockings, with bandeaux and girdles, have a most singular appearance; and when first I surveyed these loyal nymphs, it was with some difficulty I kept my features in order.

Nor is this all. Think but of the surprise of his Majesty when, the first time of his bathing, he had no sooner popped his royal head under water than a band of music, concealed in a neighbouring machine, struck up 'God save great George our King.'

One thing, however, was a little unlucky: when the Mayor and burgesses came with the address, they requested leave to kiss hands. This was graciously accorded; but, the Mayor advancing in a common way, *to take the Queen's hand*, as he might that of any lady mayoress, Colonel Gwynn, who stood by, whispered: 'You must kneel, sir!' He found, however, that he took no notice of this hint, but kissed the Queen's hand erect. As he passed him, in his way back, the Colonel said: 'You should have knelt, sir!'

'Sir,' answered the poor Mayor, 'I cannot.'

'Everybody does, sir.'

'Sir—I have a wooden leg!'

Poor man! 'Twas such a surprise! And such an excuse as no one could dispute.

But the absurdity of the matter followed—all the rest

did the same; taking the same privilege, by the example, without the same or any cause!

We have just got Mrs Piozzi's book here.[1]   My Royal mistress is reading, and will then lend it me.   Have you read it?

There is almost no general company here, as the proper season does not begin till autumn; but the party attendant on the King and Queen is large, and the principal people of the county—Lord Digby, Admiral Digby, Mr Pitt Damer, Lord Milton, Mr Rolle, etc. etc.—all are coming to and fro continually.   Our home party is just the same as it began.

A thousand thanks for your home news.

I am, most dear sir,

Affectionately and dutifully, your

F. B.

JULY 15TH. Mrs Gwynn is arrived, and means to spend the Royal season here.   She lodges at the hotel just by, and we have met several times.   She is very soft and pleasing, and still as beautiful as an angel.   We have had two or three long tête-à-têtes, and talked over, with great pleasure, anecdotes of our former mutual acquaintances —Dr Johnson, Sir Joshua Reynolds, Mrs Thrale, Baretti, Miss Reynolds, Miss Palmer, and her old admirer, Dr Goldsmith, of whom she relates—as who does not?—a thousand ridiculous traits.

The Queen is reading Mrs Piozzi's *Tour* to me, instead of my reading it to her.   She loves reading aloud, and in this work finds me an able commentator.   How like herself, how characteristic is every line!   Wild, entertaining, flighty, inconsistent, and clever!

THURSDAY, JULY 16TH. Yesterday we all went to the theatre.   The King has taken the centre front box for

[1] *Observations and Reflections made in the course of a Journey through France, Italy, and Germany.*

himself, and family, and attendants.   The side boxes are
too small.   The Queen ordered places for Miss Planta
and me, which are in the front row of a box next but one
to the Royals.   Thus, in our case, our want of rank to
be in their public suite gives us better seats than those
high enough to stand behind them!

'Tis a pretty little theatre, but its entertainment was quite
in the barn style: a mere medley—songs, dances, imitations
—and all very bad.   But Lord Chesterfield, who is here,
and who seems chief director, promises all will be better.

This morning the Royal party went to Dorchester, and I
strolled upon the sands with Mrs Gwynn.   We overtook a
lady, of a very majestic port and demeanour, who solemnly
returned Mrs Gwynn's salutation, and then addressed
herself to me with similar gravity.   I saw a face I knew,
and of very uncommon beauty; but did not immediately
recollect it was Mrs Siddons.

WEDNESDAY, JULY 29TH.   We went to the play, and saw
Mrs Siddons in Rosalind.   She looked beautifully, but too
large for that shepherd's dress; and her gaiety sits not
naturally upon her—it seems more like disguised gravity.
I must own my admiration for her confined to her tragic
powers; and there it is raised so high that I feel mortified,
in a degree, to see her so much fainter attempts and success
in comedy.

SATURDAY, AUGUST 8TH.   To-day we went to Lulworth
Castle; but not with Mrs Gwynn.   Her Majesty ordered
our Royal coach and four, and directed me to take the two
de Lucs.

Lulworth Castle is beautifully situated, with a near and
noble view of the sea.   It has a spacious and very fine
park, and commands a great extent of prospect.   It is the
property of Mr Weld, a Roman Catholic, whose eldest
brother was first husband of Mrs Fitzherbert.   A singular
circumstance, that their Majesties should visit a house in
which, so few years ago, *she* might have received them.[1]

[1] The Prince of Wales had gone through a ceremony of marriage
with Mrs Fitzherbert in 1785.

There is in it a Roman Catholic chapel that is truly elegant—a Pantheon in miniature—and ornamented with immense expense and richness. The altar is all of finest variegated marbles, and precious stones are glittering from every angle. The priests' vestments, which are very superb, and all the sacerdotal array, were shown us as particular favours; and Colonel Goldsworthy comically said he doubted not they had incense and oblations for a week to come, by way of purification for our heretical curiosity.

The castle is built with four turrets. It is not very ancient, and the inside is completely modern, and fitted up with great elegance. It abounds in pictures of priests, saints, monks, and nuns, and is decorated with crosses and Roman Catholic devices without end.

They show one room in which two of our Kings have slept; Charles II and poor James II.

We returned home to dinner, and in the evening went to the play. Mrs Siddons performed Mrs Oakley.[1] What pity thus to throw away her talents! But the Queen dislikes tragedy, and the honour to play before the Royal Family blinds her to the little credit acquired by playing comedy.

WEDNESDAY, AUGUST 12TH. This is the Prince of Wales's birthday; but it has not been kept.

THURSDAY, AUGUST 13TH. We began our western tour. We all went in the same order as we set out from Windsor.

We arrived at Exeter to a very late dinner. We were lodged at the Deanery; and Dr Buller, the dean, desired a conference with me, for we came first, leaving the Royals at Sir George Young's. He was very civil, and in high glee: I had never seen him before; but he told me he introduced himself, by this opportunity, at the express desire of Mrs Chapone [2] and Mrs Castle, who were both his relations, as well as of Dr Warton. I was glad to hear myself yet remembered by them.

---

[1] Mrs Oakly in *The Jealous Wife*, by George Colman the elder (1732–94).

[2] Hester Chapone (1727–1801), author of *Letters on the Improvement of the Mind*.

The crowds, the rejoicings, the hallooing, and singing, and garlanding, and decorating of all the inhabitants of this old city, and of all the country through which we passed, made the journey quite charming—such happy loyalty as beamed from all ranks and descriptions of men came close to the heart in sympathetic joy.

The next morning, Saturday the 15th, we quitted Exeter, in which there had been one constant mob surrounding the Deanery from the moment of our entrance.

We proceeded through a country the most fertile, varied, rural, and delightful in England, till we came to the end of our aim, Saltram. We passed through such beautiful villages, and so animated a concourse of people, that the whole journey proved truly delectable. Arches of flowers were erected for the Royal Family to pass under at almost every town, with various loyal devices, expressive of their satisfaction in this circuit. How happy must have been the King!—how deservedly! The greatest conqueror could never pass through his dominions with fuller acclamations of joy from his devoted subjects than George III experienced, simply from having won their love by the even tenor of an unspotted life, which, at length, has vanquished all the hearts of all his subjects.

THURSDAY, AUGUST 27TH. We quitted Saltram in the same order we had reached it, and returned to Exeter, where we spent the rest of the day.

MONDAY, SEPTEMBER 14TH. We all left Weymouth.

All possible honours were paid the King on his departure; lords, ladies, and sea officers lined the way that he passed, the guns of the *Magnificent* and *Southampton* fired the parting salute, and the ships were under sail.

We all set out as before, but parted on the road. The Royals went to breakfast at Redlinch, the seat of Lord Ilchester, where Mr Fairly was in waiting for them, and thence proceeded to a collation at Sherborne Castle, whither he was to accompany them, and then resign his present attendance, which has been long and troublesome and irksome, I am sure.

Miss Planta and myself proceeded to Longleat, the seat of the Marquis of Bath, late Lord Weymouth, where we were all to dine, sleep, and spend the following day and night.

Longleat was formerly the dwelling of the Earl of Lansdowne, uncle to Mrs Delany; and here, at this seat, that heartless uncle, to promote some political views, sacrificed his incomparable niece, at the age of seventeen, marrying her to an unwieldy, uncultivated country esquire, near sixty years of age, and scarce ever sober—his name Pendarves.

With how sad an awe, in recollecting her submissive unhappiness, did I enter these doors!—and with what indignant hatred did I look at the portrait of the unfeeling Earl, to whom her gentle repugnance, shown by almost incessant tears, was thrown away, as if she, her person, and her existence were nothing in the scale, where the disposition of a few boroughs opposed them! Yet was this the famous Granville—the poet, the fine gentleman, the statesman, the friend and patron of Pope, of whom he wrote:

> What Muse for Granville can refuse to sing?

Mine, I am sure, for one.

We spent all the following day here. I went to the chapel; I felt horror-struck as I looked at the altar; what an offering for ambition! what a sacrifice to tyranny!

The house is very magnificent, and of an immense magnitude. It seems much out of repair, and by no means cheerful or comfortable. Gloomy grandeur seems the proper epithet for the building and its fitting up. It had been designed for a monastery, and, as such, was nearly completed when Henry VIII dissolved those seminaries. It was finished as a dwelling-house in the reign of his son, by one of the Thynnes, who was knighted in a field of battle by the Protector Somerset.

Many things in the house, and many queer old portraits, afforded me matter of speculation, and would have filled

up more time than I had to bestow.   There are portraits
of Jane Shore and Fair Rosamond, which have some
marks of originality, being miserable daubs, yet from
evidently beautiful subjects.   Arabella Stuart is also at full
length, and King Charleses and Jameses in abundance,
with their queens, brethren, and cousins.   There are
galleries in this house of the dimensions of college halls.

The state rooms on the ground floor are very handsome;
but the queer antique little old corners, cells, recesses,
'passages that lead to nothing,' unexpected openings and
abrupt stoppages, with the quaint devices of various old-
fashioned ornaments, amused me the most.

My bedroom was furnished with crimson velvet, bed
included, yet so high, though only the second story, that
it made me giddy to look into the park, and tired to wind
up the flight of stairs.   It was formerly the favourite room,
the housekeeper told me, of Bishop Ken, who put on his
shroud in it before he died.   Had I fancied I had seen his
ghost, I might have screamed my voice away, unheard by
any assistant to lay it; for so far was I from the rest of the
habitable part of the mansion, that not the lungs of Mr
Bruce [1] could have availed me.   'Tis the room, however,
in which the present Bishop of Exeter resides when here,
and he was a favourite of my Mrs Delany; and all that
brought her to my mind without marrying her was soothing
to me.

WEDNESDAY, SEPTEMBER 16TH. We set out, amidst the
acclamations of a multitude, from Longleat for Tottenham
Park, the seat of Lord Aylesbury.   The park is of great
extent and moderate beauty.   The house is very well.

Here are many original portraits also, that offer enough
for speculation.   A 'Bloody Mary,' by Sir Anthony
More, which I saw with much curiosity, and liked better
than I expected.   The beautiful Duchesses of Cleveland
and Portsmouth, I fancy by Kneller; but we had no
cicerone.   A very fine picture of a lady in black, that I
can credit to be Vandyke, but who else can I know not.

[1] The traveller in Abyssinia.

Several portraits by Sir Peter Lely, extremely soft and pleasing, and of subjects uncommonly beautiful; many by Sir Godfrey Kneller, well enough; and many more by Sir Something Thornhill,[1] very thick and heavy.

The good lord of the mansion put up a new bed for the King and Queen that cost him nine hundred pounds.

We drove about the park in garden chairs; but it is too flat for much diversity of prospect.

Two things I heard here with concern—that my godmother, Mrs Greville, was dead; and that poor Sir Joshua Reynolds had lost the sight of one of his eyes.

FRIDAY, SEPTEMBER 18TH. We left Tottenham Court, and returned to Windsor. The Royals hastened to the younger Princesses, and I . . . to Mrs Schwellenberg. I was civilly received, however. But deadly dead sunk my heart as I entered her apartment.

JANUARY, 1790. Mr Fairly was married the 6th. I must wish happiness to smile on that day, and all its anniversaries; it gave a happiness to me unequalled, for it was the birthday of my Susanna!

One evening, about this time, Mr Fisher, now Doctor, drank tea with us at Windsor, and gave me an account of Mr Fairly's marriage that much amazed me. He had been called upon to perform the ceremony. It was by special licence, and at the house of Sir R—— F——

So religious, so strict in all ceremonies, even, of religion, as he always appeared, his marrying out of a church was to me very unexpected. Dr Fisher was himself surprised, when called upon, and said he supposed it must be to please the lady.

Nothing, he owned, could be less formal or solemn than the whole. Lady C., Mrs and Miss S., and her father and brother and sister, were present. They all dined together at the usual hour, and then the ladies, as usual, retired. Some time after, the clerk was sent for, and then, with the gentlemen, joined the ladies, who were in the drawing-room, seated on sofas, just as at any other time.

[1] Sir James Thornhill.

Dr Fisher says he is not sure they were working, but the air of common employment was such, that he rather thinks it, and everything of that sort was spread about, as on any common day—work-boxes, netting-cases, etc. etc.!

Mr Fairly then asked Dr Fisher what they were to do? He answered, he could not tell; for he had never married anybody in a room before.

Upon this, they agreed to move a table to the upper end of the room, the ladies still sitting quietly, and then put on it candles and a prayer-book. Dr Fisher says he hopes it was not a card-table, and rather believes it was only a Pembroke work-table.

The lady and Sir R. then came forward, and Dr Fisher read the service.

So this, methinks, seems the way to make all things easy!

Yet—with so little solemnity—without even a room prepared and empty—to go through a business of such portentous seriousness! 'Tis truly amazing from a man who seemed to delight so much in religious regulations and observances. Dr Fisher himself was dissatisfied, and wondered at his compliance, though he attributed the plan to the lady.

The bride behaved extremely well, he said, and was all smile and complacency. He had never seen her to such advantage, or in such soft looks before; and perfectly serene, though her sister was so much moved as to go into hysterics.

Afterwards, at seven o'clock, the bride and bridegroom set off for a friend's house in Hertfordshire by themselves, attended by servants with white favours. The rest of the party, father, sister, and priest included, went to the play, which happened to be *Benedict*.[1]

MARCH. In one of our Windsor excursions at this time, while I was in her Majesty's dressing-room, with only Mr de Luc present, she suddenly said: 'Prepare

[1] There is a touch of malice in this passage. Fanny was more hurt by 'Mr Fairly's' marriage than she allowed the diary to show.

yourself, Miss Burney, with all your spirits, for to-night you must be reader.'

She then added that she recollected what she had been told by my honoured Mrs Delany, of my reading Shakespeare to her, and was desirous that I should read a play to herself and the Princesses; and she had lately heard from Mrs Schwellenberg, 'nobody could do it better when I would.'

I assured her Majesty it was rather *when I could*, as any reading Mrs Schwellenberg had heard must wholly have been better or worse according to my spirits, as she had justly seemed to suggest.

The moment coffee was over the Princess Elizabeth came for me. I found her Majesty knotting, the Princess Royal drawing, Princess Augusta spinning, and Lady Courtown I believe in the same employment, but I saw none of them perfectly well.

'Come, Miss Burney,' cried the Queen, 'how are your spirits? How is your voice?'

'She says, ma'am,' cried the kind Princess Elizabeth, 'she shall do her best.'

This had been said in attending her Royal Highness back. I could only confirm it, and that *cheerfully*—to hide *fearfully*.

I had not the advantage of choosing my play, nor do I know what would have been my decision had it fallen to my lot. Her Majesty had just begun Colman's works, and *Polly Honeycombe* [1] was to open my campaign.

'I think,' cried the Queen most graciously, 'Miss Burney will read the better for drawing a chair and sitting down.'

'Oh, yes, mamma! I dare say so!' cried Princess Augusta and Princess Elizabeth, both in a moment.

The Queen then told me to draw my chair close to her side. I made no scruples. Heaven knows I needed not the addition of standing! But most glad I felt in being placed thus near, as it saved a constant painful effort of loud reading.

[1] 'A dramatic novel, in one act,' by George Colman the elder.

'Lady Courtown,' cried the Queen, 'you had better draw nearer, for Miss Burney *has the misfortune* of reading rather low at first.'

Nothing could be more amiable than this opening. Accordingly, I did, as I had promised, my best; and, indifferent as that was, it would rather have surprised you, all things considered, that it was not yet worse. But I exerted all the courage I possess, and, having often read to the Queen, I felt how much it behoved me not to let her surmise I had any *greater* awe to surmount.

It is but a vulgar performance; and I was obliged to omit, as well as I could at sight, several circumstances very unpleasant for reading, and ill enough fitted for such hearers.

It went off pretty flat. Nobody is to comment, nobody is to interrupt; and even between one act and another not a moment's pause is expected to be made.

I had been already informed of this etiquette by Mr Turbulent and Miss Planta; nevertheless, it is not only oppressive to the reader, but loses to the hearers so much spirit and satisfaction, that I determined to endeavour, should I again be called upon, to introduce a little break into this tiresome and unnatural profundity of respectful solemnity. My own embarrassment, however, made it agree with me, for the present, uncommonly well.

Lady Courtown never uttered one single word the whole time; yet is she one of the most loquacious of our establishment. But such is the settled etiquette.

The Queen has a taste for conversation, and the Princesses a good-humoured love for it, that doubles the regret of such an annihilation of all nature and all pleasantry. But what will not prejudice and education inculcate? They have been brought up to annex silence to respect and decorum; to talk, therefore, unbid, or to differ from any given opinion, even when called upon, are regarded as high improprieties, if not presumptions.

They none of them do justice to their own minds, while they enforce this subjection upon the minds of others.

I had not experienced it before; for when reading alone with the Queen, or listening to her reading to me, I have always frankly spoken almost whatever has occurred to me. But there I had no other examples before me, and therefore I might inoffensively be guided by myself; and Her Majesty's continuance of the same honour has shown no disapprobation of my proceeding. But here it was not easy to make any decision for myself; to have done what Lady Courtown forbore doing would have been undoubtedly a liberty.

So we all behaved alike; and easily can I now conceive the disappointment and mortification of poor Mr Garrick when he read *Lethe* to a Royal audience. Its tameness must have tamed him, and I doubt not he never acquitted himself so ill.

The next evening I had the same summons; but *The English Merchant*[1] was the play, which did far better. It is an elegant and serious piece, which I read with far greater ease, and into which they all entered with far greater interest.

The Princess Royal was so gracious when the Queen left the room, upon our next coming to town, to pay me very kind compliments upon my own part of the entertainment, though her brother the Duke of Clarence happened to be present. And the two other Princesses were full of the characters of the comedy, and called upon me to say which were my favourites, while they told me their own, at all our subsequent meetings for some time.

FRIDAY, APRIL 23RD. The anniversary of the Thanksgiving Day, a day in which my gratitude was heightened by making my acknowledgments for its blessing with my Susan by my side.

I shall add nothing at present to my Journal but the summary of a conversation I have had with Colonel Manners,[2] who, at our last excursion, was here without any other gentleman.

[1] Also by George Colman the elder.
[2] Colonel Manners was one of the Equerries.

Knowing he likes to be considered as a senator, I thought the best subject for our discussion would be the House of Commons; I therefore made sundry political inquiries, so foreign to my usual mode, that you would not a little have smiled to have heard them.

I had been informed he had once made an attempt to speak, during the Regency business, last winter; I begged to know how the matter stood, and he made a most frank display of its whole circumstances.

'Why, they were speaking away,' he cried, 'upon the Regency, and so—and they were saying the King could not reign, and recover; and Burke was making some of his eloquence, and talking; and, says he, "hurled from his throne"—and so I put out my finger in this manner, as if I was in a great passion, for I felt myself very red, and I was in a monstrous passion I suppose, but I was only going to say "Hear! hear!" but I happened to lean one hand down upon my knee, in this way, just as Mr Pitt does when he wants to speak; and I stooped forward, just as if I was going to rise up and begin; but just then I caught Mr Pitt's eye, looking at me so pitifully; he thought I was going to speak, and he was frightened to death, for he thought—for the thing was, he got up himself, and he said over all I wanted to say; and the thing is, he almost always does; for just as I have something particular to say, Mr Pitt begins, and goes through it all, so that he don't leave anything more to be said about it; and so I suppose, as he looked at me so pitifully, he thought I should say it first, or else that I should get into some scrape, because I was so warm and looking so red.'

Any comment would disgrace this; I will therefore only tell you his opinion, in his own words, of one of our late taxes.

'There's only one tax, ma'am, that ever I voted for against my conscience, for I've always been very particular about that; but that is the *bacheldor's* tax, and that I hold to be very unconstitutional, and I am very sorry I voted for it, because it's very unfair; for how can a man

help being a *bacheldor*, if nobody will have him? and,
besides, it's not any fault to be taxed for, because we did
not make ourselves *bacheldors*, for we were made so by
God, for nobody was born married, and so I think it's
a very unconstitutional tax.'

TUESDAY, MAY 18TH. This morning I again went to the
trial of poor Mr Hastings. Heavens! who can see him
sit there unmoved? not even those who think him guilty
—if they are human.

I took with me Mrs Bogle. She had long since begged a
ticket for her husband, which I could never before procure.
We now went all three. And, indeed, her original speeches
and remarks made a great part of my entertainment.

Mr Hastings and his counsel were this day most vic-
torious, I never saw the prosecutors so dismayed. Yet
both Mr Burke and Mr Fox spoke, and before the conclusion so did Mr Wyndham. They were all in evident
embarrassment. Mr Hastings's counsel finished the day
with a most noble appeal to justice and innocence, protesting that, if his client did not fairly claim the one, by proving
the other, he wished himself that the prosecutors—that the
Lords—that the nation at large—that the hand of God—
might fall heavy upon him!

This had a great and sudden effect—not a word was
uttered. The prosecutors looked dismayed and astonished;
and the day closed.

Mr Wyndham came up to speak to Misses Francis about
a *dinner*; but he only bowed to me, and with a look so
conscious—so much saying ''Tis your turn to triumph
now!'—that I had not the spite to attack him.

But when the counsel had uttered this animated speech,
Mrs Bogle was so much struck, she hastily arose, and,
clapping her hands, called out audibly, in a broad Scotch
accent: 'Oh, *chaarming*!' I could hardly quiet her till I
assured her we should make a paragraph for the newspapers!

I had the pleasure to deliver this myself to their Majesties
and the Princesses; and as I was called upon while it was

fresh in my memory, I believe but little of the general energy was forgotten. It gave me great pleasure to repeat so striking an affirmation of the innocence of so high, so injured, I believe, a character. The Queen eagerly declared I should go again at the next sitting.

WEDNESDAY, MAY 19TH. The real birthday of my Royal mistress, to whom may heaven grant many, many, and prosperous! Dressing, and so forth, filled up all the morning; and at night I had a tête-à-tête with Charles, till twelve. I got to bed about five in the morning. The sweet Princesses had a ball, and I could not lament my fatigue.

MAY 28TH. And now, my dear sisters, to a subject and narration interesting to your kind affections, because important to my future life.

The Princess Augusta condescended to bring me a most gracious message from the King, desiring to know if I wished to go to Handel's Commemoration, and if I should like the *Messiah*, or prefer any other day?

With my humble acknowledgments for his goodness, I fixed instantly on the *Messiah*; and the very amiable Princess came smiling back to me, bringing me my ticket from the King.

This would not, indeed, much have availed me, but that I fortunately knew my dear father meant to go to the Abbey. I despatched Columb to Chelsea, and he promised to call for me the next morning.

He was all himself; all his native self—kind, gay, open, and full fraught with converse.

Chance favoured me: we found so little room, that we were fain to accept two vacant places at once, though they separated us from my uncle, Mr Burney, and his brother James, who were all there, and all meant to be of the same party.

I might not, at another time, have rejoiced in this disunion, but it was now most opportune: it gave me three hours' conference with my dearest father—the only conference of that length I have had in four years.

Fortune again was kind; for my father began relating
various anecdotes of attacks made upon him for procuring
to sundry strangers some acquaintance with his daughter,
particularly with the Duchess de Biron, and the Mesdames
de Boufflers; to whom he answered, he had no power;
but was somewhat struck by a question of Madame de B.
in return, who exclaimed: 'Mais, monsieur, est-ce possible!
Mademoiselle votre fille n'a-t-elle point de vacance?'

This led to much interesting discussion, and to many
confessions and explanations on my part, never made
before; which induced him to enter more fully into the
whole of the situation, and its circumstances, than he had
ever yet had the leisure or the spirits to do; and he repeated
sundry speeches of discontent at my seclusion from the
world.

All this encouraged me to much detail: I spoke my high
and constant veneration for my Royal mistress, her merits,
her virtues, her condescension, and her even peculiar
kindness towards me. But I owned the species of life
distasteful to me; I was lost to all private comfort, dead to
all domestic endearment; I was worn with want of rest,
and fatigued with laborious watchfulness and attendance.
My time was devoted to official duties; and all that in life
was dearest to me—my friends, my chosen society, my
best affections—lived now in my mind only by recollection,
and rested upon that with nothing but bitter regret.
With relations the most deservedly dear, with friends of
almost unequalled goodness, I lived like an orphan—like
one who had no natural ties, and must make her way as
she could by those that were factitious. Melancholy was
the existence where happiness was excluded, though not
a complaint could be made! where the illustrious personages who were served possessed almost all human excellence—yet where those who were their servants, though
treated with the most benevolent condescension, could
never, in any part of the livelong day, command liberty,
or social intercourse, or repose!

The silence of my dearest father now silencing myself,

I turned to look at him; but how was I struck to see his honoured head bowed down almost into his bosom with dejection and discomfort! We were both perfectly still a few moments; but when he raised his head I could hardly keep my seat, to see his eyes filled with tears! 'I have long,' he cried, 'been uneasy, though I have not spoken . . . but . . . if you wish to resign—my house, my purse, my arms, shall be open to receive you back!'

The emotion of my whole heart at this speech—this sweet, this generous speech—oh, my dear friends, I need not say it!

We were mutually forced to break up our conference. I could only instantly accept his paternal offer, and tell him it was my guardian angel, it was Providence in its own benignity, that inspired him with such goodness. I begged him to love the day in which he had given me such comfort, and assured him it would rest upon my heart with grateful pleasure till it ceased to beat.

He promised to drink tea with me before I left town, and settle all our proceedings. I acknowledged my intention to have ventured to solicit this very permission of resigning. 'But I,' cried he, smiling with the sweetest kindness, 'have spoken first myself.'

What a joy to me, what a relief, this very circumstance! It will always lighten any evil that may, unhappily, follow this proposed step.

OCTOBER. I was ill the whole of this month, though not once with sufficient seriousness for confinement, yet with a difficulty of proceeding as usual so great, that the day was a burthen—or, rather, myself a burthen to the day. A languor so prodigious, with so great a failure of strength and spirit, augmented almost hourly, that I several times thought I must be compelled to excuse my constancy of attendance; but there was no one to take my place, except Miss Planta, whose health is insufficient for her own, and Mlle Montmoulin, to whom such an addition of duty is almost distraction. I could not, therefore, but work on while to work at any rate able.

I now drew up, however, my memorial, or rather, showed it now to my dearest father. He so much approved it, that he told me he would not have a comma of it altered. It is as respectful and as grateful as I had words at command to make it, and expressive of strong devotion and attachment; but it fairly and firmly states that my strength is inadequate to the duties of my charge, and, therefore, that I humbly crave permission to resign it, and retire into domestic life. It was written in my father's name and my own.

I had now that dear father's desire to present it upon the first auspicious moment; and oh! with what a mixture of impatience and dread unspeakable did I look forward to such an opportunity!

In this month, also, I first heard of the zealous exertions and chivalrous intentions of Mr Wyndham. Charles told me they never met without his denouncing the whole thunders of his oratory against the confinement by which he thought my health injured; with his opinion that it must be counteracted speedily by elopement, no other way seeming effectual.

But with Charlotte he came more home to the point. Their vicinity in Norfolk occasions their meeting, though very seldom at the house of Mr Francis, who resents his prosecution of Mr Hastings, and never returns his visits; but at assemblies at Aylsham and at Lord Buckingham's dinners they are certain of now and then encountering.

This summer, when Mr Wyndham went to Felbrig, his Norfolk seat, they soon met at an assembly, and he immediately opened upon his disapprobation of her sister's monastic life, adding: 'I do not venture to speak thus freely upon this subject to everybody, but to you I think I may; at least, I hope it.'

Poor dear Charlotte was too full-hearted for disguise, and they presently entered into a confidential cabal, that made her quite disturbed and provoked when hurried away.

From this time, whenever they met, they were pretty

much of a mind. 'I cannot see you,' he always cried, 'without recurring to that painful subject—your sister's situation.' He then broke forth in an animated offer of his own services to induce Dr Burney to finish such a captivity, if he could flatter himself he might have any influence.

Charlotte eagerly promised him the greatest, and he gave her his promise to go to work.

What a noble Quixote! How much I feel obliged to him! How happy, when I may thank him!

He then pondered upon ways and means. He had already sounded my father: 'but it is resolution,' he added, 'not inclination, Dr Burney wants.' After some further reflection, he then fixed upon a plan: 'I will set the Literary Club upon him!' he cried: 'Miss Burney has some very true admirers there, and I am sure they will all eagerly assist. We will present him with a petition—an address.'

Much more passed: Mr Wyndham expressed a degree of interest and kindness so cordial, that Charlotte says she quite longed to shake hands with him; and if any success ever accrues, she certainly must do it.

And now for a scene a little surprising.

The beautiful chapel of St George, repaired and finished by the best artists at an immense expense, which was now opened after a very long shutting up for its preparations, brought innumerable strangers to Windsor, and, among others, Mr Boswell.

This, I heard, in my way to the chapel, from Mr Turbulent, who overtook me, and mentioned having met Mr Boswell at the Bishop of Carlisle's the evening before. He proposed bringing him to call upon me; but this I declined, certain how little satisfaction would be given here by the entrance of a man so famous for compiling anecdotes. But yet I really wished to see him again, for old acquaintance' sake, and unavoidable amusement from his oddity and good humour, as well as respect for the object of his constant admiration, my revered Dr Johnson. I therefore told Mr Turbulent I should be extremely glad to speak with him after the service was over.

Accordingly, at the gate of the choir, Mr Turbulent brought him to me. We saluted with mutual glee: his comic-serious face and manner have lost nothing of their wonted singularity; nor yet have his mind and language, as you will soon confess.

'I am extremely glad to see you indeed,' he cried, 'but very sorry to see you here. My dear ma'am, why do you stay?—it won't do, ma'am! you must resign!—we can put up with it no longer. I told my good host the Bishop so last night; we are all grown quite outrageous!'

Whether I laughed the most, or stared the most, I am at a loss to say; but I hurried away from the cathedral, not to have such treasonable declarations overheard, for we were surrounded by a multitude.

He accompanied me, however, not losing one moment in continuing his exhortations:

'If you do not quit, ma'am, very soon, some violent measures, I assure you, will be taken. We shall address Dr Burney in a body; I am ready to make the harangue myself. We shall fall upon him all at once.'

I stopped him to inquire about Sir Joshua; he said he saw him very often, and that his spirits were very good. I asked about Mr Burke's book.[1]

'Oh,' cried he, 'it will come out next week: 'tis the first book in the world, except my own, and that's coming out also very soon; only I want your help.'

'My help?'

'Yes, madam; you must give me some of your choice little notes of the Doctor's; we have seen him long enough upon stilts; I want to show him in a new light. Grave Sam, and great Sam, and solemn Sam, and learned Sam— all these he has appeared over and over. Now I want to entwine a wreath of the graces across his brow; I want to show him as gay Sam, agreeable Sam, pleasant Sam: so you must help me with some of his beautiful billets to yourself.'

I evaded this by declaring I had not any stores at hand.

[1] *Reflections on the Revolution in France.* It came out in November.

He proposed a thousand curious expedients to get at the, but I was invincible.

Then I was hurrying on, lest I should be too late. He followed eagerly, and again exclaimed:

'But, ma'am, as I tell you, this won't do—you must resign off-hand! Why, I would farm you out myself for double, treble the money! I wish I had the regulation of such a farm—yet I am no farmer-general. But I should like to farm you, and so I will tell Dr Burney. I mean to address him; I have a speech ready for the first opportunity.'

He then told me his *Life of Dr Johnson* was nearly printed, and took a proof sheet out of his pocket to show me; with crowds passing and repassing, knowing me well, and staring well at him: for we were now at the iron rails of the Queen's Lodge.

I stopped; I could not ask him in: I saw he expected it, and was reduced to apologize, and tell him I must attend the Queen immediately.

He uttered again stronger and stronger exhortations for my retreat, accompanied by expressions which I was obliged to check in their bud. But finding he had no chance for entering, he stopped me again at the gate, and said he would read me a part of his work.

There was no refusing this; and he began, with a letter of Dr Johnson to himself. He read it in strong imitation of the Doctor's manner, very well, and not caricature. But Mrs Schwellenberg was at her window, a crowd was gathering to stand round the rails, and the King and Queen and Royal Family now approached from the Terrace. I made a rather quick apology, and, with a step as quick as my now weakened limbs have left in my power, I hurried to my apartment.

You may suppose I had inquiries enough, from all around, of 'Who was the gentleman I was talking to at the rails?' And an injunction rather frank not to admit him beyond those limits.

However, I saw him again the next morning, in coming

from early prayers, and he again renewed his remonstrances and his petition for my letters of Dr Johnson.

I cannot consent to print private letters, even of a man so justly celebrated, when addressed to myself; no, I shall hold sacred those revered and but too scarce testimonies of the high honour his kindness conferred upon me.[1] One letter I have from him that is a masterpiece of elegance and kindness united. 'Twas his last.

NOVEMBER. This month will be very brief of annals; I was so ill, so unsettled, so unhappy during every day, that I kept not a memorandum.

All the short benefit I had received from the bark was now at an end; languor, feverish nights, and restless days were incessant. My memorial was always in my mind; my courage never rose to bringing it from my letter case.

The Queen was all graciousness; and her favour and confidence and smiles redoubled my difficulties. I saw she had no suspicion but that I was hers for life; and, unimportant as I felt myself to her, in any comparison with those for whom I quitted her, I yet knew not how to give her the unpleasant surprise of a resignation for which I saw her wholly unprepared.

It is true my depression of spirits and extreme alteration of person might have operated as a preface; for I saw no one, except my Royal mistress and Mrs Schwellenberg, who noticed not the change, or who failed to pity and question me upon my health and my fatigues; but as they alone saw it not, or mentioned it not, that afforded me no resource. And thus, with daily intention to present my petition and conclude this struggle, night always returned with the effort unmade, and the watchful morning arose fresh to new purposes that seemed only formed for demolition. And the month expired as it began, with a desire the most strenuous of liberty and peace, combated by reluctance unconquerable to give pain, displeasure, or distress to my very gracious Royal mistress.

[1] There are only two references to Fanny in Boswell's *Life of Johnson*.

DECEMBER. Leaving a little longer in the lurch the late months, let me endeavour to give to my beloved friends some account of this conclusion of the year while yet in being.

My loss of health was now so notorious, that no part of the house could wholly avoid acknowledging it; yet was the terrible piquet the catastrophe of every evening, though frequent pains in my side forced me, three or four times in a game, to creep to my own room for hartshorn and for rest. And so weak and faint I was become, that I was compelled to put my head out into the air, at all hours, and in all weathers, from time to time, to recover the power of breathing, which seemed not seldom almost withdrawn.

Her Majesty was very kind during this time, and the Princesses interested themselves about me with a sweetness very grateful to me; indeed, the whole household showed compassion and regard, and a general opinion that I was falling into a decline ran through the establishment.

There seemed now no time to be lost; when I saw my dear father he recommended to me to be speedy, and my mother was very kind in urgency for immediate measures. I could not, however, summon courage to present my memorial; my heart always failed me, from seeing the Queen's entire freedom from such an expectation: for though I was frequently so ill in her presence that I could hardly stand, I saw she concluded me, while life remained, inevitably hers.

Finding my inability unconquerable, I at length determined upon consulting Mr Francis. I wrote to Charlotte a faithful and minute account of myself, with all my attacks—cough, pain in the side, weakness, sleeplessness, etc.—at full length, and begged Mr Francis's opinion how I must proceed. Very kindly he wrote directly to my father, exhorting instantaneous resignation, as all that stood before me to avert some dangerous malady.

The dear Charlotte at the same time wrote to me conjuring my prompt retreat with the most affecting earnestness.

The uneasiness that preyed upon my spirits in a task so difficult to perform for myself, joined to my daily declension in health, was now so apparent, that, though I could go no further, I paved the way for an opening, by owning to the Queen that Mr Francis had been consulted upon my health.

The Queen now frequently inquired concerning his answer; but as I knew he had written to my father, I deferred giving the result till I had had a final conference with that dear parent. I told her Majesty my father would show me the letter when I saw him.

This I saw raised for the first time a surmise that something was in agitation, though I am certain the suspicion did not exceed an expectation that leave would be requested for a short absence to recruit.

My dearest father, all kindness and goodness, yet all alarm, thought time could never be more favourable; and when next I saw him at Chelsea, I wrote a second memorial to enclose the original one.

With a beating heart, and every pulse throbbing, I returned thus armed to the Queen's house.

Mrs Schwellenberg sent for me to her room. I could hardly articulate a word to her. My agitation was so great that I was compelled to acknowledge something very awful was impending in my affairs, and to beg she would make no present inquiries.

I had not meant to employ her in the business, nor to name it to her, but I was too much disturbed for concealment or evasion.

She seemed really sorry, and behaved with a humanity I had not much reason to expect.

I spent a terrible time till I went to the Queen at night, spiriting myself up for my task, and yet finding apprehension gain ground every moment.

Mrs Schwellenberg had already been some time with her Majesty when I was summoned. I am sure she had already mentioned the little she had gathered. I could hardly perform my customary offices from excess of trepidation. The Queen looked at me with the most inquisitive solicitude. When left with her a moment I tried vainly to make an opening: I could not. She was too much impressed herself by my manner to wait long. She soon inquired what answer had arrived from Mr Francis?

That he could not, I said, prescribe at a distance.

I hoped this would be understood, and said no more. The Queen looked much perplexed, but made no answer.

The next morning I was half dead with real illness, excessive nervousness, and the struggle of what I had to force myself to perform. The Queen again was struck with my appearance, which I believe indeed to have been shocking. When I was alone with her, she began upon Mr Francis with more inquiry. I then tried to articulate that I had something of deep consequence to myself to lay before her Majesty; but that I was so unequal in my weakened state to speak it, that I had ventured to commit it to writing, and entreated permission to produce it.

She could hardly hear me, yet understood enough to give immediate consent.

I then begged to know if I might present it myself, or whether I should give it to Mrs Schwellenberg.

'Oh, to me! to me!' she cried, with kind eagerness.

She added, however, not then, as she was going to breakfast.

This done was already some relief, terrible as was all that remained; but I now knew I must go on, and that all my fears and horrors were powerless to stop me.

The Queen proposed to me to see Dr Gisburne: the King seconded the proposition. There was no refusing; yet, just now, it was distressing to comply.

The next morning, Friday, when again I was alone with the Queen, she named the subject, and told me she would rather I should give the paper to the Schwellenberg, who had been lamenting to her my want of confidence in her, and saying I confided and told everything to the Queen.

I now desired an audience of Mrs Schwellenberg. With what trembling agitation did I deliver her my paper, requesting her to have the goodness to lay it at the feet of the Queen before her Majesty left town!

Mrs Schwellenberg took it, and promised me her services, but desired to know its contents. I begged vainly to be excused speaking them. She persisted, and I then was compelled to own they contained my resignation.

How aghast she looked!—how inflamed with wrath!—how petrified with astonishment! It was truly a dreadful moment to me.

She expostulated on such a step, as if it led to destruction: she offered to save me from it, as if the peace of my life depended on averting it; and she menaced me with its bad consequences, as if life itself, removed from these walls, would become an evil.

I plainly recapitulated the suffering state in which I had lived for the last three months; the difficulty with which I had waded through even the most common fatigues of the day; the constraint of attendance, however honourable, to an invalid; and the impracticability of pursuing such a life, when thus enfeebled, with the smallest chance of ever recovering the health and strength which it had demolished.

To all this she began a vehement eulogium on the superior happiness and blessing of my lot, while under such a protection; and angrily exhorted me not to forfeit what I could never regain.

I then frankly begged her to forbear so painful a discussion, and told her the memorial was from my father as well as myself—that I had no right or authority to hesitate in delivering it—that the Queen herself was prepared to expect it—and that I had promised my father not to go again to Windsor till it was presented. I entreated her, therefore, to have the goodness to show it at once.

This was unanswerable, and she left me with the paper in her hand, slowly conveying it to its place of destination.

Just as she was gone, I was called to Dr Gisburne; or rather, without being called, I found him in my room, as I returned to it.

Think if my mind, now, wanted not medicine the most!

I told him, however, my corporeal complaints; and he ordered me opium and three glasses of wine in the day, and recommended rest to me, and an application to retire to my friends for some weeks, as freedom from anxiety was as necessary to my restoration as freedom from attendance.

During this consultation I was called to Mrs Schwellenberg. Do you think I breathed as I went along? No!

She received me, nevertheless, with complacency and smiles; she began a laboured panegyric of her own friendly zeal and goodness, and then said she had a proposal to make me, which she considered as the most fortunate turn my affairs could take, and as a proof that I should find her the best friend I had in the world. She then premised that she had shown the paper, that the Queen had read it, and said it was very modest, and nothing improper.

Her proposal was, that I should have leave of absence for six weeks, to go about and change the air, to Chelsea, and Norbury Park, and *Capitan* Phillips, and Mr Francis, and Mr Cambrick,[1] which would get me quite well; and, during that time, she would engage Mlle Montmoulin to perform my office.

I was much disturbed at this; and though rejoiced and relieved to understand that the Queen had read my memorial without displeasure, I was grieved to see it was not regarded as final. I only replied I would communicate her plan to my father.

Soon after this we set out for Windsor.

I wrote the proposal to my father. I received, by return of post, the most truly tender letter he ever wrote me. He returns thanks for the clemency with which my melancholy memorial has been received, and is truly sensible of the high honour shown me in the new proposition; but he sees my health so impaired, my strength so decayed, my whole frame so nearly demolished, that he apprehends anything short of a permanent resignation, that would ensure lasting rest and recruit, might prove

[1] Cambridge.

fatal. He quotes a letter from Mr Francis, containing his opinion that I must even be speedier in my retiring, or risk the utmost danger; and he finishes a letter filled with gratitude towards the Queen, and affection to his daughter, with his decisive opinion that I cannot go on, and his prayers and blessings on my retreat.

The term 'speedy,' in Mr Francis's opinion, deterred me from producing this letter, as it seemed indelicate and unfair to hurry the Queen, after offering her the fullest time. I therefore waited till Mrs Schwellenberg came to Windsor before I made any report of my answer.

A scene most horrible ensued, when I told Cerbera the offer was declined. She was too much enraged for disguise, and uttered the most furious expressions of indignant contempt at our proceedings. I am sure she would gladly have confined us both in the Bastille,[1] had England such a misery, as a fit place to bring us to ourselves, from a daring so outrageous against imperial wishes.

Mr Turbulent, as I have told you, won now all my good will by a visit in this my sinking and altered state, in which, with very unaffected friendliness, he counselled and exhorted me to resign my office, in order to secure my recovery.

He related to me, also, his own most afflicting story—his mortifications, disappointments, and ill-treatment; and perhaps my concern for his injuries contributed to his complete restoration in my goodwill. Adieu, my dear friends!

Adieu—undear December!

Adieu—and away for ever, most painful 1790!

JANUARY, 1791. You may suppose my recovery was not much forwarded by a ball given at the Castle on Twelfth Day. The Queen condescended to say that I might go to bed, and she would content herself with the wardrobe woman, in consideration of my weak state; but then she exhorted me not to make it known to the

---

[1] This reminds us that the French Revolution was now in progress. The Bastille fell in July, 1789.

Schwellenberg, who would be quite wretched at such a
thing.

I returned my proper thanks, but declined the proposal,
so circumstanced, assuring her Majesty that it would make
me wretched to have an indulgence that could produce
an impropriety which would make Mrs Schwellenberg
so through my means.

And now to enliven a little; what will you give me, fair
ladies, for a copy of verses written between the Queen of
Great Britain and your most small little journalist?

The morning of the ball the Queen sent for me, and
said she had a fine pair of old-fashioned gloves, white,
with stiff tops and a deep gold fringe, which she meant to
send to her new Master of the Horse, Lord Harcourt,
who was to be at the dance. She wished to convey them
in a copy of verses, of which she had composed three
lines, but could not get on. She told me her ideas, and
I had the honour to help her in the metre; and now I
have the honour to copy them from her own Royal hand:

To the Earl of Harcourt

> Go, happy gloves, bedeck Earl Harcourt's hand,
> And let him know they come from fairy-land,
> Where ancient customs still retain their reign;
> To modernize them all attempts were vain.
> Go, cries Queen Mab, some noble owner seek,
> Who has a proper taste for the antique.

Now, no criticizing, fair ladies!—the assistant was
neither allowed a pen nor a moment, but called upon to
help finish, as she might have been to hand a fan. The
Earl, you may suppose, was sufficiently enchanted.

How, or by whom, or by what instigated, I know not,
but I heard that the newspapers, this winter, had taken
up the cause of my apparent seclusion from the world,
and dealt round comments and lamentations profusely. I
heard of this with much concern.

I have now nothing worth scribbling before my terrible
illness, beginning about four o'clock in the morning of

the day preceding the Queen's birthday: and of that, and its various adventures, you, my kind and tender nurses, are fully apprised.

MAY. As no notice whatever was taken, all this time, of my successor, or my retirement, after very great harass of suspense, and sundry attempts to conquer it, I had at length again a conference with my Royal mistress. She was evidently displeased at again being called upon, but I took the courage to openly remind her that the birthday was her Majesty's own time, and that my father conceived it to be the period of my attendance by her especial appointment. And this was a truth which flashed its own conviction on her recollection. She paused, and then, assentingly, said: 'Certainly.' I then added, that as, after the birthday, their Majesties went to Windsor, and the early prayers began immediately, I must needs confess I felt myself wholly unequal to encountering the fatigue of rising for them in my present weakened state. She was now very gracious again, conscious all this was fair and true. She told me of her own embarrassments concerning the successor, spoke confidentially of her reasons for not engaging an Englishwoman, and acknowledged a person was fixed upon, though something yet remained unarranged. She gave me, however, to understand that all would be expedited; and foreign letters were dispatched, I know, immediately.

This painful task over, of thus frequently reminding my Royal mistress that my services were ending, I grew easier. She renewed, in a short time, all her old confidence and social condescension, and appeared to treat me with no other alteration than a visible regret that I should quit her—shown rather than avowed, or much indeed it would have distressed me.

JUNE 4TH. Let me now come to the 4th, the last birthday of the good, gracious, benevolent King I shall ever, in all human probability, pass under his Royal roof.

The thought was affecting to me, in defiance of my volunteer conduct, and I could scarce speak to the Queen

when I first went to her, and wished to say something upon
a day so interesting. The King was most gracious and
kind when he came into the State Dressing-Room at St
James's, and particularly inquired about my health and
strength, and if they would befriend me for the day. I
longed again to tell him how hard I would work them,
rather than let them, on such a day, drive me from my
office; but I found it better suited me to be quiet; it was
safer not to trust to any expression of loyalty, with a mind
so full, and on a day so critical.

At dinner Mrs Schwellenberg presided, attired magni-
ficently. Miss Goldsworthy, Mrs Stainforth, Messrs de
Luc and Stanhope dined with us; and, while we were still
eating fruit, the Duke of Clarence entered.[1]

He had just risen from the King's table, and waiting
for his equipage to go home and prepare for the ball.
To give you an idea of the energy of his Royal Highness's
language, I ought to set apart a general objection to
writing, or rather intimating, certain forcible words, and
beg leave to show you, in genuine colours, a Royal sailor.

We all rose, of course, upon his entrance, and the two
gentlemen placed themselves behind their chairs, while
the footmen left the room; but he ordered us all to sit
down, and called the men back to hand about some wine.
He was in exceeding high spirits and in the utmost good
humour. He placed himself at the head of the table,
next to Mrs Schwellenberg, and looked remarkably well,
gay, and full of sport and mischief, yet clever withal as well
as comical.

'Well, this is the first day I have ever dined with the King
at St James's on his birthday. Pray, have you all drunk
his Majesty's health?'

'No, your Roy'l Highness: your Roy'l Highness might
make dem do dat,' said Mrs Schwellenberg.

'Oh, by —— will I! Here, you (to the footman); bring
champagne! I'll drink the King's health again, if I die
for it! Yet, I have done pretty well already: so has the

[1] Afterwards William IV. He was the third son of George III.

King, I promise you! I believe his Majesty was never taken such good care of before. We have kept his spirits up, I promise you; we have enabled him to go through his fatigues; and I should have done more still, but for the ball and Mary—I have promised to dance with Mary!'

Princess Mary made her first appearance at Court to-day: she looked most interesting and unaffectedly lovely: she is a sweet creature, and perhaps, in point of beauty, the first of this truly beautiful race, of which Princess Mary may be called *pendant* to the Prince of Wales.

Champagne being now brought for the Duke, he ordered it all round. When it came to me I whispered to Westerhaults to carry it on: the Duke slapped his hand violently on the table and called out: 'Oh, by ——, you shall drink it!'

There was no resisting this. We all stood up, and the Duke sonorously gave the Royal toast.

'And now,' cried he, making us all sit down again, 'where are my rascals of servants? I sha'n't be in time for the ball; besides, I've got a deuced tailor waiting to fix on my epaulette! Here, you, go and see for my servants! d' ye hear? Scamper off!'

Off ran William.

'Come, let's have the King's health again. De Luc, drink it. Here, champagne to de Luc!'

I wish you could have seen Mr de Luc's mixed simper—half pleased, half alarmed. However, the wine came and he drank it, the Duke taking a bumper for himself at the same time.

'Poor Stanhope!' cried he: 'Stanhope shall have a glass, too! Here, champagne! what are you all about? Why don't you give champagne to poor Stanhope?'

Mr Stanhope, with great pleasure, complied, and the Duke again accompanied him.

'Come hither, do you hear?' cried the Duke to the servants, and on the approach, slow and submissive, of Mrs Stainforth's man, he hit him a violent slap on the back, calling out: 'Hang you! Why don't you see for my rascals?'

Away flew the man, and then he called out to Wester-haults: 'Hark 'ee! Bring another glass of champagne to Mr de Luc!'

Mr de Luc knows these Royal youths too well to venture at so vain an experiment as disputing with them; so he only shrugged his shoulders and drank the wine. The Duke did the same.

'And now, poor Stanhope,' cried the Duke; 'give another glass to poor Stanhope, d' ye hear?'

'Is not your Royal Highness afraid,' cried Mr Stanhope, displaying the full circle of his borrowed teeth, 'I shall be apt to be rather up in the world, as the folks say, if I tope on at this rate?'

'Not at all! You can't get drunk in a better cause. I'd get drunk myself if it was not for the ball. Here, champagne! Another glass for the philosopher! I keep sober for Mary.'

'Oh, your Royal Highness!' cried Mr de Luc, gaining courage as he drank, 'you will make me quite droll of it if you make me go on—quite droll!'

'So much the better! so much the better! it will do you a monstrous deal of good. Here, another glass of champagne for the Queen's philosopher!'

Mr de Luc obeyed, and the Duke then addressed Mrs Schwellenberg's George. 'Here, you! you! why, where is my carriage? Run and see, do you hear?'

Off hurried George, grinning irrepressibly.

'If it was not for that deuced tailor, I would not stir. I shall dine at the Queen's house on Monday, Miss Goldsworthy; I shall come to dine with the Princess Royal. I find she does not go to Windsor with the Queen.'

The Queen meant to spend one day at Windsor, on account of a review which carried the King that way.

Some talk then ensued upon the Duke's new carriage, which they all agreed to be the most beautiful that day at Court. I had not seen it, which, to me, was some impediment against praising it.

He then said it was necessary to drink the Queen's health.

The gentlemen here made no demur, though Mr de Luc arched his eyebrows in expressive fear of consequences.

'A bumper,' cried the Duke, 'to the Queen's gentleman usher.'

They all stood up and drank the Queen's health.

'Here are three of us,' cried the Duke, 'all belonging to the Queen: the Queen's philosopher, the Queen's gentleman usher and the Queen's son; but, thank heaven, I'm nearest!'

'Sir,' cried Mr Stanhope, a little affronted, 'I am not now the Queen's gentleman usher; I am the Queen's equerry, sir.'

'A glass more of champagne here! What are you all so slow for? Where are all my rascals gone? They've put me in one passion already this morning. Come, a glass of champagne for the Queen's gentleman usher!' laughing heartily.

'No, sir,' repeated Mr Stanhope; 'I am equerry now, sir.'

'And another glass for the Queen's philosopher!'

Neither gentleman objected; but Mrs Schwellenberg, who had sat laughing and happy all this time, now grew alarmed, and said: 'Your Royal Highness, I am afraid for the ball!'

'Hold your potato-jaw, my dear,' cried the Duke, patting her; but, recollecting himself, he took her hand and pretty abruptly kissed it, and then, flinging it hastily away, laughed aloud, and called out: 'There! that will make amends for anything, so now I may say what I will. So here! a glass of champagne for the Queen's philosopher and the Queen's gentleman usher! Hang me if it will not do them a monstrous deal of good!'

Here news was brought that the equipage was in order. He started up, calling out: 'Now, then, for my deuced tailor.'

'Oh, your Royal Highness!' cried Mr de Luc, in a tone of expostulation, 'now you have made us droll, you go!'

Off, however, he went. And is it not a curious scene? All my amaze is, how any of their heads bore such libations.

In the evening I had by no means strength to encounter the ball room. I gave my tickets to Mrs and Miss Douglas.

Mrs Stainforth was dying to see the Princess Mary in her Court dress. Mr Stanhope offered to conduct her to a place of prospect. She went with him. I thought this preferable to an unbroken evening with my fair companion, and, Mr de Luc thinking the same, we both left Mrs Schwellenberg to unattire, and followed. But we were rather in a scrape by trusting to Mr Stanhope, after all this champagne: he had carried Mrs Stainforth to the very door of the ball room, and there fixed her— in a place which the King, Queen, and suite must brush past in order to enter the ball room. I had followed, however, and the crowds of beef-eaters, officers, and guards that lined all the state rooms through which we exhibited ourselves, prevented my retreating alone. I stood, therefore, next to Mrs Stainforth, and saw the ceremony.

The passage was made so narrow by attendants, that they were all forced to go one by one. First, all the King's great state officers, amongst whom I recognized Lord Courtown, Treasurer of the Household; Lord Salisbury carried a candle!—'tis an odd etiquette. These being passed, came the King—he saw us and laughed; then the Queen's Master of the Horse, Lord Harcourt, who did ditto; then some more.

The Vice-Chamberlain carries the Queen's candle, that she may have the arm of the Lord Chamberlain to lean on; accordingly, Lord Aylesbury, receiving that honour, now preceded the Queen: she looked amazed at sight of us. The kind Princesses one by one acknowledged us. I spoke to Princess Mary, wishing her Royal Highness joy; she looked in a delight and an alarm nearly equal. She was to dance her first minuet. Then followed the Ladies of the Bedchamber, and Lady Harcourt was particularly civil. Then the Maids of Honour, every one of whom knew and spoke to us. I peered vainly for the Duke of Clarence, but none of the Princes passed us. What a crowd brought up the rear! I was vexed not to see the Prince of Wales.

Well, God bless the King! and many and many such days may he know!

I was now so tired as to be eager to go back; but the Queen's philosopher, the good and most sober and temperate of men, was really a little giddy with all his bumpers, and his eyes, which were quite lustrous, could not fix any object steadily; while the poor gentleman usher—equerry, I mean—kept his mouth so wide open with one continued grin—I suppose from the sparkling beverage—that I was every minute afraid its pearly ornaments, which never fit their case, would have fallen at our feet. Mrs Stainforth gave me a significant look of making the same observation, and, catching me fast by the arm, said: 'Come, Miss Burney, let's you and I take care of one another'; and then she safely toddled me back to Mrs Schwellenberg, who greeted us with saying: 'Vell, bin you much amused? Dat Prince Villiam—oders de Duke de Clarence—bin raelly ver merry—oders vat you call tipsy.'

July. I come now to write the last week of my royal residence. The Queen honoured me with the most uniform graciousness, and though, as the time of separation approached, her cordiality rather diminished, and traces of internal displeasure appeared sometimes, arising from an opinion I ought rather to have struggled on, live or die, than to quit her—yet I am sure she saw how poor was my own chance, except by a change in the mode of life, and at least ceased to wonder, though she could not approve.

The King was more courteous, more communicative, more amiable, at every meeting; and he condescended to hold me in conversation with him by every opportunity, and with an air of such benevolence and goodness, that I never felt such ease and pleasure in his notice before. He talked over all Mr Boswell's book, and I related to him sundry anecdotes of Dr Johnson, all highly to his honour, and such as I was eager to make known. He always heard me with the utmost complacency, and encouraged me to proceed in my accounts, by every mark of attention and interest.

He told me once, laughing heartily, that, having seen my name in the Index, he was eager to come to what was said of me; but when he found so little, he was surprised and disappointed.

I ventured to assure him how much I had myself been rejoiced at this very circumstance, and with what satisfaction I had reflected upon having very seldom met Mr Boswell, as I knew there was no other security against all manner of risks in his relations.

Tuesday morning I had a conversation, very long and very affecting to me, with her Majesty. I cannot pretend to detail it. I will only tell you she began by speaking of Mlle Jacobi,[1] whom I had the satisfaction to praise, as far as had appeared, very warmly; and then she led me to talk at large upon the nature and requisites and circumstances of the situation I was leaving.

She then conversed upon sundry subjects, all of them confidential in their nature, for near an hour; and then, after a pause, said: 'Do I owe you anything, my dear Miss Burney?'

I acquainted her with a debt or two amounting to near 70l. She said she would settle it in the afternoon, and then paused again; after which, with a look full of benignity, she very expressively said: 'As I don't know your plan, or what you propose, I cannot tell what would make you comfortable, but you know the size of my family.'

I comprehended her, and was immediately interrupting her with assurances of my freedom from all expectation or claim; but she stopped me, saying: 'You know what you now have from me: the half of that I mean to continue.'

Amazed and almost overpowered by a munificence I had so little expected or thought of, I poured forth the

---

[1] Fanny's successor as Assistant Keeper of the Robes. She came from Hanover.

most earnest disclaimings of such a mark of her graciousness, declaring I knew too well her innumerable calls to be easy in receiving it; and much more I uttered to this purpose, with the unaffected warmth that animated me at the moment. She heard me almost silently; but, in conclusion, simply, yet strongly, said: 'I shall certainly do that!' with a stress on the 'that' that seemed to kindly mean she would rather have done more.

The conference was in this stage when the Princess Elizabeth came into the room. The Queen then retired to the ante-chamber. My eyes being full, and my heart not very empty, I could not then forbear saying to her Royal Highness how much the goodness of the Queen had penetrated me. The Princess spoke feelings I could not expect, by the immediate glistening of her soft eyes. She condescended to express her concern at my retiring; but most kindly added: 'However, Miss Burney, you have this to comfort you, go when you will, that your behaviour has been most perfectly honourable.'

WEDNESDAY. In the morning Mrs Evans, the housekeeper, came to take leave of me; and the housemaid of my apartment, who, poor girl! cried bitterly that I was going to give place to a foreigner; for Mrs Schwellenberg's severity with servants has made all Germans feared in the house.

Oh, but let me first mention that, when I came from the Lower Lodge, late as it was, I determined to see my old friends the equerries, and not quit the place without bidding them adieu. I had never seen them since I had dared mention my designed retreat.

I told William, therefore, to watch their return from the Castle, and to give my compliments to either Colonel Gwynn or Colonel Goldsworthy, and an invitation to my apartment.

Colonel Goldsworthy came instantly. I told him I could not think of leaving Windsor without offering first my good wishes to all the household. He said that, when my intended departure had been published, he and all the gentlemen then with him had declared it ought to have taken place six months ago. He was extremely courteous, and I begged him to bring to me the rest of his companions that were known to me.

He immediately fetched Colonel Gwynn, General Grenville, Colonel Ramsden, and Colonel Manners. This was the then party. I told him I sent to beg their blessing upon my departure. They were all much pleased, apparently, that I had not made my exit without seeing them: they all agreed in the urgency of the measure, and we exchanged good wishes most cordially.

THURSDAY, JULY 7TH. This, my last day of office, was big and busy, joyful, yet affecting to me in a high degree.

In the morning, before I left Kew, I had my last interview with Mrs Schwellenberg. She was very kind in it, desiring to see me whenever I could in town, during her residence at the Queen's house, and to hear from me by letter meanwhile.

She then much surprised me by an offer of succeeding to her own place, when it was vacated either by her retiring or her death. This was, indeed, a mark of favour and confidence I had not expected. I declined, however, to enter upon the subject, as the manner in which she opened it made it very solemn, and, to her, very affecting.

She would take no leave of me, but wished me better hastily, and, saying we should soon meet, she hurried suddenly out of the room. Poor woman! If her temper were not so irascible, I really believe her heart would be by no means wanting in kindness.

I then took leave of Kew Palace—the same party again accompanying me, for the last time, in a Royal vehicle going by the name of *Miss Burney's coach*.

At St James's all was graciousness; and my Royal mistress gave me to understand she would have me stay to assist at her toilet after the drawing-room; and much delighted me by desiring my attendance on the Thursday fortnight, when she came again to town. This lightened the parting in the pleasantest manner possible.

When the Queen commanded me to follow her to her closet I was, indeed, in much emotion; but I told her that, as what had passed from Mrs Schwellenberg in the morning had given me to understand her Majesty was fixed in her munificent intention, notwithstanding what I had most unaffectedly urged against it——

'Certainly,' she interrupted, 'I shall certainly do it.'

'Yet so little,' I continued, 'had I thought it right to dwell upon such an expectation, that, in the belief your Majesty would yet take it into further consideration, I had not even written it to my father.'

'Your father,' she again interrupted me, 'has nothing to do with it; it is solely from *me* to *you*.'

'Let me then humbly entreat,' I cried, 'still in some measure to be considered as a servant of your Majesty, either as reader, or to assist occasionally if Mlle Jacobi should be ill.'

She looked most graciously pleased, and immediately closed in with the proposal, saying: 'When your health is restored—perhaps sometimes.'

I then fervently poured forth my thanks for all her goodness, and my prayers for her felicity.

She had her handkerchief in her hand or at her eyes the whole time. I was so much moved by her condescending kindness, that as soon as I got out of the closet I nearly sobbed. I went to help Mlle Jacobi to put up the jewels, that my emotion might the less be observed. The King then came into the room. He immediately advanced to the window, where I stood, to speak to me. I was not then able to comport myself steadily. I was forced to turn my head away from him. He stood still and silent for some minutes, waiting to see if I should turn about; but I could not recover myself sufficiently to face him, strange as it was to do otherwise; and perceiving me quite overcome he walked away, and I saw him no more.

His kindness, his goodness, his benignity, never shall I forget—never think of but with fresh gratitude and reverential affection.

They were all now going—I took, for the last time, the cloak of the Queen, and, putting it over her shoulders, slightly ventured to press them, earnestly, though in a low voice, saying: 'God Almighty bless your Majesty!'

She turned round, and, putting her hand upon my ungloved arm, pressed it with the greatest kindness, and said: 'May you be happy!'

She left me overwhelmed with tender gratitude. The three eldest Princesses were in the next room: they ran in to me the moment the Queen went onward. Princess Augusta and Princess Elizabeth each took a hand, and the Princess Royal put hers over them. I could speak to none of them; but they repeated: 'I wish you happy!—I wish you health!' again and again, with the sweetest eagerness.

They then set off for Kew.

Here, therefore, end my Court Annals; after having lived in the service of her Majesty five years within ten days—from July 17, 1786, to July 7, 1791.

PART FOUR

OCTOBER, 1791–JANUARY, 1840

PART FOUR

Oſtober, 1791–January, 1840 [1]

Chelsea College.

OCTOBER. Though another month is begun since I left my deareſt of friends, I have had no journalizing spirit; but I will give all heads of chapters, and try to do better.

I have lived altogether in the moſt quiet and retired manner possible. My health gains ground, gradually, but very perceptibly, and a weakness that makes me soon exhauſted in whatever I undertake is all of illness now remaining.

I have never been so pleasantly situated at home since I loſt the siſter of my heart and my moſt affeſtionate Charlotte. My father is almoſt conſtantly within. Indeed, I now live with him wholly; he has himself appropriated me a place, a seat, a desk, a table, and every convenience and comfort, and he never seemed yet so earneſt to keep me about him. We read together, write together, chat, compare notes, communicate projeſts, and diversify each other's employments. He is all goodness, gaiety, and affeſtion; and his society and kindness are more precious to me than ever.

Fortunately, in this season of leisure and comfort, the spirit of composition proves aſtive. The day is never long enough, and I could employ two pens almoſt incessantly, in merely scribbling what will not be repressed. This is a delight to my dear father inexpressibly great: and though I have gone no further than to let him know, from time to time, the species of matter that occupies me, he is perfeſtly contented, and patiently waits till something is quite finished, before he insiſts upon reading

[1] Vol. v, p. 261–vol. vii, p. 382.

a word. This 'suits my humour well,' as my own industry is all gone when once its intent is produced.

For the rest I have been going on with my third
tragedy.[1] I have two written, but never yet have had
opportunity to read them; which, of course, prevents their
being corrected to the best of my power, and fitted for
the perusal of less indulgent eyes; or rather of eyes less
prejudiced.

Believe me, my dear friends, in the present composed
and happy state of my mind, I could never have suggested
these tales of woe; but, having only to connect, combine,
contract, and finish, I will not leave them undone. Not,
however, to sadden myself to the same point in which I
began them; I read more than I write, and call for happier
themes from others, to enliven my mind from the dolorous
sketches I now draw of my own.

The library or study, in which we constantly sit, supplies
such delightful variety of food, that I have nothing to
wish. Thus, my beloved sisters and friends, you see me,
at length, enjoying all that peace, ease, and chosen recreation and employment, for which so long I sighed in vain,
and which, till very lately, I had reason to believe, even
since attained, had been allowed me too late. I am more
and more thankful every night, every morning, for the
change in my destiny, and present blessings of my lot;
and you, my beloved Susan and Fredy, for whose prayers
I have so often applied in my sadness, suffering, and
despondence, afford me now the same community of
thanks and acknowledgments.

November. I spent one evening with Mrs Ord, and met
our Esther, and heard sweet music from her sweet soul-
touching finger. Miss Merry, too, was of the party, she is
sister of the 'Liberty' Mr Merry,[2] who wrote the ode for our

[1] One of these three tragedies, *Edwy and Elgiva*, was acted in 1795
at Drury Lane, with Kemble and Mrs Siddons in the cast. It failed,
and was withdrawn after one performance.
[2] Robert Merry (1755–98), a poet of the 'Della Cruscan School,'
so effectively satirized by Gifford.

revolution club, and various other things, and a tragedy called *Lorenzo*, in which Miss Brunton performed his heroine so highly to his satisfaction, that he made his addresses to her, and forthwith married her.

The sister, and her aunt, which whom she lives, were much hurt by this alliance; and especially by his continuing his wife on the stage, and with their own name. She remonstrated against this indelicacy; but he answered her, she ought to be proud he had brought a woman of such virtue and talents into the family. Her virtue, his marrying her proved; and her talents would all be thrown away by taking her off the stage.

Miss Merry seems past thirty, plain, but sensible in her face, and very much the gentlewoman in her manners, with a figure remarkably good and well made. She sat next me, and talked to me a great deal. She extremely surprised me by entering speedily into French affairs, which I would not have touched upon for the world, her brother's principles being notorious. However, she eagerly gave me to understand her own were the reverse: she spoke of Mr Burke's pamphlets with the highest praise; the first of them, she said, though eloquently written, could only soothe those who already felt with him; but the appeal to the New Whigs she considered as framed to make converts of whoever was unprejudiced. Perhaps she is one of the number herself. She inveighed against the cruelties of the let-loose mob of France, and told me some scenes that had lately passed in Avignon, that were so terrible I excused myself from dwelling on the subject.

She is a sensible, cultivated, and well-read woman, and very well mannered.

Another evening, after visiting our Esther, my father took me to Sir Joshua Reynolds. I had long languished to see that kindly zealous friend, but his ill health had intimidated me from making the attempt; and now my dear father went upstairs alone, and inquired of Miss Palmer if her uncle was well enough to admit me. He returned for me immediately. I felt the utmost pleasure in again mounting his staircase.

Miss Palmer hastened forward and embraced me most cordially. I then shook hands with Sir Joshua. He had a bandage over one eye, and the other shaded with a green half-bonnet. He seemed serious even to sadness, though extremely kind. 'I am very glad,' he said, in a meek voice and dejected accent, 'to see you again, and I wish I could see you better! but I have only one eye now— and hardly that.'

I was really quite touched. The expectation of total blindness depresses him inexpressibly; not, however, inconceivably. I hardly knew how to express, either my concern for his altered situation since our meeting, or my joy in again being with him; but my difficulty was short; Miss Palmer eagerly drew me to herself, and recommended to Sir Joshua to go on with his cards. He had no spirit to oppose; probably, indeed, no inclination.

FEB. 1792. Upon the day of Sir Joshua Reynolds's death I was in my bed, with two blisters, and I did not hear of it till two days after. I shall enter nothing upon this subject here: our current letters mentioned the particulars, and I am not desirous to retrace them. His loss is as universally felt as his merit is universally acknowledged, and, joined to all public motives, I had myself private ones of regret that cannot subside. He was always peculiarly kind to me, and he had worked at my deliverance from a life he conceived too laborious for me, as if I had been his own daughter; yet, from the time of my coming forth, I only twice saw him. I had not recovered strength for visiting before he was past receiving me. I grieve inexpressibly never to have been able to pay him the small tribute of thanks for his most kind exertions in my cause. I little thought the second time I saw him would be my last opportunity, and my intention was to wait some favourable opening.

Miss Palmer is left heiress, and her unabating attendance upon her inestimable uncle in his sick room makes everybody content with her great acquisition. I am sure she loved and admired him with all the warmth of her warm heart. I wrote her a few lines of condolence, and she has sent me a very kind answer. She went immediately to the Burkes, with whom she will chiefly, I fancy, associate.

MARCH. Sad for the loss of Sir Joshua, and all of us ill ourselves, we began this month. Upon its third day was his funeral. My dear father could not attend; but Charles was invited and went. All the Royal Academy, professors and students, and all the Literary Club, attended as family mourners. Mr Burke, Mr Malone,[1] and Mr Metcalf, are executors. Miss Palmer has spared nothing, either in thought or expense, that could render the last honours splendid and grateful. It was a very melancholy day to us, though it has the alleviation and softening of a letter from our dear Charlotte, promising to arrive the next day.

MAY. I went to Mr Hastings's defence: Sarah was with me. Just before us sat Mrs Kennedy, of Windsor, with whom I renewed a meeting acquaintance, but evaded a visiting one.

The defence to-day was by Mr Markham, son of the Archbishop of York, who has repeatedly been summoned, and who bears most honourable testimony to the character, the conduct, and the abilities of Mr Hastings.

Soon after I spent a day with Mrs Ord, by invitation, for meeting the Percy family. She had also assembled Major Rennell, the Dickensons, Lady Herries, and Mr Selwyn.

Mr Selwyn I had not seen for many years. Streatham and Mrs Thrale, our constant themes, were uppermost, first and last, in all we said and all we thought. His most amiable behaviour in poor Mr Thrale's unhappy state of health I shall never forget. I met him with a glad cordiality from its remembrance, and it was very apparently mutual. He still visits, occasionally, at Streatham;

Edmund Malone (1741–1812), Shakespearian scholar and editor of Boswell's *Johnson*.

but he says the place, the inhabitants, the visitors, the way of life, are all so totally changed, it would make me most melancholy again to tread those boards.

Mrs Dickenson told me that Miss Palmer is certainly engaged to Lord Inchiquin. He is sixty-nine; but they say he is remarkably pleasing in his manners, and soft and amiable in his disposition. I am sure she has merited my wishes for her happiness, by her deep interest, upon all occasions, in mine, and I am sure she has them.

I got home to dinner to meet Mrs and Miss Mary Young,[1] who are in town for a few weeks. Miss Mary is sensible, and quick, and agreeable.

They give a very unpleasant account of Madame de Genlis, or de Sillery, or Brulard, as she is now called. They say she has established herself at Bury, in their neighbourhood, with Mlle la Princesse d'Orléans, and Pamela, and a *Circe*, another young girl, under her care. They have taken a house, the master of which always dines with them, though Mrs Young says he is such a low man he should not dine with her daughter. They form twenty with themselves and household. They keep a botanist, a chemist, and a natural historian always with them. These are supposed to have been common servants of the Duke of Orleans in former days, as they always walk behind the ladies when abroad; but, to make amends in the new equalizing style, they all dine together at home. They visit at no house but Sir Thomas Gage's, where they carry their harps, and frequently have music. They have been to a Bury ball, and danced all night; Mlle d'Orléans, with anybody, known or unknown to Madame Brulard.

What a woeful change from that elegant, amiable, high-bred Madame de Genlis I knew six years ago!—the apparent pattern of female perfection in manners, conversation, and delicacy.

There are innumerable democrats assembled in Suffolk; among them the famous Tom Paine, who herds with all

[1] Arthur Young, best known for his *Travels in France*, was a connection of the Burneys.

the farmers that will receive him, and there propagates his pernicious doctrines.

JUNE 4TH. The birthday of our truly good King.

As his Majesty had himself given me, when I saw him after the Queen's birthday, an implied reproach for not presenting myself at the palace that day, I determined not to incur a similar censure on this, especially as I hold my admission on such a national festival as a real happiness, as well as honour, when it is to see themselves.

How different was my attire from every other such occasion the five preceding years! It was a mere simple dressed undress, without feathers, flowers, hoop, or furbelows.

When I alighted at the porter's lodge I was stopped from crossing the courtyard, by seeing the King, with his three sons, the Prince of Wales, Duke of York, and Duke of Clarence, who were standing there after alighting from their horses, to gratify the people who encircled the iron rails. It was a pleasant and goodly sight, and I rejoiced in such a detention.

I had a terrible difficulty to find a friend who would make known to her Majesty that I was come to pay my devoirs.

At length, while watching in the passages to and fro, I heard a step upon the Princesses' stairs, and, venturing forward, I encountered the Princess Elizabeth. I paid my respectful congratulations on the day, which she most pleasantly received, and I intimated my great desire to see her Majesty. I am sure the amiable Princess communicated my petition, for Mr de Luc came out in a few minutes and ushered me into the Royal presence.

The Queen was in her state dressing-room, her head attired for the drawing-room superbly; but her court dress, as usual, remaining to be put on at St James's. She had already received all her early complimenters, and was prepared to go to St James's: the Princess Royal was seated by her side, and all the other Princesses, except the Princess Amelia, were in the room, with the Duchess of York. Mr de Luc, Mrs Schwellenberg, Madame la Fîte, and Miss Goldsworthy were in the background.

The Queen smiled upon me most graciously, and every Princess came up separately to speak with me. I thanked her Majesty warmly for admitting me upon such an occasion. 'Oh!' cried she, 'I resolved to see you the moment I knew you were here.'

She then inquired when I went into Norfolk, and conversed upon my summer plans, etc., with more of her original sweetness of manner than I have seen since my resignation. What pleasure this gave me! and what pleasure did I feel in being kept by her till the farther door opened, and the King entered, accompanied by the Dukes of York and Clarence!

I motioned to retreat, but, calling out: 'What, Miss Burney!' the King came up to me, and inquired how I did; and began talking to me so pleasantly, so gaily, so kindly even, that I had the satisfaction of remaining and of gathering courage to utter my good wishes and warm fervent prayers for this day. He deigned to hear me very benignly; or make believe he did, for I did not make my harangue very audibly; but he must be sure of its purport.

He said I was grown 'quite fat' since he had seen me, and appealed to the Duke of York: he protested my arm was half as big again as heretofore, and then he measured it with his spread thumbs and forefingers; and the whole of his manner showed his perfect approbation of the step I had taken, of presenting myself in the Royal presence on this auspicious day.

Mrs Phillips to Miss Burney

Mickleham, September, 1792.

We shall shortly, I believe, have a little colony of unfortunate (or rather, fortunate, since here they are safe) French noblesse in our neighbourhood. Sunday evening

Ravely informed Mr Locke that two or three families had joined to take Jenkinson's house, Juniper Hall, and that another family had taken a small house at Westhumble,[1] which the people very reluctantly let, upon the Christian-like supposition that, being nothing but French papishes, they would never pay. Our dear Mr Locke, while this was agitating, sent word to the landlord that he would be answerable for the rent; however, before this message arrived, the family were admitted. The man said they had pleaded very hard indeed, and said, if he did but know the distress they had been in, he would not hesitate.

This house is taken by Madame de Broglie, daughter of the Maréchal, who is in the army with the French Princes; or, rather, wife to his son, Victor Broglie, till very lately General of one of the French armies, and at present disgraced, and fled nobody knows where. This poor lady came over in an open boat, with a son younger than my Norbury, and was fourteen hours at sea. She has other ladies with her, and gentlemen, and two little girls, who had been sent to England some weeks ago; they are all to lodge in a sort of cottage, containing only a kitchen and parlour on the ground floor.

I long to offer them my house, and have been much gratified by finding Mr Locke immediately determined to visit them; his taking this step will secure them the civilities, at least, of the other neighbours.

At Jenkinsons are: la Marquise de la Châtre, whose husband is with the emigrants; her son; M. de Narbonne, lately Ministre de la Guerre; M. de Montmorency; Charles or Théodore Lameth; Jaucourt; and one or two more, whose names I have forgotten, are either arrived to-day, or expected. I feel infinitely interested for all these persecuted persons. Pray tell me whatever you hear of M. de Liancourt, etc. Heaven bless you!

[1] West Humble. It appears subsequently as West Hamble.

Miss Burney to Dr Burney

Halstead, October 2nd, '92.

MY DEAREST PADRE, I have just got your direction, in a letter from my mother, and an account that you seem to be in health and spirits; so now I think it high time to let you know a little about some of your daughters, lest you should forget you have any such encumbrances.

In the first place, two of them, Esther and F. B., had a safe and commodious journey hither, in the midst of pattering showers and cloudy skies, making up as well as they could for the deficiencies of the elements by the dulcet recreation of the concord of sweet sounds; not from tabrets and harps, but from the harmony of hearts with tongues.

In the second place, a third of them, Charlotte F., writes word her *caro sposo* has continued very tolerably well this last fortnight, and that she still desires to receive my visit according to the first appointment.

In the third place, a fourth of them, Sarah, is living upon French politics and with French fugitives, at Bradfield, where she seems perfectly satisfied with foreign forage.

In the fourth place, Susanna, another of them, sends cheering histories of herself and her tribe, though she concludes them with a sighing ejaculation of 'I wish I did not know there was such a country as France!'

So much for your daughters. . . .

To-day's papers teem with the promise of great and decisive victories to the arms of the Duke of Brunswick.[1] I tremble for the dastardly revenge menaced to the most injured King of France and his family. I dare hardly wish the advance and success of the combined armies, in the terror of such consequences. Yet the fate and future tranquillity of all Europe seem inevitably involved in the prosperity or the failure of this expedition. The

[1] This promise was not fulfilled, the Duke of Brunswick having already been defeated at Valmy on 20th September.

depression or encouragement it must give to political adventurers, who, at all times, can stimulate the rabble to what they please, will surely spread far, deep, and wide, according to the event of French experiment upon the minds, manners, and powers of men; and the feasibility of expunging all past experience, for the purpose of treating the world as if it were created yesterday, and every man, woman, and child were let loose to act from their immediate suggestion, without reference to what is past, or sympathy in anything that is present, or precaution for whatever is to come. It seems, in truth, no longer the cause of nations alone, but of individuals: not a dispute for a form of government, but for a condition of safety.

> Ever and ever most dutifully and
> affectionately your
> F. B.

Mrs Phillips to Miss Burney

Mickleham, November, 1792.

It gratifies me very much that I have been able to interest you for our amiable and charming neighbours.

Mrs Locke had been so kind as to pave the way for my introduction to Madame de la Châtre, and carried me on Friday to Juniper Hall, where we found M. de Montmorency, a *ci-devant duc*, and one who gave some of the first great examples of sacrificing personal interest to what was then considered the public good. I know not whether you will like him the better when I tell you that from him proceeded the motion for the abolition of titles in France; but if you do not, let me, in his excuse, tell you he was scarcely one-and-twenty when an enthusiastic spirit impelled him to this, I believe, ill-judged and mischievous act. My curiosity was greatest to see M. de Jaucourt, because I remembered many lively and spirited

speeches made by him during the time of the *Assemblée
législative*, and that he was a warm defender of my favourite hero, M. Lafayette.

Of M. de Narbonne's abilities we could have no doubt
from his speeches and letters whilst Ministre de la Guerre,
which post he did not quit till last May.   By his own desire
he then joined Lafayette's army, and acted under him;
but, on the 10th of August, he was involved, with perhaps
nearly all the most honourable and worthy of the French
nobility, accused as a traitor by the Jacobins, and obliged
to fly from his country.

M. d'Argenson was already returned to France, and
Madame de Broglie had set out the same day, November
2nd, hoping to escape the decree against emigrants.

Madame de la Châtre received us with great politeness.
She is about thirty-three; an elegant figure, not pretty,
but with an animated and expressive countenance; very
well read, *pleine d'esprit*, and, I think, very lively and
charming.

A gentleman was with her whom Mrs Locke had not
yet seen, M. d'Arblay.   She introduced him, and, when
he had quitted the room, told us he was adjutant-general
to M. Lafayette, *maréchal de camp*, and in short the first in
military rank of those who had accompanied that general
when he so unfortunately fell into the hands of the
Prussians; but, not having been one of the *Assemblée
constituante*, he was allowed, with four others, to proceed
into Holland,[1] and there M. de Narbonne wrote to him.
'Et comme il l'aime infiniment,' said Madame de la
Châtre, 'il l'a prié de venir vivre avec lui.'   He had arrived
only two days before.   He is tall, and a good figure,
with an open and manly countenance; about forty, I
imagine. . . .

[1] In spite of his services to the Revolution, Lafayette was declared
a traitor in 1792 and forced to take refuge in Liége.   He was held by
the Prussians as a political prisoner.   M. d'Arblay, who accompanied
him to Liége, was allowed to go free, since he had not been connected
with the Revolutionary movement.

Miss Burney to Mrs Locke

Chelsea, December 20th, '92.

. . . God keep us all safe and quiet! All now wears a fair aspect; but I am told Mr Windham says we are not yet out of the wood, though we see the path through it. There must be no relaxation. The pretended friends of the people, pretended or misguided, wait but the stilling of the present ferment of loyalty to come forth. . . .

The accounts from France are thrilling. Poor M. d'Arblay's speech should be translated, and read to all English imitators of French reformers. What a picture of the *now reformed*! Mr Burke's description of the martyred Duc de la Rochefoucault should be read also by all the few really pure promoters of new systems. New systems, I fear, in states, are always dangerous, if not wicked. Grievance by grievance, wrong by wrong, must only be assailed, and breathing time allowed to old prejudices, and old habits, between all that is done.

I had never heard of any *good* association[1] six months ago; but I rejoice Mr Locke had. I am glad, too, your neighbourhood is so loyal. I am sure such a colony of sufferers from state experiments, even with the best intentions, ought to double all vigilance for running no similar risks—here too, where there are no similar calls! Poor M. d'Arblay's belief in perpetual banishment is dreadful: but Chabot's horrible denunciation of M. de Narbonne made me stop for breath, as I read it in the papers.

I had fancied the letters brought for the King of France's trial were forgeries. One of them, certainly, to M. Bouillé, had its answer dated before it was written. If any have been found, others will be added, to serve any evil purposes. Still, however, I hope the King and his family will be saved. I cannot but believe it, from all I can put together. If the worst of the Jacobins hear that

[1] i.e. a loyal association in opposition to the revolutionary societies.

Fox has called him an 'unfortunate Monarch,' that Sheridan has said 'his execution would be an act of injustice,' and Grey 'that we ought to have spared that *one blast to their glories* by earlier negotiation and an ambassador,' surely the worst of these wretches will not risk losing their only abettors and palliators in this kingdom? I mean publicly: they have privately and individually their abettors and palliators in abundance still, wonderful as that is.

I am glad M. d'Arblay has joined the set at *Junipère*. What miserable work is this duelling, which I hear of among the emigrants, after such hair-breadth 'scapes for life and existence—to attack one another on the very spot they seek for refuge from attacks! It seems a sort of profanation of safety.

I can assure you people of *all* descriptions are a little alarmed here, at the successes so unbounded of the whole Jacobin tribe, which seems now spreading contagion over the whole surface of the earth. The strongest original favourers of revolutions abroad, and reforms at home, I see, are a little scared; they will not say it; but they say they are *not*, uncalled upon; which is a constant result of secret and involuntary consciousness.

F. B.

Miss Burney to Dr Burney

Norbury Park, Monday, February 4th, '93.

How exactly do I sympathize in all you say and feel, my dear sir, upon these truly calamitous times! I hear daily more and more affecting accounts of the saint-like end of the martyred Louis. Madame de Staël, daughter of M. Necker, is now at the head of the colony of French noblesse established near Mickleham. She is one of the first women I have ever met with for abilities and extraordinary intellect. She has just received, by a private letter, many particulars not yet made public, and which the Commune and Commissaries of the Temple had ordered should be suppressed. It has been exacted by those cautious men of blood that nothing should be printed that could *attendrir le peuple.*

Among other circumstances, this letter relates that the poor little Dauphin supplicated the monsters who came with the decree of death to his unhappy father, that they would carry him to the Convention, and the forty-eight Sections of Paris, and suffer him to beg his father's life.

This touching request was probably suggested to him by his miserable mother or aunt. When the King left the Temple to go to the place of sacrifice, the cries of his wretched family were heard, loud and shrill, through the courts without! Good heaven! what distress and horror equalled ever what they must then experience?

When he arrived at the scaffold, his confessor, as if with the courage of inspiration, called out to him aloud, after his last benediction: 'Fils de Saint Louis, montez au ciel!' The King ascended with firmness, and meant to harangue his guilty subjects; but the wretch Santerre said he was not there to speak, and the drums drowned the words, except to those nearest the terrible spot. To those he audibly was heard to say: 'Citoyens, je meurs innocent! Je pardonne à mes assassins; et je souhaite que ma mort soit utile à mon peuple.'

M. de Narbonne has been quite ill with the grief of this last enormity; and M. d'Arblay is now indisposed. This latter is one of the most delightful characters I have ever met, for openness, probity, intellectual knowledge, and unhackneyed manners. M. de Narbonne is far more a man of the world, and joins the most courtly refinement and elegance to the quickest repartee and readiness of wit. If anything but desolation and misery had brought them hither, we should have thought their addition to the Norbury society all that could be wished. They are bosom friends.

Your F. B.

Miss Burney to Mrs Phillips

Friday, May 31st, Chesington.

My heart so smites me this morning with making no answer to all I have been requested to weigh and decide, that I feel I cannot with any ease return to town without at least complying with one demand, which first, at parting yesterday, brought me to write fully to you, my Susan, if I could not elsewhere to my satisfaction. . . .

M. d'Arblay's last three letters convince me he is desperately dejected when alone, and when perfectly natural. It is not that he wants patience, but he wants rational expectation of better times: expectation founded on something more than mere aerial hope, that builds one day upon what the next blasts; and then has to build again, and again to be blasted.

What affects me the most in this situation is, that his time may as completely be lost as another's peace, by waiting for the effects of distant events, vague, bewildering, and remote, and quite as likely to lead to ill as to good. The very waiting, indeed, with the mind in such a state, is in itself an evil scarce to be recompensed.

My dearest Fredy, in the beginning of her knowledge of this transaction, told me that Mr Locke was of opinion that the £100 per annum[1] might do, as it does for many a curate. M. d'A. also most solemnly and affectingly declares that *le simple nécessaire* is all he requires, and here, in your vicinity, would unhesitatingly be preferred by him to the most brilliant fortune in another *séjour*.

If *he* can say that, what must *I* be not to echo it? I, who in the bosom of my own most chosen, most darling friends——

I need not enter more upon this; you all must know that to me a crust of bread, with a little roof for shelter,

[1] This was the allowance made by the Queen to Fanny upon her retirement from Court.

and a fire for warmth, near you, would bring me to peace, to happiness, to all that my heart holds dear, or even in any situation could prize. I cannot picture such a fate with dry eyes; all else but kindness and society has to me so always been nothing.

With regard to my dear father, he has always left me to myself; I will not therefore speak to him while thus uncertain what to decide.

It is certain, however, that, with peace of mind and retirement, I have resources that I could bring forward to amend the little situation; as well as that, once thus undoubtedly established and naturalized, M. d'A. would have claims for employment.

These reflections, with a mutual freedom from ambition, might lead to a quiet road, unbroken by the tortures of applications, expectations, attendance, disappointment, and time-wasting hopes and fears; if there were not apprehensions the £100 might be withdrawn. I do not think it likely, but it is a risk too serious in its consequences to be run. M. d'A, protests he could not answer to himself the hazard.

How to ascertain this, to clear the doubt, or to know the fatal certainty before it should be too late, exceeds my powers of suggestion. His own idea, to write to the Queen, much as it has startled me, and wild as it seemed to me, is certainly less wild than to take the chance of such a blow in the dark.

Yet such a letter could not even reach her. His very name is probably only known to her through myself.

In short, my dearest friends, you will think for me, and let me know what occurs to you, and I will defer any answer till I hear your opinions.

Heaven ever bless you! And pray for me at this moment.

F. B.

Dr Burney to Miss Burney

May, 1793.

DEAR FANNY, I have for some time seen very plainly that you are *éprise*, and have been extremely uneasy at the discovery. You must have observed my silent gravity, surpassing that of mere illness and its consequent low spirits. I had some thoughts of writing to Susan about it, and intended begging her to do what I must now do for myself—that is, beg, warn, and admonish you not to entangle yourself in a wild and romantic attachment, which offers nothing in prospect but poverty and distress, with future inconvenience and unhappiness. M. d'Arblay is certainly a very amiable and accomplished man, and of great military abilities I take for granted; but what employment has he for them of which the success is not extremely hazardous? His property, whatever it is, has been confiscated—*décreté*—by the Convention; and if a counter-revolution takes place, unless it be exactly such a one as suits the particular political sect in which he enlisted, it does not seem likely to secure to him an establishment in France. And as to an establishment in England, I know the difficulty which very deserving natives find in procuring one, with every appearance of interest, friends and probability; and, to a foreigner, I fear, the difficulty will be more than doubled.

As M. d'Arblay is at present circumstanced, an alliance with anything but a fortune sufficient for the support of himself and partner would be very imprudent. He is a mere soldier of fortune, under great disadvantages. Your income, if it was as certain as a freehold estate, is insufficient for the purpose; and if the Queen should be displeased and withdraw her allowance, what could you do?

I own that, if M. d'Arblay had an establishment in France sufficient for him to marry a wife with little or no fortune, much as I am inclined to honour and esteem him, I should wish to prevent you from fixing your residence there; not merely from selfishness, but for your own sake. I

know your love for your family, and know that it is reci-
procal; I therefore cannot help thinking that you would
mutually be a loss to each other. The friends, too, which
you have here, are of the highest and most desirable class.
To quit them, in order to make new friendships in a
strange land, in which the generality of its inhabitants at
present seem incapable of such virtues as friendship is
built upon, seems wild and visionary.

If M. d'Arblay had a sufficient establishment here for the
purposes of credit and comfort, and determined to settle
here for life, I should certainly think ourselves honoured
by his alliance; but his situation is at present so very remote
from all that can satisfy prudence, or reconcile to an affectionate father the idea of a serious attachment, that I
tremble for your heart and future happiness. M. d'Arblay
must have lived too long in the great world to accom-
modate himself contentedly to the little; his fate seems so
intimately connected with that of his miserable country,
and that country seems at a greater distance from peace,
order, and tranquillity now than it has done at any time
since the revolution.

These considerations, and the uncertainty of what party
will finally prevail, make me tremble for you both. You
see, by what I have said, that my objections are not
personal, but wholly prudential. For heaven's sake,
my dear Fanny, do not part with your heart too rapidly,
or involve yourself in deep engagements which it will be
difficult to dissolve; and to the last degree imprudent, as
things are at present circumstanced, to fulfil.

As far as character, merit, and misfortune demand esteem
and regard, you may be sure that M. d'Arblay will be
always received by me with the utmost attention and
respect; but, in the present situation of things, I can by
no means think I ought to encourage (blind and ignorant
as I am of all but his misfortunes) a serious and solemn
union with one whose unhappiness would be a reproach
to the facility and inconsiderateness of a most affectionate
father.

[Memorandum, this 7th of May, 1825

In answer to these apparently most just, and, undoubtedly, most parental and tender apprehensions, Susanna,
the darling child of Dr Burney, as well as first chosen
friend of M. d'Arblay, wrote a statement of the plans, and
means, and purposes of M. d'A. and F. B.—so clearly
demonstrating their power of happiness, with willing
economy, congenial tastes, and mutual love of the country,
that Dr B. gave way, and sent, though reluctantly, a
consent; by which the union took place the 31st of July
1793, in Mickleham church, in presence of Mr and Mrs
Locke, Captain and Mrs Phillips, M. de Narbonne, and
Captain Burney,[1] who was father to his sister, as Mr
Locke was to M. d'A.; and on the 1st of August the ceremony was re-performed in the Sardinian Chapel, according
to the rites of the Romish Church; and never, never was
union more blessed and felicitous; though after the first
eight years of unmingled happiness, it was assailed by
many calamities, chiefly of separation or illness, yet still
mentally unbroken.

                                          F. D'ARBLAY.]

Madame d'Arblay to Mrs ——
                              [October, 1793.]

The account of your surprise, my sweet friend, was the
last thing to create mine: I was well aware of the general
astonishment, and of yours in particular.   My own, however, at my very extraordinary fate, is singly greater than
that of all my friends united.   I had never made any vow
against marriage, but I had long, long been firmly persuaded it was for me a state of too much hazard and too
little promise to draw me from my individual plans and

---

[1] Fanny's brother, James.   It will be observed that her father was
not present.

purposes. I remember, in playing at questions and commands, when I was thirteen, being asked when I intended to marry? and surprising my playmates by solemnly replying: 'When I think I shall be happier than I am in being single.' It is true, I imagined that time would never arrive; and I have pertinaciously adhered to trying no experiment upon any other hope; for, many and mixed as are the ingredients which form what is generally considered as happiness, I was always fully convinced that social sympathy of character and taste could alone have any chance with me; all else I always thought, and now know, to be immaterial. I have only this peculiar—that what many contentedly assert or adopt in theory, I have had the courage to be guided by in practice.

We are now removed to a very small house in the suburbs of a very small village called Bookham. We found it rather inconvenient to reside in another person's dwelling, though our own apartments were to ourselves. Our views are not so beautiful as from Phenice Farm,[1] but our situation is totally free from neighbours and intrusion. We are about a mile and a half from Norbury Park, and two miles from Mickleham. I am become already so stout a walker, by use, and with the help of a very able supporter, that I go to those places and return home on foot without fatigue, when the weather is kind. At other times I condescend to accept a carriage from Mr Locke; but it is always reluctantly, I so much prefer walking where, as here, the country and prospects are inviting.

I thank you for your caution about building: we shall certainly undertake nothing but by contract; however, it would be truly mortifying to give up a house in Norbury Park; we defer the structure till the spring, as it is to be so very slight, that Mr Locke says it will be best to have it hardened in its first stage by the summer's sun. It will be very small, merely an habitation for three people, but in a situation truly beautiful, and within five minutes of

[1] Where the honeymoon was spent.

either Mr Locke, or my sister Phillips: it is to be placed just between those two loved houses.

My dearest father, whose fears and drawbacks have been my sole subject of regret, begins now to see I have not judged rashly, or with romance, in seeing my own road to my own felicity. And his restored cheerful concurrence in my constant principles, though new station, leaves me, for myself, without a wish. *L'ennui*, which could alone infest our retreat, I have ever been a stranger to, except in tiresome company, and my companion has every possible resource against either feeling or inspiring it.

As my partner is a Frenchman, I conclude the wonder raised by the connection may spread beyond my own private circle; but no wonder upon earth can ever arrive near my own in having found such a character from that nation. This is a prejudice certainly, impertinent, and very John Bullish, and very arrogant; but I only share it with all my countrymen, and therefore must needs forgive both them and myself. I am convinced, however, from your tender solicitude for me in all ways, that you will be glad to hear that the Queen and all the Royal Family have deigned to send me wishes for my happiness through Mrs Schwellenberg, who has written me 'what you call' a very kind congratulation.

F. D'A.

[In the year 1794, the happiness of the 'Hermitage' was increased by the birth of a son, who was christened Alexander Charles Louis Piochard d'Arblay; receiving the names of his father, with those of his two godfathers, the Comte de Narbonne and Dr Charles Burney.]

Madame d'Arblay to Doctor Burney

Bookham, March 22, 1794.

MY DEAR FATHER, I am at this moment returned from reading your most welcome and kind letter at our Susanna's. The account of your better health gives me a pleasure beyond all words; and it is the more essential to my perfect contentment on account of your opinion of our retreat. I doubt not, my dearest father, but you judge completely right, and I may nearly say we are both equally disposed to pay the most implicit respect to your counsel. We give up, therefore, all thoughts of our London excursion for the present, and I shall write to that effect to our good intended hostess very speedily.

I can easily conceive far more than you enlarge upon in this counsel: and, indeed, I have not myself been wholly free from apprehension of possible *embarras*, should we, at this period, visit London; for though M. d'Arblay not only could *stand*, but would *court*, all personal scrutiny, whether retrospective or actual, I see daily the extreme susceptibility which attends his very nice notions of honour, and how quickly and deeply his spirit is wounded by whatever he regards as injustice. Incapable, too, of the least trimming or disguise, he could not, at a time such as this, be in London without suffering or risking, perhaps hourly, something unpleasant. Here we are tranquil, undisturbed, and undisturbing. Can life, he often says, be more innocent than ours, or happiness more inoffensive? He works in his garden, or studies English and mathematics, while I write. When I work at my needle, he reads to me; and we enjoy the beautiful country around us in long and romantic strolls, during which he carries under his arm a portable garden chair, lent us by Mrs Locke, that I may rest as I proceed. He is extremely fond, too, of writing, and makes, from time to time, memorandums of such memoirs, poems, and anecdotes as he recollects, and I wish to have preserved. These resources for

sedentary life are certainly the first blessings that can be
given to man, for they enable him to be happy in the
extremist obscurity, even after tasting the dangerous
draughts of glory and ambition. . . .

M. d'Arblay, to my infinite satisfaction, gives up all
thoughts of building, in the present awful state of public
affairs. To show you, however, how much he is 'of
your advice,' as to *son jardin*, he has been drawing a plan
for it, which I intend to beg, borrow, or steal (all one), to
give you some idea how seriously he studies to make his
manual labours of some real utility.

This sort of work, however, is so totally new to him,
that he receives every now and then some of poor Merlin's
'disagreeable compliments';[1] for, when Mr Locke's or the
Captain's gardeners favour our grounds with a visit, they
commonly make known that all has been done wrong.
Seeds are sowing in some parts when plants ought to be
reaping, and plants are running to seed while they are
thought not yet at maturity. Our garden, therefore, is
not yet quite the most profitable thing in the world; but
M. d'A. assures me it is to be the staff of our table and
existence.

A little, too, he has been unfortunate; for, after immense
toil in planting and transplanting strawberries round our
hedge, here at Bookham, he has just been informed they
will bear no fruit the first year, and the second we may be
'over the hills and far away!'

Another time, too, with great labour, he cleared a
considerable compartment of weeds, and when it looked
clean and well, and he showed his work to the gardener,
the man said he had demolished an asparagus bed! M.
d'A. protested, however, nothing could look more like
des mauvaises herbes.

His greatest passion is for transplanting. Everything
we possess he moves from one end of the garden to
another, to produce better effects. Roses take place of

[1] Merlin was a French inventor of mechanical contrivances whom
Fanny had known long before as a visitor at her father's house.

jessamines, jessamines of honeysuckles, and honeysuckles of lilacs, till they have all danced round as far as the space allows; but whether the effect may not be a general mortality, summer only can determine.

Such is our horticultural history. But I must not omit that we have had for one week cabbages from our own cultivation every day! Oh, you have no idea how sweet they tasted! We agreed they had a freshness and a *goût* we had never met with before. We had them for too short a time to grow tired of them, because, as I have already hinted, they were beginning to run to seed before we knew they were eatable.

F. D'A.

Madame d'Arblay to Mrs ——[1]

Bookham, June 15, '95.

No, my dear M——, no—'this poor intercourse' shall never cease, while the hand that writes this assurance can hold a pen! I have been very much touched with your letter, its affection, and its—everything. Do not for the world suffer this our only communication to 'dwindle away': for me, though the least punctual of all correspondents, I am, perhaps, the most faithful of all friends; for my regard, once excited, keeps equal energy in absence as in presence, and an equally fond and minute interest in those for whom I cherish it, whether I see them but at the distance of years, or with every day's sun. . . . I love *nobody for nothing*; I am not so tindery! Therefore there must be change in the object before there can be any in me. . . .

I have a long work, which a long time has been in hand, that I mean to publish soon—in about a year. Should it succeed, like *Evelina* and *Cecilia*, it may be a little portion

---

[1] Mrs Waddington, whom the reader met at Mrs Delany's as Miss Port.

to our Bambino. We wish, therefore, to print it for ourselves in this hope; but the expenses of the press are so enormous, so raised by these late Acts, that it is out of all question for us to afford it. We have, therefore, been led by degrees to listen to counsel of some friends, and to print it by subscription. This is in many—many ways unpleasant and unpalatable to us both; but the real chance of real use and benefit to our little darling overcomes all scruples, and, therefore, to work we go!

You will feel, I dare believe, all I could write on this subject; I once rejected such a plan, formed for me by Mr Burke, where books were to be kept by ladies, not booksellers—the Duchess of Devonshire, Mrs Boscawen, and Mrs Crewe; but I was an individual then, and had no cares of times to come: now, thank heaven! this is not the case —and when I look at my little boy's dear, innocent, yet intelligent face, I defy any pursuit to be painful that may lead to his good.

Adieu, my ever dear friend!

F. D'A.

[During the years 1794 and 1795, Madame d'Arblay finished and prepared for the press her third novel, *Camilla*, which was published partly by subscription in 1796; the Dowager Duchess of Leinster, the Hon. Mrs Boscawen, Mrs Crewe, and Mrs Locke, kindly keeping lists, and receiving the names of subscribers.[1]

This work having been dedicated by permission to the Queen, the authoress was desirous of presenting the first copy to her majesty, and made a journey to Windsor for that honour.]

[1] The list of subscribers is long and impressive. Among the more humble names is that of Jane Austen.

Madame d'Arblay to Dr Burney

Bookham, July 10, 1796.

If I had as much of time as of matter, my dear father, what an immense letter should I write you! But I have still so many book oddments of accounts, examinations, directions, and little household affairs to arrange, that with baby-kissing included, I expect I can give you to-day only part the first of an excursion which I mean to comprise in four parts: so here begins.

The books were ready at eleven or twelve, but not so the tailor! The three Miss Thrales came to a short but cordial hand-shaking at the last minute, by appointment; and at about half-past three we set forward. I had written the day before to my worthy old friend Mrs Agnew, to secure us rooms for one day and night, and to Miss Planta to make known I could not set out till late.

When we came into Windsor at seven o'clock, the way to Mrs Agnew's was so intricate that we could not find it, till one of the King's footmen, recollecting me, I imagine, came forward, a volunteer, and walked by the side of the chaise to show the postilion the house. N.B.—No bad omen to worldly augurers.

Arrived, Mrs Agnew came forth with faithful attachment, to conduct us to our destined lodgings. I wrote hastily to Miss Planta, to announce to the Queen that I was waiting the honour of her Majesty's commands; and then began preparing for my appearance the next morning, when I expected a summons; but Miss Planta came instantly herself from the Queen, with orders of immediate attendance, as her Majesty would see me directly! The King was just gone upon the Terrace, but her Majesty did not walk that evening.

Mrs Agnew was my maid, Miss Planta my arranger; my landlord, who was a hairdresser, came to my head, and M. d'Arblay was general superintendent. The haste and the joy went hand in hand, and I was soon equipped, though shocked at my own precipitance in sending before I was already visible. Who, however, could have expected such prompt admission? and in an evening?

M. d'Arblay helped to carry the books as far as to the gates. My lodgings were as near to them as possible. At the first entry towards the Queen's lodge, we encountered Dr Fisher and his lady; the sight of me there, in a dress announcing indisputably whither I was hieing, was such an astonishment that they looked at me rather as a recollected spectre than a renewed acquaintance. When we came to the iron rails, poor Miss Planta, in much fidget, begged to take the books from M. d'Arblay, terrified, I imagine, lest French feet should contaminate the gravel within!—while he, innocent of her fears, was insisting upon carrying them as far as to the house, till he saw I took part with Miss Planta, and he was then compelled to let us lug in ten volumes [1] as we could.

The King was already returned from the terrace, the page in waiting told us. 'Oh, then,' said Miss Planta, 'you are too late!' However, I went into my old dining-parlour; while she said she would see if any one could obtain the Queen's commands for another time. I did not stay five minutes ruminating upon the dinners, 'gone where the chickens,' etc., when Miss Planta returned, and told me the Queen would see me instantly.

The Queen was in her dressing-room, and with only the Princess Elizabeth. Her reception was the most gracious imaginable; yet, when she saw my emotion in thus meeting her again, she was herself by no means quite unmoved. I presented my little—yet not small—offering, upon one knee, placing them, as she directed, upon a table by her side, and expressing as well as I could my devoted gratitude for her invariable goodness to me. She then began a conversation, in her old style, upon various things and people, with all her former graciousness of manner, which soon, as she perceived my strong sense of her indulgence, grew into even all its former kind-

[1] i.e. two sets. *Camilla* was published in five volumes.

ness. Particulars I have now no room for; but when, in about half an hour, she said: 'How long do you intend to stay here, Madame d'Arblay?' and I answered: 'We have no intentions, ma'am,' she repeated, laughing: 'You have no intentions! Well, then, if you can come again to-morrow morning, you shall see the Princesses.'

She then said she would not detain me at present; and, encouraged by all that had passed, I asked if I might presume to put at the door of the King's apartment a copy of my little work. She hesitated, but with smiles the most propitious; then told me to fetch the books; and whispered something to the Princess Elizabeth, who left the room by another door at the same moment that I retired for the other set.

Almost immediately upon my return to the Queen and the Princess Elizabeth, the King entered the apartment, and entered it to receive himself my little offering. . . .

Just before we assembled to dinner, Mlle Jacobi desired to speak with me alone; and, taking me to another room, presented me with a folded packet, saying: 'The Queen ordered me to put this into your hands, and said, "Tell Madame d'Arblay it is from us both."' It was a hundred guineas. I was confounded, and nearly sorry, so little was such a mark of their goodness in my thoughts. She added that the King, as soon as he came from the chapel in the morning, went to the Queen's dressing-room just before he set out for the levee, and put into her hands fifty guineas, saying: 'This is for my set!' The Queen answered: 'I shall do exactly the same for mine,' and made up the packet herself. ''Tis only,' she said, 'for the paper, tell Madame d'Arblay—nothing for the trouble!' meaning she accepted that.

The manner of this was so more than gracious, so kind, in the words *us both*, that indeed the money at the time was quite nothing in the scale of my gratification; it was even less, for it almost pained me. . . .

F. d'A.

Madame d'Arblay to Dr Burney

Bookham, Friday, October, 1796.

How well I know and feel the pang of this cruel day to my beloved father! . . . I am almost afraid to ask how my poor mother bore the last farewell. . . .

Our sorrow, however, here, has been very considerably diminished by the major's voluntary promises to Mrs Locke of certain and speedy return.[1] I shall expect him at the peace—not before. . . .

But I meant to have begun with our thanks for my dear kind father's indulgence of our extreme curiosity and interest in the sight of the reviews. I am quite happy in what I have escaped of greater severity, though my mate cannot bear that the palm should be contested by *Evelina* and *Cecilia*; his partiality rates the last as so much the highest; so does the newspaper I have mentioned, of which I long to send you a copy. But those immense men, whose single praise was fame and security—who established, by a word, the two elder sisters—are now silent. Dr Johnson and Sir Joshua are no more, and Mr Burke is ill, or otherwise engrossed; yet even without their powerful influence, to which I owe such unspeakable obligation, the essential success of *Camilla* exceeds that of the elders. The sale is truly astonishing. Charles has just sent to me that five hundred only remain of four thousand, and it has appeared scarcely three months.

The first edition of *Evelina* was of eight hundred,[2] the second of five hundred, and the third of a thousand. What the following have been I have never heard. The sale from that period became more flourishing than the publisher cared to announce. Of *Cecilia* the first edition was reckoned enormous at two thousand; and as a part of payment was reserved for it, I remember our dear

[1] Susan and her husband (now a major) had gone to Ireland.
[2] Probably a mistake for five hundred. *Camilla*, though far inferior to the two earlier novels, was much more profitable to the author. The reviews were cool, and, in Dr Burney's opinion, 'unfriendly.'

Daddy Crisp thought it very unfair. It was printed, like this, in July, and sold in October, to every one's wonder. Here, however, the sale is increased in rapidity more than a third. Charles says:

> 'Now heed no more what critics thought 'em,
> Since this you know, all people bought 'em.'

We have resumed our original plan, and are going immediately to build a little cottage for ourselves. We shall make it as small and as cheap as will accord with its being warm and comfortable. We have relinquished, however, the very kind offer of Mr Locke, which he has renewed, for his park. We mean to make this a property saleable or letable for our Alex., and in Mr Locke's park we could not encroach any tenant, if the youth's circumstances, profession, or inclination should make him not choose the spot for his own residence. M. d'Arblay, therefore, has fixed upon a field of Mr Locke's, which he will rent, and of which Mr Locke will grant him a lease of ninety years. By this means, we shall leave the little Alex. a little property, besides what will be in the funds, and a property likely to rise in value, as the situation of the field is remarkably beautiful. It is in the valley, between Mr Locke's park and Dorking, and where land is so scarce, that there is not another possessor within many miles who would part, upon any terms, with half an acre. My kindest father will come and give it, I trust, his benediction. I am now almost jealous of Bookham for having received it.

Imagine but the ecstasy of M. d'Arblay in training, all his own way, an entire new garden. He dreams now of cabbage walks, potato beds, bean perfumes, and peas blossoms. My mother should send him a little sketch to help his flower garden, which will be his second favourite object.

Alex. has made no progress in phrases, but pronounces single words a few more. Adieu, most dear sir.

F. d'A.

Madame d'Arblay to Dr Burney

Bookham, July 27, '97.

MY DEAREST PADRE, . . . I was surprised, and almost frightened, though at the same time gratified, to find you assisted in paying the last honours to Mr Burke. How sincerely I sympathize in all you say of that truly great man! That his enemies say he was not perfect is nothing compared with his immense superiority over almost all those who are merely exempted from his peculiar defects. That he was upright in heart, even where he acted wrong, I do truly believe; and it is a great pleasure to me that Mr Locke believes it too, and that he asserted nothing he had not persuaded himself to be true, from Mr Hastings's being the most rapacious of villains, to the King's being incurably insane. He was as generous as kind, and as liberal in his sentiments as he was luminous in intellect and extraordinary in abilities and eloquence. Though free from all little vanity, high above envy, and glowing with zeal to exalt talents and merit in others, he had, I believe, a consciousness of his own greatness, that shut out those occasional and useful self-doubts which keep our judgment in order, by calling our motives and our passions to account. I entreat you to let me know how poor Mrs Burke supports herself in this most desolate state, and who remains to console her when Mrs Crewe will be far off.

Our cottage is now in the act of being rough-cast. Its ever imprudent and *téméraire* builder [1] made himself very ill t'other day, by going from the violent heat of extreme hard work in his garden to drink out of a fresh-drawn pail of well-water, and dash the same over his face. A dreadful headache ensued; and two days' confinement, with James's Powders, have but just reinstated him. In vain I represent he has no right now to make so free with himself—he has such a habit of disdaining all care and

[1] M. d'Arblay.

precaution, that, though he gives me the fairest promises, I find them of no avail. Mr Angerstein went to see his field lately, and looked everywhere for him, having heard he was there; but he was not immediately to be known, while digging with all his might and main, without coat or waistcoat, and in his green leather cap. . . .

F. D'A.

Madame d'Arblay to Mrs Phillips

West Hamble, December, '97.

This moment I receive, through our dearest friend, my own Susanna's letter. I grieve to find she ever waits anxiously for news; but always imagine all things essential perpetually travelling to her, from so many of our house, all in nearly constant correspondence with her. This leads me to rest quiet as to her, when I do not write more frequently; but as to myself, when I do not hear I am saddened even here, even in my own new paradise—for such I confess it is to me; and were my beloved Susan on this side the Channel, and could I see her dear face, and fold her to my breast, I think I should set about wishing nothing but to continue just so. For circumstances—pecuniary ones I mean—never have power to distress me, unless I fear exceeding their security; and that fear these times will sometimes inflict. The new threefold assessment of taxes has terrified us rather seriously: though the necessity, and therefore justice of them, we mutually feel. My father thinks his own share will amount to 80*l.* a year! We have, this very morning, decided upon parting with four of our new windows—a great abatement of *agrémens* to ourselves, and of ornament to our appearance; and a still greater sacrifice to *l'amour propre* of my architect, who, indeed—his fondness for his edifice considered—does not ill deserve praise that the scheme had not his mere consent, but his own free proposition. . . .

We quitted Bookham with one single regret—that of leaving our excellent neighbours the Cookes. The father is so worthy, and the mother so good, so deserving, so liberal, and so infinitely kind, that the world certainly does not abound with people to compare with them. They both improved upon us considerably since we lost our dearest Susan—not, you will believe, as substitutes, but still for their intrinsic worth and most friendly partiality and regard.

We languished for the moment of removal with almost infantile fretfulness at every delay that distanced it; and when at last the grand day came, our final packings, with all their toil and difficulties and labour and expense, were mere acts of pleasantry: so bewitched were we with the impending change, that, though from six o'clock to three we were hard at work, without a kettle to boil the breakfast, or a knife to cut bread for a luncheon, we missed nothing, wanted nothing, and were as insensible to fatigue as to hunger.

M. d'Arblay set out on foot, loaded with remaining relics of things, to us precious, and Betty afterwards with a remnant glass or two; the other maid had been sent two days before. I was forced to have a chaise for my Alex. and me, and a few looking-glasses, a few folios, and not a few other oddments; and then, with dearest Mr Locke, our founder's portrait, and my little boy, off I set; and I would my dearest Susan could relate to me as delicious a journey.

My mate, striding over hedge and ditch, arrived first, though he set out after, to welcome me to our new dwelling; and we entered our new best room, in which I found a glorious fire of wood, and a little bench, borrowed of one of the departing carpenters: nothing else. We contrived to make room for each other, and Alex. disdained all rest. His spirits were so high upon finding two or three rooms totally free for his horse (alias any stick he can pick up) and himself, unencumbered by chairs and tables and such-like lumber, that he was as merry as little

Andrew and as wild as twenty colts. Here we unpacked
a small basket, containing three or four loaves, and, with
a garden knife, fell to work; some eggs had been procured
from a neighbouring farm, and one saucepan had been
brought. We dined, therefore, exquisitely, and drank
to our new possessions from a glass of clear water out of
our new well.

At about eight o'clock our goods arrived. We had our
bed put up in the middle of our room, to avoid risk of
damp walls, and our Alex. had his dear Willy's crib at our
feet.

We none of us caught cold. We had fire night and day
in the maids' room, as well as our own—or rather in my
Susan's room; for we lent them that, their own having a
little inconvenience against a fire, because it is built without
a chimney.

We continued making fires all around us the first fortnight, and then found wood would be as bad as an apothecary's bill, so desisted; but we did not stop short so soon
as to want the latter to succeed the former, or put our
calculation to the proof.

Our first week was devoted to unpacking, and exulting
in our completed plan. To have no one thing at hand,
nothing to eat, nowhere to sit—all were trifles, rather, I
think, amusing than incommodious. The house looked
so clean, the distribution of the rooms and closets is so
convenient, the prospect everywhere around is so gay
and so lovely, and the park of dear Norbury is so close
at hand, that we hardly knew how to require anything else
for existence than the enjoyment of our own situation. . . .

Thursday morning I had a letter from Miss Planta,
written with extreme warmth of kindness, and fixing the
next day at eleven o'clock for my Royal admission.

I went upstairs to Miss Planta's room, where, while I
waited for her to be called, the charming Princess Mary
passed by, attended by Mrs Cheveley. She recollected
me, and turned back, and came up to me with a fair hand
graciously held out to me. 'How do you do, Madame

d'Arblay?' she cried: 'I am vastly glad to see you again; and how does your little boy do?'

I gave her a little account of the rogue, and she proceeded to inquire about my new cottage, and its actual size. I entered into a long detail of its bare walls and unfurnished sides, and the gambols of the little man unencumbered by cares of fractures from useless ornaments, that amused her good-humoured interest in my affairs very much; and she did not leave me till Miss Planta came to usher me to Princess Augusta.

That kind Princess received me with a smile so gay, and a look so pleased at my pleasure in again seeing her, that I quite regretted the etiquette which prevented a chaste embrace. She was sitting at her toilette, having her hair dressed. The Royal Family were all going at night to the play. She turned instantly from the glass to face me, and insisted upon my being seated immediately. She then wholly forgot her attire and ornaments and appearance, and consigned herself wholly to conversation, with that intelligent animation which marks her character. She inquired immediately how my little boy did, and then with great sweetness after his father, and after my father.

My first subject was the Princess Royal, and I accounted for not having left my Hermitage in the hope of once more seeing her Royal Highness before her departure.[1] It would have been, I told her, so melancholy a pleasure to have come merely for a last view, that I could not bear to take my annual indulgence at a period which would make it leave a mournful impression upon my mind for a twelvemonth to come. The Princess said she could enter into that, but said it as if she had been surprised I had not appeared. She then gave me some account of the ceremony; and when I told her I had heard that her Royal Highness the bride had never looked so lovely, she confirmed the praise warmly, but laughingly added: ''Twas the Queen dressed her! You know what a figure she

[1] The Princess Royal had married Frederick, afterwards King of Württemberg.

used to make of herself, with her odd manner of dressing herself; but mamma said: "Now really, Princess Royal, this one time is the last, and I cannot suffer you to make such a quiz of yourself; so I will really have you dressed properly." And indeed the Queen was quite in the right, for everybody said she had never looked so well in her life.'

The word *quiz*, you may depend, was never the Queen's. I had great comfort, however, in gathering, from all that passed on that subject, that the Royal Family is persuaded this estimable Princess is happy. From what I know of her disposition I am led to believe the situation may make her so. She is born to preside, and that with equal softness and dignity; but she was here in utter subjection, for which she had neither spirits nor inclination. She adored the King, honoured the Queen, and loved her sisters, and had much kindness for her brothers; but her style of life was not adapted to the royalty of her nature, any more than of her birth; and though she only wished for power to do good and to confer favours, she thought herself out of her place in not possessing it. . . .

It would have been truly edifying to young ladies living in the great and public world to have assisted in my place at the toilette of this exquisite Princess Augusta. Her ease, amounting even to indifference, as to her ornaments and decoration, showed a mind so disengaged from vanity, so superior to mere personal appearance, that I could with difficulty forbear manifesting my admiration. She let the hair-dresser proceed upon her head without comment and without examination, just as if it was solely his affair; and when the man, Robinson, humbly begged to know what ornaments he was to prepare the hair for, she said: 'Oh, there are my feathers, and my gown is blue, so take what you think right.' And when he begged she would say whether she would have any ribbons or other things mixed with the feathers and jewels, she said: 'You understand all that best, Mr Robinson, I'm sure; there are the things, so take just what you please.' And after this she left him wholly to himself, never a moment interrupting her discourse or her attention with a single direction.

She had just begun a very interesting account of an officer that had conducted himself singularly well in the mutiny, when Miss Planta came to summon me to the Queen. I begged permission to return afterwards for my unfinished narrative, and then proceeded to the White Closet.

The Queen was alone, seated at a table, and working. Miss Planta opened the door and retired without entering. I felt a good deal affected by the sight of her Majesty again, so graciously accorded to my request; but my first and instinctive feeling was nothing to what I experienced when, after my profoundly respectful reverence, I raised my eyes, and saw in hers a look of sensibility so expressive of regard, and so examining, so penetrating into mine, as to seem to convey, involuntarily, a regret I had quitted her. This, at least, was the idea that struck me, from the species of look which met me, and it touched me to the heart, and brought instantly, in defiance of all struggle, a flood of tears into my eyes. I was some minutes recovering; and when I then entreated her forgiveness, and cleared up, the voice with which she spoke, in hoping I was well, told me she had caught a little of my sensation, for it was by no means steady. Indeed, at that moment, I longed to kneel and beseech her pardon for the displeasure I had felt in her long resistance of my resignation; for I think, now, it was from a real and truly honourable wish to attach me to her for ever. But I then suffered too much from a situation so ill adapted to my choice and disposition, to do justice to her opposition, or to enjoy its honour to myself. Now that I am so singularly, alas! nearly singularly happy, though wholly from my perseverance in that resignation, I feel all I owe her, and I feel more and more grateful for every mark of her condescension, either recollected or renewed.

She looked ill, pale, and harassed. The King was but

just returned from his abortive visit to the Nore,[1] and the inquietude she had sustained during that short separation, circumstanced many ways alarmingly, had evidently shaken her; I saw with much, with deep concern, her sunk eyes and spirits; I believe the sight of me raised not the latter. Mrs Schwellenberg had not long been dead, and I have some reason to think she would not have been sorry to have had me supply the vacancy; for I had immediate notice sent me of her death by Miss Planta, so written as to persuade me it was a letter by command. But not all my duty, all my gratitude, could urge me, even one short fleeting moment, to weigh any interest against the soothing serenity, the unfading felicity, of a Hermitage such as mine.

We spoke of poor Mrs Schwelly—and of her successor, Mlle Backmeister—and of mine, Mrs Bremyère; and I could not but express my concern that her Majesty had again been so unfortunate, for Mlle Jacobi had just retired to Germany, ill and dissatisfied with everything in England. The Princess Augusta had recounted to me the whole narrative of her retirement, and its circumstances. The Queen told me that the King had very handsomely taken care of her. But such frequent retirements are heavy weights upon the royal bounty. I felt almost guilty when the subject was started; but not from any reproach, any allusion—not a word was dropped that had not kindness and goodness for its basis and its superstructure at once.

'How is your little boy?' was one of the earliest questions. 'Is he here?' she added.

'Oh, yes,' I answered, misunderstanding her, 'he is my shadow; I go nowhere without him.'

'But *here*, I mean?'

'Oh, no! ma'am, I did not dare presume——'

I stopped, for her look said it would be no presumption. And Miss Planta had already desired me to bring him to her next time; which I suspect was by higher order than her own suggestion.

---

[1] In connection with the mutiny in the fleet.

She then inquired after my dear father, and so graciously, that I told her not only of his good health, but his occupations, his new work, a *Poetical History of Astronomy*,[1] and his consultations with Herschel.

She permitted me to speak a good deal of the Princess of Wurtemberg, whom they still all call Princess Royal. She told me she had worked her wedding garment, and entirely, and the real labour it had proved, from her steadiness to have no help, well knowing that three stitches done by any other would make it immediately said it was none of it by herself. 'As the bride of a widower,' she continued, 'I know she ought to be in white and gold; but as the King's eldest daughter she had a right to white and silver, which she preferred.' . . .

She then deigned to inquire very particularly about our new cottage—its size, its number of rooms, and its grounds. I told her, honestly, it was excessively comfortable, though unfinished and unfitted up, for that it had innumerable little contrivances and conveniences, just adapted to our particular use and taste, as M. d'Arblay had been its sole architect and surveyor. 'Then, I dare say,' she answered, 'it is very commodious, for there are no people understand enjoyable accommodations more than French gentlemen, when they have the arranging them themselves.' . . .

But what chiefly dwells upon me with pleasure is, that she spoke to me upon some subjects and persons that I know she would not for the world should be repeated, with just the same confidence, the same reliance upon my grateful discretion for her openness, that she honoured me with while she thought me established in her service for life. I need not tell my Susan how this binds me more than ever to her.

Very short to me seemed the time, though the whole conversation was serious, and her air thoughtful almost to sadness, when a page touched the door, and said something in German. The Queen, who was then standing

[1] Dr Burney subsequently destroyed this work.

by the window, turned round to answer him, and then, with a sort of congratulatory smile to me, said: 'Now you will see what you don't expect—the King!'

I could indeed not expect it, for he was at Blackheath at a review, and he was returned only to dress for the levee.

The King related very pleasantly a little anecdote of Lady ——— . 'She brought the little Princess Charlotte,' he said, 'to me just before the review. "She hoped," she said, "I should not take it ill, for, having mentioned it to the child, she built so upon it that she had thought of nothing else!" Now this,' cried he, laughing heartily, 'was pretty strong! How can she know what a child is thinking of before it can speak?'

I was very happy at the fondness they both expressed for the little Princess. 'A sweet little creature,' the King called her; 'A most lovely child,' the Queen turned to me to add; and the King said he had taken her upon his horse, and given her a little ride, before the regiment rode up to him. ''Tis very odd,' he added, 'but she always knows me on horseback, and never else.' 'Yes,' said the Queen, 'when his Majesty comes to her on horseback she claps her little hands, and endeavours to say "Gan-pa!" immediately.' I was much pleased that she is brought up to such simple and affectionate acknowledgment of relationship.

The King then inquired about my father, and with a look of interest and kindness that regularly accompanies his mention of that most dear person. He asked after his health, his spirits, and his occupations, waiting for long answers to each inquiry. . . .

There was time but for little more, as he was to change his dress for the levee; and I left their presence more attached to them, I really think, than ever. . . .

I then made a little visit to Miss Planta, who was extremely friendly, and asked me why I should wait another year before I came. I told her I had leave for an annual visit, and could not presume to encroach beyond such a permission. However, as she proposed my calling upon her, at least when I happened to be in town or at Chelsea, I begged her to take some opportunity to hint my wish of admission, if possible, more frequently. . . .

Very soon afterwards I had a letter from Miss Planta, saying she had mentioned to her Majesty my regret of the long intervals of annual admissions; and that her Majesty had most graciously answered: 'She should be very glad to see me whenever I came to town.'

Madame d'Arblay to Dr Burney

9th January, 1800.

MY MOST DEAR PADRE, My mate will say all say—so I can only offer up my earnest prayers I may soon be allowed the blessing—the only one I sigh for—of embracing my dearest Susan in your arms and under your roof. Amen.

F. D'A.

These were the last written lines of the last period—unsuspected as such—of my perfect happiness on earth; for they were stopped on the road by news that my heart's beloved sister, Susanna Elizabeth Phillips, had ceased to breathe. The tenderest of husbands—the most feeling of human beings—had only reached Norbury Park, on his way to a believed meeting with that angel, when the fatal blow was struck; and he came back to West Hamble—to the dreadful task of revealing the irreparable loss which his own goodness, sweetness, patience, and sympathy could alone have made supported.

Madame d'Arblay to Dr Burney

West Hamble, March 22, 1800.

Day after day I have meant to write to my dearest father; but I have been unwell ever since our return, and that has not added to my being sprightly. I have not once crossed the threshold since I re-entered the house till to-day, when Mr and Mrs Locke almost insisted upon taking me an airing. I am glad of it, for it has done me good, and broken a kind of spell that made me unwilling to stir.

M. d'Arblay has worked most laboriously in his garden; but his misfortunes there, during our absence, might melt a heart of stone. The horses of our next neighbouring farmer broke through our hedges, and have made a kind of bog of our meadow, by scampering in it during the wet; the sheep tollowed, who have eaten up all our greens, every sprout and cabbage and lettuce destined for the winter; while the horses dug up our turnips and carrots; and the swine, pursuing such examples, have trod down all the young plants, besides devouring whatever the others left of vegetables. Our potatoes, left, from our abrupt departure, in the ground, are all rotten or frost-bitten, and utterly spoilt; and not a single thing has our whole ground produced us since we came home. A few dried carrots, which remain from the indoor collection, are all we have to temper our viands.

What think you of this for people who make it a rule to owe a third of their sustenance to the garden? Poor M. d'A.'s renewal of toil, to supply future times, is exemplary to behold, after such discouragement. But he works as if nothing had failed; such is his patience as well as industry. . . .

I long for some further account of you, dearest sir, and how you bear the mixture of business and company, of *fag and frolic*, as Charlotte used to phrase it.

F. D'A.

[1802. The beginning of this year was attended with much anxiety to Madame d'Arblay. Her husband, disappointed in the hopes suggested by his friends, of his receiving employment as French Commercial Consul in London, directed his efforts to obtaining his half-pay on the retired list of French officers. This was promised, on condition that he should previously serve at St Domingo, where General Leclerc was then endeavouring to put down Toussaint's insurrection. He accepted the appointment conditionally on his being allowed to retire as soon as that expedition should be ended. This, he was told, was impossible, and he therefore hastened back to his family towards the end of January.

In February, a dispatch followed him from General Berthier, then Minister of War, announcing that his appointment was made out, and on his own terms. To this M. d'Arblay wrote his acceptance, but repeated a stipulation he had before made, that while he was ready to fight against the enemies of the Republic, yet, should future events disturb the peace lately established between France and England,[1] it was his unalterable determination never to take up arms against the British Government. As this determination had already been signified by M. d'Arblay, he waited not to hear the result of its repetition, but set off again for Paris to receive orders, and proceed thence to St Domingo.

After a short time he was informed that his stipulation of never taking up arms against England could not be accepted, and that his military appointment was, in consequence, annulled. Having been required at the Alien Office, on quitting England, to engage that he would not return for the space of one year, he now proposed that Madame d'Arblay, with her little boy, should join him in France.]

[1] 'The peace lately established' by the Treaty of Amiens lasted only from March 1802 to May 1803. This was an unfortunate circumstance for M. and Mme d'Arblay.

Diary resumed

Addressed to Dr Burney

I seize, at length, upon the largest paper I can procure, to begin to my beloved father some account of our journey, and if I am able, I mean to keep him a brief journal of my proceedings during this destined year or eighteen months' separation—secure of his kindest interest in all that I may have to relate, and certain he will be anxious to know how I go on in a strange land: 'tis my only way now of communicating with him, and I must draw from it one of my dearest worldly comforts, the hopes of seeing his loved hand with some return.

Thursday, April 15, 1802.

William and John conducted my little boy and me in excellent time to the inn in Piccadilly, where we met my kind Mrs Locke, and dear little Adrienne de Chavagnac.[1] The parting there was brief and hurried; and I set off on my grand expedition, with my two dear young charges, exactly at five o'clock.

Paris, April 15, 1802.

The book-keeper came to me eagerly, crying: 'Vite, vite, Madame, prenez votre place dans la diligence, car voici un monsieur anglais, qui sûrement va prendre la meilleure!' —*en effet, ce monsieur anglais* did not disappoint his expectations, or much raise mine; for he not only took the best place, but contrived to ameliorate it by the little scruple with which he made every other worse, from the unbridled expansion in which he indulged his dear person, by putting out his elbows against his next, and his knees and feet against his opposite, neighbour. He seemed prepared to look upon all around him with a sort of sulky haughtiness, pompously announcing himself as a commander of

[1] This child was returning, in Fanny's charge, to her parents in Paris.

distinction who had long served at Gibraltar and various
places, who had travelled thence through France, and
from France to Italy, who was a native of Scotland, and
of proud, though unnamed genealogy; and was now
going to Paris purposely to behold the First Consul, to
whom he meant to claim an introduction through Mr
Jackson. His burnt complexion, Scotch accent, large
bony face and figure, and high and distant demeanour,
made me easily conceive and believe him a highland
chief. I never heard his name, but I think him a gentleman born, though not gently bred.

The next to mention is a Madame *Raymond* or *Grammont*,
for I heard not distinctly which, who seemed very much a
gentlewoman, and who was returning to France, too
uncertain of the state of her affairs to know whether she
might rest there or not. She had only one defect to prevent my taking much interest in her; this was, not merely
an avoidance, but a horror of being touched by either
of my children; who, poor little souls, restless and fatigued
by the confinement they endured, both tried to fling themselves upon every passenger in turn; and though by every
one they were sent back to their sole prop, they were by
no one repulsed with such hasty displeasure as by this old
lady, who seemed as fearful of having the petticoat of
her gown, which was stiff, round, and bulging, as if lined
with parchment, deranged, as if she had been attired in a
hoop for Court.

The third person was a Madame Blaizeau, who seemed
an exceeding good sort of women, gay, voluble, good-
humoured, and merry. All we had of amusement sprang
from her sallies, which were uttered less from a desire of
pleasing others, her very natural character having none of
the high polish bestowed by the Graces, than from a jovial
spirit of enjoyment which made them produce pleasure
to herself. She soon and frankly acquainted us she had
left France to be a governess to some young ladies before
the Revolution, and under the patronage, as I think,
of the Duke of Dorset; she had *been courted*, she told us,

by an English gentleman farmer, but he would not change
his religion for her, nor she for him, and so, when everything was bought for her wedding, they broke off the
connection; and she afterwards married a Frenchman.
She had seen a portrait, set richly in diamonds, of the
King, prepared for a present to the First Consul; and described its superb ornaments and magnificence in a way to
leave no dount of the fact.   She meant to stop at St Denys,
to inquire if her mother yet lived, having received no
intelligence from or of her, these last ten eventful years!

Friday, April 16.

As we were not to sail till twelve, I had hoped to have
seen the Castle and Shakespeare's Cliff, but most unfortunately it rained all the morning, and we were confined
to the inn, except for the interlude of the custom-house,
where, however, the examination was so slight, and made
with such civility, that we had no other trouble with it
than a wet walk and a few shillings.

Our passports were examined; and we then went to the
port, and, the sea being perfectly smooth, were lifted from
the quay to the deck of our vessel with as little difficulty
as we could have descended from a common chair to the
ground.

The calm which caused our slow passage and our sickness, was now favourable, for it took us into the port of
Calais so close and even with the quay, that we scarcely
accepted even a hand to aid us from the vessel to the
shore.

The quay was lined with crowds of people, men,
women, and children, and certain amphibious females,
who might have passed for either sex, or anything else
in the world, except what they really were, European
women! Their men's hats, men's jackets, and men's
shoes; their burnt skins, and most savage-looking petticoats, hardly reaching, nay, not reaching their knees,
would have made me instantly believe any account I

could have heard of their being just imported from the wilds of America.

The vessel was presently filled with men, who, though dirty and mean, were so civil and gentle that they could not displease, and who entered it so softly and quietly that, neither hearing nor seeing their approach, it seemed as if they had availed themselves of some secret trap-doors through which they had mounted to fill the ship, without sound or bustle, in a single moment. When we were quitting it, however, this tranquillity as abruptly finished, for in an instant a part of them rushed round me, one demanding to carry Alex., another Adrienne, another seizing my *écritoire*, another my arm, and someone, I fear, my parasol, as I have never been able to find it since.

We were informed we must not leave the ship till Monsieur le Commissaire arrived to carry us, I think, to the municipality of Calais to show our passports. Monsieur le Commissaire, in white with some red trappings, soon arrived, civilly hastening himself quite out of breath to save us from waiting. We then mounted the quay, and I followed the rest of the passengers, who all followed the commissary, accompanied by two men carrying the two children, and two more carrying, one my *écritoire*, and the other insisting on conducting its owner. The quantity of people that surrounded and walked with us, surprised me; and their decency, their silence, their quiet-ness astonished me. To fear them was impossible, even in entering France with all the formed fears hanging upon its recent though past horrors.

But on coming to the municipality, I was, I own, extremely ill at ease, when upon our gouvernante's desiring me to give the commissary my passport, as the rest of the passengers had done, and my answering it was in my *écritoire*, she exclaimed: 'Vite! vite! cherchez-le, ou vous serez arrêtée!' You may be sure I was quick enough —or at least tried to be so, for my fingers presently trembled, and I could hardly put in the key.

We were all three too much awake by the new scene to try for any repose, and the hotel windows sufficed for our amusement till dinner; and imagine, my dearest sir, how my repast was seasoned, when I tell you that, as soon as it began, a band of music came to the window and struck up *God save the King*. I can never tell you what a pleased emotion was excited in my breast by this sound on a shore so lately hostile, and on which I have so many, so heartfelt motives for wishing peace and amity perpetual!

This over, we ventured out of the hotel to look at the street. The day was fine, the street was clean, two or three people who passed us made way for the children as they skipped out of my hands, and I saw such an un-expected appearance of quiet, order, and civility, that, almost without knowing it, we strolled from the gate, and presently found ourselves in the market place, which was completely full of sellers, and buyers, and booths, looking like a large English fair.

The queer, gaudy jackets, always of a different colour from the petticoats of the women, and their immense wing-caps, which seemed made to double over their noses, but which all flew back so as to discover their ears, in which I regularly saw large and generally drop gold ear-rings, were quite as diverting to myself as to Alex. and Adrienne. Many of them, also, had gold necklaces, chains, and crosses; but ear-rings all: even the maids who were scrubbing or sweeping, ragged wretches carrying burdens on their heads or shoulders, old women selling fruit or other eatables, gipsy-looking creatures with children tied to their backs—all wore these long, broad, large, shining ear-rings.

Beggars we saw not—no, not one, all the time we stayed or sauntered; and for civility and gentleness, the poorest and most ordinary persons we met or passed might be compared with the best dressed and best looking walkers in the streets of our metropolis, and still to the disadvantage of the latter. I cannot say how much this surprised me, as I had conceived an horrific idea of the populace of this country, imagining them all transformed into bloody monsters.

Sunday, April 18.

We set off for Paris at five o'clock in the morning. The country broad, flat, or barrenly steep—without trees, without buildings, and scarcely inhabited—exhibited a change from the fertile fields, and beautiful woods and gardens and civilization of Kent, so sudden and unpleasant that I only lamented the fatigue of my position, which regularly impeded my making use of this chasm of pleasure and observation for repose. This part of France must certainly be the least frequented, for we rarely met a single carriage, and the villages, few and distant, seemed to have no intercourse with each other. *Dimanche*, indeed, might occasion this stiffness, for we saw, at almost all the villages, neat and clean peasants going to or coming from mass, and seeming indescribably elated and happy by the public permission of divine worship on its originally appointed day.

I was struck with the change in Madame Raymond, who joined us in the morning from another hotel. Her hoop was no more visible; her petticoats were as lank, or more so, than her neighbours'; and her distancing the children was not only at an end, but she prevented me from renewing any of my cautions to them, of not incommoding her; and when we were together a few moments, before we were joined by the rest, she told me, with a significant smile, not to tutor the children about her any more, as she only avoided them from having something of consequence to take care of, which was removed. I then saw she meant some English lace or muslin, which she had carried in a petticoat, and, since the custom-house examination was over, had now packed in her trunk.

Poor lady! I fear this little merchandise was all her hope of succour on her arrival! She is amongst the emigrants who have twice or thrice returned, but not yet been able to rest in their own country.

Here ends the account of my journey, and if it has amused my dearest father, it will be a true delight to me to have scribbled it. My next letter brings me to the capital, and to the only person who can console me for my always lamented absence from himself.

Witness.   F. D'ARBLAY.

Diary resumed

Addressed to Dr Burney

PARIS. [*May* 5.] M. d'Arblay had procured us three tickets for entering the apartments at the Tuileries, to see the parade of General Hulin, now high in actual rank and service, but who had been a *sous-officier* under M. d'Arblay's command; our third ticket was for Madame d'Hénin,[1] who had never been to this sight—nor, indeed, more than twice to any spectacle since her return to France —till my arrival; but she is so obliging and good as to accept, nay, to seek, everything that can amuse, of which I can profit. We breakfasted with her early, and were appointed to join the party of M. le Prince de Beauveau, who had a General in his carriage, through whose aid and instructions we hoped to escape all difficulties.

Accordingly the coach in which they went was desired to stop at Madame d'Hénin's door, so as to let us get into our *fiacre*, and follow it straight. This was done, and our *precursor* stopped at the gate leading to the garden of the Tuileries. The de Beauveaus, Mademoiselle de Morte-mar, and their attending General, alighted, and we followed their example and joined them, which was no sooner done than their General, at the sight of M. d'Arblay, suddenly drew back from conducting Madame de Beauveau, and

[1] The Princess d'Hénin, one of Marie Antoinette's ladies-in-waiting. Fanny had met her during her exile in England with her lover, Lally Tollendal.

flew up to him. They had been ancient *camarades*, but had not met since M. d'A.'s emigration.

The crowd was great, but civil and well dressed; and we met with no impediment till we came to the great entrance. Alas, I had sad recollections of sad readings in mounting the steps! We had great difficulty, notwithstanding our tickets, in making our way—I mean Madame d'Hénin and ourselves, for Madame de Beauveau and Mademoiselle de Mortemar, having an officer in the existing military to aid them, were admitted and helped by all the attendants; and so forwarded that we wholly lost sight of them, till we arrived, long after, in the apartment destined for the exhibition. This, however, was so crowded that every place at the windows for seeing the parade was taken, and the row formed opposite to see the First Consul as he passed through the room to take horse, was so thick and threefold filled, that not a possibility existed of even a passing peep.

We seated ourselves now, hopeless of any other amusement than seeing the uniforms of the passing officers, and the light drapery of the stationary ladies, which, by the way, is not by any means so notorious nor so common as has been represented; on the contrary, there are far more who are decent enough to attract no attention, than who are fashionable enough to call for it.

During this interval, M. d'Arblay found means, by a ticket lent to him by M. de Narbonne, to enter the next apartment, and there to state our distress, not in vain, to General Hulin; and presently he returned, accompanied by this officer, who is, I fancy, at least seven feet high, and was dressed in one of the most showy uniforms I ever saw. M. d'Arblay introduced me to him. He expressed his pleasure in seeing the wife of his old comrade, and taking my hand, caused all the crowd to make way, and conducted me into the apartment adjoining to that where the First Consul receives the ambassadors, with a flourish of manners so fully displaying power as well as courtesy, that I felt as if in the hands of one of the seven champions who meant to mow down all before him, should any impious elf dare dispute his right to give me liberty, or to show me honour.

He put me into the first place in the apartment which was sacred to general officers, and as many ladies as could be accommodated in two rows only at the windows. M. d'Arblay, under the sanction of his big friend, followed with Madame d'Hénin; and we had the pleasure of rejoining Madame de Beauveau and Mademoiselle de Mortemar, who were at the same windows, through the exertions of General Songis.

The scene now, with regard to all that was present, was splendidly gay and highly animating. The room was full, but not crowded, with officers of rank in sumptuous rather than rich uniforms, and exhibiting a martial air that became their attire, which, however, generally speaking, was too gorgeous to be noble.

Our window was that next to the consular apartment, in which Bonaparte was holding a levee, and it was close to the steps ascending to it; by which means we saw all the forms of the various exits and entrances, and had opportunity to examine every dress and every countenance that passed and repassed. This was highly amusing, I might say historic, where the past history and the present office were known.

Sundry footmen of the First Consul, in very fine liveries, were attending to bring or arrange chairs for whoever required them; various peace officers, superbly begilt, paraded occasionally up and down the chamber, to keep the ladies to their windows and the gentlemen to their ranks, so as to preserve the passage or lane through which the First Consul was to walk upon his entrance clear and open; and several gentlemanlike-looking persons, whom in former times I should have supposed pages of the back stairs, dressed in black, with gold chains hanging round their necks, and medallions pending from them, seemed to have the charge of the door itself, leading immediately to the audience chamber of the First Consul.

But what was most prominent in commanding notice, was the array of the aides-de-camp of Bonaparte, which was so almost furiously striking, that all other vestments, even the most gaudy, appeared suddenly under a gloomy cloud when contrasted with its brightness. We were long viewing them before we could discover what they were to represent, my three lady companions being as new to this scene as myself; but afterwards M. d'Arblay starting forward to speak to one of them, brought him across the lane to me, and said: 'General Lauriston.'[1]

General Lauriston is a very handsome man, and of a very pleasing and amiable countenance; and his manly air carried off the frippery of his trappings, so as to make them appear almost to advantage.

While this variety of attire, of carriage, and of physiognomy amused us in facing the passage prepared for the First Consul, we were occupied, whenever we turned round, by seeing from the window the garden of the Tuileries filling with troops.

In the first row of females at the window where we stood, were three ladies who, by my speaking English with Mademoiselle de Mortemar and Madame de Beauveau, discovered my country, and, as I have since heard, gathered my name; and here I blush to own how unlike was the result to what one of this nation might have experienced from a similar discovery in England; for the moment it was buzzed 'C'est une étrangère, c'est une Anglaise,' every one tried to place, to oblige, and to assist me, and yet no one looked curious, or stared at me.

The best view from the window to see the marching forwards of the troops was now bestowed upon me, and I vainly offered it to the ladies of my own party, to whom the whole of the sight was as new as to myself. The three unknown ladies began conversing with me, and, after a little general talk, one of them with sudden importance of manner, in a tone slow but energetic, said:

[1] It was General Lauriston who had conveyed to England the ratification of the Treaty of Amiens.

'Avez-vous vu, Madame, le Premier Consul?'

'Pas encore, Madame.'

'C'est sans doute ce que vous souhaitez le plus, Madame?'

'Oui, Madame.'

'Voulez-vous le voir parfaitement bien, et tout à fait à votre aise?'

'Je le désire beaucoup, Madame.'

She then told me to keep my eyes constantly upon her, and not an instant lose sight of her movements; and to suffer no head, in the press that would ensue when the First Consul appeared, to intervene between us. 'Faites comme cela, Madame,' continued she; 'et vous le verrez bien, bien; car,' added she, solemnly, and putting her hand on her breast, 'moi—je vais lui parler!'

I was very much surprised, indeed, and could only conclude I was speaking to a wife, sister, or cousin at least, of one of the other consuls, or of some favourite minister. 'Et lui, Madame, il me répondra; vous l'entendrez parler, Madame, oui, vous l'entendrez! car il est bon, bon!—bon homme tout à fait et affable!—oh, affable!—oui, vous l'entendrez parler.'

I thanked her very much, but it was difficult to express as much satisfaction as she displayed herself. You may suppose, however, how curious I felt for such a conversation, and how scrupulously I followed her injunctions of watching her motions. A little squat good-humoured lady, with yellow flowers over a mob cap upon her hair; who had little sunken eyes, concise nose, and a mouth so extended by perpetual smiling, that, hardly leaving an inch for the cheek, it ran nearly into the ear, on my other side now demanded my attention also, and told me she came regularly every month to the great review, that she might always bring some friend who wanted to see it. I found by this she was a person of some power, some influence, at least, and not entirely averse to having it known. She was extremely civil to me; but as my other friend had promised me so singular a regale, I had not much voluntary time to spare for her; this, however, appeared to be no impediment to that she was so obliging as to determine to bestow upon me, and she talked on, satisfied with my acquiescence to her civility, till a sort of bustle just before us making me look a little sharp, she cried:

'Vous le voyez, Madame!'

'Qui?' exclaimed I, 'le Premier Consul?'

'Mais non!—pas encore; mais—ce—ce monsieur-là!'

I looked at her to see whom I was to remark, and her eyes led me to a tall, large figure, with a broad gold-laced hat, who was clearing the lane, which some of the company had infringed, with a stentorian voice, and an air and manner of such authority as a chief constable might exert in an English riot.

'Oui, Madame,' I answered, not conceiving why I was to look at him; 'je le vois, ce monsieur; il est bien grand!'

'Oui, Madame,' replied she, with a yet widened smile, and a look of lively satisfaction; 'il est bien grand! Vous le voyez bien?'

'Mais oui: et il est très bien mis!'

'Oui sûrement! vous êtes sûre que vous le voyez?'

'Bien sûre, Madame—mais, il a un air d'autorité, il me semble.'

'Oui, Madame; et bientôt, il ira dans l'autre appartement! il verra le Premier Consul!'

'Oh, fort bien!' cried I, quite at a loss what she meant me to understand, till at last, fixing first him, and then me, she expressively said:

'Madame, c'est mon mari!'

The grin was now distended to the very utmost limits of the stretched lips, and the complacency of her countenance forcibly said: 'What do you think of me now?' My countenance, however, was far more clever than my head, if it made her any answer. But, in the plenitude of her own admiration of a gentleman who seemed privileged to speak roughly, and push violently whoever, by a single inch, passed a given barrier, she imagined, I believe,

that to belong to him entitled her to be considered as
sharing his prowess; she seemed even to be participating
in the merits of his height and breadth, though he could
easily have put her into his pocket.

Not perceiving, as I imagine, all the delight of felicita-
tion in my countenance that she had expected, her own
fell, in a disappointed pause, into as much of length as
its circular form would admit of; it recovered, however,
in another minute, its full merry rotundity, by conjecturing,
as I have reason to think, that the niggardliness of my
admiration was occasioned by my doubt of her assertions;
for, looking at me with an expression that demanded my
attention, she poked her head under the arm of a tall
grenadier, stationed to guard our window, and trying to
catch the eye of the object of her devotion, called out, in
an accent of tenderness: 'M'Ami! M'Ami!'

The surprise she required was now gratified in full,
though what she concluded to be excited by her happiness,
was simply the effect of so caressing a public address from
so diminutive a little creature to so gigantic a big one.
Three or four times the soft sound was repeated ere it
reached the destined ear, through the hubbub created
by his own loud and rough manner of calling to order;
but, when at last he caught the gentle appellation, and
looked down upon her, it was with an eyebrow so scowl-
ing, a mouth so pouting, and an air that so rudely said:
'*What the d—— do you want?*' that I was almost afraid he
would have taken her between his thumb and finger and
given her a shake. However, he only grumbled out:
'Qu'est-ce que c'est donc?' A little at a loss what to say,
she gently stammered: 'M'Ami—le—le Premier Consul,
ne vient-il pas?' 'Oui! oui!' was blustered in reply,
with a look that completed the phrase by '*you fool, you!*'
though the voice left it unfinished.

The last object for whom the way was cleared was the
Second Consul, Cambacérès, who advanced with a stately
and solemn pace, slow, regular, and consequential; dressed
richly in scarlet and gold, and never looking to the right

or left, but wearing a mien of fixed gravity and importance. He had several persons in his suite, who, I think, but am not sure, were ministers of state.

At length the two human hedges were finally formed, the door of the audience chamber was thrown wide open with a commanding crash, and a vivacious officer, sentinel, or I know not what, nimbly descended the three steps into our apartment, and placing himself at the side of the door, with one hand spread as high as possible above his head, and the other extended horizontally, called out in a loud and authoritative voice: 'Le Premier Consul!'

You will easily believe nothing more was necessary to obtain attention; not a soul either spoke or stirred as he and his suite passed along, which was so quickly that, had I not been placed so near the door, and had not all about me facilitated my standing foremost, and being least crowd-obstructed, I could hardly have seen him. As it was, I had a view so near, though so brief, of his face, as to be very much struck by it. It is of a deeply impressive cast, pale even to sallowness, while not only in the eye but in every feature—care, thought, melancholy, and meditation are strongly marked, with so much of character, nay, genius, and so penetrating a seriousness, or rather sadness, as powerfully to sink into an observer's mind.

Yet, though the busts and medallions I have seen are, in general, such good resemblances that I think I should have known him untold, he has by no means the look to be expected from Bonaparte, but rather that of a profoundly studious and contemplative man, who 'o'er books consumes' not only the 'midnight oil' but his own daily strength, 'and wastes the puny body to decay' by abstruse speculation and theoretic plans, or rather visions, ingenious but not practicable. But the look of the commander who heads his own army, who fights his own battles, who conquers every difficulty by personal exertion, who executes all he plans, who performs even all he suggests; whose ambition is of the most enterprising, and whose bravery is of the most daring cast—this, which is the look to be expected from his situation, and the exploits which have led to it, the spectator watches for in vain. The plainness, also, of his dress, so conspicuously contrasted by the finery of all around him, conspires forcibly with his countenance, so 'sicklied o'er with the pale hue of thought,' to give him far more the air of a student than a warrior.

The intense attention with which I fixed him in this short but complete view made me entirely forget the lady who had promised me to hold him in conference. When he had passed, however, she told me it was upon his return she should address him, as he was too much hurried to be talked with at the moment of going to the parade. I was glad to find my chance not over, and infinitely curious to know what was to follow.

The review I shall attempt no description of. I have no knowledge of the subject, and no fondness for its object. It was far more superb than anything I had ever beheld; but while all the pomp and circumstance of war animated others, it only saddened me; and all of past reflection, all of future dread, made the whole grandeur of the martial scene, and all the delusive seduction of martial music, fill my eyes frequently with tears, but not regale my poor muscles with one single smile.

Bonaparte, mounting a beautiful and spirited white horse, closely encircled by his glittering aides-de-camp, and accompanied by his generals, rode round the ranks, holding his bridle indifferently in either hand, and seeming utterly careless of the prancing, rearing, or other freaks of his horse, insomuch as to strike some who were near me with a notion of his being a bad horseman. I am the last to be a *judge* upon this subject; but as a *remarker*, he only appeared to me a man who knew so well he could manage the animal when he pleased, that he did not deem it worth his while to keep constantly in order what he knew, if urged or provoked, he could subdue in a moment.

Precisely opposite to the window at which I was placed, the Chief Consul stationed himself after making his round; and thence he presented some swords of honour, spreading out one arm with an air and mien which changed his look from that of scholastic severity to one that was highly military and commanding.

Just as the consular band, with their brazen drums as well as trumpets, marched facing the First Consul, the sun broke suddenly out from the clouds which had obscured it all the morning; and the effect was so abrupt and so dazzling that I could not help observing it to my friend, the wife of *m'ami*, who, eyeing me with great surprise, not unmixed with the compassion of contempt, said:

'Est-ce que vous ne savez pas cela, Madame? Dès que le Premier Consul vient à la parade, le soleil vient aussi! Il a beau pleuvoir tout le matin; c'est égal, il n'a qu'à paraître, et tout de suite il fait beau.'

I apologized for my ignorance; but doubt whether it was forgiven.

The review over, the Chief Consul returned to the palace. The lines were again formed, and he re-entered our apartment with his suite. As soon as he approached our window, I observed my first acquaintance start a little forward. I was now all attention to her performance of her promise; and just as he reached us she stretched out her hand to present him—a petition!

The enigma of the conference was now solved, and I laughed at my own wasted expectation. *Lui parler*, however, the lady certainly did; so far she kept her word; for when he had taken the scroll, and was passing on, she rushed out of the line, and planting herself immediately before him so as to prevent his walking on, screamed, rather than spoke, for her voice was shrill with impetuosity to be heard and terror of failure: 'C'est pour mons fils! vous me l'avez promis!'

The First Consul stopped and spoke; but not loud enough for me to hear his voice; while his aides-de-camp and the attending generals surrounding him more closely,

all in a breath rapidly said to the lady: 'Votre nom,
Madame, votre nom!' trying to disengage the Consul
from her importunity, in which they succeeded, but not
with much ease, as she seemed purposing to cling to him
till she got his personal answer. He faintly smiled as he
passed on, but looked harassed and worn; while she,
turning to me, with an exulting face and voice, exclaimed:
'Je l'aurai! je l'aurai!' meaning what she had petitioned
for—'car . . . tous ces Généraux m'ont demandé mon
nom!' Could any inference be clearer?

The moment the Chief Consul had ascended the steps
leading to the inner apartment, the gentlemen in black
with gold chains gave a general hint that all the company
must depart, as the ambassadors and the ministers were
now summoned to their monthly public audience with
the Chief Consul. The crowd, however, was so great,
and Madame d'Hénin was so much incommoded, and
half ill, I fear, by internal suffering, that M. d'Arblay
procured a pass for us by a private door down to a terrace
leading to a quiet exit from the palace into the Tuileries
garden.

F. D'A.

Madame d'Arblay to Dr Burney

Passy, May 29th, 1805.[1]

Before I expected it, my promised opportunity for again
writing to my most dear father is arrived. I entirely forget whether, before the breaking out of the war stopped
our correspondence, M. d'Arblay had already obtained
his *retraite*; and, consequently, whether that is an event
I have mentioned or not. Be that as it may, he now has
it—it is 1,500 livres, or £62 10s. per annum. But all our
resources from England ceasing with the peace, we had
so little left from what we had brought over, and M.

---

[1] Fanny was in Paris when the war broke out again, and she
remained there until 1812.

d'Arblay has found so nearly nothing remaining of his natural and hereditary claims in his own province, that he determined upon applying for some employment that might enable him to live with independence, however parsimoniously. This he has, with infinite difficulty, etc., at length obtained, and he is now a *rédacteur* in the civil department of *les Bâtimens*, etc. This is no sinecure. He attends at his bureau from half-past nine to half-past four o'clock every day; and as we live so far off as Passy he is obliged to set off for his office between eight and nine, and does not return to his hermitage till past five. However, what necessity has urged us to desire, and made him solicit, we must not, now acquired, name or think of with murmuring or regret. He has the happiness to be placed amongst extremely worthy people, and those who are his *chefs* in office treat him with every possible mark of consideration and feeling.

We continue steady to our little cell at Passy, which is retired, quiet, and quite to ourselves, with a magnificent view of Paris from one side, and a beautiful one of the country on the other. It is unfurnished—indeed, un-papered, and every way unfinished; for our workmen, in the indispensable repairs which preceded our entering it, ran us up bills that compelled us to turn them adrift, and leave everything at a stand, when three rooms only were made just habitable.

Madame d'Arblay to Dr Burney, Chelsea

ce 16 septembre, 1807.

MY MOST DEAR FATHER,

I have just received a kind offer to send a few lines to the spot whence my most ardent wishes are to receive many, but whence the handwriting that most of all I sigh to behold has not blessed my sight since the return of Madame de Cadignan. Nor have I ever heard whether the last six letters I have written have as yet been received. Two of them were antiques that had waited three or four years some opportunity; a third was concerning the Institute, and M. le Breton's wish to see you installed one of the foreign members and correspondents; the two last were to reach you through a voyage by America, and therefore may not yet be arrived. I do not count the few lines sent by Maria, though to obtain even a smaller mite myself would fill me with joy and thankfulness.

21 août, 1808. The expected opportunity for which I had strung this lamentable list of unacknowledged claims, nearly a twelvemonth since, failed; another at this moment offers—may it prove more propitious! Could it but rebound to me with news of your health, such as it conveys from hence of ours, how should I bless it! But an intercourse such as that must wait for other blessings than mine — the blessings of peace — and those, the whole wounded universe would surely join to hail. My paper is so stinted, and my time so limited, that I can begin no regular account of our proceedings, which, indeed, have but little varied since we lost Maria. Oh, that any one could give me here the history of yours! I am in such terrible arrears of all such knowledge that I know not who will ever undertake to pay me. My last intelligence was that you were well, my dearest father, and that the family at large, in that at least, imitated you. But details —none, none, reach me! I have a bitter anxiety of suspense upon some subjects very near my heart. Not even the loved names of any of my family now reach me; Esther, James, Charles, Charlotte, Sally, with all their younger selves, and Richard and his boys, all are sounds strange to my ears, and my beloved friends of Norbury are banished thence with the same rigour! I am sad, sad indeed, at this deprivation; though in all else I am still and constantly happy, for in my two faithful companions I find sympathy in all my feelings, and food, sweet food for all my hopes.

F. d'A.

Journal from Paris to London

1812.

In the year 1810, when I had been separated from my dear father, and country, and native friends, for eight years, my desire to again see them became so anxiously impatient that my tender companion proposed my passing over to England alone, to spend a month or two at Chelsea. Many females at that period, and amongst them the young Duchesse de Duras, had contrived to procure passports for a short similar excursion; though no male was permitted, under any pretence, to quit France, save with the army.

Reluctantly—with all my wishes in favour of the scheme —yet most reluctantly, I accepted the generous offer; for never did I know happiness away from that companion, no, not even out of his sight! but still, I was consuming with solicitude to see my revered father—to be again in his kind arms, and receive his kind benediction.

For this all was settled, and I had obtained my passport, which was brought to me without my even going to the police office, by the especial favour of M. le Breton, the Secrétaire Perpétuel à l'Institut. The ever active services of M. de Narbonne aided this peculiar grant; though, had not Bonaparte been abroad with his army at the time, neither the one nor the other would have ventured at so hardy a measure of assistance. But whenever Bonaparte left Paris, there was always an immediate abatement of severity in the police; and Fouché, though he had borne a character dreadful beyond description in the earlier and most horrible times of the Revolution, was, at this period, when Ministre de la Police, a man of the mildest manners, the most conciliatory conduct, and of the easiest access in Paris. He had least the glare of the new Imperial Court of any one of its administration; he affected indeed all the simplicity of a plain Republican. I have often seen him strolling in the most shady and unfrequented parts of the Elysian Fields, muffled up in a plain brown rocolo,[1] and

[1] 'Roquelaure' is probably meant. Johnson defines it as 'a cloak for men.'

giving *le bras* to his wife, without suite or servant, merely taking the air, with the evident design of enjoying also an unmolested tête-à-tête. On these occasions, though he was universally known, nobody approached him; and he seemed, himself, not to observe that any other person was in the walks. He was said to be remarkably agreeable in conversation, and his person was the best fashioned and most gentlemanly of any man I have happened to see, belonging to the Government. Yet, such was the impression made upon me by the dreadful reports that were spread of his cruelty and ferocity at Lyons, that I never saw him but I thrilled with horror. How great, therefore, was my obligation to M. de Narbonne and to M. le Breton, for procuring me a passport, without my personal application to a man from whom I shrunk as from a monster.

I forget now for what spot the passport was nominated —perhaps for Canada, but certainly not for England; and M. le Breton, who had brought it to me himself, assured me that no difficulty would be made for me either to go or to return, as I was known to have lived a life the most inoffensive to Government, and perfectly free from all species of political intrigue, and as I should leave behind me such sacred hostages as my husband and my son.

Thus armed, and thus authorized, I prepared, quietly and secretly, for my expedition, while my generous mate employed all his little leisure in discovering where and how I might embark; when, one morning, when I was bending over my trunk to press in its contents, I was abruptly broken in upon by M. de Boinville, who was in my secret, and who called upon me to stop! He had received certain, he said, though as yet unpublished information, that a universal embargo was laid upon every vessel, and that not a fishing boat was permitted to quit the coast.

I pass on to my second attempt, in the year 1812. Disastrous was that interval! All correspondence with England was prohibited under pain of death! One letter only reached me, most unhappily, written with unreflecting abruptness, announcing, without preface, the death of the Princess Amelia, the new and total derangement of the King,[1] and the death of Mr Locke. Three such calamities overwhelmed me, overwhelmed us both, for Mr Locke, my revered Mr Locke, was as dear to my beloved partner as to myself. Poor Mrs —— concluded these tidings must have already arrived, but her fatal letter gave the first intelligence, and no other letter, at that period, found its way to me. She sent hers, I think, by some trusty returned prisoner.

She little knew of my then terrible situation; hovering over my head was the stiletto of a surgeon for a menace of cancer; yet, till that moment, hope of escape had always been held out to me by the Baron de Larrey [2]—hope which, from the reading of the fatal letter, became extinct.

When I was sufficiently recovered for travelling, after a dreadful operation, my plan was resumed; but with an alteration which added infinitely to its interest, as well as to its importance. Bonaparte was now engaging in a new war, of which the aim and intention was no less than —the conquest of the world. This menaced a severity of conscription to which Alexander, who had spent ten years in France, and was seventeen years of age, would soon become liable.

We agreed, therefore, that Alexander should accompany me to England, where, I flattered myself, I might safely deposit him, while I returned to await, by the side of my husband, the issue of the war, in the fervent hope that it would prove our restoration to liberty and reunion.

My second passport was procured with much less facility than the first. Fouché was no longer Minister of Police, and, strange to tell, Fouché, who, till he became that minister, had been held in horror by all France—all Europe —conducted himself with such conciliatory mildness to all ranks of people while in that office, evinced such an

---

[1] The final breakdown of the King's reason occurred in 1811.
[2] The celebrated surgeon-in-chief to the Grande Armée (1766–1842).

appearance of humanity, and exerted such an undaunted spirit of justice in its execution, that at his dismission all Paris was in affliction and dismay!

Our journey—Alexander's and mine—from Paris to Dunkirk was sad, from the cruel separation which it exacted, and the fearful uncertainty of impending events; though I was animated at times into the liveliest sensations, in the prospect of again beholding my father, my friends, and my country.

General d'Arblay, through his assiduous researches, aided by those of M de Boinville and some others, found that a vessel was preparing to sail from Dunkirk to Dover, under American colours, and with American passports and licence; and, after privately landing such of its passengers as meant but to cross the Channel, to proceed to the western continents. M. d'Arblay found, at the same time, six or seven persons of his acquaintance who were to embark in this vessel, namely, Madame and Mademoiselle de Cocherelle, Madame de Carbonière, Madame de Roncherolle, Madame de Caillebot and her son and daughter, the two Miss Potts, and Mrs Gregory.

We all met, and severally visited at Dunkirk, where I was compelled, through the mismanagement and misconduct of the captain of the vessel, to spend the most painfully wearisome six weeks of my life, for they kept me alike from all that was dearest to me, either in France or in England, save my Alexander. I was twenty times on the point of returning to Paris; but whenever I made known that design, the captain promised to sail the next morning. The truth is, he postponed the voyage from day to day and from week to week, in the hope of obtaining more passengers; and, as the clandestine visit he meant to make to Dover, *in his way to America*, was whispered about, reinforcements very frequently encouraged his cupidity.

Six weeks completely we consumed in wasteful weariness at Dunkirk; and our passage, when at last we set sail, was equally, in its proportion, toilsome and tedious.

Involved in a sickening calm, we could make no way, but lingered two days and two nights in this long-short passage. The second night, indeed, might have been spared me, as it was spared to all my fellow voyagers. But when we cast anchor, I was so exhausted by the unremitting sufferings I had endured, that I was literally unable to rise from my hammock.

Yet there was a circumstance capable to have aroused me from any torpidity, save the demolishing ravage of sea-sickness; for scarcely were we at anchor, when Alex., capering up to the deck, descended with yet more velocity than he had mounted, to exclaim: 'Oh, *maman*! there are two British officers now upon deck!'

But, finding that even this could not make me recover speech or motion, he ran back again to this new and delighting sight, and again returning, cried out in a tone of rapture: '*Maman*, we are taken by the British! We are all captured by British officers!'

Even in my immovable, and nearly insensible state, this juvenile ardour, excited by so new and strange an adventure, afforded me some amusement. It did not, however, afford me strength, for I could not rise, though I heard that every other passenger was removed. With difficulty, even next morning, I crawled upon the deck, and there I had been but a short time, when Lieutenant Harford came on board to take possession of the vessel, not as French, but American booty, war having been declared against America the preceding week.

Mr Harford, hearing my name, most courteously addressed me, with congratulations upon my safe arrival in England. These were words to reawaken all the happiest purposes of my expedition, and they recovered me from the nerveless, sinking state into which my exhaustion had cast me, as if by a miracle. My father, my brothers, my sisters, and all my heart-dear friends, seemed rising to my view and springing to my embraces, with all the joy of renovating reunion. I thankfully accepted his obliging offer to carry me on shore in his own boat;

but when I turned round, and called upon Alexander to follow us, Mr Harford, assuming a commanding air, said: 'No, madam, I cannot take that young man. No French person can come into my boat without a passport and permission from Government.'

My air now a little corresponded with his own, as I answered: 'He was born, sir, in England!'

'Oh!' cried he, 'that's quite another matter; come along, sir! We'll all go together.'

AUG. 15TH. We set off for Canterbury, where we slept, and on the 20th proceeded towards Chelsea. While, upon some common, we stopped to water the horses, a gentleman on horseback passed us twice, and then, looking in, pronounced my name; and I saw it was Charles, dear Charles! who had been watching for us several hours and *three nights* following, through a mistake. Thence we proceeded to Chelsea, where we arrived at nine o'clock at night. I was in a state almost breathless. I could only demand to see my dear father alone:[1] fortunately, he had had the same feeling, and had charged all the family to stay away, and all the world to be denied. I found him, therefore, in his library, by himself—but oh! very much altered indeed — weak, weak and changed — his head almost always hanging down, and his hearing most cruelly impaired. I was terribly affected, but most grateful to God for my arrival.

In discourse, however, he re-animated, and was, at times, all himself. But he now admits scarcely a creature but of his family, and will only see for a short time even his children. He likes quietly reading, and lies almost constantly upon the sofa, and will never eat but alone! What a change!

[1] Dr Burney's second wife had died in 1796.

Madame d'Arblay to Dr Burney

Richmond Hill, Oct. 12, 1813.

My most dear Padre will, I am sure, congratulate me that I have just had the heartfelt delight of a few lines from M. d'Arblay, dated September 5th. I had not had any news since the 17th of August, and I had the melancholy apprehension upon my spirits that no more letters would be allowed to pass till the campaign was over. It has been therefore one of the most welcome surprises I ever experienced.

He tells me, also, that he is perfectly well, and quite *accablé* with business. This, for the instant, gives me nothing but joy; for, were he not essentially necessary in some department of civil labour and use, he would surely be included in some *levée en masse*. Every way, therefore, this letter gives me relief and pleasure.

I have had, also, this morning, the great comfort to hear that my Alexander is 'stout and well' at Cambridge, where his kind uncle Charles still remains.

I am indescribably occupied, and have been so ever since my return from Ramsgate, in giving more and more last touches to my work,[1] about which I begin to grow very anxious. I am to receive merely 500*l*. upon delivery of the MS.; the two following 500*l*. by instalments from nine months to nine months, that is, in a year and a half from the day of *publication*.

If all goes well, the whole will be 3,000*l*., but only at the end of the sale of eight thousand copies. Oh, my Padre, if *you* approve the work, I shall have good hope. . . .

F. d'A.

---

[1] *The Wanderer, or Female Difficulties*, which she had begun long before and had brought with her from France. Her hopes of £3,000 were disappointed, and she had to be satisfied with £1,500 in three instalments. The book was published by Longmans.

[1814. Soon after the publication of *The Wanderer*, Madame d'Arblay wrote as follows to a friend:]

I beseech you not to let your too ardent friendship disturb you about the reviews and critiques,[1] and I quite supplicate you to leave their authors to their own severities or indulgence. I have ever steadily refused all interference with public opinion or private criticism. I am told I have been very harshly treated; but I attribute it not to what alone would affect me, but which I trust I have not excited, personal enmity. I attribute it to the false expectation, universally spread, that the book would be a picture of France, as well as to the astonishing *éclat* of a work in five volumes being all bespoken before it was published. The booksellers, erroneously and injudiciously concluding the sale would so go on, fixed the rapacious price of two guineas, which again damped the sale. But why say *damped*, when it is only their unreasonable expectations that are disappointed? for they acknowledge that 3,600 copies are positively sold and paid for in the first half year. What must I be, if not far more than contented? I have not read or heard one of the criticisms; my mind has been wholly occupied by grief for the loss of my dearest father,[2] or the inspection of his MSS., and my harassing situation relative to my own proceedings. Why, then, make myself *black bile* to disturb me further? No; I will not look at a word till my spirits and time are calmed and quiet, and I can set about preparing a corrected edition. I will then carefully read all; and then, the blow to immediate feelings being over, I can examine as well as read, impartially and with profit, both to my future surveyors and myself.

[1] *The Wanderer* was harshly reviewed in the *Quarterly*, and not less unfavourably, though more justly, by Hazlitt in the *Edinburgh*. With this unreadable work Fanny's career as a novelist came to an end.

[2] Dr Burney died in March 1814.

Presentation to Louis XVIII

1814.

While I was still under the almost first impression of grief for the loss of my dear and honoured father, I received a letter from Windsor Castle, written by Madame Beckersdorff, at the command of her Majesty, to desire I would take the necessary measures for being presented to Son Altesse Royale Madame la Duchesse d'Angoulême, who was to have a drawing-room in London, both for French and English, on the day preceding her departure for France. The letter added, that I must waive all objections relative to my recent loss, as it would be improper, in the present state of things, that the wife of a General Officer should not be presented; and, moreover, that I should be personally expected and well received, as I had been named to Son Altesse Royale by the Queen herself. In conclusion, I was charged not to mention this circumstance, from the applications or jealousies it might excite.

I had but two or three days for preparation. Lady Crewe [1] most amiably came to me herself, and missing me in person, wrote me word she would lend me her carriage to convey me from Chelsea to her house in Lower Grosvenor Street, and thence accompany me herself to the audience. When the morning arrived I set off with tolerable courage.

Lady Crewe purposed taking this opportunity of paying her own respects, with her congratulations, to Madame la Duchesse d'Angoulême. She had sent me a note from Madame de Gouvello, relative to the time, etc., for presentation, which was to take place at Grillon's Hotel, in Albemarle Street.

We went very early, to avoid a crowd. But Albemarle Street was already quite full, though quiet. We entered the hotel without difficulty, Lady Crewe having previously demanded a private room of Grillon, who had once been

[1] The reader has met her previously as Mrs Crewe.

cook to her lord. This private room was at the back of
the house, with a mere yard or common garden for its
prospect. Lady Crewe declared this was quite too stupid,
and rang the bell for waiter after waiter, till she made
M. Grillon come himself. She then, in her singularly
open and easy manner, told him to be so good as to order
us a front room, where we might watch for the arrival
of the Royals, and be amused ourselves at the same time
by seeing the entrances of the Mayor, Aldermen, and
Common Councilmen, and other odd characters, who
would be coming to pay their court to these French princes
and princesses.

M. Grillon gave a nod of acquiescence, and we were
instantly shown to a front apartment just over the street
door, which was fortunately supplied with a balcony.

I should have been much entertained by all this, and
particularly with the originality, good humour, and
intrepid yet intelligent odd fearlessness of all remark, or
even consequence, which led Lady Crewe to both say and
do exactly what she pleased, had my heart been lighter;
but it was too heavy for pleasure; and the depth of my
mourning, and the little, but sad time that was yet passed
since it had become my gloomy garb, made me hold it
a matter even of decency, as well as of feeling, to keep
out of sight. I left Lady Crewe, therefore, to the full
enjoyment of her odd figures, while I seated myself,
solitarily, at the farther end of the room.

In an instant, however, she saw from the window some
acquaintance, and beckoned them up. A gentleman,
middle-aged, of a most pleasing appearance and address,
immediately obeyed her summons, accompanied by a
young man with a sensible look; and a young lady, pretty,
gentle, and engaging, with languishing soft eyes; though
with a smile and an expression of countenance that showed
an innate disposition to archness and sport.

This uncommon trio I soon found to consist of the celebrated Irish orator, Mr Grattan,[1] and his son and daughter.

[1] Henry Grattan (1746–1820).

Lady Crewe welcomed them with all the alertness belonging to her thirst for amusement, and her delight in sharing it with those she thought capable of its participation. This she had sought, but wholly missed in me; and could neither be angry nor disappointed, though she was a little vexed. She suffered me not, however, to remain long in my seclusion, but called me to the balcony, to witness the jolting out of their carriages of the Aldermen and Common Councilmen, exhibiting, as she said, their 'fair round bodies with fat capon lined'; and wearing an air of proudly hospitable satisfaction, in visiting a King of France who had found an asylum in a street of the city of Westminster.

The crowd, however, for they deserve a better name than mob, interested my observation still more. John Bull has seldom appeared to me to greater advantage. I never saw him *en masse* behave with such impulsive propriety. Enchanted to behold a King of France in his capital; conscious that *le grand Monarque* was fully in his power; yet honestly enraptured to see that 'The King would enjoy his own again,' and enjoy it through the generous efforts of his rival, brave, noble old England; he yet seemed aware that it was fitting to subdue all exuberance of pleasure, which, else, might annoy, if not alarm, his regal guest. He took care, therefore, that his delight should not amount to exultation; it was quiet and placid, though pleased and curious; I had almost said it was gentlemanlike.

Some other friends of Lady Crewe now found her out, and she made eager inquiries amongst them relative to Madame la Duchesse d'Angoulême, but could gather no tidings. She heard, however, that there were great expectations of some arrivals downstairs, where two or three rooms were filled with company.

She desired Mr Grattan, junior, to descend into this crowd, and to find out where the Duchess was to be seen, and when, and how.

He obeyed. But, when he returned, what was the

provocation of Lady Crewe, what my own disappointment, to hear that the Duchess was not arrived, and was not expected! She was at the house of Monsieur le Comte d'Artois, her father-in-law.

'Then what are we come hither for?' exclaimed her ladyship: 'expressly to be tired to death for no purpose! Do pray, at least, Mr Grattan, be so good as to see for my carriage, that we may go to the right house.'

Mr Grattan was all compliance, and with a readiness so obliging and so well-bred that I am sure he is his father's true son in manners, though there was no opportunity to discover whether the resemblance extended also to genius.

He was not, however, cheered when he brought word that neither carriage nor footman was to be found.

Lady Crewe then said he must positively go down, and make the Duc de Duras tell us what to do.

In a few minutes he was with us again, shrugging his shoulders at his ill-success. The King, Louis XVIII, he said, was expected, and M. le Duc was preparing to receive him, and not able to speak or listen to any one.

Lady Crewe declared herself delighted by this information, because there would be an opportunity for having me presented to his Majesty. 'Go to M. de Duras,' she cried, 'and tell him Madame d'Arblay wishes it.'

'For heaven's sake!' exclaimed I, 'do no such thing! I have not the most distant thought of the kind! It is Madame la Duchesse d'Angoulême alone that I——'

'Oh, pho, pho!—it is still more essential to be done to the King—it is really important; so go, and tell the Duke, Mr Grattan, that Madame d'Arblay is here, and desires to be presented. Tell him 'tis a thing quite indispensable.'

Poor Lady Crewe seemed to think I lost a place at Court, or perhaps a peerage, by my untameable shyness, and was quite vexed. Others came to her now, who said several rooms below were filled with expectant courtiers. Miss Grattan then earnestly requested me to descend with her, as a chaperon, that she might see something of what was going forwards.

I could not refuse so natural a request, and down we went, seeking one of the commonly crowded rooms, that we might not intrude where there was preparation or expectation relative to the King.

A little hubbub soon after announced something new, and presently a whisper was buzzed around the room of 'The Prince de Condé.'

His Serene Highness looked very much pleased—as no wonder—at the arrival of such a day; but he was so surrounded by all his countrymen who were of rank to claim his attention, that I could merely see that he was little and old, but very unassuming and polite. Amongst his courtiers were sundry of the French *noblesse* that were known to Lady Crewe; and I heard her uniformly say to them, one after another: 'Here is Madame d'Arblay, who must be presented to the King.'

Quite frightened by an assertion so wide from my intentions, so unauthorized by any preparatory ceremonies, unknown to my husband, and not, like a presentation to the Duchesse d'Angoulême, encouraged by my Queen, I felt as if guilty of taking a liberty the most presumptuous, and with a forwardness and assurance the most foreign to my character. Yet to control the zeal of Lady Crewe was painful from her earnestness, and appeared to be ungrateful to her kindness; I therefore shrunk back, and presently suffered the crowd to press between us so as to find myself wholly separated from my party. This would have been ridiculous had I been more happy; but in my then state of affliction, it was necessary to my peace.

Quite to myself, how I smiled inwardly at my adroit cowardice, and was contemplating the surrounding masses of people, when a new and more mighty hubbub startled me, and presently I heard a buzzing whisper spread throughout the apartment of 'The King! Le Roi!'

Alarmed at my strange situation, I now sought to decamp, meaning to wait for Lady Crewe upstairs; but to even approach the door was impossible. I turned back, therefore, to take a place by the window, that I

might see his Majesty alight from his carriage, but how
great was my surprise when, just as I reached the top of
the room, the King himself entered it at the bottom!

I had not the smallest idea that this was the chamber
of audience; it was so utterly unornamented. But I now
saw that a large *fauteuil* was being conveyed to the upper
part, exactly where I stood, ready for his reception and
repose.

His Majesty took his seat, with an air of mingled sweetness and dignity. I then, being immediately behind him,
lost sight of his countenance, but saw that of every individual who approached to be presented. The Duc de
Duras stood at his left hand, and was le Grand Maître des
Cérémonies; Madame de Gouvello stood at his right side;
though whether in any capacity, or simply as a French lady
known to him, I cannot tell. In a whisper, from that
lady, I learned more fully the mistake of the hotel, the
Duchess d'Angoulême never having meant to quit that
of her *beau-père*, Monsieur le Comte d'Artois, in South
Audley Square.

The presentations were short, and without much mark
or likelihood. The men bowed low, and passed on;
the ladies curtsied, and did the same. Those who were
not known gave a card, I think, to the Duc de Duras;
who named them; those of former acquaintance with his
Majesty simply made their obeisance.

M. de Duras, who knew how much fatigue the King had
to go through, hurried every one on, not only with speed
but almost with ill-breeding, to my extreme astonishment.
Yet the English, by express command of his Majesty, had
always the preference and always took place of the French;
which was an attention of the King in return for the
asylum he had here found, that he seemed delighted to
display.

Early in this ceremony came forward Lady Crewe,
who being known to the King from sundry previous
meetings, was not named; and only, after curtsying,
reciprocated smiles with his Majesty, and passed on.

But instead of then moving off, though the Duke, who did not know her, waved his hand to hasten her away, she whispered, but loud enough for me to hear: 'Voilà Madame d'Arblay; il faut qu'elle soit présentée.' She then went gaily off, without heeding me.

The Duke only bowed, but by a quick glance recognized me, and by another showed a pleased acquiescence in the demand.

Retreat, now, was out of the question; but I so feared my position was wrong, that I was terribly disturbed, and felt hot and cold, and cold and hot, alternately, with excess of embarrassment.

I was roused, however, after hearing for so long a time nothing but French, by the sudden sound of English. An address in that language was read to his Majesty, which was presented by the Noblemen and Gentlemen of the county of Buckingham, congratulatory upon his happy restoration, and filled with cordial thanks for the graciousness of his manners, and the benignity of his conduct, during his long residence amongst them; warmly proclaiming their participation in his joy, and their admiration of his virtues. The reader was Colonel Nugent, a near relation of the present Duke of Buckingham. . . .

Fortunately for me, the Duc de Duras made this the moment for my presentation, and, seizing my hand and drawing me suddenly from behind the chair to the Royal presence, he said: 'Sire, Madame d'Arblay.'

How singular a change, that what, but the instant before, would have overwhelmed me with diffidence and embarrassment, now found me all courage and animation! and when his Majesty took my hand—or, rather, took hold of my fist—and said, in very pretty English: 'I am very happy to see you,' I felt such a glow of satisfaction, that, involuntarily, I burst forth with its expression, incoherently, but delightedly and irresistibly, though I cannot remember how. He certainly was not displeased, for his smile was brightened and his manner was most flattering, as he repeated that he was very glad to see me, and added that he had known me: 'though without sight, very long: for I have *read* you—and been charmed with your books—charmed and entertained. I have read them often, I know them very well indeed; and I have long wanted to know *you*!'

I was extremely surprised—and not only at these unpected compliments, but equally that my presentation, far from seeming, as I had apprehended, strange, was met by a reception of the utmost encouragement. When he stopped, and let go my hand, I curtsied respectfully, and was moving on; but he again caught my *fist*, and, fixing me, with looks of strong though smiling investigation, he appeared archly desirous to read the lines of my face, as if to deduce from them the qualities of my mind. His manner, however, was so polite and so gentle that he did not at all discountenance me; and though he resumed the praise of my little works, he uttered the panegyric with a benignity so gay as well as flattering, that I felt enlivened, nay, elevated, with a joy that overcame *mauvaise honte*.

The Duc de Duras, who had hurried on all others, seeing he had no chance to dismiss me with the same *sans cérémonie* speed, now joined his voice to exalt my satisfaction, by saying, at the next pause: 'Et M. d'Arblay, Sire, bon et brave, est un des plus dévoués et fidèles serviteurs de votre Majesté.'

The King, with a gracious little motion of his head, and with eyes of the most pleased benevolence, expressively said: 'Je le crois.' And a third time he stopped my retiring curtsy, to take my hand.

This last stroke gave me such delight, for my absent best *ami*, that I could not again attempt to speak. The King pressed my hand—wrist, I should say, for it was that he grasped—and then saying: 'Bonjour, Madame la Comtesse,' [1] let me go.

[1] This piece of politeness referred to the title which M. d'Arblay might have claimed.

My eyes were suffused with tears, from mingled emotions; I glided nimbly through the crowd to a corner at the other end of the room, where Lady Crewe joined me almost instantly, and with felicitations the most amiably cordial and lively.

We then repaired to a sideboard, on which we contrived to seat ourselves, and Lady Crewe named to me the numerous personages of rank who passed on before us for presentation. But every time any one espied her and approached, she named me also; an honour to which I was very averse. This I intimated, but to no purpose; she went on her own way. The curious stares this produced, in my embarrassed state of spirits, from recent grief, were really painful to sustain; but when the seriousness of my representation forced her to see that I was truly in earnest in my desire to remain unnoticed, she was so much vexed, and even provoked, that she very gravely begged that, if such were the case, I would move a little farther from her; saying: 'If one must be so ill-natured to people as not to name you, I had rather not seem to know who you are myself.'

*Narrative of Bonaparte's Return from Elba—Flight from Paris
—Residence at Brussels—Battle of Waterloo*

[The following narrative was written some time after the events described took place.]

I have no remembrance how I first heard of the return of Bonaparte from Elba. Wonder at his temerity was the impression made by the news, but wonder unmixed with apprehension. This inactivity of foresight was universal. A torpor indescribable, a species of stupor utterly indefinable, seemed to have enveloped the capital with a mist that was impervious. Everybody went about their affairs, made or received visits, met, and parted, without speaking, or, I suppose, thinking of this event

as of a matter of any importance.   My own participation
in this improvident blindness is to myself incomprehensible.
Ten years I had lived under the dominion of Bonaparte;
I had been in habits of intimacy with many friends of
those who most closely surrounded him; I was generously
trusted, as one with whom information, while interesting
and precious, would be inviolably safe—as one, in fact,
whose honour was the honour of her spotless husband,
and therefore invulnerable: well, therefore, by narrations
the most authentic, and by documents the most indis-
putable, I knew the character of Bonaparte; and marvellous
beyond the reach of my comprehension is my participation
in this inertia.

Whether or not M. d'Arblay was involved in the general
failure of foresight I have mentioned, I never now can
ascertain.   To spare me any evil tidings, and save me
from even the shadow of any unnecessary alarm, was the
first and constant solicitude of his indulgent goodness.
I cannot, therefore, be sure whether our apathy upon this
point were mutual, though certainly there is no other
point, from the beginning to the end of our connection,
to which the word apathy could to either of us be applied.

At this period he returned to Paris to settle various
matters for our Senlis residence.   We both now knew the
event that so soon was to monopolize all thought and all
interest throughout Europe: but we knew it without any
change in our way of life; on the contrary, we even resumed our delightful airings in the Bois de Boulogne,
whither the General drove me every morning in a light
calèche, of which he had possessed himself upon his
entrance into the King's bodyguard the preceding year;
and I have no retrospection that causes me such amazement as the unapprehensive state of mind that could urge
either of us to the enjoyment of those drives when aware
that Bonaparte had effected an invasion into France.

Brief, however, was this illusion, and fearful was the
light by which its darkness was dispersed.   In a few days
we heard that Bonaparte, whom we had concluded to be,

of course, either stopped at landing or taken prisoner, or forced to save himself by flight, was, on the contrary, pursuing unimpeded his route to Lyons.

The project upon Paris became at length obvious; yet its success was little feared, though the horrors of a civil war seemed inevitable. M. d'Arblay began to wish me away; he made various propositions for ensuring my safety; he even pressed me to depart for England to rejoin Alexander and my family: but I knew them to be in security, whilst my first earthly tie was exposed to every species of danger, and I besought him not to force me away. He was greatly distressed, but could not oppose my urgency. He procured me, however, a passport from M. le Comte de Jaucourt, his long-attached friend, who was minister *aux affaires étrangères ad interim*, while Talley-rand-Périgord was with the Congress at Vienna. M. de Jaucourt gave this passport '*pour Madame d'Arblay, née Burney*,' avoiding to speak of me as the wife of a general officer of the King, lest that might eventually impede my progress, should I be reduced to escape from Paris; while on the other hand, to facilitate my travelling with any friends or companions, he inserted, *et les personnes de sa suite*. This is dated 15 mars, 1815.

But on the 17th, hope again revived. I received these words from my best friend, written on a scrap of paper torn from a parcel, and brought to me by his groom from the palace of the Tuileries, where their writer had passed the night mounting guard:

'Nous avons de meilleures nouvelles. Je ne puis entrer dans aucun détail; mais sois tranquille, et aime bien qui t'aime uniquement.   God bless you.'

This news hung upon the departure of Marshal Ney to meet Bonaparte and stop his progress, with the memorable words uttered publicly to the King, that he would bring him to Paris in an iron cage. The King at this time positively announced and protested that he would never abandon his throne nor quit his capital, Paris.

The next day, the 18th of March, all hope disappeared. From north, from south, from east, from west, alarm took the field, danger flashed its lightnings, and contention growled its thunders: yet in Paris there was no rising, no disturbance, no confusion—all was taciturn suspense, dark dismay, or sullen passiveness. The dread necessity which had reduced the King, Louis XVIII, to be placed on his throne by foreigners, would have annihilated all enthusiasm of loyalty, if any had been left by the long underminings of revolutionary principles.

I come now to the detail of one of the most dreadful days of my existence, the 19th of March, 1815, the last which preceded the triumphant return of Bonaparte to the capital of France. Little, on its opening, did I imagine that return so near, or believe it would be brought about without even any attempted resistance. General d'Arblay, more in the way of immediate intelligence, and more able to judge of its result, was deeply affected by the most gloomy prognostics. He came home at about six in the morning, harassed, worn, almost wasted with fatigue, and yet more with a baleful view of all around him, and with a sense of wounded military honour in the inertia which seemed to paralyse all efforts to save the King and his cause. He had spent two nights following armed on guard, one at the Tuileries, in his duty of Garde du Corps to the King; the other on duty as artillery captain at the barracks. He went to bed for a few hours; and then, after a wretched breakfast, in which he briefly narrated the state of things he had witnessed and his apprehensions, he conjured me, in the most solemn and earnest manner, to yield to the necessity of the times, and consent to quit Paris with Madame d'Hénin, should she ultimately decide to depart.

We knelt together, in short but fervent prayer to heaven for each other's preservation, and then separated. At the door he turned back, and with a smile which, though forced, had inexpressible sweetness, he half-gaily exclaimed: 'Vive le Roi!' I instantly caught his wise wish that we should part with apparent cheerfulness, and reechoed his words—and then he darted from my sight.

This had passed in an ante-room; but I then retired to my bedchamber, where, all effort over, I remained for some minutes abandoned to an affliction nearly allied to despair, though rescued from it by fervent devotion.

But an idea then started into my mind that yet again I might behold him. I ran to a window which looked upon the inward courtyard. There, indeed, behold him I did, but oh! with what anguish! just mounting his warhorse, a noble animal, of which he was singularly fond, but which at this moment I viewed with acutest terror, for it seemed loaded with pistols, and equipped completely for immediate service on the field of battle; while Deprez, the groom, prepared to mount another, and our cabriolet was filled with baggage and implements of war.

I was now sufficiently roused for action, and my first return to conscious understanding was a desire to call in and pay every bill that might be owing, as well as the rent of our apartments up to the present moment, that no pretence might be assumed from our absence for disposing of our goods, books, or property of any description. As we never had any avoidable debts, this was soon settled; but the proprietor of the house was thunderstruck by the measure, saying, the King had reiterated his proclamation that he would not desert his capital. I could only reply that the General was at his Majesty's orders, and that my absence would be short. I then began collecting our small portion of plate, etc.; but while thus occupied, I received a message from Madame d'Hénin, to tell me I must bring nothing but a small change of linen, and one band-box, as by the news she had just heard, she was convinced we should be back again in two or three days, and she charged me to be with her in an hour from that time. I did what she directed, and put what I most valued, that was not too large, into a hand-basket, made by some French prisoners in England, that had been given me by my beloved friend, Mrs Locke. I then swallowed, standing, my neglected dinner, and, with Madame Deprez, and my small allowance of baggage, I got into a fiacre, and drove to General Victor de la Tour Maubourg.

It was about nine o'clock at night, and very dark. I sent on Madame Deprez to the Princesse, and charged her not to return to summon me till the last moment.

I found the house of the Marquis Victor de la Tour Maubourg in a state of the most gloomy dismay. No *portier* was in the way, but the door of the *porte cochère* was ajar, and I entered on foot, no *fiacre* being ever admitted into *les cours des hôtels*. Officers and strangers were passing to and fro, some to receive, others to resign commissions, but all with quick steps, though in dead silence. Not a servant was in the way, and hardly any light; all seemed in disorder. I groped along till I came to the drawing-room, in which were several people, waiting for orders, or for an audience; but in no communication with each other, for here, also, a dismal taciturnity prevailed.

Presently, what was my emotion at the sudden and abrupt entrance into the room of an officer of the King's Garde du Corps! in the self-same uniform as that from which I had parted with such anguish in the morning! A transitory hope glanced like lightning upon my brain, with an idea that the bodyguard was all at hand; but as evanescent as bright was the flash! The concentrated and mournful look of the officer assured me nothing genial was awaiting me; and when the next minute we recognized each other, I saw it was the Count Charles de la Tour Maubourg, and he then told me he had a note for me from M. d'Arblay.

The Count Charles had obtained leave of absence for one hour to see his wife (Mademoiselle de la Fayette) and his children; but M. d'Arblay, who belonged to the artillery company, could not be spared even a moment. He had therefore seized a cover of a letter of M. de Bethizy, the commandant, to write me a few words.

I now read them, and found:

'Ma chère amie—Tout est perdu! Je ne puis entrer dans aucun détail—de grâce, partez! le plus tôt sera le mieux.

'A la vie et à la mort,

'A. D'A.'

Scarcely had I read these lines when I was told that Madame d'Hénin had sent me a summons.

Arrived at Madame la Princesse d'Hénin's, all was in a perturbation yet greater than what I had left, though not equally afflicting. Madame d'Hénin was so little herself, that every moment presented a new view of things, and urged her impatiently, nay imperiously, to differ from whatever was offered.

But what a new and terrible commotion was raised in her mind upon receiving a pencil billet from M. de Lally, brought by a confidential servant, to announce that Bonaparte was within a few hours' march of Paris! He begged her to hasten off, and said he would follow in his cabriolet when he had made certain arrangements, and could gain some information as to the motions of the King.

She now instantly ordered horses to her berlin, which had long been loaded, and calling up all her people and dependants, was giving her orders with the utmost vivacity, when intelligence was brought her that no horses could now be had, the Government having put them all in requisition.

Madame d'Hénin was now almost distracted, but this dreadful prospect of indefinite detention, with all the horrors of captivity, lasted not long; Le Roy, her faithful domestic from his childhood, prevailed upon some stable friend to grant the use of his horses for one stage from Paris, and the berlin and four was at the *porte cochère* in another moment. The servants and dependants of Madame d'Hénin accompanied her to the carriage in tears; and all her fine qualities were now unmixed, as she took an affectionate leave of them, with a sweetness the most engaging, suffering the women to kiss her cheek, and smiling kindly on the men, who kissed her robe.

We now rushed into the carriage, averse, yet eager, between ten and eleven o'clock at night, 19th March, 1815.

I come now to busier scenes, and to my sojourn at Brussels during the opening of one of the most famous campaigns upon record; and the battle of Waterloo, upon which, in great measure, hung the fate of Europe.

I was awakened in the middle of the night by confused noises in the house, and running up and down stairs. I listened attentively, but heard no sound of voices, and soon all was quiet. I then concluded the persons who resided in the apartments on the second floor, over my head, had returned home late, and I tried to fall asleep again.

I succeeded; but I was again awakened at about five o'clock in the morning, Friday, 16th June, by the sound of a bugle horn in the Marché aux Bois; I started up, and opened the window. But I only perceived some straggling soldiers, hurrying in different directions, and saw lights gleaming from some of the chambers in the neighbourhood; all again was soon still, and my own dwelling in profound silence, and therefore I concluded there had been some disturbance in exchanging sentinels at the various posts, which was already appeased; and I retired once more to my pillow, and remained till my usual hour.

I was finishing, however, a letter for my best friend, when my breakfast was brought in, at my then customary time of eight o'clock; and, as mistakes and delays and miscarriages of letters had caused me much unnecessary misery, I determined to put what I was then writing in the post myself, and set off with it the moment it was sealed.

In my way back from the post office, my ears were alarmed by the sound of military music, and my eyes

equally struck with the sight of a body of troops marching
to its measured time.   But I soon found that what I had
supposed to be an occasionally passing troop was a
complete corps; infantry, cavalry, artillery, bag and baggage, with all its officers in full uniform, and that uniform
was black.

This gloomy hue gave an air so mournful to the procession, that, knowing its destination for battle, I contemplated it with an aching heart.   On inquiry, I learned it
was the army of Brunswick.   How much deeper yet
had been my heartache had I foreknown that nearly all
those brave men, thus marching on in gallant though dark
array, with their valiant royal chief at their head, the
nephew of my own King, George the Third, were amongst
the first destined victims to this dreadful contest, and that
neither the chief, nor the greater part of his warlike
associates, would, within a few short hours, breathe again
the vital air!

My interrogations were answered with brevity, yet
curiosity was all awake and all abroad; for the procession
lasted some hours.   Not a door but was open; not a
threshold but was crowded, and not a window of the
many-windowed Gothic, modern, frightful, handsome,
quaint, disfigured, fantastic, or lofty mansions that diversify the large market place of Brussels, but was occupied
by lookers-on.   Placidly, indeed, they saw the warriors
pass; no kind greeting welcomed their arrival; no warm
wishes followed them to combat.   Neither, on the other
hand, was there the slightest symptom of dissatisfaction;
yet even while standing thus in the midst of them, an
unheeded, yet observant stranger, it was not possible for
me to discern, with any solidity of conviction, whether
the Belgians were, at heart, Bourbonists or Bonapartists.
The Bonapartists, however, were in general the most open,
for the opinion on both sides, alike with good will and
with ill, was nearly universal that Bonaparte was invincible.

What a day of confusion and alarm did we all spend
on the 17th!   In *my* heart the whole time was Trèves!

Trèves! Trèves![1]   That day, and June 18th, I passed in
hearing the cannon!   Good heaven! what indescribable
horror to be so near the field of slaughter! such I call it,
for the preparation to the ear by the tremendous sound
was soon followed by its fullest effect, in the view of the
wounded, the bleeding martyrs to the formidable contention that was soon to terminate the history of the war.
And hardly more afflicting was this disabled return from
the battle, than the sight of the continually pouring forth
ready-armed and vigorous victims that marched past my
windows to meet similar destruction.

But what a day was the next—*June* 18*th*—the greatest,
perhaps, in its result, in the annals of Great Britain!

My slumbers having been tranquillized by the close
of the 17th, I was calmly reposing, when I was awakened
by the sound of feet abruptly entering my drawing-room.
I started, and had but just time to see by my watch that
it was only six o'clock, when a rapping at my bedroom
door, so quick as to announce as much trepidation as it
excited, made me slip on a long kind of domino always,
in those times, at hand, to keep me ready for encountering
surprise, and demand what was the matter? 'Open your
door! there is not a moment to lose!' was the answer, in
the voice of Miss Ann Boyd.   I obeyed, in great alarm,
and saw that pretty and pleasing young woman, with
her mother, Mrs Boyd, who remembered having known
and played with me when we were both children, and
whom I had met with at Passy, after a lapse of more than
forty years.   They both eagerly told me that I must be
with them at eight o'clock, to proceed to the wharf, and
set sail for Antwerp, whence we must sail on for England,
should the taking of Brussels by Bonaparte endanger
Antwerp also.

To send off a few lines to the post, with my direction
at Antwerp, to pack and to pay, was all that I could attempt,
or even desire; for I had not less time than appetite for
thinking of breakfast.   My host and my maid carried my

[1] Where General d'Arblay was stationed.

small package, and I arrived before eight in the rue d'Assault. We set off for the wharf on foot, not a *fiacre* or chaise being procurable. Mr and Mrs Boyd, five or six of their family, a governess, and I believe some servants, with bearers of our baggage, made our party.

Though the distance was short, the walk was long, because rugged, dirty, and melancholy. Now and then we heard a growling noise, like distant thunder, but far more dreadful.

Arrived at the wharf, Mr Boyd pointed out to us our barge, which seemed fully ready for departure; but the crowd already come and still coming so incommoded us, that Mr Boyd desired we would enter a large inn, and wait till he could speak with the master, and arrange our luggage and places. We went therefore, into a spacious room and ordered breakfast, when the room was entered by a body of military men of all sorts; but we were suffered to keep our ground till Mr Boyd came to inform us that we must all decamp!

If this intelligence filled us with the most fearful alarm, how much more affrighting still was the sound of cannon which next assailed our ears! The dread reverberation became louder and louder as we proceeded. Every shot tolled to our imaginations the death of myriads; and the conviction that the destruction and devastation were so near us, with the probability that if all attempt at escape should prove abortive, we might be personally involved in the carnage, gave us sensations too awful for verbal expression; we could only gaze and tremble, listen and shudder.

Yet, strange to relate! on re-entering the city, all seemed quiet and tranquil as usual! and though it was in this imminent and immediate danger of being invested, and perhaps pillaged, I saw no outward mark of distress or disturbance, or even of hurry or curiosity.

Having re-lodged us in the rue d'Assault, Mr Boyd tried to find some land carriage for our removal. But not only every chaise had been taken, and every diligence secured; the cabriolets, the calèches, nay, the wagons and the carts, and every species of caravan, had been seized for military service. And, after the utmost efforts he could make, in every kind of way, he told us we must wait the chances of the day, for that there was no possibility of escape from Brussels either by land or water.

We then separated; I was anxious to get home, to watch the post, and to write to Trèves.

My reappearance produced no effect upon my hosts; they saw my return with the same placid civility that they had seen my departure.

But even apathy, or equanimity—which shall I call it?—like theirs was now to be broken; I was seated at my bureau and writing, when a loud 'hurrah!' reached my ears from some distance, while the daughter of my host, a girl of about eighteen, gently opening my door, said the fortune of the day had suddenly turned, and that Bonaparte was taken prisoner.

At the same time the 'hurrah!' came nearer. I flew to the window; my host and hostess came also, crying: '*Bonaparte est pris! le voilà! le voilà!*'

I then saw on a noble war-horse in full equipment, a general in the splendid uniform of France; but visibly disarmed, and to all appearances, tied to his horse, or, at least, held on, so as to disable him from making any effort to gallop it off, and surrounded, preceded, and followed by a crew of roaring wretches, who seemed eager for the moment when he should be lodged where they had orders to conduct him, that they might unhorse, strip, pillage him, and divide the spoil.

His high, feathered, glittering helmet he had pressed down as low as he could on his forehead, and I could not discern his face; but I was instantly certain he was not Bonaparte, on finding the whole commotion produced by the rifling crew above-mentioned, which, though it might be guided, probably, by some subaltern officer, who might have the captive in charge, had left the field of battle at a moment when none other could be spared, as all the attendant throng were evidently among the refuse of the army followers.

The dearth of any positive news from the field of battle, even in the heart of Brussels, at this crisis, when everything that was dear and valuable to either party was at stake, was at one instant nearly distracting in its torturing suspense to the wrung nerves, and at another insensibly blunted them into a kind of amalgamation with the Belgic philosophy. At certain houses, as well as at public offices, news, I doubt not, arrived; but no means were taken to promulgate it; no gazettes, as in London, no bulletins, as in Paris, were cried about the streets; we were all left at once to our conjectures and our destinies.

The delusion of victory vanished into a merely passing advantage, as I gathered from the earnest researches into which it led me; and evil only met all ensuing investigation; retreat and defeat were the words in every mouth around me! The Prussians, it was asserted, were completely vanquished on the 15th, and the English on the 16th, while on the day just passed, the 17th, a day of continual fighting and bloodshed, drawn battles on both sides left each party proclaiming what neither party could prove—success.[1]

Not above a quarter of an hour had I been restored to my sole occupation of solace, before I was again interrupted and startled; but not as on the preceding occasion by riotous shouts; the sound was a howl, violent, loud, affrighting, and issuing from many voices. I ran to the window, and saw the Marché aux Bois suddenly filling with a populace, pouring in from all its avenues, and hurrying on rapidly, and yet as if unconscious in what direction; while women with children in their arms, or clinging to their clothes, ran screaming out of doors; and cries, though not a word was ejaculated, filled the air, and from

[1] The campaign began on the 15th, and on the 16th the battles of Ligny and Quatre-Bras were fought; on the 17th the Prussians retreated to Wavre and Wellington to the Waterloo position, where, on the 18th, the final battle took place.

every house, I saw windows closing, and shutters fastening; all this, though long in writing, was presented to my eyes in a single moment, and was followed in another by a burst into my apartment, to announce that *the French were come*!

I know not even who made this declaration; my head was out of the window, and the person who made it scarcely entered the room and was gone.

How terrific was this moment! My perilous situation urged me to instant flight; and, without waiting to speak to the people of the house, I crammed my papers and money into a basket, and throwing on a shawl and bonnet, I flew downstairs and out of doors.

My intention was to go to the Boyds, to partake their fate; but the crowd were all issuing from the way I must have turned to have gained the rue d'Assault, and I thought, therefore, I might be safer with Madame de Maurville, who, also, not being English, might be less obnoxious to the Bonapartists. To la rue de la Montagne I hurried, in consequence, my steps crossing and crossed by an affrighted multitude; but I reached it in safety, and she received me with an hospitable welcome.

The *alerte* which had produced this effect, I afterwards learnt, though not till the next day, was utterly false; but whether it had been produced by mistake or by deceit I never knew. The French, indeed, were coming; but not triumphantly; they were prisoners, surprised and taken suddenly, and brought in, being disarmed, by an escort; and, as they were numerous, and their French uniform was discernible from afar, the almost universal belief at Brussels that Bonaparte was invincible, might perhaps, without any intended deception, have raised the report that they were advancing as conquerors.

Madame de Maurville now told me that an English commissary was just arrived from the army, who had assured her that the tide of success was completely turned to the side of the Allies. She offered to conduct me to his apartment, which was in the same hotel as her own, and in which he was writing and transacting business; gravely assuring me, and, I really believe, herself, that he could not but be rejoiced to give me, in person, every particular I could wish to hear. I deemed it, however, but prudent not to put his politeness to a test so severe.

When the night of this memorable day arrived, I took leave of Madame de Maurville to join the Boyds; for though all accounts confirmed the victory of the Duke of Wellington, we had so little idea of its result, that we still imagined the four days already spent in the work of carnage must be followed by as many more, before the dreadful conflict could terminate.

I found the Boyds still firm for departure. The news of the victory of the day, gained by the Duke of Wellington and Prince Blücher, had raised the highest delight; but further intelligence had just reached them that the enemy, since the great battle, was working to turn the right wing of the Duke of Wellington, who was in the most imminent danger; and that the capture of Brussels was expected to take place the next morning, as everything indicated that Brussels was the point at which Bonaparte aimed, to retrieve his recent defeat. Mr Boyd used every possible exertion to procure chaises or diligence, or any sort of land conveyance, for Antwerp, but every horse was under military requisition; even the horses of the farmers, of the nobility and gentry, and of travellers. The hope of water carriage was all that remained. We were to set off so early, that we agreed not to retire to rest.

A gentleman, however, of their acquaintance, presently burst into the room with assurances that the enemy was flying in all directions.

This better news reanimated my courage for Brussels and my trust in the Duke of Wellington; and when the Boyd family summoned me the next morning at four or five o'clock to set off with them for Antwerp, I permitted my repugnance to quitting the only spot where I could receive letters from Trèves to conquer every obstacle,

and begged them to excuse my changed purpose. They
wondered at my temerity, and probably blamed it; but
there was no time for discussion, and we separated.

It was not till Tuesday, the 20th, I had certain and
satisfactory assurances how complete was the victory.
At the house of Madame de Maurville I heard confirmed
and detailed the matchless triumph of the matchless
Wellington, interspersed with descriptions of scenes of
slaughter on the field of battle to freeze the blood, and
tales of woe amongst mourning survivors in Brussels to
rend the heart.

I met at the Embassade an old English officer who gave
me most interesting and curious information, assuring
me that in the carriage of Bonaparte, which had been
seized, there were proclamations ready printed, and even
dated from the palace of Lachen, announcing the downfall
of the Allies, and the triumph of Bonaparte!

But no satisfaction could make me hear without deadly
dismay and shuddering his description of the field of
battle. Piles of dead! Heaps, masses, hills of dead
bestrewed the plains!

We were all at work more or less in making lint. For
me, I was about amongst the wounded half the day, the
British, s'entend! The rising in France for the honour of
the nation now, and for its safety in independence hereafter, was brilliant and delightful, spreading in some
directions from la Manche to la Méditerranée: the focus
of loyalty was Bordeaux. *Le Roi* left Gand the 22nd.
All Alost, etc., surrounded, followed, or preceded him.
The noble Blücher entered France at Mortes le Château.
'Suivez-les vite,' he cried, 'mes enfans! ou demain nous les
aurons encore sur les bras!' *On dit* that the Duke of Wellington avowed he more than once thought the battle lost!
The efforts made by Bonaparte were stupendous, and his
Imperial Guards fought with a *dévouement*, an enthusiasm,
that showed they thought victory and their leader must be
one. It was not till six o'clock that the Duke felt his real
advantage. He was everywhere in the field, and ran the

most terrible risks, for which he is equally blamed and
admired: but the stake was so prodigious! the victory or
defeat so big with enormous consequences!

Meanwhile, to put a stop as much as possible to the
alarming putrid exhalations, three thousand peasants were
employed all at once in burying the heaps of dead on the
plains!

This, at least, was the current account at Brussels.

About the middle of July—but I am not clear of the
date—the news was assured and confirmed of the brilliant
re-enthronement of Louis XVIII, and that Bonaparte
had surrendered to the English.

Brussels now became an assemblage of all nations,
from the rapturous enthusiasm that pervaded all to view
the field of battle, the famous Waterloo, and gather upon
the spot details of the immortal victory of Wellington.

PARIS, OCT. On the eve of setting out for England, I
went round to all I could reach of my intimate acquaintance, to make—as it has proved—a last farewell!

M. de Talleyrand came in to Madame de Laval's drawing-
room during my visit of leave-taking. He was named
upon entering; but there is no chance he could recollect
me, as I had not seen him since the first month or two after
my marriage, when he accompanied M. de Narbonne
and M. de Beaumetz to our cottage at Bookham. I
could not forbear whispering to Madame de Laval how
many *souvenirs* his sight awakened! M. de Narbonne was
gone, who made so much of our social felicity during
the period of our former acquaintance; and Mr Locke
was gone, who made its highest intellectual delight; and
Madame de Staël, who gave it a zest of wit, deep thinking,
and light speaking, of almost unexampled entertainment;
and my beloved sister Phillips, whose sweetness, intelligence, grace, and sensibility won every heart; these were
gone, who all, during the sprightly period in which I
was known to M. Talleyrand, had almost always made
our society.

Madame de Laval sighed deeply, without answering me,
but I left M. de Talleyrand to Madame la Duchesse de
Luynes, and a sister of M. le Duc de Luxembourg, and
another lady or two while I engaged my truly amiable
hostess, till I rose to depart: and then, in passing the chair
of M. de Talleyrand, who gravely and silently, but politely
rose and bowed, I said: 'M. de Talleyrand m'a oubliée:
mais on n'oublie pas M. de Talleyrand.' I left the room
with quickness, but saw a movement of surprise by no
means unpleasant break over the habitual placidity, the
nearly imperturbable composure, of his *made-up* countenance.

Our journey was eventless, yet sad; sad, not solely,
though chiefly, from the continued sufferings of my
wounded companion,[1] but sad, also, that I quitted so
many dear friends, who had wrought themselves, by
innumerable kindnesses, into my affections, and who knew
not, for we could not bring ourselves to utter words that
must have reciprocated so much pain, that our intended
future residence was England. The most tender and
generous of fathers had taken this difficult resolution for
the sake of his son, whose earnest wish had been repeatedly expressed for permission to establish himself in
the land of his birth. That my wishes led to the same
point, there could be no doubt, and powerfully did they
weigh with the most disinterested and most indulgent of
husbands.

Madame d'Arblay to Mrs Locke

Bath, November 10, 1816.

I wish to live at Bath, wish it devoutly; for at Bath we
shall live, or no longer in England. *London* will only
do for those who have *two* houses, and of the *real country*

---

[1] The expression is slightly misleading. General d'Arblay had
taken no part in the fighting, but had been kicked on the leg by a colt
which he was training.

I may say the same; for a cottage, now Monsieur d'Arblay cannot, as heretofore, brave all the seasons, to work, and embellish his wintry hours by embellishing *anticipatingly* his garden, would be too lonely, in so small a family, for the long evenings of cold and severe weather; and would lose us Alexander half the year, as we could neither expect nor wish to see him begin life as a recluse from the world. Bath, therefore, as it eminently agrees with us all, is, in England, the only place for us, since here, all the year round, there is always town at command, and always the country for prospect, exercise, and delight.

Therefore, my dear freind, not a word but in favour of Bath, if you love me. Our own finishing finale will soon take root here, or yonder; for Alex. will take his degree in January, and then, his mind at liberty, and his faculties in their full capacity for meditating upon his lot in life, he will come to a decision what mountain he shall *climb*, upon which to fix his staff; for all that relates to worldly prosperity will to him be up-hill toil and labour. Never did I see in youth a mind so quiet, so philosophic, in mundane matters, with a temper so eager, so impetuous, so burningly alive to subjects of science and literature. The Tancred scholarship [1] is still in suspense. The Vice-Chancellor is our earnest friend, as well as our faithful Dr Davy, but the trustees have come to no determination; and Alex. is my companion—or rather, I am Alex.'s flapper [2]—till the learned doctors can agree. At all events, he will not come out *in Physic*; we shall rather enter him at another college, with all the concomitant expenses, than let him, from any economy, begin his public career under false colours. When he entered this institution, I had not any notion of this difficulty; I was ignorant there would be any objection against his turning which way he pleased when the time for taking the degree should arrive. . . .

---

[1] Alex. had been awarded a Tancred scholarship in 1813.
[2] Alluding to the Laputa section of *Gulliver's Travels*.

Madame d'Arblay to her Son

Bath, Friday, April 25, 1817.

Why, what a rogue your are! four days in town! As there can be no scholarship—*hélas!* it matters not; but who knew that circumstance when they played truant? Can you tell me that, hey! Mr Cantab? Why, you *dish* me as if I were no more worth than Paley or Newton, or such-like worthies!

Your dear Padre is very considerably better, *surtout* in his looks, but by no means re-established; for cold air—too much exertion—too little—and all sorts of nourishment or beverage that are not precisely adapted to the present state of the poor shattered frame, produce instant pain, uneasiness, restlessness, and suffering. Such, however, is the common condition of convalescence, and therefore I observe it with much more concern than surprise; and Mr Hay assures me all is as well as can possibly be expected after so long and irksome an illness.

> 'The scholarship is at an end—
> So much for that!'

pretty cool, my friend!

Will it make you double your diligence for what is *not* at an end? hey, *mon petit monsieur?*

But I am sorry for your disappointment in the affair you mention, my dear Alex.: though your affections were not so far engaged, methinks, but that your *amour propre* is still more *blessé* than your heart! hey? However, 'tis a real loss, though little more than of an ideal friend, at present. But no idea is so flattering and so sweet, as that which opens to expectation a treasure of such a sort. I am really, therefore, sorry for you, my dear Alex.

Your determination to give way to no *sudden* impulse in future is quite right. Nothing is so pleasant as giving way to impulse; nothing so hazardous.

Madame d'Arblay to Alex. d'Arblay, Esq.

Bath, November 9, 1817.

We have here spent nearly a week in a manner the most extraordinary, beginning with hope and pleasure, proceeding to fear and pain, and ending in disappointment and grief.

The joy exhibited on Monday, when her Majesty and her Royal Highness arrived, was really ecstatic; the illumination was universal. The public offices were splendid; so were the tradespeople's who had promises or hopes of employment; the nobles and gentles were modestly gay, and the poor eagerly put forth their mite. But all was flattering, because voluntary. Nothing was induced by power, or forced by mobs. All was left to individual choice. Your Padre and I patrolled the principal streets, and were quite touched by the universality of the homage paid to the virtues and merit of our venerable Queen, upon this her first progress through any part of her domains by herself. Hitherto she has only accompanied the poor King, as at Weymouth and Cheltenham, Worcester and Exeter, Plymouth and Portsmouth, etc.; or the Prince Regent, as at Brighthelmstone. But here, called by her health, she came as principal, and in her own character of rank and consequence. And, as Mr Hay told me, the inhabitants of Bath were all even vehement to let her see the light in which they held her individual self, after so many years witnessing her exemplary conduct and distinguished merit.

She was very sensible to this tribute; but much affected, nay, dejected, in receiving it, at the beginning; from coming without the King where the poor King had always meant himself to bring her; but just as he had arranged for the excursion, and even had three houses taken for him in the Royal Crescent, he was afflicted by blindness. He would not then come; for what, he said, was a beautiful city to him who could not look at it? This was continually in the remembrance of the Queen during the honours of her reception; but she had recovered from the melancholy recollection, and was cheering herself by the cheers of all the inhabitants, when the first news arrived of the illness of the Princess Charlotte.[1] At that moment she was having her diamonds placed on her head for the reception of the mayor and corporation of Bath, with an address upon the honour done to their city, and upon their hopes from the salutary spring she came to quaff. Her first thought was to issue orders for deferring this ceremony; but when she considered that all the members of the municipality must be assembled, and that the great dinner they had prepared to give to the Duke of Clarence could only be postponed at an enormous and useless expense, she composed her spirits, finished her regal decorations, and admitted the citizens of Bath, who were highly gratified by her condescension, and struck by her splendour, which was the same as she appeared in on the greatest occasions in the capital. The Princess Elizabeth was also a blaze of jewels. And our good little Mayor (not four feet high) and Aldermen and Common Councilmen were all transported. The Duke of Clarence accepted their invitation, and was joined by the Marquis of Bath and all the Queen's suite. But the dinner was broken up. The Duke received an express with the terrible tidings: he rose from the table, and struck his forehead as he read them, and then hurried out of the assembly with inexpressible trepidation and dismay. The Queen also was at table when the same express arrived, though only with the Princess and her own party: all were dispersed in a moment, and she shut herself up, admitting no one but her Royal Highness. She would have left Bath the next morning; but her physician, Sir Henry Halford, said it would be extremely dangerous that she should travel so far, in her state of health, just in the first perturbation of affliction. She would see no one but her

[1] Being the only child of the Prince of Wales, she was heiress presumptive to the throne. She died in childbirth.

immediate suite all day, and set out the next for Windsor
Castle, to spend the time previous to the last melancholy
rites in the bosom of her family. All Bath wore a face
of mourning. The transition from gaiety and exultation
was really awful. What an extinction of youth and happiness! The poor Princess Charlotte had never known a
moment's suffering since her marriage. Her lot seemed
perfect. Prince Leopold [1] is, indeed, to be pitied. I have
left no room for your Padre; but the turn was fairly mine;
and both are so delighted with your new spirit of correspondence, that whichever holds the pen, the heart of both
writes in truest affection to the dearest of sons.

Madame d'Arblay to Mrs Piozzi

Bath, February 26, 1818.

There is no situation in which a kind remembrance
from you, my dear Madam, would not awaken me to some
pleasure; but my poor sufferer was so very ill when your
note came, that it was not possible for me to answer it.
That I think him so *very bad*, is that I see him perpetually
in pain nearly insupportable; yet I am assured it is local
and unattended with danger while followed up with
constant care and caution. This supports my spirits,
which bear me and enable me to help him through a
malady of anguish and difficulty. It is a year this very
month since he has been in the hands of Mr Hay as a
regular patient. Mr Hay was recommended to us by
Mrs Locke and Mrs Angerstein, whom he attends as
physician, from their high opinion of his skill and discernment. But, alas! all has failed here; and we have called
in Mr Tudor, as the case terminates in being one that
demands a surgeon. Mr Tudor gives me every comfort

[1] Afterwards Leopold I, King of the Belgians.

in prospect, but prepares me for long suffering, and slow, slow recovery. . . .

Believe me, dear Madam, with unalterable affection,

Your ever obliged and obedient,

F. D'ARBLAY.

I hope you were a little glad that my son has been among the high Wranglers.

Extract from Pocket-Book Diary

May 17, 1818.[1]

This melancholy second Sunday since my irreparable loss I ventured to church. I hoped it might calm my mind and subject it to its new state—its lost—lost happiness. But I suffered inexpressibly; I sunk on my knees, and could scarcely contain my sorrows — scarcely rise any more! But I prayed—fervently—and I am glad I made the trial, however severe. Oh, *mon ami! mon tendre ami!* if you looked down! if that be permitted, how benignly will you wish my participation in your blessed relief!

From Mrs Piozzi to Madame d'Arblay

Bath, October 20 [1820].

It was very gratifying, dear Madam, to find myself so kindly remembered, and with all my heart I thank you for your letter. My family are gone to Sandgate for the purpose of bathing in the sea, this wonderfully beautiful October; and were you not detained in London by such a son as I hear you are happy in, I should wish you there too. Apropos to October, I have not your father's admirable verses upon that month; those upon June 1

[1] M. d'Arblay had died on 3rd May.

saw when last in Wales; could you get me the others? It would be such a favour, and you used to like them best.

How changed is the taste of verse, prose, and painting! since *le bon vieux temps*, dear Madam! Nothing attracts us but what terrifies, and is within—*if* within—a hair's breadth of positive disgust. The picture of Death on his Pale Horse,[1] however, is very grand certainly—and some of the strange things they *write* remind me of Squoire Richard's visit to the Tower Menagerie, when he says 'Odd, they are *pure* grim devils'—particularly a wild and hideous tale called *Frankenstein*.[2] Do you ever see any of the friends we used to live among? Mrs Lambart is yet alive, and in prosperous circumstances; and Fell, the bookseller in Bond Street, told me a fortnight or three weeks ago, that Miss Streatfeild lives where she did in his neighbourhood—Clifford Street, S. S. still.

Old Jacob and his red night-cap are the only live creatures, as an Irishman would say, that come about *me* of those you remember, and death alone will part us—he and I both lived longer with Mr Piozzi than we had done with Mr Thrale. . . .

Once more, farewell! and accept my thanks for your good-natured recollection of poor

H. L. P.

Madame d'Arblay to Mrs Burney

February 29, 1823.

Thanks for that kind jump of joy for the success of Alex. at Lee, and for my hopes from St Paul's. You ask who named him *Preacher for the 5th Sunday in Lent?* How could I omit telling you 'twas the Bishop of London himself? This has been brought about by a detail too

---

[1] Benjamin West's *Death on the Pale Horse*, first exhibited in 1817.

[2] *Frankenstein* had appeared in 1818. This letter shows Mrs Piozzi, now eighty years old, to have lost none of her vivacity. She died in 1821.

long for paper, but it is chiefly to my faithful old friends
Bishop Fisher of Salisbury and the Archdeacon of
Middlesex that we owe this mark of attention; for Alex.
has never been presented to the Bishop of London.

You still ask about my health, etc. . . .

The chief changes, or reforms, from which I reap benefit
are: 1st. Totally renouncing for the evenings all revision
or indulgence in poring over those letters and papers
whose contents come nearest to my heart, and work upon
its bleeding regrets. Next, transferring to the evening,
as far as is in my power, all of sociality, with Alex., or my
few remaining friends, or the few he will present to me
of new ones. 3rd. Constantly going out every day—
either in brisk walks in the morning, or in brisk jumbles
in the carriage of one of my three friends who send for
me, to a 'tête-à-tête' tea-converse. 4th. Strict attention
to diet. . . .

You ask me the history of the Rev. Dr Vyse.[1] He
pensioned off his ill-taken rib; a connection formed in a
luckless hour, and repented ever after, and never made
known but by the provisions of his will, as he survived
her! Sir William and Sir Lucas Pepys, who alone, of all
the Streatham set, have lived, and found me out in Bolton
Street, except the three daughters of the house, now and
then give me the pleasure of an hour's social recollection
of old time, that is interesting to us all.

Adieu, my dearest Esther—remember me kindly to all
who kindly remember me—if such, after this long absence,
be found.

God bless you ever, prays your ever affectionate and
faithful,

F. D'A.

Although Madame d'Arblay's intercourse with society
was now usually confined to that of her relations, and of

[1] Sophy Streatfeild had been in love with Dr Vyse.

old and established friends, she yet greeted with admiration and pleasure Sir Walter Scott, who was brought to her by Mr Rogers. Sir Walter, in his Diary for Nov. 18th, 1826, thus describes the visit: 'I have been introduced to Madame d'Arblay, the celebrated authoress of *Evelina* and *Cecilia*—an elderly lady with no remains of personal beauty, but with a simple and gentle manner, a pleasing expression of countenance, and apparently quick feelings. She told me she had wished to see two persons—myself, of course, being one, the other George Canning. This was really a compliment to be pleased with—a nice little handsome pat of butter made up by a neat-handed Phillis of a dairy-maid, instead of the grease fit only for cart-wheels which one is dosed with by the pound. . . . I trust I shall see this lady again.'

From the year 1828 to 1832 Madame d'Arblay was chiefly occupied in preparing for the press the *Memoirs* of her father.[1]

1835 to 1838

Madame d'Arblay's letters were now very few. A complaint in one of her eyes, which was expected to terminate in a cataract, made both reading and writing difficult to her. The number of her correspondents had also been painfully lessened by the death of her eldest sister, Mrs Burney, and that of her beloved friend, Mrs Locke; and she had sympathised with other branches of her family in many similar afflictions, for she retained in a peculiar degree not only her intellectual powers, but the warm and generous affections of her youth.

[1] Dr Burney left behind him an enormous mass of papers, including the MS. of an autobiography. The *Memoirs*, as edited by Fanny, appeared in 1832. Although Southey wrote her a complimentary letter, the work was unfavourably received.

'Though now her eightieth year was *past*,' she took her wonted and vivid interest in the concerns, the joys, and sorrows of those she loved.

At this time her son formed an attachment which promised to secure his happiness, and to gild his mother's remaining days with affection and peace; and at the close of the year 1836 he was nominated minister of Ely Chapel, which afforded her considerable satisfaction. But her joy was mournfully short-lived. That building, having been shut for some years, was damp and ill-aired. The Rev. Mr d'Arblay began officiating there in winter, and during the first days of his ministry he caught the influenza, and on the 19th of January, 1837, in three weeks from his first seizure, the death of this beloved son threw Madame d'Arblay again into the depths of affliction.

The following paragraph is taken from her private notebook:

'1837. On the opening of this most mournful—most *earthly* hopeless, of any and of all the years yet commenced of my long career! Yet, humbly I bless my God and Saviour, not hopeless; but full of gently-beaming hopes, countless and fraught with aspirations of the time that may succeed to the dread infliction of this last irreparable privation, and bereavement of my darling loved, and most touchingly loving, dear, soul-dear Alex.'

In November, 1839, Madame d'Arblay was attacked by an illness which showed itself at first in sleepless nights and nervous imaginations. During the earlier part of her illness she had listened with comfort to some portions of St John's Gospel, but she now said to her niece: 'I would ask you to read to me, but I could not understand one word—not a syllable! but I thank God my mind has not waited till *this* time.'

At another moment she charged the same person with affectionate farewells and blessings to several friends, and with thanks for all their kindness to her. Soon after she said: 'I have had some sleep.' 'That is well,' was the reply; 'you wanted rest.' '*I shall have it soon, my dear,*' she answered emphatically: and thus, aware that death was approaching, in peace with all the world, and in holy trust and reliance on her Redeemer, she breathed her last on the 6th of January, 1840; the anniversary of that day she had long consecrated to prayer, and to the memory of her beloved sister Susanna.

INDEX

INDEX